Advanced
Korean

T0351644

by Ross King, PhD, Chungsook Kim, PhD,
Jaehoon Yeon, PhD, and Donald Baker

TUTTLE Publishing

Tokyo | Rutland, Vermont | Singapore

Books to Span the East and West

Our core mission at Tuttle Publishing is to create books which bring people together one page at a time. Tuttle was founded in 1832 in the small New England town of Rutland, Vermont (USA). Our fundamental values remain as strong today as they were then—to publish best-in-class books informing the English-speaking world about the countries and peoples of Asia. The world is a smaller place today and Asia's economic, cultural and political influence has expanded, yet the need for meaningful dialogue and information about this diverse region has never been greater. Since 1948, Tuttle has been a leader in publishing books on the cultures, arts, cuisines, languages and literatures of Asia. Our authors and photographers have won many awards and Tuttle has published thousands of titles on subjects ranging from martial arts to paper crafts. We welcome you to explore the wealth of information available on Asia at **www.tuttlepublishing.com**.

Published by Tuttle Publishing, an imprint of Periplus Editions (HK) Ltd.

www.tuttlepublishing.com

Copyright © 2015 by Ross King, Jaehoon Yeon, Chungsook Kim and Donald Baker

ISBN 978-0-8048-4249-5

Distributed by

North America, Latin America & Europe
Tuttle Publishing
364 Innovation Drive
North Clarendon, VT 05759-9436 U.S.A.
Tel: 1 (802) 773-8930
Fax: 1 (802) 773-6993
info@tuttlepublishing.com
www.tuttlepublishing.com

Asia Pacific
Berkeley Books Pte. Ltd.
3 Kallang Sector #04-01
Singapore 349278
Tel: (65) 6741-2178
Fax: (65) 6741-2179
inquiries@periplus.com.sg
www.tuttlepublishing.com

Second edition
23 22 21 20   10 9 8 7 6 5 3   2012VP

Printed in Malaysia

TUTTLE PUBLISHING° is a registered trademark of Tuttle Publishing, a division of Periplus Editions (HK) Ltd.

CONTENTS

PREFACE

This book is an updated and improved version of 한국어 3, first published in 1986 by the (then) 민족문화연구소 or Research Center for Korean Culture at Korea University (고려대학교) in Seoul. Since that time, the Research Center has grown in scale and scope of activity, and has been renamed the 민족문화연구원 or Institute of Korean Culture; and over the years, the original version of this book has gone through at least three major revisions and multiple reprintings, all of which testify to the popularity of the book in Korean language programs, not just in Korea, but outside Korea as well.

When Ross King and Jaehoon Yeon were still teaching Korean together at the School of Oriental and African Studies (SOAS), University of London, in the early 1990s, they found that 한국어 3 provided a useful combination of review material and new materials for learners who had mastered King & Yeon's *Elementary Korean* and *Continuing Korean* (both available from Tuttle Publishing), and since taking up his post at the University of British Columbia (UBC), Ross King has used 한국어 3 as the main textbook for "Korean 300," UBC's third-year Korean course.

But 한국어 3 in its original state was unsatisfactory for Anglophone learners. Like many textbooks produced in Korea for use in Korean university programs, the original 한국어 3 lacks detailed vocabulary lists and grammar notes. Indeed, there is no English in it at all. Thus, *Advanced Korean* takes the core materials in 한국어 3 and adds to them the annotational apparatus—vocabulary lists, grammatical explanations, English translations for the example sentences, comprehensive glossaries—necessary to create a more user-friendly textbook for learners using the book outside of Korea and / or for self-study. Unsure at first how to name our reincarnation of 한국어 3, we settled on *Advanced Korean*. This textbook is ideal for learners already familiar with King & Yeon's *Elementary Korean* and *Continuing Korean*, but lends itself to use by a variety of learners and programs.

The division of labor amongst the three coauthors has been as follows: Chungsook Kim was the lead author of the large team of textbook developers at Korea University that created their original six-level textbook series. Thus, she is responsible for the bulk of the Korean language content in the book as well as for the main contours of the grammar pattern sequencing. Ross King and Jaehoon Yeon have developed all the grammar notes for *Advanced Korean*; partly on the basis of work begun at SOAS in the early 1990s on a sequel volume to King & Yeon's *Elementary Korean* and *Continuing Korean*, and partly on the basis of new work by Ross King at UBC. All the vocabulary lists, example sentence translations, and glossaries, as well as the compilation of new exercises, along with all the inputting, formatting, and editing, were done by Ross King in conjunction with research assistants at UBC (and with feedback from both Chungsook Kim and Jaehoon Yeon).

In addition to, and parallel with the two volumes of *Advanced Korean*, Ross King, Chungsook Kim, and Donald Baker have developed *Advanced Korean: Sino-Korean Companion* as an optional online supplement for those learners wishing to undertake the study of Chinese characters as they are used in Korean. The *Sino-Korean Companion* is a sort of Sino-Korean "parallel universe" for *Advanced Korean*, and assumes a knowledge of the main texts and structural patterns introduced in *Advanced Korean*; it introduces 500 Chinese characters (한자) in their Korean readings with a view to helping students teach themselves 한자 in order to improve their knowledge of Sino-Korean vocabulary. Readers are invited to refer to the prefatory material for the *Sino-Korean Companion* on page 340 of this book for further information. The Sino-Korean Companion can be accessed at **www.tuttlepublishing.com/advanced-korean**

Most of the hard work in preparing *Advanced Korean* has been carried out by research assistants working with Ross King at UBC: Kiyoe Minami, Sinae Park, and Jung Hwang in the first phase of work; in the second phase, both Sunah Cho and Leif Olsen put in many hours of work on the files and made numerous helpful suggestions concerning content and format; in the third phase, UBC Lecturer in Korean, Eurie Shin, has also made countless improvements to the book as a result of her own experience teaching from the beta version. Finally, UBC PhD student in Korean Language and Linguistics, Scott Wells, and Visiting Lecturer in Korean Language, Youngmi Cho, provided invaluable assistance in preparing the files for the publisher. Moreover, several cohorts of UBC students have suffered through beta versions of *Advanced Korean* since 1995. The authors are grateful to all these students for their patience and feedback. The 2003–2004 UBC "Korean 300" cohort deserves special thanks (Shiho Maeshima, Wayne Taylor, Tina Lee, Janie Hong, Frank Rausch, Christine Kim, and David Lee), as does the 2005–2006 cohort (David Bae, Sunny Oh, Sally Suh, Yoon Chung, Mike Whale, and Andrew Pugsley). The authors wish to thank Daniel Martig and Stefan Ewing for invaluable comments, as well.

The authors also owe a debt of thanks to several colleagues who have published useful reference manuals and textbooks in recent years. Thus, Ihm, Hong, and Chang's *Korean Grammar for International Learners* (2001), which Ross King had the privilege of translating into English, has been invaluable for the occasional example sentence, and both this work and the accompanying workbook in Korean by the same authors (1997) have been useful for generating exercises for certain grammar points not originally presented in 한국어 3. Likewise for 백봉자 (1999) and 이희자 & 이종희 (2001), two other manuals of Korean grammar full of useful explanations and example sentences—we have borrowed and adapted numerous examples from these works. The excellent, but now out-of-print Myongdo textbooks—the *Intermediate Korean, Part I* volume, in particular—have provided the inspiration for the Main Text in Lesson Six on proverbs. Finally, the authors wish to register their gratitude to the Korea Foundation for the teaching materials development grant that funded this project at UBC, and to UBC MA student Sean Bussell for proofreading the final page proofs..

References

Ihm, Ho Bin, Kyung Pyo Hong, and Suk In Chang. 2001. *Korean grammar for international learners (new edition)*. Seoul: Yonsei University Press.

Kim, Nam-Kil. 2000. *Modern Korean: An intermediate reader*. Honolulu, HI: University of Hawai'i Press.

King, Ross and Jaehoon Yeon. 2000. *Elementary Korean*. Tokyo, Japan and Rutland, Vermont: Tuttle Publishing Co.

King, Ross and Jaehoon Yeon with Insun Lee. 2002. *Continuing Korean*. Tokyo, Japan and Rutland, Vermont: Tuttle Publishing Co.

Myongdo Language Institute, Franciscan Friars. 1977. *Intermediate Korean: Part I*. Seoul: Myongdo Language Institute.

백봉자. 1999. *외국어로서의 한국어 문법 사전*. 서울: 연세대학교 출판부.

이희자 & 이종희. 2001. *한국어 학습용 어미-조사 사전*. 서울: 한국문화사.

임호빈, 홍경표 & 장숙인. 1997. *외국인을 위한 한국어 문법 Workbook (신개정)*. 서울: 연세대학교 출판부.

About the Authors

Ross King completed his BA in linguistics and political science at Yale in 1983, then his MA (1985) and PhD (1991) in linguistics at Harvard. Currently he is professor of Korean and head of department in the Department of Asian Studies, University of British Columbia, Vancouver, Canada. His email: ross.king@ubc.ca.

Chungsook Kim completed her BA in Korean language and literature at Korea University in 1984 and subsequently earned her MA (1986) and PhD (1992) from the same institution. Currently, she is a professor at Korea University in Seoul. Her email: kmjane@korea.ac.kr

Jaehoon Yeon completed his BA (1984) and MA (1986) in linguistics at Seoul National University, and then PhD (1994) in linguistics at the University of London. Currently he is professor of Korean language and linguistics at the School of Oriental and African Studies (SOAS), University of London. He is the author of many books for Korean language learners. His email: jyl@soas.ac.uk

Donald Baker is professor of Korean civilization in the Department of Asian Studies, University of British Columbia, Vancouver, Canada. A cultural historian, he has published extensively on religion, philosophy, and traditional science in pre-modern Korea. His email: don.baker@ubc.ca

MORE ABOUT THIS BOOK

Structure and Contents

The authors see *Advanced Korean* as ideal for self-study, but also as a relatively solid backbone around which any resourceful teacher could teach an "advanced" course. Thus, *Advanced Korean* is not necessarily targeted at the university classroom market, but is, we would maintain, suitable enough for it.

Advanced Korean consists of twenty lessons, where Lessons Five, Ten, Fifteen, and Twenty are short sentence pattern reviews and the other lessons consist of the following sections:

–Main Text
–Vocabulary
–Patterns (usually from 5–8 structural patterns)
–Exercises (Comprehension Questions, Pattern Practice, Field Work / Composition)

Needless to say, if used as part of a university course, *Advanced Korean* can (and should) be supplemented by other activities as and when the teacher feels appropriate.

Advanced Korean does not contain any explicit sections on culture, but cultural points touched on in the Main Texts are: Korean humor and jokes, proverbs, mythology, daily life, cross-cultural encounters and comparisons, and letter writing. It is essentially a reader in a light vein, not a conversation book, and it is to the credit of the original text's authors that it does not fixate on "high culture" and obvious national icons. It is also not particularly time-bound, meaning that the contents are unlikely to sound dated at any time soon.

About the Exercises

The exercises at the end of each lesson are designed primarily as written homework, not as oral exercises for the classroom. We have deliberately omitted oral pattern drills from the lessons because we feel such drills take up unnecessary space and can easily be constructed by the teacher.

Target Audience

This book, along with its (optional) companion online volume, *Advanced Korean: Sino-Korean Companion* (available at **www.tuttlepublishing.com/advanced-korean**), is targeted in the first instance at those highly motivated learners of Korean who have completed two years of college-level Korean instruction or the equivalent, and wish to continue with their studies, whether through self-study or in a formal course. In the latter case, the question arises as to how best to use this book in an Anglophone university setting. Most university Korean courses in the United States, Canada, United Kingdom, Australia, and New Zealand meet four or five hours per week. At this pace, the authors would recommend covering one lesson every six to ten classroom hours (i.e., one lesson every two weeks), in which the students have at least a thirty-minute quiz at the end of every other week. But the authors recognize that different students and different courses proceed at different paces, and more hours would be necessary if the *Sino-Korean Companion* were also included as part of the course. Indeed, at UBC, the *Sino-Korean Companion* is covered as a separate, stand-alone course taken either simultaneously with, or after, completion of *Advanced Korean*.

About Vocabulary

Advanced Korean introduces a lot of vocabulary—more than a thousand items in all. The authors are skeptical of approaches to introducing vocabulary based on statistical frequency lists, since these frequency lists are never based on the vocabulary needs of university students, businessmen, or travelers learning Korean. Our book includes many sophisticated, intellectual vocabulary items—the sorts of words that mature adults would like to be able to say early in their Korean learning career. Furthermore, since Korean does not give the English speaker as many shortcut vocabulary "freebies" as does French or Spanish or German, it is a hard fact of life that students need to spend more time on vocabulary building.

It is also the view of the authors that some vocabulary items cost more than others to learn. This view is reflected occasionally in the layout of the vocabulary sections, where certain words are indented beneath others to indicate that these items are related to the main vocabulary item in question, and thus cost less to learn.

Other features of the vocabulary sections to be borne in mind are these: (1) all verb bases are given in the special notation introduced in King & Yeon's *Elementary Korean* (see "About Verbs" below); (2) processive and descriptive bases are distinguished from each other by their English glosses—descriptive verbs are always preceded by *be* (e.g., be blue, be sad), while processive verbs are not; (3) vocabulary items in each lesson are listed in the order in which they occur in the lesson; to aid the learner in navigating these lists, they are broken up according to "Vocabulary from the Main Text," "Vocabulary from the Example Sentences," and "Vocabulary from the Exercises." All vocabulary items from each lesson can also be found in *alphabetical* order in the glossaries at the back of the book; (4) some vocabulary items are illustrated with full sentences and glossed with English translations in *italics* in the vocabulary sections; (5) most Sino-Korean vocabulary items in *Advanced Korean* are given along with their Chinese characters in parentheses. These are *not* part of the *Advanced Korean* course, and are given as a courtesy and aid to those (increasingly many) learners who already have some knowledge of Chinese characters through prior exposure to either Japanese or Chinese. Users of the book with no knowledge of these languages can ignore the Chinese characters.

About Verbs

This book follows King & Yeon's *Elementary Korean* and *Continuing Korean* in its treatment of the so-called "irregular" verbs and in its notations for verb base types in the vocabulary lists and glossaries. This is most significant for the ㅂ ~w verbs and ㄷ ~ ㄹ verbs, but also applies to the ㄹ-extending verbs. Verbs with the ㅂ ~w alternation end in final ...w–: 더w– (덥다) *be hot*; verbs with the ㄷ ~ ㄹ alternation end in final ...ㄹ - : 들 - (듣다) *listen*; and ㄹ-extending verbs end in - ㄹ - : 드 - ㄹ - (들다) *enter; lift/hold*. But because not all users of this book will be familiar with this system, we also give traditional dictionary forms in - 다. For example, 더w– (덥다) *be hot*, 들 - (듣다) *listen*, 드 - ㄹ - (들다), etc. In this system (covered in King & Yeon's *Elementary Korean*), students learn a rule which changes **w** to ㅂ before consonants, e.g., hot 더w– + - 다 → 덥다 (see below for use of linguistic symbols in this book). The **w** counts as a consonant, and students also learn the rule that **w** + 으 gives 우: 더w– + - 으세요 → 더우세요.

In the case of verbs like 들 - (듣다) *listen*, we take the form with ㄹ as the base (들 -), and students learn a rule which changes ㄹ to ㄷ before consonants: 들 - + - 다 → 듣다. Verbs like 사 - ㄹ - (살다) *live* are treated as a special kind of "ㄹ-extending" vowel base (사 - ㄹ -) which requires the addition of an ㄹ in front of certain verb endings. This is because verbs like these always select that shape of two-shape endings (endings like ﹣면 ~ ﹣으면 that occur with or without ﹣으 depending on whether the preceding base ends in a vowel or consonant) which is appropriate to vowel bases. Thus, in this system, verbs like 사﹣ㄹ﹣ (살다) live are a special kind of vowel base that sometimes insert a ㄹ before certain endings, but always select ending shapes appropriate for vowel bases. (In the traditional Korean system, they are a kind of irregular consonant base).

Of course, by the time students are ready for *Advanced Korean*, they should already have mastered the basics of Korean verb + ending mechanics, and thus this book does not actually delve into the analyses hinted at here. But for those learners (and teachers) who care to think about it, our analysis of the ㅂ ~**w** verbs actually saves the student one rule in comparison to the traditional treatment, and in general our analysis completely disposes of the traditional Korean notion of "irregular verb" for what are more productively thought of as different conjugation classes. It is this prejudicial notion of "irregular verb" which leads some Korean teachers (and students) to regard them as difficult, and tackle them far too late in a student's career.

About the English Translations and Glosses

In a number of cases the English translations of Korean expressions and patterns are structured to resemble as closely as possible the Korean meaning. In some cases, students and teachers may feel that certain English renditions are not typical English usage. The authors ask for indulgence on this matter.

About Linguistic Symbols

Our use of linguistic symbols amounts to a special kind of code which is designed to streamline the learning process for the student, and to streamline the book presentation. Once the teacher and students have mastered the few simple symbols below, they should have no trouble following the exposition in the book.

SYMBOL	COMMENTS
–	The hyphen is used to demarcate boundaries and bound forms. Because the abstract Korean verb stems (called "bases") to which endings attach are all bound forms (that is, they cannot be used and do not occur in real speech without some ending), verbs in each lesson's Vocabulary List are listed as a base (bound form) followed by a hyphen to its right (e.g., 사﹣ㄹ﹣ *live*). The same goes for all verb endings in Korean—they are abstract notions which only occur when attached to a verb base; they are bound forms, and always appear in the book with a hyphen to their left. We continue to refer to verb bases and endings in the grammar notes in this way, too.
+	The plus sign means "plus" or "added to / in combination with."
[...]	Phonetic notations are enclosed by square brackets. This notation is used to indicate the actual pronunciation of a Korean form when this is not indicated in the Korean orthography. Another usage of the square brackets is to indicate optional material.
*	The asterisk is used to mark grammatically unacceptable utterances.

→   This arrow sign means "becomes/gives/yields/produces."

←   This arrow sign means "comes from / is a product of / derives from."

~   The tilde is used to represent 1) an alternation, and means "in alternation with"; or 2) a glossary item repeated in a glossary definition.

How to Download the Online Contents for this Book.

1. Make sure you have an Internet connection.
2. Type the URL below into your web browser.

        http://www.tuttlepublishing.com/advanced-korean

For support, you can email us at info@tuttlepublishing.com.

그 사람이 왜 그러는지 알 수가 없었다

지난 겨울, 춘천 근처에 있는 청평사에 놀러 갔을 때에 있었던 일이다.

평일인데다가 소양댐에서 첫배를 탔기 때문에 청평사로 가는 사람이 나 말고는 아무도 없었다. 그런데 5분쯤 올라가다 보니 앞에 한 남자가 걸어가고 있는 것이 보였다.

나는 전날 그 근처에서 묵은 여행객일 거라고 생각했다. 그 사람도 내가 따라오고 있는 것을 느꼈는지 뒤를 돌아다보았다. 그리고는 내가 자기보다 앞서 갈까 봐 걸음을 재촉하는 것이었다. 호기심이 생겨서 내가 열심히 따라갔더니 그 사람은 더 빨리 걷는 것이었다. 나는 도대체 그 사람이 왜 그러는지 알 수가 없었다.

그런데 잠시 후 아직 문을 열지 않은 청평사 매표소가 나타났을 때 의문이 풀렸다. 그 사람은 거기서 표를 파는 사람이었다.

NEW VOCABULARY

Vocabulary from the Main Text

춘천(春川)	Ch'unch'ŏn (place name)	그리고는	and then; after which; after that
청평사(淸平寺)	Ch'ŏngp'yŏng Temple	앞서	in advance of, ahead of
평일(平日)	working day, weekday	앞서 가 -	go ahead of, precede
평일(平日)에	on weekdays	걸음	one's steps; one's pace; gait; walking (nominal form in the two-shape ending –(으)ㅁ from 걷다, 걸어요)
소양댐	Soyang Dam		
첫배	the first boat		
나 말고는	except for / other than me; besides me		
전(前) 날	the previous day	재촉(을) 하 -	urge on; urge (sb or sth) to hurry up; *here:* hasten (one's steps)
묵 -	spend the night; lodge; put up at	호기심(好奇心)	curiosity
여행(旅行)	traveling; journey, trip	매표소(賣票所)	ticket office; ticket booth
여행(旅行)(을) 하 -	travel	표(票)	ticket
여행객(旅行客)	traveler	나타나 -	appear
느끼 -	feel; sense	의문(疑問)	doubt
돌아다보 -	turn around and look, look back, look behind oneself	의문이 풀리 -	one's doubts are dispelled, removed, cleared away

Vocabulary from the Example Sentences

서두르 -	rush; rush about	모자라 -	be not enough; be insufficient (NB: processive)
그녀	she (formal / written)		
넘어지 -	fall down; slip and fall; fall over	당황(唐慌) 하 -	be confused; feel at a loss as to what to do; be flustered, bewildered (NB: processive)
늘	always; constantly		
꼭대기	summit, peak		
내용(內容)	contents	장소(場所)	place; venue
알아들 - (알아듣다)	understand, catch (sth said)	자꾸	continually; all the time; keep on ...–ing
즐거w– (즐겁다)	be enjoyable, fun	이해(理解)(가) 되 -	"get it"; understand
낡 -	be old (things / objects); old and worn out	이해(理解)	understanding
		이해(理解)(를) 하 -	understand
고장(故障)(이) 나 -	break; break down	비결(秘訣)	the secret, key, or knack to sth; the "trick"
경제적(經濟的)	economical		
경제(經濟)	economy	비밀(秘密)	secret you might tell sb
안전(安全) 하 -	be safe	첫눈에 반하 -	fall in love at first sight ("at first eye")
안전(安全)	safety		
집들이	housewarming (party / celebration)	정(情)(이) 드 - ㄹ - (들다)	grow fond of, attached to ("affection enters"); come to love sb (but not necessarily romantically)
한꺼번에	all at once; in one go; in one breath; in one stroke		

게으르 -	be lazy
요즘	lately
고민 (苦悶)	anguish; worry; mental agony
고민 (을) 하 -	worry, agonize over
연락 (連絡) (을) 하 -	contact; get in contact with
출장 (出張) (을) 가 -	go away on an official trip; go away on business
출장 (出張)	official trip; business trip
살 (이) 빠지 -	lose weight
유명 (有名) 하 -	be famous
아무렇게나	any old which way, in any manner
성격 (性格) [- 격]	character; personality
어울리 -	(people) get along with, go well together; (clothes) go well with, match; be appropriate for; suit

더러 **w**- (더럽다)	be dirty, filthy, unkempt
늦잠 (을) 자 -	sleep late; sleep in
길 (이) 막히 -	road is blocked, jammed (with traffic), congested
도착 (到着) (을) 하 -	arrive at; reach
취직 (就職)	getting / landing a job; finding employment
취직 (을) 하 -	get / find a job
시험 (試驗) 에 붙 -	"stick to," i.e., pass an exam
시험에 떨어지 -	fail an exam
바닷가	the seaside
가 버리 -	leave; take off; get up and go
흉 (을) 보 -	speak ill of; disparage; criticize; run down
계속 (繼續)	continuously

Vocabulary from the Exercises

갑자기	suddenly
안색 (顔色)	complexion; the color of one's face
보고서 (報告書)	written report
병 (이) 나 -	get sick (not to be confused with 병 (이) 나 (ㅅ) - , 나아: *sickness gets better*)
지루하 -	be boring
다치 -	hurt oneself
생각 (이) 나 -	recall; sth comes to mind
화 (火) (가) 나 -	get angry
인기 (人氣) (가) 있 - [인끼]	be popular (used with people)
걸어 다니 -	go about / attend on foot; walk around
요리 (料理)	cooking; cuisine; dish or main course
솜씨	skill or dexterity (usually involving the hands)
기침 (을) 하 -	cough

부 (ㅅ) - (붓다, 부어)	swell, swell up
버리 -	discard, throw away
새벽	dawn; daybreak
승객 (乘客)	a passenger
시청 (市廳)	city hall
잃어버리 -	lose sth
반말	Intimate or Plain Style speech
존댓말 [존댄말]	Polite or Formal Style speech
다행 (多幸)	great fortune
다행 (多幸) 이에요	*It is a great fortune; it is fortunate*
다행히 (도)	fortunately; as good luck would have it
지갑 (紙匣)	wallet; pocketbook; purse
두고 오 -	leave sth behind (usually by accident)
그대로	just as it is / was; intact; just as you are
다이어트 (를) 하 -	diet; go on a diet

PATTERNS

1. Startling Close-ups with -더니

The one-shape ending ‐더니 is a kind of "zoom shot" ending which has the effect of zooming in like a camera on what is to be said in the following clause, which is usually about something startling or interesting. It can attach to Past Bases (in which the subject cannot be second-person "you" and is usually first-person "I" or "we") or to Plain Bases (in which case the subject is usually not in the first person). ㄹ-extending bases like 사‐ㄹ‐ (살다) *live* and 파‐ㄹ‐ (팔다) *sell* retain their ‐ㄹ‐. Here are some examples (taken from the Yonsei 『외국인을 위한 한국어문법』):

1. 친구가 가자는 대로 갔더니 노래방이었어요.
    I went along with my friend, as requested, and it turned out to be a karaoke room.

2. 금방 결혼할 것처럼 서두르더니 아직 소식이 없죠?
    They were rushing headlong into an imminent marriage—still no news?

3. 과일에 채소까지 샀더니 너무 무거워.
    I bought vegetables in addition to the fruit, and now [my bag] is too heavy.

4. 덥더니 비가 오는구먼.
    It was hot, but now it's raining!

5. 대학에 입학했나 했더니 어느새 졸업이군요.
    I was thinking maybe she had just entered college, but [whadda ya know—] she's graduating already!

6. 음식을 만들어다가 친구한테 주었더니 좋아하던데요.
    I made some food and took it to my friend, and [whadda ya know—] he liked it!

7. 연습을 열심히 했더니 이젠 잘 해요.
    We practiced hard, and [whadda ya know—] now we're pretty good.

8. 수미 씨는 열심히 공부하더니 시험을 잘 봤어요.
    Sumi studied hard, and [now—whadda ya know—] she did well on her test.

9. 그녀가 편지를 읽더니 울기 시작했습니다.
    She was reading the letter, and then [—whadda ya know—] she started crying.

10. 그 애가 과식을 하더니 배탈이 난 모양이죠.
    He was eating too much, so now [—whadda ya know—] it seems he has a stomach ache.

2. Transferentive -다(가)

Transferentive verb forms, with the ending -다 (optionally followed by 가), indicate a shift or transfer in action—either a change of the verb action itself, of its direction, or of the recipient of its benefit.

Attached to a Plain Base, the ending makes the form mean when *so-and-so* happens, which is then followed by another action that interrupts, transfers, or shifts the trend of the first situation to that of the second situation. (It is not specified by the construction alone whether the original action is later resumed.)

Attached to a Past Base, the past transferentive form -었다(가) conveys the meaning when *so-and-so happened* or something *came full circle, and then*, followed by a verb that tells of something contradictory or unanticipated that happened right after the first action indicated by the past transferentive form.

11. 어디 갔다 오셨어요?
    Where have you been?

12. 뛰어가다가 넘어졌어요.
    He was running and then fell down.

13. 아이가 울다가 잤어요.
    The baby cried itself to sleep.

14. 아기가 자다가 깨서 기분이 안 좋은 것 같아요.
    The baby woke up from a [deep] sleep, and doesn't seem to be in a good mood.

15. 시장에 가다가 우체국에 들렀어요.
    We stopped at the post office on the way to the market.

16. 시장에 갔다가 우체국에 들를까요?
    Shall we go to the market [first] and then drop by the post office?

17. 삼 개월 전에 새 컴퓨터를 샀다가 팔았습니다.
    Three months ago I bought a new computer but then sold it [again].

18. 준비를 하시다가 질문이 있으시면 언제든지 전화하십시오.
    If, in the course of preparing, you [suddenly] have any questions, call me any time.

19. 사무실에서 다른 걸 찾다가 만 원짜리를 하나 찾았어요.
    I was looking for something in the office when I found a 10,000-wŏn note.

Another construction involving transferentive forms employs two such forms, of opposite or contrasting meaning (either in the present or, more commonly, in the past) rounded off by a form of 하-, 해요 or 그러-, 그래요. This construction means that the two actions keep interrupting each other.

For example:

20. 편지를 썼다가 지웠다가 했어요.
    Going back and forth, I wrote a letter, and then erased it.

21. 달은 한 달마다 커지다가 작아지다가 해요. or
    달은 한 달마다 커졌다가 작아졌다가 해요.
    The moon waxes and wanes each month. or
    The moon gets bigger and smaller each month.

22. 시장에 갔다 우체국에 갔다 해서 저녁이 늦어지면 어떻게 해요?
    What will we do if dinner is late because of our going to the market and [going] to the post office and so on?

23. 이 하나가 늘 아팠다 괜찮았다 그래요.
    One of my teeth aches on and off.

24. 불을 켰다가 껐다가 그러지 말아요!
    Stop turning the lights on and off!

It is important not to confuse the past-tense transferentive form 갔다(가) *went, and then...* with the abbreviation 갖다(가)←가져다(가) *carry / bring and then [shift]* as seen here:

25. 이 국을 할아버지께 갖다 드려요.
    Take this soup and give it to Grandfather.

The form 갖다(가) conveys the meaning *take and shift [the position of]*. Thus, 갖다 주십시오 means *Please bring it to me*, a useful expression when ordering food in a restaurant.

The transferentive form 있다(가), meaning *stays [for a while] and then*, is the etymological source for the adverb 이따(가), which means *in a little while* or *later on*.

Here are more examples of transferentive forms:

On Plain Bases:
26. 어제는 수학 선생님의 강의를 듣다가 잤어요.
    Yesterday, I was listening to the math teacher's lecture and fell asleep.

27 길을 걸어가다가, 피곤해서 버스를 탔어요.
    While I was walking along the street, I got tired and got on a bus.

On Past Bases:
28. 대사관에 갔다 왔어요.
    I've been to the embassy. [I went to the embassy and then came back.]

29. 갔다가 바로 오세요.
    Come right back!
30. 싼 것을 샀다가 비싼 것으로 바꿨어요.
    I bought a cheap one, but exchanged it for an expensive one.

Repeated Actions:

31. 사람들이 들어왔다 나갔다 하네요.
    People keep coming in and going out.

32. 수저를 그렇게 들었다 놓았다 하지 말아요!
    Stop picking up and putting down your spoon and chopsticks like that!

33. 비가 오다 말다 하네요.
    It's raining on and off. [It keeps raining and then stopping.]

The last example shows that you can use the auxiliary 마 - ㄹ - (말다) *desist* (which is often put after Suspective - 지) to make negative commands and suggestions when you want to use a negative form of the same verb instead of using a completely different second verb. Another example:

34. 비가 오다 말았어요.
    It started to rain and then stopped.

3. *On top of ...–ing, [what's more...]* with -(으)ㄴ / -는데다(가)

First, it would be useful to learn the following adverb: 그런데다(가) *on top of that; what's more; to make matters worse.*

This pattern combines the circumstantial pattern - (으)ㄴ데, - 는데 with the transferentive particle - 에다(가). This transferentive particle emphasizes or calls attention to a shift in time, action, or space. Here the composite meaning of the ending - (으)ㄴ데 / - 는데 plus the particle - 에다(가) can be described as *on top of / in addition to the circumstance, [SHIFT—something else unexpected or noteworthy happens]*. (Note that you never see the - 에 and have to imagine that it is hiding, or has been sucked into the 데.)

35. A: 왜 꼭대기까지 올라가지 않았습니까?
       Why didn't you go up to the summit?

    B: 바람이 많이 부는데다가 눈까지 와서 꼭대기까지 올라갈 수 없었습니다.
       On top of there being lots of wind, it was snowing, so we couldn't go up to the summit.

36. A: 강의 내용을 많이 알아들었습니까?
       Did you understand much of the contents of the lecture?

    B: 말을 빨리 하는데다가 어려운 단어를 많이 써서 알아듣기 힘들었습니다.
       In addition to talking [too] fast, she used a lot of difficult words, so it was difficult to understand.

37. A: 여행 즐거웠습니까?

    Was your trip enjoyable?

    B: 버스가 낡은데다가 에어컨이 고장 나서 고생을 많이 했습니다.

    On top of the bus being old and decrepit, the air-conditioning was broken, so I had a really tough time.

38. A: 무슨 차를 사는 게 좋겠습니까?

    What kind of car would be best to buy?

    B: 모닝이 경제적인데다가 안전하니까 모닝을 사십시오.

    In addition to being economical, the Morning is [also] safe, so buy a Morning.

39. A: 집들이 잘 했습니까?

    Did you have a successful housewarming party?

    B: 손님이 한꺼번에 온데다가 음식이 모자라서 애를 많이 먹었습니다.

    On top of the guests coming all at once, we were short of food, so I had a tough time.

40. A: 앨버트 씨 한국말 많이 늘었지요?

    Albert's Korean has improved a lot, hasn't it?

    B: 네, 머리도 좋은데다가 열심히 하니까 금방 느는 것 같습니다.

    Yes. On top of being smart, he [also] works hard, so he seems to improve right away.

---

4. *If / when one tries doing it over a period of time, then [the next thing one knows]...* **with -다(가) 보니**

This pattern is a combination of the transferentive pattern ‑(으)니(까) with the verb 보‑ – *see* (functioning more like the auxiliary 보‑ in the exploratory pattern ‑어 보‑ *does it [to check out what it's like]; does it [and takes stock after giving it a try]*). This pattern is encountered much more often as ‑다 보니 than as ‑다가 보니. Note that the pattern can occur with descriptive verbs, too, where the meaning is more along the lines of reflecting (보니) on this [descriptive] state of affairs, I find that...

41. A: 약속 장소를 금방 찾았습니까?

    Were you able to find the meeting place right away?

    B: 네, 버스에서 내려서 조금 걸어가다(가) 보니 보였습니다.

    Yes. I saw it [it was visible] after I got off the bus and walked a bit.

42. A: 이 책 어렵지요? 다 이해했습니까?

    This book is difficult, isn't it? Did you understand all of it?

    B: 네, 처음에는 너무 어려워서 이해할 수 없었는데 자꾸 읽다 보니 이해가 되었습니다.

    Yes. At first it was very difficult so I wasn't able to understand it, but after I kept reading it, I got it.

43. A: 왜 이렇게 늦었습니까?

      Why are you so late?

   B: 친구들하고 얘기하다 보니 늦었습니다.

      I was talking with my friends, and [before I knew it] I was late.

44. A: 한국말이 많이 늘었네요. 무슨 비결이 있습니까?

      Your Korean has improved a lot! Is there some sort of secret?

   B: 한국 사람하고 자주 이야기하다 보니 늘었습니다.

      I have been talking frequently with Koreans, and [before I knew it] I improved.

45. A: 첫눈에 반해서 결혼했습니까?

      Did you get married after falling in love at first sight?

   B: 아니요. 자꾸 만나다 보니 정이 들어서 결혼했습니다.

      No. We got together often, and [next thing we knew] we grew fond of each other and got married.

46. 제가 게으르다 보니 전화도 못했네요.

      I'm so lazy I didn't even get around to calling.

5. *Perhaps because...* with -(으)ㄴ지, -는지

This is the oblique question pattern -(으)ㄴ지, -는지 used in an idiomatic way. The best way to understand this pattern is as an abbreviation of the longer -(으)ㄴ지, -는지 [도] [모르지만]... *maybe / perhaps is, does, did.* This pattern means *Perhaps it is a question of...* or *Perhaps because... [but I don't really know].* More idiomatically, it expresses *It might /must be the case that...* (followed by the result or situation which has led one to this supposition).

47. A: 준호 일어났습니까?

      Is Chunho up?

   B: 오늘은 수업이 없는지 일어나지 않습니다.

      Maybe he doesn't have class today—he's not getting up.

48. A: 요즘 정민이 왜 저래요?

      Why is Chŏngmin like that lately?

   B: 글쎄요. 무슨 고민이 있는지 웃지를 않습니다.

      Good question. She must have something on her mind—she doesn't smile.

49. A: 영호 씨가 요즘 바쁜지 연락을 안 합니다.

      Yŏngho must be busy lately—he hasn't been in touch.

   B: 영호 씨 출장 간 거 모르십니까?

      You didn't know that Yŏngho had gone away on a business trip?

50. A: 철민이 뭐 합니까?

   What's Ch'ŏlmin doing?

   B: 여행을 가려고 하는지 여행 가방에 이것저것 넣고 있습니다.

   He must be getting ready to travel or something, as he's putting this and that into his travel bag.

51. A: 수잔 한국말 많이 늘었습니까?

   Has Susan's Korean improved a lot?

   B: 아니요, 그동안 한국말을 안 썼는지 전보다 더 못하는 것 같았습니다.

   No. She must not have used Korean for a while—her Korean seems worse than before.

52. A: 요즘 경호 보셨습니까?

   Have you seen Kyŏngho lately?

   B: 아까 만났는데 그 동안 어디 아팠는지 살이 많이 빠졌던데요.

   I met him just a short while ago; he must have been sick recently, because he's lost a lot of weight.

6. *No... at all* with 아무...도 and *any... at all* with 아무...(이)나

The pattern 아무 NOUN도 means *no NOUN at all* (the option of any other NOUN is closed off). On the other hand, the pattern 아무 NOUN(이)나 means *any NOUN at all* (the options are open ended, and any and every NOUN is a possibility).

There are two slight tricks with these patterns. The first is that the default NOUN is *person*. Thus, 아무도 (with no NOUN tucked in between 아무 and 도) followed by a negative verb means *nobody at all*, and 아무나 (with no NOUN tucked in between 아무 and 나) means *anybody at all*. The second is that the particles 도 and (이)나 that bracket these patterns actually bracket *everything*—including any relevant particles. Thus, in the example sentence below, *[I never fought] with anybody* is 아무하고도, with the particle 하고 tucked in between 아무 and 도. See below for more examples.

53. 나는 지금까지 아무하고도 싸워 본 적이 없습니다.

   I have never fought with anybody until now.

54. 내가 왔을 때 여기에 아무도 없었습니다.

   There was nobody here when I came.

55. 아침부터 지금까지 아무것도 못 먹었습니다.

   I haven't eaten a thing since morning until now.

56. 아직 아무한테도 말 안 했습니다.

   I haven't told anybody yet.

57. 열심히 찾았지만 아무데도 없습니다.

   I searched high and low, but it was nowhere [to be found].

58. 아무 데서나 담배를 피우면 안 됩니다.
    One shouldn't smoke just anywhere [i.e., one shouldn't smoke in any old, arbitrary place—there are designated areas for this!].
    (This would be said to somebody as a way of scolding them for smoking somewhere they shouldn't.)

59. 유명한 식당이니까 근처에 와서 아무한테나 물어 보십시오.
    It's a well-known restaurant, so ask anybody once you get close [to the vicinity].

60. 아무렇게나 하십시오.
    Do as you please. [Do it any way you please.]

61. 배가 고프니까 아무 것이나 먹을 것을 주십시오.
    I'm hungry, so please give me something to eat—anything at all.

62. 가고 싶은 사람은 아무나 다 가도 됩니다.
    Anybody [at all] who wants to go—[all] can go.

63. 정아는 성격이 좋아서 아무하고나 잘 어울립니다.
    Chŏng'a has such a pleasant personality, she gets along well with anybody.

64. 바지가 더러워지니까 아무 데나 앉지 마십시오.
    Your trousers will get dirty, so don't just sit any-old-where. [Be careful where you sit!]

65. 항상 집에 있으니까 아무 때나 전화하십시오.
    I'm always at home, so call any time.

7. *For fear that / lest...* with -(으)ㄹ까 봐(서)

The best way to understand this pattern is as an abbreviation of the longer -(으)ㄹ까 봐(서) 걱정했는데... *was worried that / lest [something untoward might happen].*

66. 손님이 생각보다 많이 왔습니다.
    More guests came than I had expected.

    음식이 모자랄까 봐 걱정을 많이 했습니다.
    I was really worried that there might not be enough food.

67. 늦잠을 잤습니다.
    I slept late.

    회사에 늦을까 봐 걱정했는데 길이 안 막혀서 일찍 도착했습니다.
    I was worried that I might be late to the office, but the roads weren't congested, so I arrived early.

68. 취직 시험에 붙었습니다.
    I passed the company entrance examination.

    그동안 시험에 떨어질까 봐 걱정을 많이 했습니다.
    I was worried for a while that I might fail the exam.

69. 바닷가에 왔습니다.
    We arrived at the seaside.

    낮에는 덥지만 밤에는 추울까 봐 두꺼운 옷을 가지고 왔습니다.
    I brought thick clothes for fear that it might be hot in the daytime but cold at night.

70. 약속 시간에 30분이나 늦었습니다.
    I was a good thirty minutes late for the appointment.

    친구가 가 버렸을까 봐 걱정을 했는데 기다리고 있었습니다.
    I was afraid that my friend would have taken off [already], but she was waiting for me.

71. 선영이 흉을 보는데 어떤 사람이 계속 쳐다봅니다.
    Some person kept [keeps] staring at me when I was saying critical things about Sŏnyŏng.

    선영이를 아는 사람일까 봐 걱정이 되었습니다.
    I was worried that it might be somebody who knew [knows] her.

EXERCISES

Exercise 1: Reading Comprehension

Write out answers to the following questions.

1. 나는 언제, 어디에 놀러 갔습니까?
2. 청평사에 가는 사람이 많이 있었습니까? 왜 그랬습니까?
3. 나는 앞에 가는 남자가 어떤 사람일 거라고 생각했습니까?
4. 그 사람은 나를 보고 어떻게 했습니까?
5. 내가 열심히 따라갔더니 그 사람은 어떻게 했습니까?
6. 앞에 가던 사람은 무엇을 하는 사람이었습니까?
7. 그 사람은 왜 나보다 먼저 가려고 했습니까?

Exercise 2: Practice with -더니

The clauses in the following sentences are joined with -었는데. Replace -었는데 with either -더니 or -었더니 as appropriate and translate the resulting sentences into English.

1. 하루 종일 날이 흐렸는데 저녁부터 비가 내리기 시작했습니다.
2. 며칠 잠을 못 잤는데 좀 피곤하네요.
3. 어제 저녁을 많이 먹었는데 배가 아파요.
4. 오랜만에 만났는데 많이 컸더라.
5. 어제는 추웠는데 오늘은 덥네요.
6. 어젠 전화 목소리가 힘이 없었는데 오늘은 기분이 많이 좋아진 것 같네요.
7. (네가) 빵을 사 왔는데 왜 (네가) 밥을 먹니?
8. (내가) 빵을 사 왔는데 왜 (네가) 밥을 먹니?
9. (내가) 수미를 오랜만에 만났는데 못 알아보겠어.
10. (네가) 수미를 오랜만에 만났는데 할 이야기가 그렇게 많았니?

Exercise 3: Practice with -다(가)

Each item below contains two sentences. Link the two sentences together with the transferentive -다(가), to show the meaning *someone does or did something, and then... [shift]*. Then translate the resulting sentence. For example, the first one would be 로비에서 한 시간 기다리다가 그냥 갔어요. *I waited for an hour in the reception room and then left.*

1. 로비에서 한 시간 기다렸어요. 그냥 갔어요.
2. 밥을 먹었어요. 갑자기 안색이 이상해졌어요.
3. 젓가락을 썼어요. 포크로 바꿨어요.
4. 밤 늦게까지 보고서를 썼어요. 잤어요.
5. 버스에서 내렸어요. 넘어졌어요.
6. 생선만 며칠 동안 먹었어요. 병이 났어요.
7. 뉴스를 봤어요. 너무 지루해서 텔레비전을 그냥 껐어요.
8. 집에 갔어요. 도서관에 들러야겠어요.
9. 학교에 왔어요. 영진 씨를 만났어요.
10. 비가 왔어요. (갑자기 그쳤어요)
11. 한국에서 회사에 다녔어요. 캐나다에 왔습니다.
12. 도서관에 갔어요. 친구를 만났어요.
13. 사무실을 청소했어요. 이 사진을 찾았어요.
14. 운동을 했어요. 다리를 다쳤어요.
15. 음악을 들었어요. 여자친구 생각이 났어요.

Exercise 4: Practice with -(으)ㄴ / -는데다(가)

Answer the following questions using the pattern -(으)ㄴ / -는데다(가).

1. 모임이 재미있었습니까?
2. 가방 샀습니까?
3. 이 식당에는 언제나 이렇게 손님이 많습니까?
4. 영진 씨, 어제 왜 그렇게 화가 났습니까?
5. 수미 씨는 왜 그렇게 친구들한테 인기가 있습니까?
6. 앨버트 씨 한국말 많이 늘었지요?

Exercise 5: Practice with -다 보니

Answer the following questions with a verb form -다 보니.

1. A: 왜 이렇게 늦었습니까?
   B: _____.
2. A: 어떻게 해서 테니스를 이렇게 잘 치게 되었습니까?
   B: _____.
3. A: 어떻게 여기까지 오게 되었습니까?
   B: _____.
4. A: 요즘 회사까지 걸어 다니십니까?
   B: _____.
5. A: 선영 씨, 요리 솜씨가 많이 늘었습니다.
   B: _____.
6. A: 수미 씨, 살이 많이 빠진 것 같습니다.
   B: _____.

Exercise 6: Practice with -(으)ㄴ지, -는지

Fill in the blanks below with an appropriate form or clause -(으)ㄴ지 or -는지.

1. A: 준영 씨 오늘 이상하지요?
   B: 네, _____ 말을 안 합니다.
2. A: 선주가 요즘도 자주 전화합니까?
   B: 아니요, _____.
3. A: 영호가 오늘은 일찍 자네요.
   B: _____ 저녁을 먹자마자 잡니다.
4. A: 경선 씨하고 창민 씨가 요즘 안 만나는 것 같지요?
   B: _____ 안 만나는 것 같습니다.
5. A: 아까 선영 씨를 만났습니다.
   B: 그런데 _____ 자꾸 기침을 했습니다.
6. A: 선미 씨한테 안 좋은 일이 있습니까?
   B: _____ 눈이 많이 부었던데요.

Exercise 7: Practice with 아무

Fill in the blanks below with an appropriate phrase using either 아무...도 or 아무...(이)나.

1. 하루 종일 _____ 못 먹었습니다.
2. 비밀이니까 _____ 말하지 마십시오.
3. 계속 집에 있을 거니까 _____ 전화하십시오. ["anytime"]
4. 내일 우리 집에 오고 싶은 사람은 _____ 다 오십시오.
5. _____ 휴지를 버리면 안 됩니다.
6. 새벽에 버스를 탔더니 승객이 나 말고는 _____ 없었습니다.
7. 나는 지금까지 _____ 싸워 본 적이 없습니다.
8. 이 근처에 있는 커피숍은 다 괜찮으니까 _____ 갑시다.
9. 그 식당은 유명하니까 그 근처에 가서 _____ 물어 보면 가르쳐 줄 겁니다.
10. 죄송합니다. 시간이 없어서 _____ 했습니다. ["any old which way"]
11. 열쇠를 잃어버려서 집안을 샅샅이 찾아보았지만 _____ 없었습 니다.
12. 영민아, _____ 반말을 하면 안 돼.

Exercise 8: Practice with -(으)ㄹ까 봐(서)

Why were you worried? Fill in the blanks below using an appropriate form -(으)ㄹ까 봐(서).

1. 손님이 많이 와서 _____.
2. _____ 이겨서 다행입니다.
3. 오늘 시험이 있어서 어제 밤을 새웠습니다. _____ 다행 히 시험을 잘 봤습니다.
4. 도서관 책상 위에 지갑을 두고 왔습니다. _____ 가 보니 그대 로 있었습니다.
5. 약속 시간에 40분 늦었습니다. _____ 아직도 기다리고 있었습니다.
6. 나는 요즘 다이어트를 하고 있습니다. _____ 초콜릿하고 아이스크림 같 은 것을 먹지 않습니다.

로마에 가면 로마법을 따르라는 말이 있잖아요

　나는 전에 2년 동안 로마에 가서 산 적이 있었다. 그때 제일 힘들었던 것이 로마 사람들의 운전 습관에 익숙해지는 것이었다.

　언젠가 한번은 교황청 근처에서 큰 교통사고가 나는 바람에 차들이 많이 밀렸다. 그래서 나는 꼼짝도 못 하고 차 안에서 30분이나 앉아 있었다. 그때 주위에 있던 차들이 유턴을 하기 시작했다. 나는 다른 날 같았으면 좀 더 기다렸을 텐데 그 날은 중요한 약속이 있었기 때문에 남들처럼 차를 돌렸다. 그때 어디서 나타났는지 경찰관이 다가와서 나에게 차를 길옆에 세우라고 명령했다. 그리고는 운전 면허증을 보여 달라고 했다. 나는 약간 걱정이 되었지만 그동안 배운 이탈리아말로 이렇게 말했다.

　"로마에 가면 로마법을 따르라는 말이 있잖아요. 나는 단지 로마 사람들이 한 것처럼 했을 뿐이에요."

　그러나 그 말은 경찰관에게 통하지 않았다. 그래서 결국 나는 딱지를 떼이고 말았다.

NEW VOCABULARY

Vocabulary from the Main Text

습관 (習慣)	custom; habit
습관이 됐어요.	*I'm used to it.*
익숙해지 -	get accustomed / used to
언젠가 (는)	once; sometime or other (I don't remember); some day
cf. 무언가	sth or other
누군가	sb or other
어디선가	(happening at) some place or other
교황청 (敎皇廳)	the Vatican
교황 (敎皇)	the pope
~청 (~廳)	administrative headquarters
시청 (市廳)	city hall
밀리 -	*lit.:* be / get pushed; *here:* get backed up, jammed, clogged (said of work or traffic)
꼼짝도 못 하 -	can't even budge; can't move an inch
유턴	U-turn
다른 날 같았으면	*if it had been ("like") any other day...*
좀 더 기다렸을 텐데	*I would have waited a bit more.*
남들처럼	like the others
돌리 -	turn sth; make sth turn

차를 돌렸다	*I turned my car around.*
경찰관 (警察官)	police officer
경찰 (警察)	the police
경찰서 (警察署)	police station
경찰국가 (警察國家)	police state
다가오 -	approach; come near; come up to
세우 -	stop (a car); bring to a stop
명령 (命令) (을) 하 -	order; command
운전면허증 (運轉免許證) [- 쯩]	driver's license
약간 (若干)	a bit, a little; somewhat
로마법 (法) [- 뻡]	the ways ("law") of Rome
따르 - , 따라	follow (NB: Note that this base is not ㄹ - doubling—it is irregular.)
단지 (但只)	just; only; merely; simply
했을 뿐이에요	*all / the only thing I did was (to do as the Romans do)*
(말이) 통 (通) 하 -	(one's words) get through (as in communicate with; get through to)
마음 (이) 통하 -	communicate well; understand each other
결국 (結局) (에)	ultimately; in the end
딱지 (를) 떼이 -	get a ticket
딱지를 떼이고 말았다	*I ended up getting a ticket.*

Vocabulary from the Example Sentences

잘못 타 -	get in the wrong vehicle ("ride in error")
잘못	means (1) error, mistake, e.g., 내 잘못이에요. *It's my mistake,* or (2) mistakenly, in error (adv.) (as in 잘못 타 -)
조용히	quietly
조용히 하세요!	*Please be quiet!*
일등 (一等) (을) 하 -	get first place / prize

일등 (一等)	first class; first place
달리 -	run; race along
제주도 (濟州道)	Cheju Island
미리	beforehand; in advance; ahead of time
미리미리	(same as above; more common in colloquial Korean)
강아지	puppy; doggie
갖다 주 -	bring to / for

용(用)돈 [- 똔]	spending money; pocket money
번호(番號)	number
전화번호(電話番號)	telephone number
주민등록번호 (住民登錄~)	one's (Korean) citizen registration number (all Koreans born in Korea have one)
외국인등록번호 (外國人登錄~)	one's foreigner registration number (for foreigners residing in Korea)
물가(物價)	price(s) (of sth)
해(서) 오 -	do sth before one comes; do sth and then come; come having done sth
신경(神經)(을) 쓰 -	get worked up about sth, worry about; stress about

신경을 쓰지 마세요.	*Don't worry about it.*
사이	*lit.:* "the space between"; relationship
애인(愛人) 사이	dating relationship
친구(親舊) 사이	"just friends" relationship
제 시간(時間)에	on time
모두	all; everyone; in all cases
취(醉)하 -	get drunk (NB: processive)
취했어요.	*I'm drunk.*
식사(食事)	meal
끝내 -	finish sth
입맛(을) 잃어버리 -	lose one's appetite
초대(招待)(를) 하 -	invite
부부(夫婦)	married couple, husband and wife

Vocabulary from the Exercises

법규(法規)	rules, regulations; legislation
교통법규(交通法規)	traffic rules / regulations
처벌(處罰)(을) 하 -	punish
법규에 따라 처벌하 -	punish according to / in accordance with the law
위반(違反)	violation; infringement, infraction
위반(違反)(을) 하 -	violate; infringe; break
그건 규칙 위반이 에요.	*That's against the regulations.*
잘 봐 주 -	give sb a break
이유(理由)	reason
웬일로...?	*Why... ? What for? On account of what (thing)? For what reason ... ?*
웬일이세요?	*What's the matter (with you)?*
웬일로 늦었어요?	*Why were you late? What were you late for?*
모임	meeting; gathering; get-together
경기(競技)	athletic competition
야구경기(野球競技)	baseball game
경기대회(競技大會)	athletic meet, competition

연습경기(練習競技)	practice game
경기장(競技場)	stadium; track and field
중단(中斷)(이) 되 -	be / get suspended, broken off, or interrupted
찌개	stew
김치찌개	kimch'i stew
된장찌개	*twenjang* stew
순두부찌개	soft tofu stew
고춧가루	red hot pepper powder
들고 다니 -	carry around
섭섭하 -	be sad that sb is leaving; be disappointed; be regrettable; be / feel sorry
섭섭하게도	to one's regret
과장(課長)	section chief; section head; manager
염려(念慮)	worry, concern
염려(念慮)(를) 하지 마세요.	*Don't worry.*
안심(安心)하 -	be / feel at ease; feel unworried
실망(失望)(을) 하 -	feel disappointed
반드시	for sure; certainly; without fail
후추	black pepper

집 -	pick up, take up (with the fingers); *here: Please pass (the pepper).*	이혼(離婚)	divorce	
		이혼(離婚) (을) 하 -	divorce, get divorced from	
마르 -	lose weight; be thin, skinny (NB: processive)	남편과 이혼했다.	*[She] got divorced from her husband.*	
진호는 너무 말랐다. *Chinho is too skinny.*		깨뜨리 -	break sth	
모양(模樣)	appearance; shape; form	부탁 (을) 들어 주 - (듣다)	do the favor that sb asks	
동전(銅錢)	coins; change	의견(意見)	opinion	
특별(特別) 하 -	be special, particular	찬성(贊成) (을) 하 -	endorse, agree with	
밤 (을) 새우 -	stay up all night	의견에 찬성(을) 하 -	agree with an opinion	
어지러**w**– (어지럽다)	be / feel dizzy			
성공(成功) (을) 하 -	achieve success; succeed	설거지	the dishes; the washing up	

PATTERNS

1. *Because / on account of* with -(으)ㄴ / -는 바람에

This pattern was covered in Lesson 24 of *Continuing Korean*, and usually implies that something unpleasant, negative or undesirable happens to the speaker because of whatever transpires in the clause with - (으) ㄴ / - 는 바람에.

1. A: 왜 이렇게 늦었습니까?
    Why are you so late?

    B: 버스를 잘못 타는 바람에 늦었습니다.
    I'm late because I got on the wrong bus.

2. A: 영진아, 좀 조용히 해. 네가 큰 소리로 얘기하는 바람에 못 들었잖아.
    Yŏngjin, please be quiet! I couldn't hear because of how loudly you're talking.

    B: 미안해.
    Sorry.

3. A: 수미 씨한테서 빌린 책 다 읽었습니까?
    Did you finish reading the book you borrowed from Sumi?

    B: 아니요, 어제 밤에 잠이 드는 바람에 다 못 읽었습니다.
    No. I couldn't read all of it because I fell asleep last night.

4. A: 어떻게 김진호 선수가 마라톤에서 1등을 했습니까?
    How did athlete Kim Chinho get first place in the marathon?

    B: 1등으로 달리던 신영동 선수가 다리에 쥐가 나는 바람에 김진호 선수가 1등을 했습니다.
    He got first place on account of athlete Sin Yŏngdong, who was in first, getting a cramp in his leg.

5. A: 제주도 여행 재미있었습니까?
    Was your trip to Cheju Island fun?

    B: 비가 오는 바람에 고생만 많이 하고 왔습니다.
    All we did was suffer a lot because of the rain.

6. A: 어제 저녁 늦게까지 일하셨지요?
    You worked until late last night, didn't you?

    B: 네, 할 일이 많아지는 바람에 늦게까지 일하게 됐어요.
    Yeah, I had to work late on account of the growing list of things to be done.

2. **[It is the expectation / intention that] someone would be / do, would have been / done with -(으)ㄹ 텐데(요)**

This is a combination of two patterns. The first is the pattern -(으)ㄹ 터(이)- where the post-modifier 테 (or 터) means roughly *intention; expectation*. The second is the Imminent Elaboration pattern -(으)ㄴ / -는데. (The "(이)-" in our notation here is the copula, which, as you will recall, deletes after vowels in colloquial Korean.)

Korean has three different but related patterns that use the pattern -(으)ㄹ 터(이)-.

2.1. Expressing Intentions with -(으)ㄹ 테(이)-.

The expression -(으)ㄹ 터(이)- is used to mean *expect; (fully) intend; be supposed to,* and originally came from -(으)ㄹ 터(이)- *it is (in) a position [= basis for planning] to happen,* where 터 is a word (now functioning as a postmodifier, i.e., as a grammatical element privileged to occur after modifiers in a grammatical pattern or structure) meaning *site; place.* Nowadays -(으)ㄹ 터(이)- *it is the site for ...-ing* is limited to sentences like the following:

7. 여기는 집을 지을 터다.
    This is the site where we will build the house.

Compare this with the following example:

8. 우리가 여기에 집을 지을 테다.
    We expect to build a house here.

You will find that some Korean texts write -(으)ㄹ 테- as -(으)ㄹ 터이-, but you can treat these as simple spelling variants. The variant in -(으)ㄹ 테- is most common in colloquial, spoken Korean. Here are some more examples of -(으)ㄹ 테-:

9. 먹을 테냐, 안 먹을 테냐?
    Do you expect / intend to eat or not?

10. 오늘 가는 것이 좋을 테지요.
    It will be better to go today, you know.

11. 그 사람도 거기서 만나게 될 테지요.
    I expect to get to see him there, too.

12. 어떤 일을 할 테냐?
    What sort of work do you expect / intend to do?

13. 연구소를 세울 테야.
    I expect / intend to set up a research institute.

14. 음악회가 7시 30분부터 시작할 테면 빨리 먹고 가야겠네.
    If the concert is [supposed] to start at 7:30, we'll have to eat in a hurry [and go].

15. 갈 테면 가세요.
    lit.: If it is your intention to go, [then] go.
    (i.e., Go if you must. or Go if you will. or Go if you insist.)

16. 같이 갈 테야?
    Are you going to go with me? / Do you want to go with me?
    [Is it your intention to go with me?]

2.2. *It is the expectation / intention that...* [*but / and* elaboration] with -(으)ㄹ 텐데(요)

This pattern—the one exemplified in our lesson and the one you are likely to encounter most frequently—is typically used in the second half of an *If... then...* construction, especially when the conditional sentence is contrary to fact. Note that it can be used with Past Bases, too.

17. A: 진호는 시간이 없어서 못 간답니다.
       Chinho says he can't go because he doesn't have time.

    B: 그러게 말이에요. 같이 가면 좋을 텐데요.
       No kidding. It would be nice / good if he could go with us.
       [The expectation is that it would be good if...]

18. A: 말이 빨라서 못 알아듣겠습니다.
       The words are so fast I can't catch what's being said.

    B: 그렇지요? 말을 조금만 천천히 하면 알아들을 수 있을 텐데요.
       Yeah—if he were to speak just a little bit slower, we'd be able to catch it.

19. A: 6년 전에 아들이 교통사고로 죽었습니다.
       Their son died six years ago in an automobile accident.

    B: 네, 그 아이가 그 때 죽지 않았으면 지금 15살일 텐데요.
       Yes, if he hadn't died then, he'd be fifteen years old now.

20. A: 왜 철민이를 안 도와줬습니까?

    Why didn't you help Ch'ŏlmin?

    B: 글쎄요. 나한테 얘기했으면 가서 도와주었을 텐데요.

    Well, if he had said something to me, I would have gone and helped him.

21. A: 철민 씨 회사에 갔더니 철민 씨는 출장을 가고 없었습니다.

    When I went to Ch'ŏlmin's company, he was away on a business trip.

    B: 미리 확인했으면 좋았을 텐데요.

    You should have confirmed beforehand.

22. A: 박 선생님 계십니까?

    Is Mr. Pak in?

    B: 조금만 일찍 왔으면 만날 수 있었을 텐데요.

    If you had come just a little earlier, you would have been able to see him.

23. A. 그 집이 도둑을 맞았대.

    I hear that house was broken into.

    B. 그런 집에 귀중품도 없을 텐데 도둑이 뭘 가져 갔을까?

    You wouldn't expect a house like that to have any valuables in it, so what would the thief have taken?

24. A. 철민이가 퇴원했어요?

    Is Ch'ŏlmin out of the hospital?

    B. 글쎄요. 지금쯤은 병원에서 나왔을 텐데...

    He must have gotten out by now, but... [I haven't seen him]

2.3. *Because / seeing as it is the expectation / intention that... with* -(으)ㄹ 테니(까)

This pattern combines the intention / expectation pattern -(을) 테- with the sequential pattern -(으)니(까) (here meaning *because* or *since*). Note that in this particular combination, the first clause using -(을) 테니(까) is almost always followed by a command in the second clause.

25. 내일 아침 수술할 테니까 오늘 하루 종일 아무것도 먹지 마세요.

    Please don't eat anything at all today since they will be operating on you tomorrow morning.

3. Quoted Commands with -(으)라고 (말)하-, 달라고 하-

These patterns for indirect commands and requests were covered in Lessons 27 and 28 of *Continuing Korean*. The pattern 달라고 하- quotes an incoming request which, when originally uttered, had the verb 주- *give [to me, the speaker]*. In the example sentences below, pay close attention to who is speaking to whom: Speaker A, Speaker B, and me.

26. [Speaker A to Speaker B]
빨리 일어나세요.
Hurry up and get up!
→ 빨리 일어나라고 (말) 했다.
     A told B to hurry up and get up.

27. [Speaker A to Speaker B]
앉으십시오.
Please sit down.
→ 앉으라고 했다.
     A told B to sit down.

28. [Speaker A to Speaker B]
늦지 마세요.
Please don't be late.
→ 늦지 말라고 했다.
     A told B not to be late.

29. [Speaker A to Speaker B]
강아지한테 물 좀 줘.
Give the doggie some water.
→ 강아지한테 물 좀 주라고 했다.
     A told B to give the doggie some water.
     [The verb 주 - *give* is in the quoted sentence, but is not incoming, i.e., not directed to *me, the speaker.*]

30. [Speaker A to Speaker B]
수미한테 이것 좀 갖다 줘.
Please take this over to Sumi.
→ 수미한테 이것 좀 갖다 주라고 했다.
     A told B to take this over to Sumi.
     [The verb 주 - *give* is in the quoted sentence, but is not incoming, i.e., not directed to *me, the speaker.*]

31. [Speaker A to Speaker B]
영준 씨한테 수미 씨 전화번호를 가르쳐 주지 마십시오.
Please don't tell Yŏngjun Sumi's phone number.
→ 영준 씨한테 수미 씨 전화번호를 가르쳐 주지 말라고 했습니다
     Speaker A told [Speaker B = somebody unspecified] not to tell Yŏngjun Sumi's phone number.
     [The verb 주 - *give* is in the quoted sentence, but is not incoming, i.e., not directed to *me, the speaker.*]

32. [Me (the speaker) to somebody else (Mom)]

    엄마, 용돈 좀 주세요.

    Mom, please give me some pocket money.

    → 엄마한테 용돈 좀 달라고 했습니다.

    > *I asked Mom to give me some pocket money.*
    > [The verb 주 - *give* is in the quoted sentence, **and** it is incoming, i.e., directed to *me, the speaker*; hence, 주 - is quoted as 달라(고).]

33. [Me (the speaker) to somebody else (Sŏnyŏng)]

    선영 씨, 좀 도와주십시오.

    Sŏnyŏng, please help me.

    → 선영 씨한테 도와 달라고 했습니다.

    > *I asked Sŏnyŏng to help me.*
    > [The verb 주 - *give* is in the quoted sentence, **and** it is incoming, i.e., directed to *me, the speaker*; hence, 주 - is quoted as 달라(고).]

4. Rhetorical Retorts with -잖아(요)

This pattern for rhetorical retorts was covered in Lesson 13 of *Elementary Korean*. Originally, this pattern was an abbreviation of the long negation pattern - 지 않아(요), used as a question. This was shortened to - 잖아(요) and then to - 잖아(요). The meaning now is a sort of rhetorical question: *Is it not the case that...?* [answer: *Duh—of course, it is!*]. Note that it can be used with both Past and Future Bases.

34. A: 앨버트 씨 한국말 많이 늘었지요?

    Albert's Korean has improved a lot, hasn't it?

    B: 언제나 열심히 공부하잖아요.

    Sure, but isn't he studying hard all the time?

35. A: 차가 왜 이렇게 더러워졌지요?

    How did the car get so dirty like this?

    B: 아까 비가 왔잖아요.

    It rained just a little while ago [don't you remember?].

36. A: 돈이 왜 이것밖에 안 남았지요?

    Why is this all the money I have left?

    B: 아까 점심 값하고 커피 값 냈잖아요.

    Duh—you just paid for lunch and coffee!

37. A: 진호가 왜 이렇게 안 들어오죠?

    Why isn't Chinho [coming] back yet?

    B: 늦게 들어올 거라고 아침에 얘기했잖아요.

    Duh—he said this morning that he'd get in late.

38. A: 이 식당에는 항상 손님이 많습니다.
   There are always lots of customers in this restaurant.

   B: 음식이 싸고 맛있잖아요.
   Sure—the food is cheap and it tastes good!

39. A: 물가가 너무 비싸서 걱정입니다.
   I'm worried that these prices are so high.

   B: 여기는 물가가 비싼 곳이잖아요.
   What do you expect? This is an expensive place.

5. *It is only / simply a case of NOUN* with NOUN뿐이- and *all one does / did is / was...* with -(으)ㄹ 뿐이-

As a particle, 뿐 means *only*, as in this example:

40. 준비를 안 해 온 사람은 저뿐이었습니다.
   The only person who didn't come prepared was me ["was only I"].

As a postmodifier, 뿐 occurs only after the prospective modifier -(으)ㄹ (though this may occur on a Past Base). Note that in Korean spelling, particles are usually written flush with the noun they attach to with no intervening space, whereas postmodifiers are typically separated from the modifier they follow by a space.

41. 농담으로 말한 것뿐이니까 너무 신경 쓰지 마십시오.
   I said it just as a joke, so don't get all concerned about it.

42. 머리만 조금 아플 뿐이니까 걱정하지 마십시오.
   I just have a slight headache, so don't worry [about me].

43. 애인 사이는 아니고 마음이 잘 통하는 친구 사이일 뿐입니다.
   We're not boyfriend and girlfriend; we're just friends who understand each other well.

44. 제 시간에 영미만 왔을 뿐, 다른 사람들은 모두 늦게 왔습니다.
   Yŏngmi was the only one to arrive on time, and the others all arrived late.

45. 소주 한 잔 마셨을 뿐인데 취하네요.
   All I drank was a glass of soju, but I'm getting tipsy!

6. Eventual Development of an Action with -고 마-ㄹ-

The pattern -고 + auxiliary verb 마-ㄹ-(말다) implies the eventual outcome of an action or series of actions, or the final development of an action. It often gets translated as *ends up doing; finally does; gets around to doing; ultimately does*. When the particle 야 *only if* intervenes (in other words, -고

야 마 - ㄹ -), this sometimes yields a new and different pattern, the translation of which comes out as *simply has to* [= must]; *is / am [absolutely] determined to* [= will definitely]. For example:

> 46. 이 숙제를 내일까지 내고야 말겠다.
>   *I am simply determined to hand this homework in by tomorrow.*

This meaning could be more literally rendered as something like *Only if it's by handing in this homework by tomorrow will I end the matter.* Here are some examples of ‑ 고 말아요.

> 47. 빨리 식사를 끝내고 말았지요.
>   *I finished up my meal in a hurry.*

> 48. 나는 생선을 먹으면 언제나 배탈이 나고야 말아요.
>   *I [invariably] end up getting a stomachache every time I eat fish.*

> 49. 입맛을 잃어버리고 말았어요.
>   *I have completely lost my appetite.*

> 50. 참, 내일이면 내가 마흔 살이나 되고 말겠군요!
>   *Whadda ya know, I will be forty years old tomorrow!*

> 51. 그 여자가 저녁에 초대한 것을 잊어버리고 말았으니 어떻게 하지요?
>   *What shall I do? I completely forgot that she had invited me to dinner.*

> 52. 그 부부는 어제 벌써 미국으로 떠나고 말았지요.
>   *The couple had already left for the U.S. yesterday, you see.*

Another pattern using ‑ 고 + auxiliary 마 ‑ ㄹ ‑ involves two consecutive ‑ 고 forms. The first can be formed from any verb and the second always uses 말고, with the meaning *of course...!* as in:

> 53. 알고 말고요.
>   *Of course she knows!*

A sentence ends in 요 if one is talking in the Polite Style. If you drop the 요, the sentence has the same meaning, but now it is in the Intimate Style. In Seoul, the ending ‑ 고 is often pronounced ‑ 구. Since the expressions with ‑ 고 말고 are so colloquial, you are likely to hear them more often as ‑ 구 말구: 알구 말구요! Here are some more examples:

> 54. 먹고 말고요.
>   *Of course I'm eating!*

55. A: 오늘 학교에 갑니까?

   Are you going to school today?

   B: 가고 말고요!

   Of course I'm going.

56. A: 오늘 저녁에 주무시겠습니까?

   Are you going to go to bed tonight?

   B: 자고 말고요.

   Of course I am!

57. A. 크고 좋습니까?

   Is it nice and big?

   B. 크고 좋고 말고요.

   Of course it is.

58. 중요한 규칙은 가르치고 말고요.

   Of course they teach the important rules.

EXERCISES

Exercise 1: Reading Comprehension

Write out answers to the following questions.

1. 나는 지금 로마에 살고 있습니까?
2. 로마에 살 때 제일 어려운 문제는 무엇이었습니까?
3. 이 날은 왜 길이 밀렸습니까?
4. 나는 자주 교통법규를 위반합니까?
5. 이 날 나는 왜 교통법규를 위반했습니까?
6. 언제 교통 경찰관이 나타났습니까?
7. 교통 경찰관이 나한테 와서 뭐라고 했습니까?
8. 나는 경찰관에게 뭐라고 했습니까?
9. 경찰관은 내 말을 듣고 나를 잘 봐 주었습니까?

Exercise 2: Practice with -(으)ㄴ / -는 바람에

The "A" questions and statements below all call for an explanation. Write out responses using an appropriate form -(으)ㄴ / -는 바람에.

1. A: 수잔 씨, 오늘은 웬일로 늦었습니까?

   B: _____

2. A: 성호 씨, 오늘 모임 재미있었습니까?

   B: _____

3. A: 약속 장소에 30분이나 일찍 도착하셔서 기다리셨다고 들었습니다.

   B: _____

4. A: 왜 야구 경기가 중단되었습니까?

   B: _____

5. A: 어제 혼자서 늦게까지 일하셨지요?

   B: _____

6. A: 그동안 왜 연락하지 않았습니까?

   B: _____

Exercise 3: Practice with -(으)ㄹ 텐데(요), -(으)ㄹ 테니(까), and -(으)ㄹ 테야

In items 1–6 below, an opportunity was missed. Use the pattern -(으)ㄹ 텐데(요) to express what should have happened.

1. 찌개가 너무 맵지요?

   고춧가루를 _____.

2. 우산 들고 다니기가 귀찮습니다.

   아침에 우산을 _____.

3. 수미 씨도 우리하고 같이 제주도에 _____.

   _____ 섭섭합니다.

4. 박 과장님은 방금 나가셨습니다.

   조금만 일찍 _____.

5. 정은 씨한테 연락이 안 됩니다.

   준형 씨가 온 것을 알면 _____.

6. 늦어서 미안합니다.

   지하철을 _____ 늦었습니다.

Now use the pattern -(으)ㄹ 테니(까) to set up an introduction or explanation for your command in the second clause.

7. 내가 점심을 살게—나가자.

8. 그럼 약을 드릴게요—드세요.

9. 아이들은 제가 볼게요—염려 마세요.

10. 이제는 별 일 없을 거야—안심해.

11. 건강이 곧 좋아질 거예요—너무 실망하지 말아요.

Finally, replace -(으)ㄹ래 and -(으)ㄹ 거야 in items 12–17 below with the pattern -(으)ㄹ테야 to express an even stronger intention (or to ask somebody about *their* strong intention):

12. 난 나중에 먹을래.

13. 오늘은 샤워하지 않을래.

14. 네가 죽으면 나도 따라 죽을래.
15. 내년에 한국에 꼭 갈 거야.
16. 나 혼자라도 반드시 찾을 거야.
17. 영화 보러 갈래?

Exercise 4: Quoting Commands in 주- with 달라(고)

The following sentences are verbatim quotes of commands that 나 I [*the speaker*] gave to somebody. Quote the commands using the indirect quotation pattern. Be careful to use 달라고 in those sentences when the original (quoted) command used the verb 주 - with reference to *me* [*the speaker*].

1. 만구 씨, 저쪽에 가서 앉으세요.
2. 주연 씨, 후추 좀 집어 주십시오.
3. 수잔 씨, 내일 약속을 잊어버리지 마십시오.
4. 엄마, 용돈 좀 주세요.
5. 선영아, 아무한테도 얘기하지 마.
6. 수미 씨, 미진이한테 물 좀 주세요.
7. 앨버트 씨, 사전 좀 빌려 주십시오.

In the following imagined exchanges, fill in the blanks with the appropriate indirect quotation form based on the conversation you imagine you had.

8. A: 이 사진 왜 가지고 왔습니까?
   B: 선영 씨가 어릴 때 사진을 _____.
9. A: 무슨 일이 생겼습니까? 좀 이야기해 주십시오.
   B: 준호 씨가 아무한테도 _____.
10. A: 모리 씨, 사전 좀 빌려 주세요.
    모리: 지금 없습니다. 스즈키 씨가 _____ 빌려 줬습니다.
    ["because he asked me to lend it to him"]

Exercise 5: Practice with -잖아(요)

Respond to the "A" sentences using the form - 잖아 (요) to remind "A" of something that he or she was supposed to know already.

1. A: 영준 씨가 왜 저렇게 말했지?
   B: _____
2. A: 어제 모임에 왜 안 왔습니까?
   B: _____
3. A: 오늘 여기에 왜 이렇게 사람들이 많습니까?
   B: _____
4. A: 선희가 내일도 일찍 올까?
   B: _____

5. A: 이 가방 모양이 별로 안 예쁜데 왜 샀니?

    B: _____

6. A: 만호 씨한테 도와 달라고 부탁하십시오.

    B: _____

Exercise 6: Practice with 뿐이-

Convert sentences 1–3 below, using the pattern 뿐이 - .

1. 동전이 이것밖에 없습니다.
2. 내일 아침 일찍 나올 수 있는 사람은 우리밖에 없습니다.
3. 나를 정말로 걱정해 주는 사람은 부모님밖에 없습니다.

For items 4–6 combine the two sentences into one sentence, again using the appropriate form of the pattern 뿐이 - .

4. 그냥 한두 번 만나 보았습니다. 특별한 사이가 아닙니다.
5. 아픈 데는 없고 그냥 좀 피곤합니다. 그러니까 걱정하지 마십시오.
6. 어제 밤을 새웠습니다. 그런데 좀 어지럽습니다.

Exercise 7: Practice with -고 마-ㄹ- and -고 말고(요)

In the following sentences, change the final verb into - 고 말겠 - or - 고 말았 - to show the determination to do something or the eventual outcome of something.

1. 나는 꼭 성공할 거다.
2. 이번 야구경기에서 꼭 이길 거야.
3. 아무리 어려워도 한국말을 꼭 배울 거야.
4. 조심했지만 감기에 걸렸다.
5. 두 사람이 결국 이혼을 했어요.
6. 여자친구가 준 지갑을 잃어버렸어요.
7. 설거지를 하다가 그릇을 깨뜨렸어요.

Now answer the following questions using the - 고 말고 (요) pattern to mean *of course!*

8. 제 부탁을 들어 주실 거예요?
9. 우리 의견에 찬성하세요?
10. 정말이에요?
11. 그렇게 해도 돼요?
12. 제 생일 파티에 오실 거지요?
13. 한국어 수업이 재미있어요?

다시는 영어로 말하지 말아야지

오늘로 내가 한국에 온 지 꼭 1 년이 되었습니다. 처음 한국에 왔을 때는 말이 통하지 않아서 무척 고생을 했습니다. 그때 있었던 재미있던 일을 한 가지 이야기해 보겠습니다.

한국에서는 한국 사람들이 길을 걸어가다가 모르는 사람한테도 자주 길을 물어봅니다. 나는 일본 사람인데 한국 사람과 비슷하게 생겨서 그런지 나한테도 가끔 길을 물어보는 사람들이 있었습니다. 그 때마다 나는 대답을 못하고 쩔쩔맸습니다.

그러던 어느 날 아주 좋은 생각이 떠올랐습니다. 질문을 받을 때 한국말로 대답하려고 애쓸 것이 아니라 영어로 대답하면 되겠다는 생각이었습니다. 그 후 며칠이 지나서 어떤 아주머니가 나한테 길을 물어 보았습니다. 내가 "미안합니다. 나는 한국말을 못합니다."라고 영어로 말했더니 그 아주머니는 깜짝 놀라면서 가 버렸습니다. 그 후에도 나는 몇 번 그런 식으로 곤란한 순간을 넘겼습니다.

　그런데 어느 날 예상하지 못했던 일이 벌어졌습니다. 친구를 만나러 종로에 있는 다방에 가는 길이었습니다.

　갑자기 어떤 사람이 나한테 뭐라고 말을 했습니다. 나는 알아듣지 못하는 표정을 지으면서 한국어를 못한다고 영어로 말했습니다. 내가 영어로 대답했더니 그 사람이 영어로 다시 질문을 했습니다. "아, 이 사람은 영어를 잘 하나보다."

　나는 너무나 당황했습니다. 그렇지만 아무렇지도 않은 척하면서 머릿속으로 열심히 작문을 해서 그 사람에게 영어로 대답해 주었습니다. 그리고 그 사람이 가고 난 후 식은 땀을 닦으면서 결심했습니다. "다시는 영어로 말하지 말아야지."

NEW VOCABULARY

Vocabulary from the Main Text

오늘로	as of today	그런 식 (式) 으로	in such a way / manner
꼭	(adv.) exactly	한국식으로	in the Korean way / Korean style
무척	very much (so); terribly; awfully	곤란 (困難) 하 -	be awkward, embarrassing; feel ill at ease; be complicated, vexing, problematic
비슷하 -	be similar		
비슷하게	in a similar fashion / way	순간 (瞬間)	moment
생기 -	*here:* turn out a certain way; "look" a certain way (always in the past tense if sentence-final)	순간적 (瞬間的) 으로	momentarily
		넘기 -	get past, through, or over sth unpleasant; "weather the storm" (get through a trying moment)
잘 생겼어요	*is handsome*		
쩔쩔매 -	be flustered; be at a complete loss as to what to do; be at one's wits' end (NB: processive)	예상 (豫想) (을) 하 -	foresee; predict
		벌어지 -	(sth) happens; (an event) develops, unfolds
뜨 -	float; rise up	종로 (鐘路)	Chongno ("Bell Road"), a main boulevard in downtown Seoul
생각 (이) 떠오르 -	a thought occurs to (sb), a thought "floats up" (into sb's head)		
		표정 (表情)	facial expression (a verbal expression is 표현)
애 (를) 쓰 -	make an effort; try hard		
며칠	a few days; several days; *also: How many days?*	표정 (을) 지 (ㅅ) - (짓다)	make a face; make a facial expression
지나 -	(it) passes (cf. 지난 주일 *last ["past"] week*)	너무나	ever so (much); terribly; very
		아무렇지도 않 -	be cool as a cucumber, unaffected by events
깜짝 놀라 -	be gobsmacked, utterly surprised, amazed (NB: processive)	머릿속으로	in sb's mind ("inside sb's head")

작문(作文)(을) 하 -	write a composition; compose a sentence	식은 땀	a cold sweat
가고 난 후(後)	after going (cf. also: 가고 나서 *after going*)	닦 -	wipe sth; brush (one's teeth)
식 -	go cold, cool off / down	결심(決心)(을) 하 -	resolve (to do); make a resolution (to do); make up one's mind (to do)
식기 전에 많이 드세요.	*Eat up before it gets cold.*		

Vocabulary from the Example Sentences

후배(後輩)	one's junior at school or work	자기(自己)	self; *here: She seems to be sleeping in her [own] room.*
선배(先輩)	one's senior at school or work	사 주었는데도	*despite my having bought for you; in spite of my having bought you (sth)*
어머니날	Mother's Day (no such day in Korea)	사람이 많은 것을 보니	*judging by ("seeing / viewing") the fact that there are many people...*
어버이날	Parents' Day (celebrated in Korea)		
아르바이트(를) 하 -	do part-time work on the side (usually said of students)	차가 없는 것을 보니	*judging from the fact that there are no cars...*
		수박	watermelon
들르 -	stop in; drop by	수박 한 통	one watermelon
들렀다 가 -	drop in, stop by, drop by (and then be on one's way again)	급(急)하 -	be urgent
		급하게	urgently; hurriedly; in a rush
우연(偶然)히	coincidentally; by chance	수영장(水泳場)	swimming pool
퇴근(退勤)(을) 하 -	leave work for home	수영(을) 하 -	swim
산소(山所)	family or clan burial site (often used as the honorific equivalent of 무덤 "grave")	상징(象徵)	symbol
		상징(을) 하 -	symbolize
		이따가	in a while; a little while later
착하 -	be good (at heart) (often used of dogs and children ["Good boy!"], or of anybody who is a good-hearted, honest person); be good-natured	남	others; other people
		끊 -	cut off; sever
		담그 -	soak; steep; prepare; pickle (as with kimch'i)
적자(赤字)	financial deficit; (with - 이 -) be in the red	잘나 -	*lit.:* "turn out nice," i.e., be handsome, good-looking; be great, distinguished (usually Past Tense)
흑자(黑字)	financial surplus; (with - 이 -) be in the black		
여기저기	here and there	잘난 척하 -	put on airs; pretend to be sth great
미성년(未成年)	minor, underage person		

Vocabulary from the Exercises

반응(反應)(을) 보이 -	give ("show / reveal") a reaction		one's day-to-day life
태연(泰然)하 -	be / remain as if nothing happened; remain unaf- fected (NB: descriptive)	시키 -	order sth (as in a restau- rant)
생신(生辰)	birthday (honorific equivalent of 생일)	뚱뚱하 -	be fat, chubby
		설날	New Year's Day
여러분	"Ladies and gentlemen!" "Y'all" (if you're from the American south). Polite way of addressing many people, or in this case, the readers of this book.	설	the New Year; New Year's Day
		내내	continuously; all through- out
		거의	virtually, nearly (all, etc.)
		지각(遲刻)(을) 하 -	arrive late
신사숙녀 여러분!	"Ladies and gentlemen!" (very formal)	분위기(雰圍氣)	atmosphere
		창(窓)	window
신사(紳士)	gentleman	펴 -	open; lay out; spread open
숙녀(淑女)	lady	막내	youngest child; youngest (son, daughter)
꿈속에서	in one's dreams	자기 뜻대로	as one intends; in accord with one's wishes
세탁(洗濯)(을) 하 -	do the laundry		
세탁기(洗濯機)	laundry machine; washing machine	적 -	write down; take note of; jot down
세탁소(洗濯所)	laundromat; launderette	내버리 -	leave alone; "leave be"
아니면	or... (if that is not the case, then...)		
생활(生活)(을) 하 -	*lit.*: "do living," i.e., conduct		

PATTERNS

1. *It is not the case that... [but rather...]* **with NOUN이 / 가 아니라**

You have already learned that the opposite or negation of the pattern NOUN이 - *It is a NOUN* is NOUN이 / 가 아니 - *It is not a NOUN*, where NOUN can optionally take the particle 이 / 가 (with no difference in meaning). The pattern introduced here is exactly the same construction, with just a minor difference in that the negative copula 아니 - occurs in a special, nonsentence-final form: 아니라. The resulting pattern NOUN이 / 가 아니라 means something like *It is not the case that... [but rather...]*.

1. A: 이 우산 선영 씨 겁니까?
    Is this umbrella Sŏnyŏng's?

   B: 아니요, 선영 씨 것이 아니라 수미 씨 겁니다.
    No, it's not Sŏnyŏng's—it's Sumi's.

2. A: 준호 씨가 영진 씨 후배입니까?

       Is Chunho Yŏngjin's hubae?

   B: 아니요, 후배가 아니라 선배입니다.

       No, he's not her hubae, *rather he's her* sŏnbae.

3. A: 내일이 어머니날이지요?

       Is tomorrow Mother's Day?

   B: 어머니날이 아니라 어버이날입니다.

       It's not Mother's Day, but Parents' Day.

4. A: 이 옷이 손님한테 잘 어울릴 것 같습니다.

       I think these clothes will suit you well.

   B: 제가 입으려는 것이 아니라 동생한테 선물할 겁니다.

       They're not for me to wear, but to give as a present to my younger sibling.

5. A: 성호 씨, 내일 안 오실 거지요?

       Sŏngho, you're not coming tomorrow, are you?

   B: 안 오는 것이 아니라 못 오는 겁니다.

       *It's not by choice—I **can't** come.*

6. A: 갑자기 손님이 오신다고 하는데 어떻게 하지요?

       They say guests are coming suddenly; what shall we do?

   B: 걱정만 하고 있을 게 아니라 빨리 준비합시다.

       Let's not just sit around worrying—let's hurry up and prepare!

2.   Instrumental Particle (으)로

The instrumental particle (으)로 has a wide range of meanings and usages, many of which can be found in *Elementary Korean*, Lesson 8.5. Nouns ending in consonants (other than ㄹ) take 으로, and nouns ending in vowels or ㄹ take 로. Observe the various meanings of this particle in the example sentences below.

7. A: <u>영어로</u> 말해도 됩니까?

       May I speak <u>in English</u>?

   B: 안 됩니다. <u>한국말로</u> 하십시오.

       No. Please speak <u>in Korean</u>.

8. A: 꼭 <u>연필로</u> 써야 됩니까?

       *Do I absolutely **have** to write <u>with a pencil</u>?*

   B: 아니요, <u>볼펜으로</u> 써도 됩니다.

       No, it's OK to write <u>with a ballpoint pen</u>.

9. A: 학교에 무엇을 타고 왔습니까?
        What did you ride to school in?

    B: 보통 버스를 타고 다니는데, 오늘은 <u>택시로</u> 왔습니다.
        Usually I ride the bus, but today I came <u>by taxi</u>.

10. A: <u>어떤 책으로</u> 공부했습니까?
        <u>What book</u> did you study <u>with</u>?

    B: <u>이 책으로</u> 공부했습니다.
        I studied <u>with this book</u>.

11. A: 이 컴퓨터 아주 좋은데요.
        Say, this is a really nice computer!

    B: 내가 아르바이트 해서 번 <u>돈으로</u> 산 겁니다.
        I bought it <u>with money</u> I earned from part-time work.

12. A: 도와 드릴까요?
        May I help you?

    B: 아니요, <u>제 힘으로</u> 해 보겠습니다.
        No, I'll give it a try all on my own [<u>"with my own strength"</u>].

3. *On the way to... / one is just on the way to... with* -는 길에 / -는 길이-

The word 길 means *street; road; path; way*. As a postmodifier following a verb of motion (가 - , 오 - , and compounds built on these two verbs, etc.), it combines with either the particle 에 to or the copula - 이 - to mean *on the way to...* or *is on the way to...*, respectively. This pattern is also explained in *Continuing Korean*, Lesson 19.4.

13. A: 내일 우리 집에 잠깐 들렀다 가십시오.
        Please stop by my place tomorrow.

    B: 네, 오전에 시내에 가는 길에 잠깐 들르겠습니다.
        Sure. I'll drop by in the morning on my way downtown.

14. 집에 오는 길에 우연히 친구를 만났습니다.
    On my way home, I happened to meet a friend.

15. 오늘 퇴근하는 길에 술 한 잔 합시다.
    Let's have a drink on the way home from work today.

16. 고향에 가는 길에 할아버지 산소에 들렀습니다.
    On the way to my hometown, I stopped by my grandfather's grave.

17. A: 어디 가십니까?
     Where are you going?

     B: 회사에 가는 길입니다.
     I'm on my way to the office ["company"].

18. A: 여행 갔다 오십니까?
     Are you on your way back from a trip?

     B: 네, 제주도에 갔다 오는 길입니다.
     Yes, I'm on my way back from Cheju Island.

4. Quoted Statements with -다고

Indirect quotations were covered in detail in *Continuing Korean*, Lesson 27, but quoted statements can be summarized as follows.

First, all indirect quotations are built on the Plain Style (한다 Style) by adding the indirect quotation particle ﹣고.

Plain Style Statements

Plain Processive Bases

﹣ㄴ다 / ﹣는다:

> ﹣ㄴ다 after Processive Bases ending in vowels: 간다, 친다, etc.
>
> ﹣는다 after Processive Bases ending in consonants: 먹는다, 찾는다, etc.

All Other Bases

﹣다:

Plain Descriptive Bases	좋다, 비싸다, ﹣이다 (copula), etc.
All Past Bases	갔다, 쳤다, 먹었다, 좋았다, 비쌌다, ﹣이었다, etc.
All Future Bases	가겠다, 먹겠다, 좋겠다, 비싸겠다, ﹣이겠다, etc.
있﹣ *have / exist* and 없﹣	있다, 없다

Second, there are three types of indirect quotation:

1) Expanded Quotations,
2) Simple Quotations, and
3) Contracted Quotations.

Expanded Quotations have the indirect quotation particle ﹣고, Simple Quotations drop the indirect quotation particle ﹣고, and Contracted Quotations end in ㅐ(요) (in the Polite 해요 and Intimate 해 Styles) or ﹣ㅂ니다 (in the Formal 합니다 Style).

Plain Style Indirect Quotations: Expanded

The basic rule is to add ‑ 고 해요 to the Plain Style form.

Plain Processive Bases

Vowel Bases	‑ ㄴ다고 해요	간다고 해요, 친다고 해요, etc.
Consonant Bases	‑ 는다고 해요	먹는다고 해요, etc.

All Other Bases

Plain Descriptive Bases	좋다고 해요, 비싸다고 해요, etc. *The nonpast copula is irregular:* ‑ 이라고 해요
All Past Bases	갔다고 해요, 쳤다고 해요, 먹었다고 해요, 좋았다고 해요, 비쌌다고 해요, ‑ 이었다고 해요, etc.
All Future Bases	가겠다고 해요, 먹겠다고 해요, 좋겠다고 해요, 비싸겠다고 해요, ‑ 이겠다고 해요, etc.
있 ‑ *have / exist* and 없 ‑	있다고 해요, 없다고 해요

Plain Style Indirect Quotations: Simple

The basic rule is to drop the ‑ 고 from ‑ 고 해요.

Processive **Vowel Bases**	‑ ㄴ다 해요 ‑ ㄴ다 합니다	간다 해요, 친다 해요, etc. 간다 합니다, 친다 합니다, etc.	
Processive **Consonant Bases**	‑ 는다 해요 ‑ 는다 합니다	먹는다 해요, etc. 먹는다 합니다, etc.	
Descriptive Bases	좋다 해요, 비싸다 해요, etc. 좋다 합니다, 비싸다 합니다, etc.		
Nonpast Copula **(still irregular)**	‑ 이라 해요 ‑ 이라 합니다		
All Past Bases	갔다 해요 갔다 합니다	쳤다 해요 쳤다 합니다	먹었다 해요 먹었다 합니다
	좋았다 해요 좋았다 합니다	비쌌다 해요 비쌌다 합니다	‑ 이었다 해요 ‑ 이었다 합니다
All Future Bases	가겠다 해요 가겠다 합니다	먹겠다 해요 먹겠다 합니다	좋겠다 해요 좋겠다 합니다
	비싸겠다 해요 비싸겠다 합니다	‑ 이겠다 해요, etc. ‑ 이겠다 합니다, etc.	
있 ‑ *have / exist* and 없 ‑	있다 해요 있다 합니다	없다 해요 없다 합니다	

Plain Style Indirect Quotations: Contracted

There are two main types of contraction: 해(요)-type and 합니다-type. Using the verb 하다 as our model, these two types can be schematized as follows:

해(요)-type	합니다-type
- ㄴ다 해(요) → - ㄴ대(요)	- ㄴ다 합니다 → - ㄴ답니다
- 는다 해(요) → - 는대(요)	- 는다합니다 → - 는답니다
- 다 해(요) → - 대(요)	- 다 합니다 → - 답니다
- (이)라 해(요) → - (이)래(요)	- (이)라 합니다 → - (이)랍니다

Processive Vowel Bases	- ㄴ대요 - ㄴ답니다	간대요, 친대요, etc. 간답니다, 친답니다, etc.	
Processive Consonant Bases	- 는대요 - 는답니다.	먹는대요, etc. 먹는답니다, etc	
Descriptive Bases	좋대요, 비싸대요, etc. 좋답니다, 비싸답니다, etc.		
Nonpast Copula (irregular as ever)	- 이래요 - 이랍니다		
All Past Bases	갔대요 갔답니다 좋았대요 좋았답니다	쳤대요 쳤답니다 비쌌대요 비쌌답니다	먹었대요 먹었답니다 - 이었대요, etc. - 이었답니다, etc.
All Future Bases	가겠대요 가겠답니다 비싸겠대요 비싸겠답니다	먹겠대요 먹겠답니다 - 이겠대요, etc. - 이겠답니다, etc.	좋겠대요 좋겠답니다
있 - *have / exist* and 없 -	있대요 있답니다	없대요 없답니다	

Here are some examples of 합니다-type Contracted Indirect Quotations:

19. 수미는 착합니다.
    Sumi is a good kid.
    수미는 착하다고 합니다. (→ 착하답니다)

20. 그 영화는 재미없습니다.
    That film is boring.
    그 영화는 재미없다고 합니다. (→ 재미없답니다)

21. 정아는 친구한테 편지를 씁니다.
    Chŏng'a is writing a letter to her friend.
    정아는 친구한테 편지를 쓴다고 합니다. (→ 쓴답니다)

22. 진호는 전화를 겁니다.
    Chinho is making a phone call.
    진호는 전화를 건다고 합니다. (→ 건답니다)

23. 선영이는 친구를 만나러 갔습니다.
    Sŏnyŏng went to meet a friend.
    선영이는 친구를 만나러 갔다고 합니다. (→ 갔답니다)

24. 어제는 아주 피곤했습니다.
    Yesterday I was really tired.
    어제는 아주 피곤했다고 합니다. (→ 피곤했답니다)

25. 아침 일찍 가겠습니다.
    He'll go early in the morning.
    아침 일찍 가겠다고 합니다. (→ 일찍 가겠답니다)

26. 비가 올 것 같습니다.
    It looks like it will rain.
    비가 올 것 같다고 합니다. (→ 올 것 같답니다)

27. 영수는 키가 크지 않습니다.
    Yŏngsu isn't tall.
    영수는 키가 크지 않다고 합니다. (→ 크지 않답니다)

28. 진호는 담배를 피우지 않습니다.
    Chinho doesn't smoke.
    진호는 담배를 피우지 않는다고 합니다. (→ 피우지 않는답니다)

29. 토마스 씨는 독일 사람입니다.
    Thomas is German.
    토마스 씨는 독일 사람이라고 합니다. (→ 독일 사람이랍니다)

30. 지난달에는 적자였습니다.
    Last month we ran a deficit.
    지난달에는 적자였다고 합니다. (→ 적자였답니다)

31. 친구를 만나러 나갈 것입니다.
    She's going to go out to meet her friend.
    친구를 만나러 나갈 것이라고 합니다. (→ 나갈 것이랍니다)

32. 여기저기 여행하고 싶습니다.
    I want to travel around here and there.
    여기저기 여행하고 싶다고 합니다. (→ 싶답니다)

5.   *Seems...* with -나 보- ~ -(으)ㄴ / -는가 보-

This lesson presents two new patterns for *seem*, built on the two patterns for questions presented in *Continuing Korean*, Lesson 29: - 나(요)? and - (으)ㄴ가(요) / - 는가(요)? The mechanics of the pattern - 나 보 - are easy, insofar as - 나(요) is a one-shape ending and attaches in this one shape to any and all bases. The mechanics for the pattern - (으)ㄴ / - 는가 보 - are more complex:

Descriptive Plain Bases:	- (으)ㄴ가 보 -
Processive Plain Bases:	- 는가 보 -
있 - and 없 - :	- 는가 보 -
Past (and Future) Bases:	- 는가 보 -

Note that the auxiliary verb 보 - *see* in this pattern behaves like a descriptive verb.

5.1. Modifier + -(으)ㄴ / -는가 보-

보 - is an auxiliary descriptive verb. It is **descriptive** because the plain form is 보다, not 본다 (which is the processive verb *sees*), and it is an **auxiliary** because it always follows either the Familiar Question Form in - 나 or a modifier plus the question postmodifier 가. The meaning of the expression is *it looks as if; it seems.* Thus, this pattern is very similar in meaning to the expressions made up of a modifier + 것 같아요 *it seems; it looks as if.*

33. a. 비가 오는가 봐요.
    b. 비가 오나 봐요.   *It seems to be raining.*
    c. 비가 오는 것 같아요.

34. a. 비가 왔는가 봐요.
    b. 비가 왔나 봐요.   *It seems to have rained.*
    c. 비가 온 것 같아요.

35. a. 비가 오겠는가 봐요.
    b. 비가 오겠나 봐요.   *It looks as if it might rain.*
    c. 비가 올 것 같아요.

Note that many speakers nowadays shun the combination of Future-Presumptive - 겠 - with - 는가 보 - or - 나 보 - . Thus, (35a) and (35b) are more naturally expressed as 비가 오려나 봐요 or 비가 올 건가 봐요.

36. a. 날이 좋은가 봐요.
    b. 날이 좋나 봐요.   *The weather seems to be nice.*
    c. 날이 좋은 것 같아요.

Here are some more examples of a modifier + 가 보 - :

37. 미성년인가 봐요.
   He seems to be a minor.

38. 누가 왔는가 보다.
   I think someone's here.

39. 그 영화가 재미있는가 보다.
   That movie looks interesting.

40. 밖이 추운가 보다.
   It seems cold out.

41. 아빠가 화났는가 보다.
   Dad seems to have lost his temper.

5.2. Base + -나 보-

Usually this pattern is reserved for processive bases, or for 있 - and 없 - as well as ALL Past (- 었 -) and Future (- 겠 -) Bases. However, one will also occasionally hear - 나 보 - used on a descriptive base. Note that while copula - 이 - rarely occurs with the Plain Base + - 나 보 - , forms - 이었나 보 - on the Past Base are perfectly acceptable.

42. A: 선영이는 뭐 합니까?
   What is Sŏnyŏng doing?

   B: 자기 방에서 자나 봅니다.
   She seems to be sleeping in her room.

43. A: 옷을 사 주었는데도 별로 안 좋아하는 것 같지요?
   Even though you bought her clothes, she doesn't seem to like them much, right?

   B. 옷이 별로 마음에 안 드나 봅니다.
   Seems she doesn't like the clothes.

44. A: 저 영화 재미있을까요?
   Do you think that movie might be interesting?

   B: 사람이 많은 것을 보니 영화가 재미있나 봅니다.
   Judging by all the people in line, it would appear to be interesting.

45. A: 윤주 씨 어디 갔습니까?
   Where did Yunju go?

   B: 차가 없는 것을 보니 멀리 나갔나 봅니다.
   Judging by the fact her car is not there, she seems to have gone far away.

46. A: 수박 좀 줄래?

    Please give me some watermelon.

    B: 냉장고 안에 없는데요. 아까 아이들이 다 먹었나 봐요.

    There isn't any in the fridge. It seems the kids ate it all a little while ago.

47. A: 준호는 왜 저렇게 밥을 급하게 먹습니까?

    Why is Chunho eating in such a rush?

    B: 시간이 없어서 점심을 못 먹었나 봅니다.

    Looks like he didn't have time to eat lunch.

48. A: 수영장에 갔다 온다고 했는데, 왜 이렇게 빨리 왔답니까?

    He said he was going to the pool; why is he back so soon?

    B: 수영장에 사람이 너무 많아서 일찍 돌아왔나 봅니다.

    Seems he came back early because there were too many people at the swimming pool.

49. A: 어제 그 시계 누구 것이었습니까?

    Whose watch was that yesterday?

    B: 성준 씨 것이었나 봅니다.

    Seems to have been Sŏngjun's.

50. 호랑이는 한국을 상징하나 봐요.

    It seems that the tiger symbolizes Korea.

51. 그 사람은 돈이 없나 봐요.

    That man looks as if he has no money.

52. 어머님이 오늘 저녁에 집에 계시겠나 봐요.

    It looks as if Mother is going to stay home this evening.

53. 일찍 잤나 봐요.

    It looks as if he's gone to bed early.

54. 눈이 더 오지 않나 봐요.

    It doesn't seem to be snowing anymore.

55. 이 학교에서 공부한 일이 있나 봐요.

    It seems that he once studied at this school.

6. *Has to / must do [of course / don't ya know, i.e., emphatic]* with -아 / -어야 [하-]지(요)

You already know the *have to / must* pattern – 어야 하 – (processive). When combined with the pattern – 지 (요), this yields – 어야 하지 (요) *has to / must [of course, don't you know, etc.].* This pattern, in turn, can undergo contraction by deleting the 하 – of 하지요, which yields a highly colloquial pattern – 어야지요 (sometimes spelled – 어야죠). A similar contraction is also widespread for the pattern – 어야 하겠 – *shall have to; probably ought to*, which contracts to – 어야겠 – . Here are some examples:

56. 속이 안 좋으니까 오늘은 술 마시지 말아야겠다.
    My stomach doesn't feel well, so I'd better not drink today.

57. 내일부터는 일찍 일어나야지.
    Starting tomorrow, you'd better get up early.

58. 올해는 담배를 꼭 끊어야지.
    This year, you definitely have to quit smoking.

59. 아침에 일찍 일어나서 운동을 해야지.
    In the morning, I should get up early and exercise.

60. 이따가 진영이한테 잊어버리지 말고 꼭 전화해야지.
    I should definitely not forget to call Chinyŏng in a little bit.

61. 오늘부터는 한국말만 써야지.
    From today on, I should use just Korean.

62. 남들한테 화내지 말아야지.
    You shouldn't get angry with others.

7. Three New Auxiliary Verbs: 놓-, 버리-, 두-

Examine the following sentences:

63. 공부를 잘 해 놓아야지요.
    I have to do my studying well [in preparation for something].

64. 입맛을 잃어 버렸습니다.
    I lost my appetite [completely].

65. 그 위에다가 소금을 뿌려 둡니다.
    You sprinkle salt over them [and get that out of the way].

Certain Korean verbs mean one thing when they are used by themselves, but combine into phrases with infinitives in - 아 / - 어 to mean something different. You have learned the following:

봐요　　*sees*　　해 봐요　　*does [to see what it's like]*
줘요　　*gives*　　해 줘요　　*does [as a favor for someone]*
드려요　*gives*　　해 드려요　*does [as a favor for someone esteemed]*

Three more such combinations are made by putting together an infinitive in - 아 / - 어 with another verb (all processive). The combinations all mean various shades of *finish doing* or *do it [in anticipation of some later use for the action]*:

놓아요　*puts; places*　　　　　해 놓아요　　　　　*gets it done; does it now [in anticipation of a later need]; does it for later*

버려요　*throws away; discards*　해 버려요　　　　　*does it totally, completely, or exhaustively*

두어요　*puts or leaves [somewhere]*　해 두어요 (둬요)　*does sth and gets it out of the way; does it and gets it over with; finishes up*

For the pattern - 어 놓아요, note that the auxiliary verb is often heard as 놔요, and for the pattern - 어 버려요, note that the pronunciation with ㅃ (뻐려요) is livelier. But in writing, they are always just 놓아요 and 버려요.

　　Observe how each verb is used by itself below:

66. 어디에 놓을까요?
　　Where shall I put it?

67. 얼마 후에 소금물을 버리고... [instructions on a cooking show]
　　Somewhat later you throw away the brine and after that...

68. 한 사흘 두었다가 먹습니다.
　　You leave it for about three days and then eat it.

Here are some more examples of the verbs used in phrases with infinitives:

69. 우리가 채소를 사 놓으면 김 선생님 부인이 김치를 만들어 주시겠대요.
　　If we buy vegetables [in advance, ahead of time], Mrs. Kim says she'll make the kimch'i for us.

70. 음식을 잘 준비해 놓았습니다.
　　We've prepared the food well [ahead of time].

71. 그 음식이 너무 맛이 있어서, 다 먹어 버렸습니다.
　　That food tasted so good that I ate it all.

72. 저녁 후에 바로 집으로 가 버립시다.
　　Let's go home right after dinner.

73. 젊었을 때 공부를 해 두어야 합니다.
    You have to study while you are still young.

74. 지금 다 먹어 둬요.
    You'd better eat all of it now.

75. 한국 사람은 김치를 가을에 담가 두었다가 겨울 동안 늘 먹지요.
    Koreans make kimch'i in the fall, and have it throughout the winter.

Note that the two verbs 잊어버리 – *forget* and 잃어버리 – *lose* derive etymologically from this pattern, but are now treated as single, unitary verbs (no space in the spelling):

76. 저는 잊어버리고, 책을 못 가지고 왔어요.
    I completely forgot to bring [forgot and didn't bring] the book.

77. 김 선생님이 백화점에서 지갑을 잃어버리셨대요.
    Mr. Kim says he lost his wallet at the department store.

8.   *Pretends to...* with -(으)ㄴ / -는 척하-

The postmodifier 척 means *pretense*. In combination with the (processive) auxiliary verb 하 – and the – (으)ㄴ and – 는 modifiers, it forms the two patterns – (으)ㄴ 척하 – *pretend to be a certain way* (with descriptive verbs) or *pretend to have done* (with processive verbs) and – 는 척하 – *pretend to do / be doing something* (with processive verbs). Note that you may also encounter 체 instead of 척 in this pattern.

78. 바쁜 척하지 말고 나 좀 도와줘요.
    Stop pretending to be busy and [instead] help me.

79. 수지는 보고도 못 본 척하고 그냥 지나갔다.
    Even though she saw it, Suji pretended not to and just passed by.

80. 잘난 척하지 마.
    Stop showing off ["pretending to be great"].

81. 그 사람은 바보인 척한다.
    He pretends to be a fool.

82. 그냥 모르는 척하세요.
    Just ignore him ["pretend not to know him"].

EXERCISES

Exercise 1: Reading Comprehension

Write out answers to the following questions.

1. 나는 한국에 온 지 얼마나 되었습니까?
2. 처음 한국에 왔을 때 무엇 때문에 고생을 많이 했습니까?
3. 한국 사람들은 길을 모를 때 어떻게 합니까?
4. 한국 사람들이 왜 나한테 길을 물어 보는 것 같습니까?
5. 사람들이 나한테 길을 물어 보았을 때 나는 잘 가르쳐 주었습니까?
6. 그래서 나는 어떻게 하면 되겠다고 생각했습니까?
7. 길을 묻는 아주머니한테 내가 영어로 말했더니 아주머니는 어떤 반응을 보였습니까?
8. 내가 예상하지 못했던 일은 어떤 것이었습니까?
9. 영어로 질문을 받고 나는 태연했습니까?
10. 그 사람한테 어떻게 대답해 주었습니까?
11. 그 사람이 가고 난 후 나는 어떤 결심을 했습니까?

Exercise 2: Practice with NOUN이 / 가 아니라

Answer the "A" questions below using the pattern NOUN이 / 가 아니라.

1. A: 이 핸드폰 수미 씨 겁니까?
   B: _____
2. A: 이 그림 저쪽 벽에 걸 겁니까?
   B: _____
3. A: 영진 씨는 내일 안 가실 거지요?
   B: _____
4. A: 할아버지 생신이 내일입니까?
   B: _____
5. A: 이 꽃 저한테 줄 겁니까?
   B: _____
6. A: 저 사람이 진호 씨 형입니까?
   B: _____

Exercise 3: Practice with (으)로

Answer the questions below using the particle (으)로.

1. 요즘 꿈속에서 무슨 말로 이야기합니까?
2. 편지 쓸 때 무엇을 많이 사용합니까?
3. 여러분 손으로 직접 세탁을 합니까? 아니면 다른 사람이 해 줍니까?

4. 지금 누구 돈으로 생활하고 있습니까? 직접 자기 힘으로 번 돈입니까? 아니면 다른 사람한테서 받은 돈입니까?

5. 무슨 샴푸로 머리를 감습니까?

6. 어떤 책으로 한국어를 공부하고 계십니까?

Exercise 4: Practice with -는 길이- and -는 길에

Use the patterns ‑는 길이‑ and ‑는 길에 to answer the questions below.

1. A: 어디 가십니까?

   B: _____

2. A: 오늘은 좀 늦으셨네요.

   B: _____

3. A: 어디에 갔다 오십니까?

   B: _____

4. A: 저 시장에 가는데, 뭐 시킬 일 없습니까?

   B: _____

5. A: 이따 오후에 시간 있으면 저희 집에 잠깐만 다녀가세요.

   B: _____

6. A: 여보, 저녁에 집에 올 때 책 좀 한 권 사 가지고 오세요.

   B: _____

Exercise 5: Composition

처음 외국에 갔을 때 그 나라의 언어를 못해서 힘든 일이나 웃기는 일은 없었습니까? 있으면 이야기해 보세요.

Exercise 6: Practice with Quoted Statements

Convert the following sentences to (a) Expanded Indirect Quotations, then (b) Contracted Indirect Quotations, all in the 합니다 Formal Style as indicated in the 보기 below.

보기: 비가 옵니다. → 비가 온다고 합니다. (→ 온답니다)

1. 수미는 머리가 깁니다.
2. 말이 빨라서 알아들을 수 없습니다.
3. 정아는 친구한테 전화를 겁니다.
4. 진호는 아침마다 수영을 배우러 다닙니다.
5. 선영이는 영화를 보러 갔습니다.
6. 어제는 아주 바빴습니다.
7. 내일부터는 늦지 않겠습니다.
8. 비가 올 것 같습니다.
9. 영수는 뚱뚱하지 않습니다.

10. 진호는 술을 별로 좋아하지 않습니다.
11. 내일은 한글날입니다.
12. 어제는 설날이었습니다.
13. 친구를 만나러 갈 것입니다.
14. 집에 가서 쉬고 싶습니다.

Exercise 7: Indirect Quotations (again)

Convert example sentences 19–32 from Pattern 4 to the 해요 Style. For example, sentence 19 would go as follows: 착해요 → 착하대요.

Exercise 8: Practice with -나 보- and -(으)ㄴ / -는가 보-

A. Use the pattern -나 보- to fill in the blanks.

1. 주희는 어제 _____.
   눈이 많이 부었습니다.
2. 아까부터 영호 방이 조용합니다.
   _____.
3. 진수는 기분이 나쁜지 말을 안 합니다.
   _____.
4. 앨버트 씨는 수업 시간 내내 좁니다.
   _____.
5. 어제 성준 씨하고 선영 씨가 수미 씨 집에 놀러 갔다고 합니다.
   어제가 _____.
6. 세용 씨는 오늘도 수박을 한 통 사 가지고 갔습니다.
   _____.

B. Now convert the following sentences from the -나 보- pattern to the -(으)ㄴ / -는가 보- pattern.

7. 진호는 전화를 거나 봅니다.
8. 선영이는 친구를 만나러 갔나 봅니다.
9. 어제는 아주 피곤했나 봅니다.
10. 아침 일찍 가겠나 봅니다.
11. 비가 오나 봅니다.
12. 영수는 키가 크지 않나 봅니다.

Exercise 9: Practice with -아 / -어야지

Following the 보기 below, convert the sentences to statements using -아 / -어야지.

보기: 지금까지는 매일 늦게 일어났다.
   → 내일부터는 일찍 일어나야지.

1. 지금까지는 매일 밤늦게 집에 들어갔다.
2. 지금까지는 술을 너무 많이 마셨다.
3. 지금까지는 아주 게을렀다.
4. 그동안 살이 많이 쪘다.
5. 지금까지는 거의 매일 지각했다.
6. 지금까지는 수업 시간에 많이 졸았다.

Exercise 10: Practice with -아 / -어 놓-, -아 / -어 버리-, and -아 / -어 두-

Recast the underlined verbs in the following sentences using the pattern -아 / -어 놓-, -아 / -어 버리- or -아 / -어 두-, then translate the results into English. (Some sentences allow more than one of these patterns.)

1. 치료하지 않고 그냥 <u>놓으면</u> 병이 더 심해져요.
2. 창문을 <u>열고</u> 잘 테야?
3. 이 표현을 꼭 <u>외우세요</u>.
4. 옷은 가방에다가 <u>넣었어요</u>.
5. 텔레비전을 <u>켜고</u> 거기서 뭘 하니?
6. 너 혼자 다 <u>먹으면</u> 어떡해?
7. 책을 <u>펴세요</u>.
8. 막내도 미국으로 대학을 <u>보내면</u> 섭섭하시겠습니다.
9. 자기 뜻대로 안 되면 <u>울어요</u>.
10. 여기에다 이름을 먼저 <u>쓰고</u> 들어가세요.
11. 기분 나쁜 일은 그냥 <u>잊으세요</u>.
12. 손님들은 하나씩 <u>떠나고</u> 집이 다시 조용해졌다.
13. 일을 다 <u>끝냈어요</u>.
14. 잊어버리지 않게 <u>적었어요</u>.
15. 내가 그것을 어디에다 <u>놓았지</u>?
16. 점심 준비를 다 <u>했으니</u> 이따가 잡수세요.
17. 한국 사람들은 겨울 동안 먹을 김치를 한꺼번에 <u>담급니다</u>.
18. 지금은 너무 피곤하니까 나를 그냥 <u>내버리세요</u>.

Exercise 11: Practice with -(으)ㄴ / -는 척하-

Recast the underlined verbs in the following sentences using the *pretend* pattern -(으)ㄴ / -는 척하-.

1. 선희는 나를 보고도 <u>못 봤다고 한다</u>.
2. 알고도 <u>모른다고 합니다</u>.
3. 벌써 먹고는 <u>안 먹었다고 한다</u>.
4. 남자친구가 <u>잘났다는</u> 바람에 분위기가 나빠졌어요.
5. 잘 알지도 못하면서 뭘 그렇게 <u>안다고 하나</u>?
6. 우리 수영장에서 만나면 서로 <u>모른다고 합시다</u>.
7. 영숙이는 지금 책을 안 읽고 있으면서도 <u>읽고 있다고 한다</u>.

우리 나라에는 보드카가 마시고 남을 만큼 흔합니다

러시아인, 쿠바인, 미국인 세 명이 미국인 변호사와 같이 기차로 여행을 하고 있었다.

한참 재미있게 이야기를 하고 가다가 러시아 사람이 큰 보드카 병을 꺼냈다. 그러더니 사람들에게 한 잔씩 따라주고 아직도 술이 반이나 남은 병을 창밖으로 던져 버렸다. 깜짝 놀란 미국인이 아까운 걸 왜 버리느냐고 물었다. 그랬더니 러시아 사람은 자기네 나라에는 보드카가 마시고 남을 만큼 흔하다고 말했다.

조금 후에 쿠바 사람이 시가를 사람들에게 하나씩 나눠 주었다. 그리고 자기도 두어 모금 피우다가 창밖으로 던져 버렸다.

"아니. 쿠바는 형편이 어렵다고 들었는데 왜 다 피우지 않고 버립니까?"

"우리 쿠바에는 시가가 피우고 남을 정도로 흔합니다."

그 말을 들은 미국인은 벌떡 일어나더니 미국인 변호사를 번쩍 들어 창밖으로 던져 버렸다.

NEW VOCABULARY

Vocabulary from the Main Text

러시아	Russia	아까w– (아깝다)	be regrettable, pitiful; be (too) precious or valuable (to discard)
러시아인(~人)	Russian (person)		
미국인(美國人)	American (person)		
변호사(辯護士)	lawyer	그랬더니	whereupon
기차(汽車)	train	자기네 나라에는	in their (own) country
기차사고(汽車事故)	train accident	흔하 –	be common, plentiful
한참	for quite a while	시가	cigar
꺼내 –	take out, produce (from sb's pocket, a bag, etc.); bring up (a subject); broach	나누 –	divide, share
		나눠 주 –	share sth with sb
		두어	two or three; a few
		모금	mouthful; sip
그러더니	whereupon	형편(形便)	the situation, state of affairs
따르 –, 따라	pour, pour out (NB: Note that this base is *not* ㄹ – doubling—it is irregular.)	형편 없다	be a mess; be in a sorry state (said of a country's economy, for example)
		벌떡 일어나 –	stand up abruptly, suddenly
던지 –	throw; toss	번쩍 드 – ㄹ – (들다)	lift sth up briskly

Vocabulary from the Example Sentences

접시	plate, dish	빠지 –	be absent; fail to turn up (NB: processive)
천장(天障)	ceiling		
닿 –	sth reaches, goes as far as	진영 씨 덕분입니다	*It is thanks to Chinyŏng.*
마음 놓고	with peace of mind; without anxiety; free from care	전(前)부터	from the very beginning
예쁘다면서요?	*Is it true that she is pretty? Did sb / you say she was pretty?*	원래(原來 / 元來)	originally; actually; as a matter of fact
		약속(約束)(을) 지키 –	keep an appointment or promise
돌아보 –	look back; turn around and look	넘치 –	overflow
과목(科目)	subject, course (at school)	경부(京釜) 고속도로 (高速道路)	the Seoul-Pusan Highway
지치 –	get exhausted, tired, worn out	고속(高速)	"high speed"
		고속버스	highway bus; coach
푹 쉬 –	have a good rest	눈(을) 뜨 –	open one's eyes
하도 안 보여서	*because sth / sb was so not-to-be-seen, i.e., never showed up*	끔찍하 –	be disgusting (in a horrific, scary way); give one the creeps; be horrid, horrible
뒷모습	one's appearance from behind	사투리	dialect; brogue; regional accent

심 (甚) 하 -	be severe, intense, extreme; be strict, stern, harsh	어떨 때는	sometimes; on some occasions
심 (甚) 하게	in a grave / serious way; terribly; (e.g. "he uses dialect something terrible!")	하숙 (下宿)	boarding; staying as a long-term lodger
		하숙비 (下宿費)	boarding expenses; lodging fees

Vocabulary from the Exercises

휴가 (休暇)	leave of absence; holiday; vacation	학자 (學者)	scholar
일억 (一億)	a hundred million	단골집	one's regular or favorite restaurant / bar
참 -	put up with sth; be patient; "bear it"; suffer sth; endure sth	단골손님	regular customer
		파산 (破産)	bankruptcy; insolvency
놀라w– (놀랍다)	be surprising, amazing	파산 (破産) (을) 하 -	go bankrupt
세 -	count	몸조리 (~調理) (를) 하 -	take good care of oneself (usually after sickness or childbirth)
살 (을) 빼 -	lose weight		
비 (를) 맞 -	get rained on	대통령 (大統領)	president (of a country)
웬일이십니까?	*What's the matter?*	선언 (宣言) (을) 하 -	declare
실수 (失手) (를) 하 -	make an error, mistake; commit an indiscretion	장가 (杖家) (를) 가 -	(man) get married
		시집 (을) 가 -	(woman) get married
엉뚱한 실수 (失手)	stupid mistake; silly gaffe	얌전하 -	be gentle, modest, nice, well brought up, pleasant, well behaved
복권 (福券)	lottery ticket		
당첨 (當籤) (이) 되 -	get selected in a drawing	논문 (論文)	thesis; scholarly paper
복권에 당첨 (이) 되 -	win the lottery; win on a lottery ticket	제출 (提出) (을) 하 -	hand in; submit
날씬하 -	be slim, slender		

PATTERNS

1. Quoted Questions with -냐고

This section reviews the indirect quotation patterns found in *Continuing Korean*, Lesson 27, and continues the ongoing review of indirect / reported speech in the first lessons of this course. Here we focus on the expanded indirect quotation of questions in the Formal 합니다 Style. (You will have an opportunity to practice other Styles in the exercises at the end of the lesson.) Finally, note that in colloquial Korean, there is a growing tendency to replace the three different forms - 느냐고~으냐고~ 냐고 with just - 냐고 everywhere.

1. 무엇을 합니까? What are you doing? →
   (a) Expanded: 무엇을 하느냐고 합니다 (Present: *asks*)
   (→ Contracted: 무엇을 하느냡니다).

   (b) Expanded: 무엇을 하느냐고 했습니다 (Past: *asked*)
   (→ Contracted: 무엇을 하느냈습니다).

2. 누구를 만나러 갑니까? Who are you going to meet? →
   누구를 만나러 가느냐고 물었습니다.

3. 무슨 책을 읽습니까? What book are you reading? →
   무슨 책을 읽느냐고 물었습니다.

4. 무슨 생각을 하고 있습니까? What are you thinking about? →
   무슨 생각을 하고 있느냐고 물었습니다.

5. 그 책 재미있습니까? Is that book interesting? →
   그 책 재미있느냐고 물었습니다.

6. 어디 아픕니까? Where does it hurt? →
   어디 아프냐고 물었습니다.

7. 기분 좋습니까? Are you in a good mood? →
   기분 좋으냐고 물었습니다.

8. 쉬고 싶습니까? Do you want to rest? →
   쉬고 싶으냐고 물었습니다.

9. 비가 올 것 같습니까? Does it look like it's going to rain? →
   비가 올 것 같으냐고 물었습니다.

10. 피곤하지 않습니까? Aren't you tired? →
    피곤하지 않으냐고 물었습니다.

11. 진수 씨는 오지 않습니까? Isn't Chinsu coming? →
    진수 씨는 오지 않느냐고 물었습니다.

12. 저 사람 누구입니까? Who is that? →
    저 사람 누구냐고 물었습니다.

13. 토마스 씨는 어느 나라 사람입니까? What country is Thomas from? →
    토마스 씨는 어느 나라 사람이냐고 물었습니다.

14. 어제 뭐 했습니까? What did you do yesterday? →
    어제 뭐 했느냐고 물었습니다.

15. 많이 아팠습니까? Did it hurt a lot? →
    많이 아팠느냐고 물었습니다.

16. 전에도 여기가 커피숍이었습니까? Was this a coffee shop before too? →
    전에도 여기가 커피숍이었느냐고 물었습니다.

17. 뭐 먹겠습니까? What would you like to eat? →
    뭐 먹겠느냐고 물었습니다.

18. 저 영화 재미있겠습니까? Do you think that movie will be interesting? →
    저 영화 재미있겠느냐고 물었습니다.

2. *As much as / as... as NOUN* with *NOUN만큼* and *to the extent that...* with *-(으)ㄹ 만큼*

The word 만큼 has two functions. As a particle following a noun, it means *as much as; equal to*:

19. A: 얼마나 더 가지고 올까요?
    How much more should I bring?

    B: 이 접시 위에 있는 것만큼 가지고 오십시오.
    Please bring as much as there is on this plate.

20. A: 모리 씨는 한국말을 잘합니까?
    Does Mori speak Korean well?

    B: 네, 수잔 씨만큼 잘합니다.
    Yes, he speaks as well as Susan.

21. A: 제주도가 정말 그렇게 아름답습니까?
    Is Cheju Island really so beautiful?

    B: 글쎄요, 제가 생각했던 것만큼은 아름답지 않았습니다.
    Well, it wasn't as beautiful as I had thought.

As a postmodifier following the prospective modifier in -(으)ㄹ, it creates a pattern that means *to the extent that...*:

22. A: 앨버트 씨는 키가 커요?
    Is Albert tall?

    B: 네, 머리가 버스 천장에 닿을 만큼 큽니다.
    Yes, so much so that his head reaches the ceiling on the bus.

23. A: 한국말 많이 늘었습니까?

    Has your Korean improved a lot?

    B: 네, 이제는 마음 놓고 다닐 수 있을 만큼 늘었습니다.

    Yes, it has improved now to the extent that I can get around without much worry.

24. A: 진우 씨 부인이 그렇게 예쁘다면서요?

    Is it true that Chinu's wife is so pretty?

    B: 네, 지나가던 사람들이 다시 한 번 돌아볼 만큼 예쁩니다.

    Yes, so much so ["to the extent"] that people passing by turn around to get a second look.

In this latter postmodifier usage, the pattern －(으)ㄹ 만큼 is similar to －(으)ㄹ 정도(로). Another use of this －(으)ㄹ 만큼 pattern has the meaning of *enough to*, as shown below:

25. 큰 집을 지을 만큼 돈이 없다.

    I don't have enough money to build a big house.

26. 나는 이 과목을 가르칠 만큼 아는 것이 없다.

    I don't have enough knowledge to teach this subject.

3. Startling Close-ups with -더니 Again

We have already examined this form in Lesson 1. Recall that Plain Base + －더니 is usually used for non-first persons (*you, he, she, it, they*), Past Base + －더니 cannot be used with second-person *you* as the subject, and Past Base + －더니 is usually used with first-person *I* or *we*. A good translation strategy is to think of the meaning *"whereupon."*

27. (내가) 어제 산에 갔다 왔더니 다리가 아픕니다.

    I went hiking yesterday, and [now I discover] my legs hurt.

28. (철민 씨가) 어제 산에 갔다 오더니 다리가 아픈가 봅니다.

    Ch'ŏlmin went hiking yesterday, and [whadda ya know, now] it seems his legs hurt.

29. 급하게 먹더니 배탈이 난 것 같습니다.

    He ate in such a rush it seems he has a tummy-ache [now].

30. 열심히 공부하더니 시험에 붙었나 봅니다.

    He studied so hard [and look!]—seems he's passed the exam.

31. 철민 씨가 며칠 밤을 새우더니 지쳤나 봅니다.

    Ch'ŏlmin stayed up several nights in a row, which probably explains why he seems exhausted.

32. 며칠 푹 쉬더니 몸이 좋아졌나 봅니다.

    He had a good rest for several days, whereupon his body seems to have recovered.

33. 하루 종일 수영을 하고 오더니 피곤한가 봅니다.
    After coming home from swimming all day long, she seems tired.

34. 경철 씨가 선주를 며칠 동안 안 만나더니 보고 싶은가 봅니다.
    After not seeing Sŏnju for several days, it seems Kyŏngch'ŏl misses her.

4. Postmodifier 줄

4.1. *Know-how* with -(으)ㄹ 줄

In one common pattern, the noun 줄 has the meaning *know-how*. In this pattern, it has the prospective modifier -(으)ㄹ in front of it and 아 - ㄹ - *know* or 모르 - *not know* after it. The expression as a whole means *knows (doesn't know) how to...* Because the 줄 serves as the object of 아 - ㄹ - / 모르 -, it can optionally take particles like 을, 은, etc. Here are some examples:

35. 어떻게 할 줄(을) 모르겠어요.
    I don't know what to do.

36. 설거지를 할 줄 알아요?
    Do you know how to wash dishes?

37. 음식도 할 줄 알아요.
    I know how to cook, too.

38. 아무것도 할 줄을 몰라요.
    He doesn't know how to do anything.

39. 부산에 혼자 갈 줄 몰라요.
    He doesn't know how to get to Pusan by himself.

40. 한국말을 읽을 줄 아세요?
    Do you know how to read Korean?

41. 젓가락으로 먹을 줄 몰라요.
    We don't know how to eat with chopsticks.

Notice that this construction is often translated to mean *can* (or *can't*) in English: *I can eat with chopsticks, I can't speak Japanese*, etc. Thus, the English *can(not)* has three separate equivalents in Korean:

a.   can = it is possible: -(으)ㄹ 수(가) 있 -
     음식을 할 수 있어요 (없어요).
     He can [can't] cook.

b.   can = knows how to: - (으)ㄹ 줄 (을) 아 - ㄹ -
한국말을 읽을 줄 알아요 (몰라요).
She can [can't] read Korean.

c.   can = has permission to: - 아 / - 어도 좋 - , - 아 / - 어도 되 -
극장에 가도 좋아요 (가면 안 돼요).
They can [can't] go to the theatre.

4.2. *Thinks /assumes that...* with 줄(로) 아-ㄹ- and *not know /realize that...* with 줄(을) 모르-
Yet another meaning of the postmodifier 줄 is *assumption; presumed fact*. In this pattern, 줄 can follow any of the basic modifiers. When used with 아 - ㄹ - (알다) *know* and optionally followed by the particle 로, the meaning concerns presumptions rather than hard facts: *One thought or presumed (wrongly) that...* or *One assumes, presumes, thinks, or feels that [so-and-so is the case].* When used with 모르-, the particle 을 is preferred over 로, and yields a pattern with the meaning *One didn't know or realize that [so-and-so is / was the case].*

On a Past Modifier:
42. 안 오신 줄 알았습니다.
I thought / assumed you hadn't / didn't come [but I now know you did].

On a Descriptive Modifier:
43. A: 그동안 어떻게 지냈습니까?
How have you been doing?

B: 여행 좀 갔다 왔습니다.
I was traveling for a while.

A: 그동안 하도 안 보여서 어디 아픈 줄 알았습니다.
I hadn't seen you for so long I thought you were sick or something [but obviously I was wrong!].

On a Processive Modifier:
44. A: 영진이 지금 자니까 내일 아침에 다시 전화하십시오.
Yŏngjin is asleep now, so please call again tomorrow morning.

B: 엄마 저 안 자요.
Mom, I'm not asleep.

A: 너무 조용해서 자는 줄 알았다.
You were so quiet I thought [wrongly] you were sleeping.

On a Prospective Modifier:
45. A: 진호 씨는 오늘도 늦나 봅니다.
Looks like Chinho is late again today.

B: 그럴 줄 알았습니다. 한 번도 제 시간에 온 적이 없으니까요.
I knew it! ["I had assumed he would do that."] After all, he hasn't come on time even once.

More examples:

46. A: 야, 선주야.
    Hey, Sŏnju!

    B: 누구세요?
    Who are you?

    A: 어머, 죄송합니다. 뒷모습만 보고 제 친구인 줄 알았습니다.
    Oh, I'm so sorry. Just seeing you from behind, I thought you were my friend.

47. A: 철민 씨, 어제 모임에 왜 안 왔습니까?
    Ch'ŏlmin, why didn't you come to the meeting yesterday?

    B: 갔다가 일이 있어서 좀 일찍 나왔습니다.
    I went, but then something came up so I left early.

    A: 그렇습니까? 저는 안 오신 줄 알았습니다.
    Really? I thought you hadn't come.

48. A: 어머, 용필 씨. 바빠서 못 오실 줄 알았는데 오셨군요.
    Oh, Yongp'il! I thought you were too busy to come, but you're here!

    B: 이런 데에 제가 빠지면 되겠습니까?
    How could I not come to an event like this?

49. 나쁜 것을 안 가르칠 줄(로) 압니다.
    I assume they wouldn't teach anything bad.

50. 나쁜 일을 안 가르쳤을 줄로 압니다.
    I feel certain that they didn't teach anything bad.

51. 내일 올 줄로 알고 있습니다.
    I think [I'm assuming] he'll be [= come] back tomorrow.

52. 내일 오는 줄로 알고 있습니다.
    I think [I'm assuming] he's coming back tomorrow.

53. 내일 올 줄로 알았습니다.
    I thought he was coming tomorrow [but now I realize that I was wrong, and in fact he will come some other time].

54. 지금 집에 없는 줄로 알고 있는데요.
    My understanding is that he's not at home now.

Note that when you use 몰랐 - , as in the next few examples, 로 cannot be used.

55. A: 앨버트 씨가 한국말을 이렇게 잘하는 줄 정말 몰랐습니다.
    I really had no idea that Albert spoke Korean so well.

    B: 다 진영 씨 덕분입니다.
    It's all thanks to Chinyŏng.

56. A: 수미가 그렇게 착한 줄을 몰랐어요.
    I had no idea Sumi was such a good person.

    B: 제가 전부터 착하다고 이야기했잖아요.
    Come on—I've been telling you how nice she is since forever!

57. 그 집에 애들이 있는 줄 몰랐습니까?
    Didn't you know they had children in that family?

58. A: 상현이가 약속을 하고 안 올 줄 정말 몰랐습니다.
    I had no idea Sanghyŏn would promise to come and then not show up.

    B: 상현이는 원래 약속을 잘 안 지킵니다.
    Sanghyŏn has never been good at keeping appointments.

5. *To the extent that...* with -(으)ㄹ 정도이- and -(으)ㄹ 정도로

This pattern was covered in detail in *Continuing Korean*, Lesson 28. The basic meaning of the noun 정도 is *extent*, e.g., 어느 정도까지 *to a certain extent* or *to what extent?* As a postmodifier following the prospective modifier in -(으)ㄹ, it creates two patterns: (a) -(으)ㄹ 정도이- *lit.: It is to the extent that...*, and (b) -(으)ㄹ 정도로 *to the extent that...* (adverbially).

59. A: 요즘도 바쁘십니까?
    Still busy?

    B: 네, 밥 먹을 시간이 없을 정도입니다.
    Yes, so much that ["to the extent that"] I don't have time to eat.

60. A: 지난 여름에 서울에 비가 많이 왔습니까?
    Did it rain a lot in Seoul last summer?

    B: 네, 한강이 넘칠 정도로 많이 왔습니다.
    Yes, it rained so much ["to the extent that"] the Han River overflowed its banks.

61. A: 앨버트 씨 한국말 많이 늘었습니까?
    Has Albert's Korean improved much?

    B: 네, 놀랄 정도로 늘었습니다.
    Yes, to a surprising extent.

62. A: 어제 경부고속도로에서 큰 사고가 났다고 들었습니다.

   I heard there was a big accident on the Seoul Pusan Highway yesterday.

   B: 저도 뉴스에서 보았는데, 정말 눈을 뜨고 볼 수 없을 정도로 큰 사고였습니다.

   I saw it on the news, too, and it really was one of those accidents that was so horrible you can't bear to look.

63. A: 선호 씨는 사투리를 심하게 씁니까?

   Does Sŏnho use a lot of dialect?

   B: 네, 어떨 때는 저도 알아들을 수 없을 정도로 심하게 씁니다.

   Yes, so much that sometimes even I can't understand.

64. A: 어제 술 많이 마셨습니까?

   Did you drink a lot yesterday?

   B: 네, 오늘 아침 일어났을 때 어떻게 집에 왔는지 기억이 안 날 정도로 많이 마셨습니다.

   Yes, so much that when I got up this morning, I couldn't remember how I got home.

6. **Is it true that...? with -다면서(요)? ~ -(이)라면서(요)?**

These two related patterns are built on the indirect quotation patterns introduced in *Continuing Korean*, Lesson 27, and reviewed in this course in Lesson 3. In other words, these patterns are originally contractions from the expanded indirect quotation pattern, and one could "spell out" or expand them as -다[고 하-]면서(요)? and -(이)라[고 하-]면서(요)? However, this is by now simply a historical or etymological fact, and nobody uses the fully expanded source form—you should use only the contracted forms.

   Note that in highly colloquial Korean, these patterns can be contracted even further, as (a) -다며 (요)? and -(이)라며(요)? or (b) (even more colloquially) -다메(요)? and -(이)라메(요)? These highly contracted forms are restricted mostly to the Plain (한다) and Intimate (해) Styles (in other words, you are unlikely to hear them followed by the Polite 요 and are not normally used in writing.

65. A: 지난 주에 여행 갔다 왔다면서요?

   Is it true you went on a trip last week?

   B: 네, 어디서 들었어요?

   Yes, where did you hear about it?

66. A: 저 음식점 갈비탕이 맛있다면서?

   Is it true that restaurant has good kalbit'ang?

   B: 응, 정말 맛있더라.

   Yeah, it is really good.

67. A: 저 연극 재미있다면서?

    Is it true that play is interesting?

    B: 응, 정말 재미있어.

    Yeah, it's really interesting.

68. A: 저 사람이 가수라면서?

    Is it true she's a singer?

    B: 응, 정말 노래 잘하더라.

    Yeah, she sings really well.

69. A: 저 사람이 너네 옆집에 산다면서?

    Is it true he lives next door to you?

    B: 응.

    Yep.

70. A: 요새 하숙비가 비싸다면서?

    Is it true that lodging prices have been expensive lately?

    B: 응, 또 올랐어.

    Yeah, they went up again.

EXERCISES

Exercise 1: Reading Comprehension

Write out answers to the following questions.

1. 몇 명이 여행을 했습니까? 또 어느 나라 사람들입니까?
2. 러시아 사람은 보드카 병을 꺼내서 어떻게 했습니까?
3. 그것을 본 미국 사람은 어떻게 했습니까?
4. 러시아 사람은 왜 술이 든 보드카 병을 창밖으로 던졌습니까?
5. 쿠바 사람은 시가를 꺼내서 어떻게 했습니까?
6. 왜 시가를 다 피우지 않고 버렸습니까?
7. 미국 사람은 왜 변호사를 창밖으로 던져 버렸습니까?

Exercise 2: Practice Quoting Questions

Quote the questions below as expanded indirect quotations in the Formal (합니다) Style, following the "보기" below.

보기: 비가 많이 옵니까? → 비가 많이 오느냐고 물었습니다.

1. 날씨 좋습니까?
2. 어디에 가고 싶습니까?
3. 어제 누구를 만났습니까?
4. 이번 휴가 때 뭐 할 겁니까?
5. 누구한테 전화 겁니까?
6. 비가 올 것 같습니까?
7. 기분이 어떻습니까?
8. 1억 원이 생기면 뭐 하겠습니까?
9. 수미 씨가 아는 사람입니까?
10. 영화를 좋아합니까?
11. 여기가 어디입니까?
12. 오늘 아침 버스에 사람이 많았습니까?
13. 기분이 좋지 않습니까?
14. 개를 좋아하지 않습니까?
15. 갈비를 맛있게 구웠습니까?
16. 오후에 어디에 갈 겁니까?
17. 언제 한국에 왔습니까?
18. 보통 몇 시에 일어납니까?
19. 어제 만난 여자 어땠습니까?
20. 가방이 무겁습니까?

Exercise 3: More Practice Quoting Questions

Rewrite the questions in example sentences 1–18 from Pattern 1 in the Contracted form (both Present and Past tenses), as shown in Example 1 below, and translate the original questions into English.

1. 무엇을 합니까? What are you doing? →
   (a) 무엇을 하느냡니다. (Present: *asks*)
   (b) 무엇을 하느냈습니다. (Past: *asked*)

Exercise 4: Practice with 만큼

Answer the questions below using 만큼.

1. A: 앨버트 씨는 한국말을 잘합니까?
   B: _____
2. A: 진호 씨는 키가 큽니까?
   B: _____
3. A: 아기가 많이 컸지요?
   B: _____
4. A: 지난 겨울에 눈이 많이 왔지요?
   B: _____
5. A: 얼마나 더 가지고 오면 되겠습니까?
   B: _____
6. A: 내일 모임에 손님이 200명쯤 온다면서요?
   B: _____

Now translate the following sentences as indicated, using 만큼.

7. Probably nobody takes as much medicine as I do.
8. There is probably no country that likes sons as much as Korea.
9. There is probably no guy that takes as good care of his girlfriend as I do.
10. We were so upset we couldn't stand it.

11. The students here study surprisingly hard.

12. I'm so exhausted I can't even budge.

13. So many people came I couldn't count [them all].

Exercise 5: Practice with -더니

Finish off the sentences below to reveal the noteworthy occurrence with a clause - 더니.

1. _____ 체했나 봅니다.
2. _____ 살이 좀 빠졌나 봐요.
3. _____ 다리 무척이나 아프네요.
4. _____ 감기에 걸렸어요.
5. _____ 반갑게 인사를 했어요.
6. _____ 감기가 다 나았어요.

Exercise 6: Practice with 줄 아-ㄹ- / 모르-

Write an appropriate response for the blanks below using the pattern 줄 아 - ㄹ - / 모르 -. Then translate all the exchanges into English.

1. A: 어, 진호 씨 여기서 일하십니까?
   B: 네, 얼마 전에 이 회사에 취직했습니다.
   A: _____.

2. A: 영진 씨는 지금 없으니까 30분 후에 다시 전화하십시오.
   B: 저 여기 있는데요.
   A: _____.

3. A: 진호 씨는 오늘도 안 올 건가 봅니다.
   B: _____.
   ["I knew it!"]
   힘든 일을 할 때는 한 번도 나온 적이 없잖아요.

4. A: 어, 영준 씨 여기에 웬일이십니까?
   B: 누구 좀 만나러 왔습니다.
   A: 이런 데서 영준 씨를 _____.
   ["I had no idea I'd meet you in a place like this..."]

5. A: 나 어제 길에서 실수했어.
   B: 어떤 실수?
   A: 어떤 사람 뒷모습이 너랑 너무 비슷해서 _____.
   ["I thought it was you"]

6. A: 늦게 와서 미안합니다. 제가 너무 늦어서 _____?

   ["you thought I wasn't coming, right?"]

   B: 무슨 일이 있었습니까?

Use 줄 in the sense of "know-how" with -(으)ㄹ to translate items (7)–(9) into Korean.

7. I don't know how to make kimch'i.
8. Do you know how to use chopsticks?
9. Do you know how to get downtown?

Now try your hand at translating the following sentences with either 줄(로) 아-ㄹ- / 모르- or 줄(을) 아-ㄹ- / 모르-.

10. I had no idea that Chinho would really come to our house.
11. I had no idea I would win the lottery.
12. Who would have known that it would snow like this?
13. I had absolutely no idea she was going abroad to study.
14. I didn't know you were such a good cook!
15. I didn't know it had rained.
16. I didn't know it was raining.
17. I didn't know it would rain.
18. I thought the kids were little, but they're not at all!

Exercise 7: Practice with -(으)ㄹ 정도

Answer the questions below using the pattern -(으)ㄹ 정도.

1. A: 지난 겨울에 눈이 많이 왔습니까?
   B: _____.
2. A: 오늘 날씨가 춥습니까?
   B: _____.
3. A: 수미 씨가 아주 날씬해졌다고 들었는데 사실입니까?
   B: _____.
4. A: 정미는 착합니까?
   B: _____.
5. A: 선호 씨는 말을 빨리 합니까?
   B: _____.
6. A: 전에는 술을 아주 좋아하셨다고 들었습니다.
   B: _____.

Exercise 8: Practice with -다면서(요)? and -(이)라면서(요)?

Use this new pattern to ask what was originally said or reported. For example, in number 1, 선영 will ask 진희: 다음 주일에 미국에 간다면서요? *Is it true you're going to the States next week?* Translate the results into English.

1. 진희 → 호철: 다음 주일에 미국에 가요.
   선영 → 진희: _____.

2. 만호 → 호철: 그 술집은 이 교수님의 단골집입니다.
   진희 → 만호: _____.

3. 진희 → 호철: 내일 눈이 올 겁니다.
   선영 → 진희: _____.

4. 진희 → 호철: 전쟁 때 고생을 많이 했습니다.
   선영 → 진희: _____.

5. 진희 → 호철: 그런 영화는 보기 싫습니다.
   선영 → 진희: _____.

6. 진희 → 호철: 에릭 씨 아버님이 유명한 학자십니다.
   선영 → 진희: _____.

7. 진희 → 호철: 아버지가 수영하러 가고 싶어하십니다.
   선영 → 진희: _____.

8. 진희 → 호철: 민희 씨가 지금 밖에서 가방을 들고 있습니다.
   선영 → 진희: _____.

9. 진희 → 호철: 수철 씨는 교통사고로 죽었습니다.
   선영 → 진희: _____.

10. 진희 → 호철: 김치 없으면 못 삽니다.
    선영 → 진희: _____.

11. 진희 → 호철: 회사가 파산을 해서 난리가 났습니다.
    선영 → 진희: _____.

12. 진희 → 호철: 병이 나았지만 몸조리를 잘 못하고 있습니다.
    선영 → 진희: _____.

13. 진희 → 호철: 대통령을 모시러 갑니다.
    선영 → 진희: _____.

14. 진희 → 호철: 결국에는 오래 가지 못하고 파산을 선언했어요.
    선영 → 진희: _____.

15. 진희 → 호철: 친구가 장가를 갑니다.
    선영 → 진희: _____.

16. 진희 → 호철: 저 여자분은 아주 얌전하십니다.
    선영 → 진희: _____.

17. 진희 → 호철: 4월에 논문을 제출해야 합니다.
    선영 → 진희: _____.

18. 진희 → 호철: 상범이하고 수영 배우러 다녀요.
    선영 → 진희: _____.

Exercise 9: 작문

Fieldwork: Using a combination of interviews with Koreans you know and web-based searches, find four or five jokes in Korean. Write them out in a composition, and also be prepared to retell them orally.

제 **5** 과 　복습 I

Review the example sentences below. Then, for each one, write a new sentence that uses the same pattern.

1.　-더니 (First Pass)

1.　철민 씨가 열심히 공부하더니 시험에 붙었나 봅니다.
2.　내가 열심히 공부했더니 시험에 붙었습니다.

2.　-다(가)

3.　영호 씨는 군대에 갔다가 이번 가을 학기부터 복학을 했나 봅니다.
4.　간식을 먹으려고 하다가 말았어요. 살 좀 빼야지요.
5.　커피를 마시다가 다음 주일의 동창회 생각이 났다.
6.　평소에는 잘 하다가 시험만 보면 왠지 엉뚱한 실수를 많이 합니다.

3.　-(으)ㄴ / -는데다(가)

7.　A: 왜 꼭대기까지 올라가지 않았습니까?
　　B: 바람이 많이 부는데다가 눈까지 와서 꼭대기까지 올라갈 수 없었습니다.
8.　A: 여행 즐거웠습니까?
　　B: 버스가 낡은데다가 에어컨이 고장 나서 고생을 많이 했습니다.
9.　A: 무슨 차를 사는 게 좋겠습니까?
　　B: 모닝이 경제적인데다가 안전하니까 모닝을 사십시오.

4.　-다(가) 보니

10.　A: 약속 장소를 금방 찾았습니까?
　　B: 네, 버스에서 내려서 조금 걸어가다(가) 보니 보였습니다.
11.　A: 이 책 어렵지요? 다 이해했습니까?
　　B: 네, 처음에는 너무 어려워서 이해할 수 없었는데 자꾸 읽다 보니 이해가 되었습니다.

12. A: 처음에는 다 못 마실 것 같았는데 다 마셨네요.
　　B: 글쎄 말입니다. 마시다 보니 다 마셨네요.

5. -(으)ㄴ / -는지

13. A: 준호 일어났습니까?
　　B: 오늘은 수업이 없는지 일어나지 않습니다.
14. A: 영호 씨가 요즘 바쁜지 연락을 안 합니다.
　　B: 영호 씨 출장 간 거 모르십니까?
15. A: 요즘 경호 보셨습니까?
　　B: 글쎄요. 그 사이에 여자친구가 생겼는지 약속을 잘 안 지키고 모임에도 안 나타나네요.
16. A: 학생들이 모르는 게 없는지 질문을 안 하네요.
　　B: 모르는 게 없는 게 아니라, 무엇을 모르고있는지도 몰라서 그래요.

6. 아무...도, 아무... -(이)나

17. 아침부터 지금까지 아무 것도 못 먹었습니다.
18. 내가 왔을 때 여기에 아무도 없었습니다.
19. 아직 아무한테도 말 안 했습니다.
20. 열심히 찾았지만 아무 데도 없습니다.
21. 아무렇게나 하십시오.
22. 배가 고프니까 아무 것이나 먹을 것을 주십시오.
23. 유명한 식당이니까 근처에 와서 아무한테나 물어 보십시오.
24. 가고 싶은 사람은 아무나 다 가도 됩니다.
25. 바지가 더러워지니까 아무 데나 앉지 마십시오.
26. 항상 집에 있으니까 아무 때나 전화하십시오.

7. -(으)ㄹ까 봐(서)

27. 손님이 생각보다 많이 왔습니다. 음식이 모자랄까 봐 걱정을 많이 했습니다.
28. 늦잠을 잤습니다. 회사에 늦을까 봐 걱정했는데 길이 안 막혀서 일찍 도착했습니다.
29. 약속 시간에 30분이나 늦었습니다. 친구가 가 버렸을까 봐 걱정을 했는데 학교 정문 앞에서 기다리고 있었습니다.

8. -(으)ㄴ / -는 바람에

30. A: 왜 이렇게 늦었습니까?
　　B: 버스를 잘못 타는 바람에 늦었습니다.
31. A: 수미 씨한테서 빌린 책 다 읽었습니까?
　　B: 아니요, 어제 밤에 불이 나가는 바람에 다 못 읽었습니다.
32. A: 표를 다 사셨지요?
　　B: 아니요, 매표소가 문을 일찍 닫는 바람에 못 샀습니다.

9. -(으)ㄹ 텐데(요)

33. 진아는 시간이 없어서 못 간답니다. 같이 가면 좋을 텐데요.
34. 5년 전에 아들이 교통사고로 죽었습니다. 그 아이가 그 때 죽지 않았으면 지금 15살일 텐데요.
35. 왜 도와 달라고 말하지 않았습니까? 나한테 얘기했으면 가서 도와주었을 텐데요.

10. -(으)라고 (말)하-, 달라고 하-

36. 6 시까지 일어나세요. → 6 시까지 일어나라고 (말) 했다.
37. 늦지 마시오. → 늦지 말라고 했다.
38. 엄마, 용돈 좀 주세요. → 엄마한테 용돈 좀 달라고 했습니다.
39. 선영 씨, 좀 도와주십시오. → 선영 씨한테 도와 달라고 했습니다.
40. 영준 씨한테 수미 씨 전화번호를 가르쳐 주지 마십시오.
    → 영준 씨한테 수미 씨 전화번호를 가르쳐 주지 말라고 했습니다.

11. -잖아(요)

41. A: 앨버트 씨 한국말 많이 늘었지요?
    B: 언제나 열심히 공부하잖아요.
42. A: 차가 왜 이렇게 더러워졌지요?
    B: 아까 비가 왔잖아요.
43. A: 돈이 왜 이것밖에 안 남았지요?
    B: 아까 점심 값하고 커피 값 냈잖아요.

12. 뿐이-, -(으)ㄹ 뿐이-

44. 준비를 안 해 온 사람은 저뿐이었습니다.
45. 농담으로 말한 것뿐이니까 너무 신경 쓰지 마십시오.
46. 머리만 조금 아플 뿐이니까 걱정하지 마십시오.
47. 애인 사이는 아니고 마음이 잘 통하는 친구 사이일 뿐입니다.

13. -고 마-ㄹ-, -고야 말겠-

48. 대단한 미인이었지만 결국 삼촌은 그 여자하고 이혼하고 말았다.
49. 이번에는 운전 시험에 꼭 붙고야 말겠다.

14. NOUN(이 / 가) 아니라

50. A: 이 인형 선영 씨 겁니까?
    B: 아니요, 선영 씨 것이 아니라 수미 씨 겁니다.
51. A: 내일이 어머니날이지요?
    B: 어머니날이 아니라 아버이날입니다.
52. A: 이 옷이 손님한테 잘 어울릴 것 같습니다.
    B: 제가 입으려는 것이 아니라 동생한테 선물할 겁니다.

15.　(으)로

53. A: 영어로 말해도 됩니까?

　　B: 안 됩니다. 한국말로 하십시오.

54. A: 꼭 만년필로 써야 됩니까?

　　B: 아니요, 볼펜으로 써도 됩니다.

55. A: 학교에 무엇을 타고 왔습니까?

　　B: 보통 버스를 타고 다니는데, 오늘은 택시로 왔습니다.

16.　-는 길에, -는 길이-

56. 공장에 오는 길에 공대에 들렀습니다.

57. 오늘 기분이 좋네요. 오늘 퇴근하는 길에 술 한 잔 합시다.

58. A: 어디 가십니까?

　　B: 종로에 후배를 만나러 가는 길입니다.

17.　-다고

59. 엉뚱한 질문에도 수미는 언제나 명답을 합니다.

　　엉뚱한 질문에도 수미는 언제나 명답을 한다고 합니다 ~ 했습니다.

60. 수미는 수력학을 전공합니다.

　　수미는 수력학을 전공한다고 합니다.

61. 선영이는 선배를 만나러 갔습니다.

　　선영이는 선배를 만나러 갔다고 합니다.

62. 서비스를 일시 중지를 하겠습니다.

　　아침 일찍 표를 사겠댔습니다.

63. 생전 처음 눈을 봤습니다.

　　생전 처음 눈을 봤다고 합니다.

64. 영수는 생일이 멀지 않습니다.

　　영수는 생일이 멀지 않다고 합니다.

65. 진호는 평일에는 담배를 피우지 않습니다.

　　진호는 평일에는 담배를 피우지 않는다고 합니다.

66. 토마스 씨는 영국 사람입니다.

　　토마스 씨는 영국 사람이라고 합니다.

67. 지난달에는 적자였습니다.

　　지난달에는 적자였다고 합니다.

18.　-나 보-, -(으)ㄴ / -는가 보-

68. A: 선영이는 뭐 합니까?

　　B: 자기 방에서 공부하나 봅니다.

69. A: 윤주 씨 어디 갔습니까?

    B: 차가 없는 것을 보니 멀리 나갔나 봅니다.

70. A: 어제 그 시계 누구 것이었습니까?

    B: 성준 씨 것이었나 봅니다.

71. 저 학생이 호기심이 굉장히 강한가 봐.

19. -아 / -어야지

72. 내일부터는 일찍 일어나야지.

73. 내년부터는 일어도 열심히 배워야지.

74. 미안하지만, 너같이 뚱뚱한 아이는 아침 일찍 일어나서 운동을 해야지.

75. 할아버지, 변소는 옛날 말이잖아요. "화장실"이라고 하셔야지요.

20. -아 / -어 버리-, -아 / -어 놓-, -아 / -어 두-

76. 선배: 다방을 아직도 하고 계십니까?

    후배: 아니요, 일 년 전에 팔아 버렸습니다.

77. 사촌동생이 자기 뜻대로 안 되는 일이 있으면 그냥 울어 버리는 버릇이 있습니다.

78. 차를 여기에 주차해 놓으십시오.

79. A: 아이들한테 줄 선물을 다 준비해 놓았어요?

    B: 인형 오십 개를 만들어 놓았으니 걱정 마십시오.

80. 제오과의 모든 한자를 꼭 외워 두세요.

21. -(으)ㄴ / -는 척하-

81. 열심히 공부하는 척만 하지 말고 제대로 해!

82. 김 선생님 부인은 계속 창문 밖을 보는 척하십니다.

83. 저 여자는 성형수술을 해 가지고 계속 예쁜 척하네.

84. 우리 한국어 선생님한테 영어를 쓰면 못 들은 척하십니다.

22. -냐고

85. 영국에는 남녀평등이 잘 돼 있습니까?

    영국에는 남녀평등이 잘 돼 있느냐고 물었습니다.

86. 내일 일기예보에 의하면 비가 옵니까?

    내일 일기예보에 의하면 비가 오느냐고 물었습니다.

87. 그 책 인기 있습니까?

    그 책 인기 있느냐고 물었습니다.

88. 거기 경제 형편이 어렵습니까?

    거기 경제 형편이 어려우냐고 물었습니다.

89. 한국의 인구가 얼마입니까?

    한국의 인구가 얼마냐고 물었습니다.

90. 다른 방법이 없니?
    다른 방법이 없느냐고 물었습니다.
91. 저 사람 중국 사람입니까?
    저 사람 중국 사람이냐고 물었습니다.
92. 방이 몇 평방 미터니?
    방이 몇 평방 미터냐고 물었습니다.
93. 한약을 가끔 드세요?
    한약을 가끔 드시느냐고 물었습니다.
94. 한국에 화산이 많나요?
    한국에 화산이 많으냐고 물었습니다.
95. 언제 복학을 하겠습니까?
    언제 복학을 하겠느냐고 물었습니다.

23. NOUN만큼, -(으)ㄹ 만큼

96. A: 얼마나 더 가지고 올까요?
    B: 이 접시 위에 있는 것만큼 가지고 오십시오.
97. A: 모리 씨는 한국말을 잘합니까?
    B: 네, 수잔 씨만큼 잘합니다.
98. A: 앨버트 씨는 키가 커요?
    B: 네, 머리가 버스 천장에 닿을 만큼 큽니다.

24. -더니 (Second Pass)

99. 급하게 먹더니 배탈이 난 것 같습니다.
100. 며칠 푹 쉬더니 몸이 좋아졌나 봅니다.

25. -(으)ㄴ / -(으)ㄹ 줄 아-ㄹ- / 모르-

101. A: 그 동안 어떻게 지냈습니까?
     B: 여행 좀 갔다 왔습니다.
     A: 그 동안 하도 안 보여서 어디 아픈 줄 알았습니다.
102. A: 철민 씨, 어제 모임에 왜 안 왔습니까?
     B: 갔다가 일이 있어서 좀 일찍 나왔습니다.
     A: 그렇습니까? 저는 안 오신 줄 알았습니다.

26. (으)ㄹ 정도이-, -(으)ㄹ 정도로

103. A: 요즘도 바쁘십니까?
     B: 네, 밥 먹을 시간이 없을 정도입니다.
104. A: 지난 여름에 서울에 비가 많이 왔습니까?
     B: 네, 한강물이 넘칠 정도로 많이 왔습니다.

27.   **-다면서(요)? ~ -(이)라면서(요)?**

105. A: 자녀 분이 많으시다면서요?

  B: 네, 아들 하나, 딸 다섯입니다.

106. 이 식당 후식들이 그렇게 맛있다면서요?

107. 성균관 대학교가 캐나다에 분교를 만든다면서요?

108. 밴쿠버는 수질도 토질도 좋다면서요?

109. 저 학생이 삼학년이라면서요?

110. 한국인들은 한국어를 하다 보면 무심코 쓰는 일본어 단어들이 있다면서요?

속담

어느 나라 말에나 속담이 있습니다. 속담은 누가 생각해 냈는지 그리고 언제부터 생겼는지는 알 길이 없습니다. 그렇지만 속담은 옛 선조들로부터 내려오면서 민족의 경험에 의해서 만들어진 지혜의 말이라고 할 수 있겠습니다.

속담은 짧은 말로 되어 있지만, 우리가 속담을 한번 듣고서 잘 잊어버리지 않는 이유는 짧은 말 속에 그 뜻이 분명하게 나타나 있기 때문입니다. 또 속담에는 지난날 우리 선조들의 생활과 생각이 들어 있기 때문에 속담은 우리가 생활하는 데에 많은 교훈을 줍니다.

"서당 개 삼년이면 풍월 읊는다"라는 속담이 있습니다. 이 속담은 무식한 사람도 글 잘하는 사람과 오래 있게 되면 자연 견문이 생긴다는 뜻입니다. "꼬리가 길면 밟히는 법이다"라고 하는 속담도 있습니다. 한두 번은 남을 속일 수 있지만 계속해서 반복하다가는 꼭 들키게 된다는 말이지요.

그 밖에 "낫 놓고 기역자도 모른다"는 속담이 있습니다. 낫의 모양은 한글의 기역자와 비슷합니다. 그 낫을 보고도 기역자도 모른다면 무식하다는 뜻이 아니겠습니까?

"종로에서 뺨 맞고 한강에 가서 화풀이 한다"는 속담을 아십니까? 욕을 당한 그 자리에서는 아무 말도 못하고 화풀이를 엉뚱한 곳에 가서 한다는 뜻입니다. 또, 입에서 입으로 전해지는 소문이 눈 깜짝하는 사이에 널리 퍼지게 됩니다. 그래서 "발 없는 말이 천리를 간다"는 말이 있는 것처럼 한 번 소문이 퍼지면 아무도 막을 수 없습니다.

"고생 끝에 낙이 온다"는 속담을 들어 보셨습니까? 어려운 일이나 괴로운 일을 겪은 후에 즐겁고 좋은 일도 반드시 온다는 뜻인데 고생하는 친구에게 용기를 줄 때 쓸 수 있습니다.

이 밖에 주로 한자로 구성된 속담도 여러 가지 있습니다. 예를 들어, "금강산도 식후경"이라는 말이 있는데 아무리 재미있는 일이라도 배가 불러야 흥이 난다는 말입니다. 또, "일석이조"라는 말은 한 개의 돌로 새 두 마리를 잡는다는 뜻이고, "백문이 불여일견"이라는 속담은 백 번 듣는 것이 한 번 보는 것만 못하다는 뜻입니다. 즉, 여러 번 말로만 듣는 것보다 실제로 한 번 보는 것이 더 낫다는 말입니다.

NEW VOCABULARY

Vocabulary from the Main Text

속담 (俗談)	proverb	무식 (無識) 하 -	be ignorant; lack learning
NOUN (으)로부터	from NOUN, by way of NOUN	글 (을) 잘하 -	be good in studies (NB: processive)
민족 (民族)	a people, race, nation, ethnic group	오래	for a long time
		자연 (自然)	nature; naturally, as a matter of course
경험 (經驗)	experience		
NOUN에 의해서	based on NOUN; by NOUN	견문 (見聞)	one's personal experience (things "seen and heard")
지혜 (智慧)	wisdom	견문 (이) 생기 -	gain / acquire experience; broaden one's horizons
분명 (分明) 하 -	be clear, obvious		
선조 (先祖)	ancestor	꼬리	tail
교훈 (教訓)	moral (to a story)	속이 -	cheat, fool, deceive
서당 (書堂)	traditional village school-house for learning the Chinese classics	속 -	be / get cheated, fooled, deceived
		반복 (反復) (을) 하 -	repeat, reiterate
풍월 (風月)	"wind and moon"; poetry	들키 -	be / get caught
읊 -	recite (poetry)	낫	Korean sickle

종로(鐘路)	Chongno ("Bell Road"), a main boulevard in downtown Seoul	겨-	suffer; experience; undergo
		반드시	for sure; definitely, certainly
뺨	cheek	용기(勇氣)	courage
맞-	get hit, smacked	용기(를) 주-	give courage to; encourage
화풀이(를) 하-	vent one's anger; take out one's anger	주(主)로	for the most part; in the main; mainly
욕(辱)	humiliation, abuse; swearing, "cussing"	구성(構成)(이) 되-	be / get composed of, made up of
욕(을) 당하-	suffer humiliation, be humiliated	예(例)	example
		예(例)를 들어(서)	for example; for instance
엉뚱하-	be "random"; be farfetched, outrageous	금강산(金剛山)	the Diamond Mountains
		흥(興)	merriment, mirth
널리	far and wide	흥(이) 나-	feel merry / excited
퍼지-	spread (intransitive)	한 번 보는 것만 못하다	*isn't as good as seeing [it] once*
천리(千里)	1000 *li* (one *li* = one-third of a mile)		
		즉(卽)	namely; to wit; that is to say
막-	stop, block		
고생(苦生)	suffering	실제(實際)로	in actual fact; in real life
끝	end; tip; "the end"	나(ㅅ)- (낫다)	be preferable, be better than
낙(樂)	joy, pleasure		
괴로w- (괴롭다)	be tormenting, onerous; feel tormented, out of sorts		

Additional 속담

Here are some additional 속담 that are frequently used in Korea.

1. 낮말은 새가 듣고 밤말은 쥐가 듣는다.
   Birds hear words spoken in daytime, and mice hear words spoken at nighttime.

낮	daytime

2. 바늘 도둑이 소 도둑 된다.
   The needle thief becomes a cattle rustler.

바늘	needle
도둑	thief

3. 가는 말이 고와야 오는 말이 곱다.
   Say something nice, hear something nice in return.

고w- (곱다, 고와)	be pretty, beautiful

4. 콩 심은 데 콩 나고 팥 심은 데 팥 난다.
   Plant black beans, and you get black beans; plant red beans, and you get red beans. (Reap what you sow.)

콩	black beans
팥	red beans
심 -	plant something

5. 호랑이도 제 말하면 온다.
   Speak of the devil.

호랑이	tiger
제	one's own, self's

6. 시장이 반찬이다.
   Hunger is the best sauce.

시장	hunger
반찬(飯饌)	side dishes to accompany rice

7. 남의 떡이 더 커 보인다.
   The grass is greener on the other side of the fence (lit.: "others' rice cakes look bigger").

8. 뱁새가 황새를 따라가면 다리가 찢어진다.
   If a crow-tit tries to keep up with a stork, its legs will get torn.

뱁새	crow-tit; parrotbill (a bird the size of a sparrow or chickadee)
황새	stork

9. 쇠뿔도 단 김에 빼라.
   Remove the cow's horn when [the iron] is hot. (i.e., Strike while the iron is hot.)

쇠뿔	cow's horn; ox horn
다 - ㄹ - (달다)	get heated, become very hot
빼 -	take out, extract, remove

10. 원숭이도 나무에서 떨어지는 수(가) 있다.
    Even monkeys sometimes fall out of trees. (i.e., Even experts sometimes make mistakes.)

원숭이	monkey

Vocabulary from the Example Sentences

믿 -	believe in; rely on	여성(女性)	women; the female gender
목(이) 쉬 -	get a hoarse throat	임금(賃金)	wage(s)
헤드라인	headline	남성(男性)	men; the male gender
머리기사(~記事)	lead story	절반(折半)	half

끼 -	put on (glasses)	점 (點)	birthmark
공약 (公約) (을) 하 -	make a public pledge or promise	레이저	laser
어른	elder or adult	제거 (除去) (를) 하 -	remove, get rid of
닮 -	take after; resemble	사망자 (死亡者) :	a casualty, victim, dead person
Person한테 혼 (이) 나 -	get in trouble with somebody	고혈압 (高血壓)	high blood pressure
부자 (富者)	rich person	사망률 (死亡率)	death rate
오해 (誤解) (를) 받 -	be misunderstood	꽤	quite; rather
등산 (登山) (을) 하 -	hike; go hiking	일기예보 (日氣豫報)	weather forecast
부엌	kitchen	짖 -	bark
이야기 (를) 꺼내 -	bring up / raise a subject	조언 (助言)	advice
드라이브	(computer) drive	움직이 -	move; behave
저장 (貯藏) (을) 하 -	save (a computer file)	쓰이 -	be / get used
고급 (高級) 스러w– (~스럽다)	high-class; refined	석유 (石油)	gasoline
		수입 (輸入) (을) 하 -	import
말라리아	malaria	강 (强) 하 -	be strong
모기	mosquito	국가 (國家)	nation, nation-state
감염 (感染) (이) 되 -	be / get infected	다루 -	handle; take care of; deal with
질병 (疾病)	disease; affliction; ailment	글씨	writing; handwriting
건축가 (建築家)	architect	시험지 (試驗紙)	test; test paper
설계 (設計) (가) 되 -	be / get designed		

Vocabulary from the Exercises

게으름 (을) 피우 -	act like a lazy bum; be lazy	사치 (奢侈) 스러w– (~스럽다)	be luxurious, extravagant
물건 (物件)	thing; item; goods	사치 (奢侈)	luxury, extravagance
갈아입 -	change (apparel)	매번 (每番)	every time; all the time
죄 (罪) (를) 지 (ㅅ) - (짓다)	commit a crime / sin	얻어 먹 -	get free meals; freeload
벌 (罰) (을) 받 -	be / get punished	빚 (을) 지 -	incur debt; go into debt
죄와 벌	crime and punishment	제사 (祭祀) (를) 지내 -	conduct a ritual ceremony
갚 -	pay back; repay	데이터	data
복 (福) (을) 받 -	be blessed / fortunate (*lit.*: "receive blessings," i.e., processive)	사과 (謝過) (를) 하 -	apologize
		우정 (友情)	friendship; bonds of friendship
후회 (後悔) (를) 하 -	regret	지켜 나가 -	maintain (into the future)
뒤떨어지 -	fall behind	예의 (禮儀)	courtesy; decorum; propriety
도끼	axe		
발등 [- 뜽]	top of the foot	동방예의지국 (東方禮義之國)	Eastern Country of Propriety (i.e., Korea)
찍히 -	be / get chopped	노력 (努力)	endeavor; exertion; effort
꼴	(pitiful / derogatory) shape, form, appearance, sight	노력 (努力) (을) 하 -	make effort(s); exert oneself

방법(方法)	method; means; way	삭제(削除)(를) 하 -	delete
꾸준하 -	be consistently persistent, steadfast, unflagging	신장(腎臟)	kidneys
선진국(先進國)	advanced country	손상(損傷)(이) 되 -	be / get damaged, injured
나라(를) 발전(發展) 시키 -	develop the country	결과(結果)	result(s)
장어	eel	밟 -	tread on; step on
정력(精力)	virility	주의(注意)(를) 하 -	pay attention; be cautious of
정력(精力)(을) 돋우 -	boost virility	길(을) 잃어버리 -	get lost; lose one's way
취소(取消)(를) 하 -	cancel; annul	보약(補藥)	tonic, restorative
사정(事情)	(extenuating) circum- stance	체질(體質)	one's physical constitution
		체질에 맞 -	fit / match one's physical constitution
형성(形成)(이) 되 -	be / get formed	오히려	contrary to expectations; contrary to what one might think / expect
환경(環境)	environment		
유전(遺傳)	genetics; heredity		
유전자(遺傳子)	gene	해(害)(가) 되 -	be injurious, harmful (NB: processive)
야구중계(野球中繼)	baseball (re)broadcast		
방송국(放送局)	broadcasting station	닫히 -	be / get closed
결정(決定)(이) 되 -	be / get decided, determined	굳 -	be hard, solid, firm (functions both as proces- sive and descriptive)
독자(讀者)	reader	생겨나 -	come about; come into being
뽑 -	select; choose; hire		
국민투표(國民投票)	popular vote	조선시대(朝鮮時代)	the Chosŏn era
부장(部長)	chief of section / depart- ment / division	세우 -	set up, establish
		지우 -	erase
게시판(揭示板)	bulletin board	벗기 -	remove, [make] take off (clothing); undress (sb)
관리자(管理者)	manager; webmaster		

PATTERNS

---

1. -고 + 서 **and** -고 + 도

1.1. After ... –ing with -고서

The Main Text above contains the following phrase:

> 우리가 속담을 한 번 <u>듣고서</u> 잘 잊어버리지 않는 이유는...
> *The reason we don't forget a proverb after hearing it [just] once is...*

Lesson 16.1 in *Continuing Korean* introduced the one-shape ending - 고 and noted that there are two different kinds of - 고 used to join sentences. In other words, - 고 can take on two meanings:

(a) *does or is [so-and-so], and...* [i.e., ***and also***]
(b) *having done or been [so-and-so], and...* [i.e., ***and then***]

As you may recall, with the (a) usage of ‑고 (the ***and also*** usage) there are tenseless (plain) ‑고 forms, made by attaching the ending ‑고 to the Plain Base of the verb (가 ‑ *go:* 가고), and past-tense and future-tense ‑고 forms, made by attaching ‑고 to the Past and Future Bases, respectively:

Plain Base:	가 ‑	*go*
Past Base:	갔 ‑	
Past ‑고 form:	갔고 [가꼬]	*went and...*
Future Base:	가겠 ‑	
Future ‑고 form:	가겠고 [가게꼬]	*will go and...*

But the ***and then*** ‑고 only attaches to the Plain Base. In the new pattern being introduced in this lesson, the ‑고 form plus 서 removes any potential ambiguity as to the meaning of the ‑고 form—it can only mean ***and then***. And just like the ‑고 form in its *and then* meaning, ‑고서 appears only on Plain (or honorific) Bases, and never on Past or Future Bases:

Plain Base:	가 ‑	*go*
‑고서 form:	가고서	*goes* or *went and then...*
Honorific Base:	가시 ‑	
‑고서 form:	가시고서	
Past Base:	갔 ‑	
Past ‑고서 form:	*갔고서 [nonexistent]	
Future Base:	가겠 ‑	
Future ‑고서 form:	*가겠고서 [nonexistent]	

Here are some examples of the pattern ‑고서:

1. 이야기를 다 듣고서 이해가 되었어요.
    After hearing her out, he understood.

2. 문을 열고서 보세요.
    Open the door and take a look.

3. 경찰이 누군가에게 전화를 하고서 이곳을 왔다갔다 하고 있다.
    The police phoned somebody and are now coming and going.

4. 목욕을 하고서 저녁을 먹었다.
    She took a bath and then ate supper.

5. 노래방에서 세 시간 내내 노래를 부르고서 목이 쉬었답니다.
    He says his throat is hoarse after singing for three hours straight in a noraebang.

6. 그렇게 배부르게 먹고서 또 배가 고프다고 하니?
   You eat your fill like that, and then say you're hungry again?

7. 누구를 믿고서 여기에 왔어요?
   In whom have you trusted in coming here?

In general, then, you can think of ‑ 고서 as an emphatic or fortified version of ‑ 고 in its **and then** meaning.

1.2. Even after … –ing with -고도

We observed in Section 1.1 above that placing 서 after the ending ‑ 고 forces the *and then* meaning for ‑ 고. In a similar manner, placing 도 after the ending ‑ 고 also yields a new ending with the *and then* meaning, but in this case reinforced with the *even / even though* meanings of 도. Thus, the ending ‑ 고도 can mean *even after … –ing* or *even though one does it / finishes doing it*. (It is similar, though not identical to the pattern in ‑ 어도.) Here are some examples:

8. [오늘의 헤드라인] 같은 일 하고도 여성 임금은 남성의 "절반"
   [today's headline] *Even Though Performing the Same Work, Women's Wages are "Half".*

9. 안경을 끼고도 잘 안 보인다고요?
   You mean, even when you put your glasses on you can't see well?

10. 대통령은 국민에게 공약을 하고도 지키지 않는다.
    The president, even after having made public pledges to the people of the nation, is not honoring them.

11. 그녀에게는 졸업을 하고도 연락을 하고 찾아오는 학생들이 많답니다.
    They say she has lots of former students who, even after graduating, stay in touch and come to see her.

2. Generalized Truths with Modifier + 법이-

The Main Text includes the proverb 꼬리가 길면 밟히는 법이다. Literally, this means something like *If your tail is [too] long, it's bound to get stepped on*, meaning more generally that if something is overly conspicuous, cocky, or otherwise draws too much attention to itself, it is bound to pay a price.

The Sino-Korean word 법 (法) literally means *law; regulation; rule; good reason; justification; propriety; (pre)ordained way*. When it follows a modifier, it creates a pattern meaning *such-and-such is the invariable or universal nature of things; such-and-such is the preordained state of affairs; it is fitting and proper that…*, etc. As postmodifier, 법 can follow any of the three main modifiers (i.e., ‑ (으) ㄴ, ‑ 는, and ‑ (으) ㄹ), but usually you will encounter it on the processive modifier ‑ 는.

12. 어른한테 그렇게 말하는 법이 아니야!
    That's no way to speak to your elders!

13. 아이들은 부모를 닮는 법이다.
    Children usually take after their parents.

14. 사람은 누구에게나 아주 친한 친구가 몇 명은 있는 법이다.
    Every person has [at least] a few close friends.

15. 그런 법이 어디 있느냐?
    Where do you find justification for that?

Note that the universalizing or generalizing aspect of this pattern makes it particularly appropriate for proverbs:

16. 작은 고추가 매운 법이다.
    It is in the nature of things for small peppers to be hot.

3. Warnings with -다가는

The Main Text includes the proverb 반복하다가는 들키게 마련입니다. Literally, this means *If you keep on doing something, you are bound to end up getting caught.* The pattern ‑게 마련이‑ means *it inevitably ends up a certain way* and we will be examining it more later.

For now, let us focus on the ending in ‑다가는, which is made up of the transferentive ending ‑다(가) plus particle ‑는. As with just transferentive ‑다(가), the ending ‑다가는 can attach to either Plain or Past Bases, and creates the first clause of a warning: *If one does blah-blah-blah, [then some bad result will come about].* In other words, the ending ‑다가는 retains some of the transferentive or interruptive sense of just ‑다가, and we can think of it as meaning *if one keeps on doing... [then suddenly AND unfortunately]...* Here are some examples:

17. 잘못하다가는 다칠 수 있으니까, 조심하세요.
    You might get hurt if you make a mistake, so be careful.

18. 사장님에게 잘못 보였다가는 혼이 나지요.
    If you make a bad impression on the boss, you'll get in big trouble.

19. 일은 안 하고 놀기만 하다가는 부자가 못 돼요!
    Carry on not working and fooling around, and you'll never get rich.

20. 잘못하다가는 오해를 받기가 쉽지.
    One mistake, and it's easy to be misunderstood.

21. 그렇게 버릇없게 굴다가는 아빠한테 [선생님께] 혼나지.
    Keep misbehaving like that, and you'll get in big trouble with Dad [the teacher].

22. 늘 잘난 척만 하다가는 친구들과 멀어진다.
    Act like a hotshot all the time, and you'll lose your friends.

23. [등산하면서] 여기서 실수를 했다가는 저 아래로 떨어진다.
   [while hiking] One false step here, and you fall down there.

4. *While you're at it...* with -(으)ㄴ / -는 김에

The list of additional proverbs above contains the expression 쇠뿔도 단 김에 빼라, literally: *Remove the cow's horn when [the iron] is hot* (i.e., *Strike while the iron is hot*). The *while you're at it...* pattern -(으)ㄴ / -는 김에 was covered in Lesson 22.7 of *Continuing Korean*. As you will recall, a processive verb followed by a past modifier -(으)ㄴ or a processive modifier -는 followed by 김에 means *incidental to VERBing; seeing as one is VERBing or has VERBed anyway...* Such clauses can be preceded by the adverb 이왕, which we can translate as *anyway; anyhow*. Here are some examples:

24. 부엌에 가는 김에 맥주 한 병 (물 한 잔) 가져다줄래?
   Since you're going to the kitchen anyway, would you mind bringing me a beer (a cup of water)?

25. 부엌을 청소하는 김에 화장실도 청소했어요.
   Since we were cleaning the kitchen anyway, we cleaned the bathroom, too.

26. 이야기를 꺼낸 김에 하고 싶은 이야기를 다 해 버렸어요.
   Seeing as I had brought up the subject anyway, I got everything I wanted to say off my chest.

5. *In the course of ... –ing* with -는 데에

The Main Text contains the phrase 생활하는 데에 많은 교훈을 줍니다 *provides us with many lessons for our lives*. More literally, it means something like *gives us lessons in the course of our living*. The pattern -는 데에 should remind you of the Imminent Elaboration pattern with Circumstantial -는데(요), -(으)ㄴ데(요) covered in *Continuing Korean*, Lesson 23.1.

In the pattern introduced here, the Circumstantial 데 occurs as a quasi-free noun (that is, a noun that cannot begin a sentence but must always be modified by something in front of it) with the meaning *course [of doing sth]; circumstance; occasion*. The locative particle 에 spells out the sense of *in the course or circumstance of ...–ing*, and the following clause usually has expressions like 도움을 주 - *help*, 도움이 되 - *be a help*, 좋은 참조가 되 - *serve as a good reference*, 쓰 - / 사용하 - *use sth*, 필요하 - *be necessary*, 중요하 - *be important*, etc. Here are some examples:

27. A: 이 C-드라이브는 무엇에 쓰는 거예요?
     What's this C-drive used for?

   B: 프로그램을 저장하는 데에 써요.
     For saving programs.

28. A: 이 지팡이는 무슨 지팡이예요?
     What sort of cane is this?

   B: 그것은 등산하는 데에 사용하는 등산용 지팡이예요.
     That's a walking stick used for hiking.

29. 순두부찌개 만드는 데에 뭐가 필요합니까?

    What do you need to make sundubu tchigae *[soft-tofu stew]?*

30. 텔레비전을 보는 데에 너무 시간을 버리지 마십시오.

    Don't spend too much time watching TV.

31. 한국음식을 만드는 데에 시간이 많이 걸립니다.

    It takes a long time to make Korean food.

32. 이 많은 한자를 외우는 데 한 달이나 걸렸습니다.

    It took me a whole month to memorize all these Chinese characters.

33. 고급스러운 한국말을 배우는 데에 가장 중요한 것은 한자 공부입니다.

    The most important thing in learning high-class Korean is studying Chinese characters.

6. *According to* and *by* with NOUN 에 의해(서)

Lesson 27.7 in *Continuing Korean* introduced the pattern NOUN에 의하면... *according to NOUN...* Technically speaking, there is a verb 의 (依) 하 - *follow; accord with; be according to; be pursuant to; be based on; depend on; be due to, owing to, because of,* but usually one encounters it as either NOUN에 의하면 or as NOUN에 의해서 (NOUN에 의하여 in more formal written contexts). This latter form appears in the Main Text of this lesson in the phrase 민족의 경험에 의해서 만들어진 지혜의 말 *words of wisdom created by the experience of the people.*

Thus, one of the main functions of NOUN에 의해서 is to mark the "*by* phrase" in passive constructions:

34. 이슬람이 칼에 의해서 전해졌는가?

    Was Islam spread by the sword?

35. [dictionary definition] 말라리아: 모기에 의해서 감염되는 질병

    malaria: a disease contracted through mosquitoes

36. 이태리 건축가에 의해서 설계되었다.

    It was designed by an Italian architect.

37. 점은 레이저에 의하여 쉽게 제거됩니다.

    Birthmarks are easily removed via laser.

Note that 의하 - can also occur in past modifier form:

38. 자동차 사고에 의한 사망자가 계속 늘어나고 있습니다.

    Deaths [dead persons] by automobile accident continue to increase.

39. 고혈압에 의한 사망률이 꽤 높답니다.
    They say the death rate from high blood pressure is quite high.

Finally, as a review, here are some examples of NOUN에 의하면 meaning *according to...* Note that it is common to cast the entire sentence in the indirect quotation pattern:

40. 일기예보에 의하면 내일은 갠답니다.
    According to the weather report, ["they say"] it will be clear tomorrow.

41. 소문에 의하면 그 사람이 죽었다고 한다.
    According to the rumors, ["they say"] he's dead.

7. *Sometimes stuff happens* with -는 수(가) 있다

The list of additional proverbs above includes this one: 원숭이도 나무에서 떨어지는 수(가) 있다 *even monkeys sometimes fall out of trees* (i.e., *even experts sometimes make mistakes*). The pattern in question is based on the little word 수 *possibility; likelihood; eventuality; case; circumstance* which occurs in another pattern introduced in Lesson 18.5 of *Continuing Korean*: ‑(으)ㄹ 수 있‑ / 없‑ *can / cannot do.*

But, while in this latter pattern the modifier is the Prospective Modifier ‑(으)ㄹ, here we have the Processive Modifier ‑는 (examples with ‑(으)ㄴ are also possible, but rare). Thus, the literal meaning of the pattern is something like *the possibility or cases of... –ing exist(s)*. And of course, the cases of even monkeys falling to their deaths from trees must exist: 그러는 수도 있겠지요, 뭐...

This pattern should also remind you of the postmodifier patterns ‑는 일이 있어요, ‑는 적이 있어요 / ‑는 일이 없어요, ‑는 적이 없어요 for *ever does; sometimes does / never does*, etc. (Lesson 19.4.2.2 in *Continuing Korean*). Here are some more examples:

42. 겨울에는 스키를 타다가 다쳐서 병원을 찾아오는 수가 많다.
    There are many cases in the winter of [people] hurting themselves while skiing and then coming to the hospital.

43. 운동하다가 이렇게 다치는 수가 많아요.
    There are many case of [people] injuring themselves like this during exercise.

44. 개는 모르는 사람을 보면 크게 짖는 수가 있습니다.
    Dogs are likely to bark loudly when they see somebody they don't know.

45. 그러나 그 조언대로만 움직이다간 실패하는 수가 있다.
    But if you go around just following their advice there is the danger of failure.

46. 보통 일찍 오지만 길이 막히면 늦게 오는 수도 있어요.
    Usually I arrive early, but if traffic is bad, there are times when I arrive late, too.

8. Pseudo-passives with -아 / -어지-

Lesson 18.4 in *Continuing Korean* introduced the Infinitive pattern ⁻아 / ⁻어 + 지⁻ meaning *get / become* with descriptive verbs (e.g., 나빠요 *is bad* → 나빠져요 *gets worse*, 흐려요 *is cloudy* → 흐려져요 *gets cloudy; clouds up*, 피곤해요 *is tired* → 피곤해져요 *gets tired*, etc.).

The Main Text in this lesson has the two following phrases 경험에 의해서 만들어진 지혜의 말 *words of wisdom created by experience* and 입에서 입으로 전해지는 소문 *rumors that get transferred from mouth to mouth*, but the verbs 만드⁻ㄹ⁻ (만들다) *make; create* and 전하⁻ *transfer; pass on* are processive verbs, not descriptive. This means we are dealing here with a slightly different pattern (or a new twist on an old pattern).

In essence, the pattern ⁻아 / ⁻어 + 지⁻ with processive verbs makes a kind of passive form: *gets so that...; becomes...,* etc. But note that this "passive form" (if we can really call it that) can occur on top of "true" passive patterns, as found in ⁻히⁻, ⁻이⁻, ⁻리⁻, ⁻기⁻, etc. The difference signaled by the presence or absence of ⁻아 / ⁻어지⁻ on these already passive verbs (see Example 47 below) is often hard to discern. For some speakers, the difference seems to be this: the presence of ⁻아 / ⁻어지⁻ implies that nobody cares who the original agent, actor, or culprit responsible for the action was (or, at least, nobody has a specific agent in mind). Thus, in Example 47, gasoline gets used in our lives, but we don't really care (for the purposes of this sentence) by whom—hence, 쓰여지⁻ rather than the "true passive" 쓰이⁻ (which would imply that we have a specific agent or "user" in mind).

47. 우리 생활에 쓰여지는 석유는 모두 외국으로부터 수입되는 것이에요.
    The gasoline used in our lives is all imported from abroad.

48. 강한 국가는 어떻게 만들어지는가?
    How are strong nations made?

49. 친구와 통화하고 있는데 갑자기 전화가 끊어졌다.
    I was talking to my friend on the phone when suddenly we were cut off.

50. 제6과에서 다루어지는 문법은 다소 어렵다.
    The grammar dealt with in Chapter 6 is a bit tough.

With some intransitive processive verbs, putting them into this ⁻아 / ⁻어지⁻ pattern gives the effect of potentiality or of a reflexive verb in languages like French and Spanish:

51. 이 볼펜이 글씨가 잘 써지네요.
    This pen sure writes well.

52. 차가 잘 가지네.
    The car is running nicely!

Finally, note that this same ⁻아 / ⁻어지⁻ pattern can be found fossilized in some verbs, e.g., 떨어지⁻ *fall:*

53. A: 여기 있던 시험지가 어디 갔지요?

   Where did the exam paper that was here go?

   B: 바람이 불어서 떨어졌어요.

   It fell off because of the wind.

EXERCISES

Exercise 1: Reading Comprehension

Write out answers to the following questions.

1. 영어나 프랑스말에도 속담이 있습니까?
2. 속담은 누가 생각을 해냈고 또 언제부터 생겼습니까?
3. 우리가 속담을 한 번만 들어도 왜 잊어버리지 않습니까?
4. 속담 속에 어떤 것들이 들어 있습니까?
5. 속담은 우리가 생활하는 데에 어떤 도움을 줍니까?
6. 발 없는 말이 어떻게 천리를 갈 수가 있을까요?
7. 고생을 하는 친구에게 용기를 주고 싶으면 무슨 속담을 쓰는 게 좋을까요?
8. 한 개의 돌로 두 마리의 새를 잡는 것을 한자로 표현하면 무엇이라고 합니까?

Exercise 2: Practice with -고서 and -고도

Each of the following items contains two sentences connected with 그리고 *and*. Combine these into a single sentence by using －고서, and then translate the sentence. For example, the first item would be: 아침에 먼저 세수를 하고서 머리를 감아요. *In the morning, first I wash my face and then I shampoo my hair.*

1. 아침에 먼저 세수를 해요. 그리고 머리를 감아요.
2. 거짓말을 했어요. 얼굴이 확 빨개지더군요.
3. 옷을 입어요. 그리고 아침을 먹지요.
4. 식사 후 이를 닦아요. 그리고 버스 정류장으로 나가요.
5. 그렇게 게으름을 피워요. 언제 일을 다 끝내겠어요?
6. 학교에 와서 도서관에서 숙제를 마쳐요. 그리고 수업에 들어가요.
7. 돈을 다 내지 않아요. 물건을 가지고 가면 되나요?
8. 오후에는 피아노를 연습해요. 그리고 운동장에 나가요.
9. 옷을 갈아입어요. 그리고 운동을 좀 하지요.
10. 남의 물건을 훔쳐요. 부끄러운 줄을 모르나 봐요.
11. 저녁에는 집에 와서 쉬어요. 그리고 부엌에서 저녁식사를 준비해요.

Each of the following items contains two sentences connected with 그리고도 *yet nevertheless*. Combine these into a single sentence by using －고도, and then translate each sentence.

12. 엄마가 부르는 소리를 들었어요. 그리고도 못 들은 척했어요.
13. 마셨어요. 그리고도 안 마신 척했어요.
14. 진수는 시험에 떨어졌어요. 그리고도 놀기만 하네요.
15. 아까 그렇게 많이 먹었어. 그리고도 벌써 배가 고프니?

Finally, what do you suppose this very common proverb means?

16. 젊어서 하는 고생은 돈을 주고도 못 산다.

Exercise 3: Practice with ...-는 법이-

Convert the sentences below into (nearly) universal truths using the pattern modifier + 법이 - . Then translate the resulting sentences into English.

1. 죄를 지으면 벌을 받아요.
2. 돈을 빌리면 반드시 갚아야 돼요.
3. 착한 사람은 복을 받아요.
4. 약속은 꼭 지켜야 해요.
5. 공부를 하지 않으면 시험을 못 봐요.
6. 교통 법규를 어기면 딱지를 떼여요.
7. 아프면 집 생각이 나요.
8. 밥을 자주 굶고 잠도 제대로 못 자면 건강이 나빠져요.
9. 공부를 열심히 하면 성공해요.
10. 여름은 덥고 겨울은 추워요.

Exercise 4: Practice with Warnings with -다가는

Change the underlined verb forms in - (으)면 below to the warning pattern - 다가는. Translate the resulting sentences into English.

1. 그렇게 게으르게 시간을 <u>보내면</u> 후회하는 날이 꼭 올 거야.
2. 게으름을 <u>피우면</u> 시험에 떨어지는 수가 있어.
3. 그렇게 신경을 많이 <u>쓰면</u> 병이 나고 마는 법이다.
4. 그렇게 놀기만 <u>하면</u> 남한테 뒤떨어지기가 쉬워.
5. 그 사람만 <u>믿으면</u> 믿는 도끼에 발등 찍히는 꼴이 될 거야.
6. A: 고향으로 돌아가신다고요?
   B: 예, 조금 더 <u>있으면</u> 돌아가기가 싫어질 것 같아서요.
7. A: 술을 끊으셨다고요?
   B: 예, 이렇게 날마다 술을 <u>마시면</u> 건강이 나빠질 것 같아서요.
8. A: 왜 식사를 조금씩만 하세요?
   B: 계속해서 많이 <u>먹으면</u> 뚱뚱해질 것 같아서요.
9. A: 왜 여기서 TV를 보면 안 돼요?
   B: 그렇게 가까이에서 TV를 <u>보면</u> 눈이 나빠질 테니까요.

10. A: 왜 갑자기 컴퓨터를 배우려고 하세요?

    B: 컴퓨터를 <u>모르면</u> 뒤떨어질 것 같아서요.

11. A: 늦을 때마다 집에 연락하세요?

    B: 그럼요. <u>전화하지 않으면</u> 어머니한테 야단을 맞을까 봐서요.

12. 그렇게 사치스럽게 <u>살면</u> 돈을 곧 다 써 버릴 겁니다.

13. 매번 얻어먹기만 <u>하면</u> 친구들이 싫어해요.

14. 운동은 하지 않고 먹기만 <u>하면</u> 살이 쪄요.

15. 돈을 벌지 않고 쓰기만 <u>하면</u> 빚을 지는 법이다.

Exercise 5: Practice with -(으)ㄴ / -는 김에

Each item below contains two sentences. Link the two together with the pattern -(으)ㄴ / -는 김에, so that the combined sentence conveys the meaning *now that...; seeing as...; while one is at it...* Then translate the sentence. For example, the first sentence would be: 시내에 나온 김에 백화점에 들러서 쇼핑이나 할까요? *Seeing as we're downtown, shall we drop in at a department store and do some shopping?*

1. 시내에 나왔어요. 백화점에 들러서 쇼핑이나 할까요?
2. 생각이 났어요. 그 사람한테 전화나 겁시다.
3. 이왕 준비를 해요. 보고서를 잘 씁시다.
4. 이왕 사요. 괜찮고 보기 좋은 것을 삽시다.
5. 영국까지 가요. 프랑스 구경도 좀 하고 옵시다.
6. 도서관에 왔어요. 신문이나 보고 가야겠어요.
7. 우리 집에 오셨어요. 점심이나 드시고 가시지요.
8. 청소를 해요. 내 방도 좀 청소할래요?
9. 빨래를 해요. 이 바지도 좀 빨아 줄래요?
10. 한국어를 배워요. 한자도 좀 배워야겠지요?
11. 일어났어. 그 창문 좀 닫아 줄래?
12. 우체국에 가세요. 이 편지도 부쳐 주실래요?
13. 떡을 보았습니다. 제사를 지냅시다. [속담!]
14. 말이 나왔습니다. 이 일도 좀 해 주세요.
15. 생각났어. 친구 부모님도 찾아뵈었어.

Exercise 6: Practice with -는 데에

Look at the example answer given for 1 below. Complete all of the "B" sentences accordingly and then translate the resulting sentences into English.

1. A: 이 약은 어디에 쓰는 약이에요? (모기를 잡아요)

    B: 그 약은 모기를 잡는 데에 쓰는 약이에요.

2. A: 이 USB 드라이브는 뭐에 써요? (데이터를 저장해요)

    B: 그것은 _____ 사용하는 드라이브예요.

3. A: 친구 사이에 사과란 것을 꼭 해야 하나요? (우정을 지켜 나가요)

    B: 그럼요. _____ 필요한 예의는 반드시 지켜야죠.

4. A: 한국말 배우는 게 이렇게 시간이 많이 걸릴 줄은 몰랐어요. (외국어를 배워요)
   B: _____ 가장 필요한 건 시간과 노력이라고요.
5. A: 한 번에 시험에 붙는 좋은 방법이 없을까요? (시험을 잘 봐요)
   B: _____ 가장 중요한 건 꾸준한 노력이랍니다.
6. A: 선진국이 되기 위해서 무엇이 필요하다고 생각하세요? (나라를 발전시켜요)
   B: _____ 국민이 모두 노력해야 합니다.
7. A: 이거 하면 어떻게 도움이 되는 겁니까? (선택을 하세요)
   B: 여러분께서 _____ 도움이 될 것입니다.
8. A: 사람들이 장어를 왜들 그렇게 좋아하지요? (정력을 돋워요)
   B: 장어는 _____ 좋다고 알려졌어요.
9. A: 숙제를 하는 데에 도움이 있었습니까? (보고서를 써요)
   B: _____ 한국인 룸메이트한테 도움을 좀 받았습니다.

Exercise 7: Practice with NOUN에 의해(서)

Look at the example answer given for item 1 below. Complete all of the "B" sentences accordingly and then translate the resulting sentences into English.

1. A: 무슨 일로 예약을 취소하게 되었어요? (사정)
   B: 사정에 의해서 여행을 못 가게 되었어요.
2. A: 사람의 성격은 어떻게 형성되지요? (환경과 유전)
   B: 대개 _____.
3. A: TV에서 6시에 야구중계를 한다고 신문에 나와 있는데, 왜 안 할까요? (방송국 사정)
   B: _____.
4. A: 좋은 책과 나쁜 책은 어떻게 결정됩니까? (독자)
   B: 그건 _____.
5. A: 한국에서 대통령은 어떻게 뽑아요? (국민투표)
   B: 대통령은 _____.
6. A: 사장님은 분명히 내일 가라고 하셨는데요. (부장님 명령)
   B: 나는 _____.
7. A: [웹사이트 게시판에서] 이쪽 글이 왜 안 보이지요? (관리자)
   B: _____. (use 삭제되-)
8. A: 사람이 똑똑하고 똑똑하지 못한 것은 어떻게 결정되지? (유전자)
   B: _____.
9. A: 그 사람 신장이 나쁘다면서요? (고혈압)
   B: 네. _____. (use 손상되-)

Exercise 8: Practice with -는 수(가) 있-

Change the underlined verb forms below, using the pattern - (으) ㄴ / - 는 수 (가) 있 - . Then translate the resulting sentences.

1. 열심히 노력했지만 결과가 좋지 않게 <u>나타납니다</u>.
2. 요즘같이 교통이 복잡할 때는 택시보다 지하철이 더 <u>빠릅니다</u>.
3. 복잡한 버스 안에서는 잘못해서 다른 사람의 발을 <u>밟습니다</u>.
4. 시험 볼 때 당황하면 아는 문제도 <u>틀립니다</u>.
5. 거짓말을 많이 하면 들키게 <u>됩니다</u>.
6. 일하지 않고 잘 <u>삽니까</u>?
7. A: 비행기 도착 시간이 10분이나 지났는데 왜 소식이 없지요?
     B: 날씨가 나쁘면 원래 도착 시각보다 늦게 <u>도착합니다</u>.
8. A: 지난번엔 그 집을 못 찾아서 아주 고생했어요.
     B: 그 곳은 비슷한 곳이 많아서 주의하지 않으면 길을 <u>잃어버립니다</u>.
9. A: 김 선생님을 찾아 갔는데 못 뵈었어요.
     B: 바쁘신 분이라서 미리 약속을 하지 않으면 <u>못 만납니다</u>.
10. A: 이 과목은 꼭 하는 건가요?
     B: 학생이 너무 적으면 <u>취소됩니다</u>.
11. A: 이 보약이 몸에 좋다는데 한번 먹어볼까요?
     B: 체질에 맞지 않으면 오히려 해가 <u>됩니다</u>.
12. A: 믿을 수 있는 사람이니까 걱정 안 하셔도 돼요.
     B: 그러다가 믿는 도끼에 발등을 <u>찍힙니다</u>. [속담!]

Exercise 9: Practice with -아 / -어지-

Convert the underlined verb forms, using the - 아 / - 어지 - pattern. Then translate the resulting sentences into English, paying special attention to the nuances of this pattern. (Note that sentences 3, 6, 7, and 8 are ungrammatical until and unless you change the form!)

1. 고장이 났는지 문이 잘 안 <u>닫히는데요</u>.
2. 잉크가 <u>굳어서</u> 쓸 수가 없어요.
3. 불이 <u>끄고</u> 영화가 곧 시작 되었다.
4. 잘 <u>쓰는</u> 볼펜 있으면 좀 빌려 주세요.
5. A: 한글은 언제 생겨났어요?
     B: 조선시대 때 <u>만들었어요</u>.
6. A: 연세대학교가 언제 <u>세웠어요</u>?
     B: 1885년에 언더우드라는 사람에 의해 <u>세웠어요</u>.
7. A: 티셔츠에 뭐라고 쓰여 있어요?
     B: 학교 티셔츠인데 오래 되어서 글씨가 다 <u>지웠어요</u>.
8. A: 어디에서 모자를 잃어버리셨어요?
     B: 모르겠어요. 지하철 안에서 <u>벗겼나</u> 봐요.

9. A: 이 책은 언제 <u>쓰인</u> 책이에요?

    B: 이 책은 지금으로부터 100년 전에 <u>쓰인</u> 것이에요.

Exercise 10: 속담 숙제

There are numerous websites for Koreans dedicated to the study and enjoyment of 속담. Using your favorite search engine, find half a dozen 속담 that appeal to you, bring them to class, and introduce them to your classmates. Help your classmates by defining any new vocabulary items or grammatical patterns, and be sure you know *when* to use the proverb.

애니 네 생각이 많이 나더라

보고 싶은 애니에게.

어떻게 지내고 있니, 애니. 나는 잘 지내고 있어.

네가 한국을 떠난 지도 벌써 두 달이 다 되어 가는구나. 세월이 참 빠르지? 서울에서 같이 지내던 때가 엊그제 같은데도 말이야. 지금도 눈을 감으면 너하고 같이 지냈던 날들이 눈에 선해.

여기 소식 좀 알려 줄게. 기초반에서 우리를 가르쳐 주신 최 선생님 생각나지? 그 선생님이 십이월 이십오일에 결혼하신대. 요즘은 뭐가 그렇게 좋은지 싱글벙글하셔.

그리고 얼마 전에는 우리 반 애들이랑 같이 도봉산에 갔다 왔어. 꼭대기까지 올라가느라고 얼마나 고생을 했는지 몰라. 내려올 때는 다리가 후들후들 떨려서 혼났어.

너도 같이 갔으면 좋았을 텐데, 네 생각이 많이 나더라.

넌 어떻게 지내? 학교생활은 재미있어? 어떻게 지내는지 궁금하니까 이 편지 받는 대로 답장 써, 알겠지?

빨리 만나고 싶어. 내년 여름에 꼭 다시 올 거지?

그럼 애니, 답장 쓰는 거 잊지 말고 건강하게 잘 지내.

2004년 10월 28일 서울에서 모리가

NEW VOCABULARY

Vocabulary from the Main Text

어떻게 지내고 있니	*How are you getting along?*	싱글벙글하 -	be all smiles (NB: processive)
벌써 두 달이 되어 가는구나	*(I suddenly realize that) it is nearly two months.*	얼마 전에는	not too long ago
세월 (歲月)	time (as in "time flies")	얼마나 고생을 했는지 몰라	*You have no idea how much he suffered.*
엊그제	a few days ago	후들후들	(shaking, trembling) terribly, like a leaf
엊그제 같은데 말이야	*I mean, it seems like (only) the other day.*	떨리 -	shake; tremble (intransitive)
눈에 선하 -	be fresh / vivid "before one's eyes"; be fresh in one's mind / memory	혼나 -	have a hard time of it
소식 (消息)	news; tidings; word	궁금하 -	it causes concern, is worrisome; I am curious to know about (NB: descriptive)
알리 -	inform; let know		
기초 (基礎)	fundament; basis; foundation		
기초반 (基礎班)	basic course; basic class; elementary class	받는 대로	*as soon as you receive it*
		답장 (答狀)	a reply letter
뭐가 그렇게 좋은지	*I have no idea what she was so happy about, but...*	건강 (健康) 하 -	be healthy

Vocabulary from the Example Sentences

점점 (漸漸)	gradually; bit by bit	심부름 (을) 가 -	go on an errand
걱정거리 [- 꺼리]	a matter for concern	심부름꾼	errand boy
웃음거리 [- 꺼리]	laughingstock; butt of ridicule	출발 (出發) (을) 하 -	set off, depart
		갑 (匣)	(cigarette, match) case, box
국거리	the makings / ingredients for soup	줄이 -	cut down on (e.g., cigarettes, booze); reduce; diminish; lessen
이야깃거리	subject of talk, topic		
일거리 [- 꺼리]	a piece of work; job	이상 (異常) 하 -	be strange, odd
갖추 -	have a thing ready, in stock; equip, furnish	이상 (異常) 하게	strangely, oddly
		문병 (問病)	a visit to sb who it sick
소리를 치 -	call out, yell, shout	개원 (開院)	an opening (of a school, business, hospital, etc.)
심부름	errand		

폐원 (閉院)	a closing (of a school, business, hospital, etc.)	국민학교	old term for elementary school (now 초등학교)
입맛에 맞 -	suit one's tastes	하도	so (much so that)
쌀쌀하 -	be chilly	전 (傳) 하 -	pass (a message) on
늦가을	late autumn	사 주는 거 있지	*You know (how) he buys / bought me...?*

Vocabulary from the Exercises

무리 (無理) 하 -	overdo it; go over the top in one's efforts, exert oneself unreasonably	졸리 -	be / feel sleepy
		애 (가) 타 -	worry oneself sick; anxious
끝마치 -	finish sth	애타게	anxiously
먼저들 다녀오십시오	*You (all) go ahead first.* (Note that the plural marker 들 can latch on to just about anything except a sentence- or clause-final verb.)	등 (等)	and so on; and so forth; and the like; etc.
		늘어나 -	increase; be on the increase
		초기 (初期)	first stage(s); early stage(s); initial period
음식 나오려면	*lit.: "if the food intends to appear"*	치매 (癡呆)	senile dementia
		환자 (患者)	patient; sb suffering from a disease
아직 멀었습니까?	*Is it still far off? (here: Is it still a long time until the food comes?)*	치매환자 (癡呆患者)	sb suffering from senile dementia
장마	the seasonal rains, monsoons	시력 (視力)	one's eyesight
		근시 (近視)	nearsightedness
장마철	the rainy season	난시 (亂視)	astigmatism
쫓아다니 -	follow (sb) around	원시 (遠視)	farsightedness
입고 다니 -, 쓰고 다니 -	wear around	익명 (匿名)	anonymous; anonymity
		익명의 NOUN	anonymous NOUN
들고 다니 -	carry around (e.g., an umbrella)	익명으로	anonymously
		한창	in full swing; in full bloom; at its peak
굽	heel; hoof	고조 (高潮) (가) 되 -	be / get heightened; reach a high point / climax
상당 (相當) 히	quite; rather		

PATTERNS

1. **Moving Away from the Speaker (in time) with -아 / -어 가-**

The verb 가 - *go* as an auxiliary after the infinitive lends the nuance that an action is going forward in time, away from the speaker's position on an imaginary time line, and often approaching an end-point.

1. A: 아직도 할 일이 많이 남았습니까?
      Do you still have a lot left to do?

   B: 아니요, 다 끝나 갑니다.
      No, it's nearly finished. [Or: *I'm getting there.*]
      (That is, it is proceeding forward in time to the point where it will soon be finished.)

2. A: 아직도 그 책을 다 못 읽었습니까?
      You still haven't finished that book yet?

   B: 거의 다 읽어 갑니다.
      I'm nearly finished reading it.
      (That is, I'm proceeding forward in time with my reading to the point where I will soon be done.)

3. A: 고기 다 구울까요?
      Shall I cook up all the meat?

   B: 한꺼번에 다 굽지 말고 먹어 가면서 구웁시다.
      Don't cook it all at once; let's cook it up as we eat [*while we carry on eating (the meat)*]
      (That is, proceeding forward in time along with our eating.)

4. A: 전에는 몰랐는데 교장 선생님하고 교장 선생님 사모님이 많이 닮은 것 같습
      니다.
      I wasn't aware of this before, but the principal and his wife resemble each other a lot.

   B: 부부는 점점 닮아 간다고 하잖아요.
      Couples gradually come [*"go" in Korean!*] *to resemble each other over time.*

5. A: 영호 씨, 무슨 걱정거리가 있습니까?
      Yŏngho, is something worrying you?

   B: 그런 건 아니고요, 며칠 전에 고향에 갔다 왔거든요.
      부모님이 점점 늙어 가시는 모습을 보니까 마음이 아파서요.
      It's not that, it's just that a few days ago I went to my family home, you know?
      It hurts me to see my parents gradually getting older.

6. A: 수미 씨는 결혼할 때 모든 것을 다 가지고 시작하고 싶습니까?

   Sumi, when you get married do you want to start with everything in hand?

   B: 아니요, 저는 처음부터 다 갖추고 사는 것보다 살아 가면서 하나씩 갖추며 사는 것이 재미도 있고 좋을 것 같습니다.

   No, I think it would be better and more interesting to acquire things in the course of living than have everything right from the start.

   (That is, acquire things as one is proceeding forward in time with one's living.)

2. *I mean, in spite of the fact that...* with -(으)ㄴ / -는데(도) 말이-

2.1. Usage of 말이-

The word 말 (or its formal equivalent 말씀) usually means *words; what is said* or the like, but sometimes it is better translated as *meaning [of the words]*. Korean has a number of patterns that use 말 + a form of the copula as a kind of interpolation that is functionally equivalent to such English expressions as *I mean, you know, you see, uh, that is...* and the like. Overuse of this form (like overuse of the corresponding English fillers) sounds irritating to many people, so it should be used sparingly. Here are some examples:

7. 오늘은 비가 오니까 말이야, 나갈 수 없단 말이다.

   It's raining today, uh, so we can't go out, you see.

8. 찾아가니까 말야, 자고 있더라 말이야.

   When I went, uh, to call on him, you know, he was asleep.

9. 내일 말야, 우리 영화 보러 가면 어떨까?

   How about us—uh—taking in a movie tomorrow?

10. 글쎄 말입니다.

    Yes, I know what you mean. Or: I quite agree. Or: Hear, hear.

In another closely related pattern, 말 is preceded by a quoted sentence that has been turned into a modifier: - 다[고 하] - , - (이)라[고 하] - , etc., are adnominalized to 말 with modifier - 는 to give - 다는 말이 - , - (이)라는 말이 - , etc., and these in turn are often contracted to just - 단 말 이 - , - (이)란 말이 - , etc. The translation is *I [You] mean...* This is a very common way to specify, elaborate on, or amplify one's remarks in Korean. Observe the following examples:

11. 집 비우지 말라고 소리치고 갔단 말이야.

    I mean, [my wife] left calling out to me not to leave the house empty.

12. 그럼, 자네는 그 사람하고 싸우겠다는 말인가?

    So, do you mean to say [are you telling me] you'd fight with him?

13. 그와 나와 결혼한단 말이지.

    I mean, he and I are getting married, you see.

14. 돈을 다 써버렸단 말씀입니까?

    You mean you spent all the money?

15. 십 분 더 기다려야 한단 말이에요.

    What I mean is we'll have to wait another ten minutes.

16. 적어도 삼 년은 걸릴 것이란 말이에요.

    It will take—well—at least three years.

2.2. Usage of -(으)ㄴ / -는데(도) 말이-

You have previously learned the pattern -(으)ㄴ / -는데(도) meaning *in spite of the fact that...* When this pattern is combined with the *I mean* tag ...말이- seen above, the result is as you might predict: *I mean, in spite of the fact that...* Here are some examples:

17. 엄마가 심부름 좀 갔다오래. 피곤하다고 얘기했는데도 말이야.

    Mom says to go run an errand—even though I said I was tired.

18. 미안해요. 오늘도 또 늦었어요. 집에서 일찍 출발했는데도 말이에요.

    I'm sorry. I'm late again today—in spite of leaving home early.

19. 남편이 아직도 담배를 하루에 두 갑이나 피웁니다.
    좀 줄이라고 그렇게 얘기했는데도 말입니다.

    My husband still smokes two packs of cigarettes a day.
    In spite of me telling him to cut down, I mean.

20. 아버지가 오늘은 이상하게 화를 안 내십니다. 우리가 다 늦게 들어왔는데도 말입니다.

    Oddly, father isn't getting angry today—in spite of the fact that we all came home late.

21. 얼굴이 많이 탔어. 그렇게 선크림을 발랐는데도 말이야.

    Your face is really burnt [tanned]. In spite of having put on all that sunscreen.

3. *Because of ... –ing* with -느라(고)

This pattern was covered in *Continuing Korean*, Lesson 26, Section 7. Here is an abbreviated guide to its usage. The one-shape ending -느라(고) occurs only with processive verbs. This ending typically has the meaning *what with ... –ing, on account of the process of ... –ing, as a result of ... –ing*, or *because of ... –ing*. Note that the subject of the two clauses is always the same, the verb denotes some sort of process with a duration (rather than a one-off action), and the outcome in the second clause is typically undesirable. Here are some representative verb bases with this ending:

Base	Meaning	-느라(고) Form	Pronunciation
하 -	do	하느라(고)	same
기다리 -	wait	기다리느라(고)	same
노 - ㄹ - (놀다)	play	노느라(고)	same
들 - (듣다)	listen	듣느라(고)	든느라(고)
받 -	receive	받느라(고)	반느라(고)
벗 -	take off (clothes)	벗느라(고)	번느라(고)
찾 -	look for	찾느라(고)	찬느라(고)
있 -	stay	있느라(고)	인느라(고)
놓 -	put	놓느라(고)	논느라(고)
지 (ㅅ) - (짓다)	make	짓느라(고)	진느라(고)
구w - (굽다)	broil	굽느라(고)	굼느라(고)

Sometimes you will hear this ending without the 고, as in the following:

22. 공부하느라, 편지를 쓰느라, 참 바쁘다.
    What with studying and writing letters, I'm very busy.

But usually it is followed by 고, with no change in meaning.

23. A: 일요일 날 바빴니?
    Were you busy on Sunday?

    B: 응, 할머니를 문병 가느라고, 아무것도 못했지.
    Yep. What with visiting my sick grandmother [and all], I didn't get anything done.

24. 점심 먹느라고 늦었어.
    What with eating lunch and all I was late [i.e., Lunch made me late].

25. 대학교에 다닐 때, 연애하느라고 공부를 못 했어.
    I was so busy dating when I was in college that I didn't [couldn't] study.

26. 편지를 쓰느라고 뉴스를 놓쳤다.
    Trying to get a letter written, I missed the news.

27. 자동차를 고치느라고 애를 썼다.
    I've made efforts to repair the automobile. [I tried to get the car fixed. = I had a rough time (in the process of) getting the car fixed].

28. A: 내가 부탁한 것 가지고 왔니?

    Did you bring the thing I asked [you to do as a favor for me] for?

    B: 미안해, 급히 오느라고 잊어버렸어.

    Sorry, I was in such a rush coming (here) that I forgot.

29. A: 아기가 어디 있냐?

    Where's the baby?

    B: 저기서 노느라고 정신이 없지.

    He's absorbed in playing over there.

30. A: 어제 텔레비전에서 축구시합을 봤나?

    Did you see the soccer game on TV yesterday?

    B: 아니, 자느라고 못 봤어.

    No, I missed it because I was sleeping.

31. A: 들고 오느라고 힘들었지?

    It must have been difficult to carry it here.

    B: 안 무거우니까, 괜찮았어.

    It isn't heavy, so it was no problem.

32. 어머니: 술 마시느라고 매일 집에 이렇게 늦게 들어오지!

    Mother: *You're coming home late like this every day because you're drinking, aren't you!*

    아들: 네, 엄마. 미안해요.

    Son: *Yes, Mom. I'm sorry.*

33. 이렇게 추운데 오시느라고 수고하셨어요.

    It's so cold out—thank you for taking the trouble to come.

34. 회의하느라고 그분을 만나지 못 했다.

    I wasn't able to meet him because I was in a conference.

35. 늦잠 자느라고 이도 닦지 못 하고 왔어.

    I overslept, so I came without even brushing my teeth.

36. 전화를 기다리느라고 나가지도 못 했지.

    Because I was waiting for a phone call, I couldn't even go out.

4. Retrospective Aspect

The Main Text for this lesson contains the following phrases:

37. 서울에서 같이 지내<u>던</u> 때
   The times we used to spend together in Seoul...

38. 너하고 같이 지냈<u>던</u> 날들이
   The days I spent together with you...

39. 네 생각이 많이 나<u>더라</u>.
   [As I recall] I kept thinking about you.

Each of the underlined forms in the three examples above contains the "Retrospective" marker -더-. As the name "Retrospective" implies, this marker provides a grammatical means of showing that what you're saying is a kind of "looking back" in time, or recollection of a past experience or sensation. There is a long section on "Retrospectives" in *Continuing Korean*, Lesson 28, Section 1, but we will review it again here.

4.1. Retrospective Sentences

Korean has a wide variety of Retrospective verb endings occurring throughout the various speech styles. A Retrospective ending at the end of a statement may be translated (pedantically, that is—it is hard to translate these, as English doesn't have this grammatical concept) as *it has been observed that*, or *I have sensory evidence to the effect that [so-and-so happens]* rather than the matter-of-fact *so-and-so happens* of other statement endings. Making a statement about a past event absolves the speaker of any conclusive responsibility for what he or she is reporting, as if to say: *That's my understanding as to what happened—but I wouldn't swear to it in court.* Thus, Retrospective statements are not compatible with adverbs like 틀림없이 *without question; for sure.* Likewise, Retrospective questions mean something like *has it been observed?* or *has [someone] noticed / does someone have sensory evidence to the effect that [so-and-so was happening]?* rather than simply *does or did so-and-so happen?*

Because Retrospective forms normally imply that the speaker has some sort of sensory evidence (however shaky) for what is being reported, it is normally a bit odd to use them for reporting anything based on prolonged experience or on something one is dead certain about. Thus, it is usually odd to refer to oneself, close family members, or others with whom one is intimate using a Retrospective form:

*우리 집사람은 내가 20년을 같이 살아서 아는데 코를 엄청 골더라.
   My wife—and I know because we've lived together for 20 years—is quite the snorer.

This is not to say, though, that Retrospectives cannot be used with a first-person (I) subject. In this case, the Retrospective implies that the speaker is reporting on his or her past feelings or actions as a kind of passive or involuntary participant; the sensations or actions being reported happened despite oneself. The following title of a popular song serves as an example of this:

난 김치 볶음밥을 잘 만드는 여자가 좋더라.
   I've found that I just can't help liking women who make good kimch'i pokkŭmbap.

Retrospective endings tend to go on Plain Bases (하 - , 하시 -), but you can also attach them to a Past (했 - , 하셨 -) or Future (하겠 - , 하시겠 -) Base if, at the time in the past you are "looking back" on, **what you said to yourself then** would have used a Past or Future Base. For example, imagine that last week you met somebody for the first time, and as it turns out, this person had a really huge nose. At the time, you said to yourself, 와, 코가 진짜 크다! *Wow, what a huge nose!* Today, you meet a friend and are recounting this past experience to her. You tell your friend, 지난 주일에 어떤 사람을 만났는데 코가 진짜 크더라! *Last week I met this person, and boy was his nose huge!*

Now imagine that last week you saw an old family friend for the first time in over a year. Their eleven-year-old son Chinho had really grown a lot taller since the last time you had seen him. At the time, you thought to yourself, 와, 많이 컸구나! *Wow, he sure has grown a lot!* Today, you meet a friend and are recounting this past experience to him. You say, 지난 주일에 진호를 만났는데 진짜 많이 컸더라! *Last week I met Chinho, and boy had he grown!*

Now imagine that last week you were vacationing in Arizona, where it was blazing hot. At the time, you thought to yourself, 와, 못 견디겠다! *Wow, I don't think I'm going to be able to handle this!* Today, you meet a friend and are recounting this past experience to him. You say, 지난 주일에 애리조나를 갔는데 더워서 못 견디겠더라. *Last week I went to Arizona, and it was so hot I couldn't bear it.* So:

Base	When it happened, you thought	Recalling it later, you say
Plain	코가 크다	코가 크더라
Past	많이 컸구나!	많이 컸더라
Future	못 견디겠다	못 견디겠더라

Here are the Retrospective endings for the various styles:

	Statement	Question	Apperceptive
Formal Style Plain Base	- 습디다 [after cons.] - ㅂ디다 [after vowel]	- 습디까? - ㅂ디까?	- 더군요!
Past Base	- 었습디다	- 었습디까?	- 었더군요!
Future Base	- 겠습디다	- 겠습디까?	- 겠더군요!
Polite Style Plain Base	- 데요 (- 더라고요, - 던데요)	- 던가요?	- 더군요!
Past Base	- 었데요	- 었던가요?	- 었더군요!
Future Base	- 겠데요	- 겠던가요?	- 겠더군요!
Plain Style Plain Base	- 더라	- 더냐?, - 디?	- 더군!
Past Base	- 었더라	- 었더냐?, - 었디?	- 었더군!
Future Base	- 겠더라	- 겠더냐?, - 겠디?	- 겠더군!

Here are some more examples with ‒더라 in the Plain Style:

40. A: 수미 씨 봤어?
    Have you seen Sumi?

    B: 응, 아까 저기서 영진이하고 얘기하고 있더라.
    Yeah. I recall seeing her just a short while ago over there talking with Yŏngjin.

41. A: 그 집 음식 맛있어?
    Is that restaurant's food tasty?

    B: 응, 내 입맛에 맞더라.
    Yep. As I remember, I thought it was delicious.

42. A: 야, 진섭이 여자 친구 어떠니?
    Hey, what's Chinsŏp's girlfriend like?

    B: 예쁘고 착해 보이더라.
    As I recall, she's quite pretty and looks like a really nice person.

43. A: 어제 진호랑 같이 모임에 갔니?
    Did you go to the meeting yesterday with Chinho?

    B: 아니, 같이 가려고 전화했는데 진호는 벌써 나갔더라.
    Nope, I called him in the hopes of going together, but he had already left [as I recall].

44. A: 너는 어떤 날씨가 좋니?
    What kind of weather do you like?

    B: 나는 좀 쌀쌀한 늦가을 날씨가 좋더라.
    I've always liked slightly chilly, late autumn weather.

45. Younger 할아버지: 오랜만에 초등학교 동창들 만나서 기분이 좋았겠습니다.
    Younger old man: It must have felt good to meet up with old elementary school classmates after such a long time.

    Older 할아버지: 그런데 하도 오래간만에 만났더니 이름이 잘 생각이 안 납디다.
    Elder old man: But because we hadn't met for such a long time, I couldn't really remember their names [now that I think back on it].

In this last example, note that the Formal Style Retrospectives ‒(스)ㅂ디까 and ‒(스)ㅂ디다 are now used primarily by older-generation speakers who are in their fifties, sixties, and older. You should not be surprised to hear such a form from a Korean of this generation, but wait until you're much older (and speaking to somebody younger) to use these forms yourself!

As you can see from the table above, the Retrospective form in the Polite Style is ‒데요. However, this rather colloquial form can sound rude if used to one's elders. Moreover, it can sound the same in colloquial, spoken Korean, as the contracted quotations in － 대요. So what do you do when you want to avoid these pitfalls when you say something retrospectively in the Polite Style? The most usual way is to rephrase the sentence to take advantage of the Retrospective modifier － 던 and say something like *it's a fact that it has been observed that it happened*: － 던데요 (see Section 4.3 below). Another common strategy is to quote the Plain Style Retrospective － 더라, i.e., － 더라고, and then round it off with the polite particle 요: － 더라고요 (see Section 4.4 below).

Here are some more sentences ending with Retrospective forms:

46. 언제 가겠다고 하던가요?
    Did you hear him say when he's going? [According to your recollection, when did he say he would go?]

47. 금강산은 참 굉장한 산이더라고요!
    The Diamond Mountains are incredible mountains indeed [I was there]!

48. 그런 사람이 많이 있던데요!
    I've been given to understand that there are many such people.

4.2. The Retrospective Modifier with -던

The Retrospective modifier － 던 functions as the modifier equivalent to the progressive pattern － 고 있었어요 *was doing*. Thus, 사과를 먹고 있었어요 *was eating an apple*, but 내가 먹던 사과 *the apple I was [in the process of] eating*. In this latter function, － 던 attaches only to Plain (nonpast, i.e., 하 － , 하시 －) Bases. However, － 던 can also attach to Past Bases (－ 았 － / － 었 －), in which case it implies that the action of the verb carried on for a while in the past, then ceased. Retrospective － 던 on a Plain Base does not imply that the action actually came full circle, whereas － 던 on a Past Base can sometimes imply completion of the action. Thus, the special phrase 갔던 길에 means *on the way **back** [from having gone somewhere]* and contrasts with the processive modifier phrase 가는 길에, which means *on the way [going to a place]*. (가던 길에 is also possible, as long as the sentence is in the past tense.) With some verbs, there is little or no difference in meaning between － 던 and － 았 / － 었 던, other than perhaps the latter implying a more remote past tense. Here are some more examples of － 던 on Past Bases:

49. 어제 왔던 사람이 또 왔습니다.
    That person I saw come yesterday is here again.

50. 시장에 갔던 길에 진호를 만났습니다.
    On the way back from the market, I met Chinho.

51. 옛날에 유명했던 오페라극장이 이 자리에 있었어요.
    An opera house, which used to be famous in prior days, used to be at this spot.

52. 그 사람이 전에 파티에 가서 만났던 사람 아니에요?
    Isn't that the person we met at that party one time?

4.3. -던데(요)

This pattern combines two forms you already know—the Retrospective marker ‑더‑ and the imminent elaboration pattern ‑는／(으)ㄴ데(요). This combined pattern preserves the original meanings of both composite elements. Thus, verbs with this form in statements mean something like *[it has been observed that] so-and-so happened ／ is happening ／ will happen, [and ／ but there is more I could tell you about it]*.

> 53. 선배: 수진 씨 집에 있냐?
> Senior: *Is Sujin at home?*
>
> 후배: 아까 없던데요.
> Junior: *She wasn't there just a moment ago [would you like more info?].*

> 54. 아침에 종로에서 좋은 구두를 팔던데, 한 번 가볼까?
> *They were selling some nice shoes on Chongno in the morning; shall we go and take a look?*

> 55. A: 호철 씨도 갈까요?
> *Do you think Hoch'ŏl will go, too?*
>
> B: 못 가겠던데요.
> *[I'm afraid] it seemed he wouldn't be able to go [would you like more elaboration?].*

4.4. -더라고(요)

As explained above, this highly colloquial pattern is often used as a kind of escape hatch when speakers need to produce a Retrospective form in the Polite Style (해요), but balk at using the ending ‑데요 because of its potential ambiguity with condensed quotations in ‑대요. Here are some more examples:

> 56. 아버지: [맥주 캔을 따면서] 안주로 먹을 게 없나?
> Father: *[opening a can of beer] Do we have any beer snacks?*
>
> 아들: 어머니가 육포를 사 오셨더라고요.
> Son: *I seem to recall Mother bought some jerky.*

> 57. 어제는 퍽 춥더라고요.
> *It was quite cold yesterday [I found].*

> 58. 사흘만 있으면 꽃이 피겠더라고요!
> *In three days the flowers will be in bloom [from what I have seen of them].*

5. *As soon as...; in accordance with...* with -(으)ㄴ／-는 대로

This pattern was covered in *Continuing Korean*, Lesson 24.9, but is worth reviewing here. The postmodifier 대 is used with the particle 로 after it in two kinds of constructions.

5.1. *As soon as...* with -는 대로

The pattern -는 대로 combines with Plain Bases to mean *as soon as [so-and-so] happens.*

59. 김 사장님이 나오시는 대로 알려 주세요.
    Please let me know as soon as Company President Kim comes out.

60. 수미한테 들어오는 대로 저희 집에 전화하라고 전해 주십시오.
    Please tell Sumi to call our house as soon as she gets home.

61. 일이 끝나는 대로 바로 집으로 오십시오.
    As soon as the work is finished, come straight home.

62. 물건이 나오는 대로 보내 드리겠습니다.
    As soon as the goods are ready ["come out"], we'll send them to you.

63. 영진 씨를 만나는 대로 즉시 전하겠습니다.
    As soon as I meet Yŏngjin I'll pass it along [tell her] right away.

64. 돈이 생기는 대로 갚을 테니까 10만 원만 빌려 주십시오.
    I'll pay you back as soon as I get some money, so please lend me 100,000 wŏn.

65. 약속 시간이 결정되는 대로 알려 드리겠습니다.
    I'll let you know as soon as the appointment time is settled.

Recall there is another way to say *as soon as:* -자(마자).

5.2. *According to; in accordance with...* with -(으)ㄴ / -는 대로

With modifiers of any appropriate tense, 대로 means *according to; in accordance with; as; with [something] still as it was.* Here are some examples:

66. 하고 싶은 대로 하세요.
    [Do according to what you will do =] Do as you like.

67. 들은 대로 말해 보세요.
    [Speak according to what you heard =] Tell what you heard!

68. 선생님이 말씀하시는 대로 하세요.
    Do as the teacher says.

The expression 될 수 있는 대로 means *as much as possible [= according to what is possible; in line with what can be done]; insofar as it is possible.*

69. 될 수 있는 대로 빨리 가십시오.
   [As much as possible, go quickly =] Go as quickly as possible.

70. 운동을 될 수 있는 대로 매일 하십시오.
   Please do your best to exercise every day.

The expression 대로 is also used after a few nouns, with similar meaning.

마음대로	*[following one's mind =] as [one] wants, wishes, likes*
뜻대로	*[in line with the intention or meaning =] as [one] hoped or wished for*
선생님 말씀대로	*[in accordance with the teacher's words =] as the teacher says; just like you say*
사실대로	*according to the facts*
그대로	*just as it is [like that]; just like that*

71. 사실대로 말하십시오.
   [Speak according to =] Stick to the facts.

72. 그대로 두세요.
   Leave it as it is.

Finally, note that 대로 sometimes even occurs with a prospective modifier in -(으)ㄹ:

73. 좋으실 대로 하십시오.
   Do as you like ["in accordance with what might be / would be best"].

6. ..., *you see?* Lead-ins and Follow-ups with -거든(요)

The verb ending -거든(요) is a one-shape ending and can occur with any base, though usually you will encounter it on Plain (하-, 하시-) and Past (했-, 하셨-) Bases more than on Future (하겠-, 하시겠-) Bases. L-extending bases appear in their extended form before this ending: 사-ㄹ- → 살거든(요). The ending -거든(요) implies an explanation and works in one of three ways: (1) in direct response to a query (as a response to *Why...?*); (2) as a lead-in—something volunteered by the speaker in the course of initiating a conversation or telling a story; or (3) as a kind of follow-up explanation to what has just been said or implied (often as a kind of damage control, in case the person you are talking to has suddenly missed a connection or been left in the dark about what you just said). For this latter usage, a literal spelling out of its effect might be: *I hasten to give you an explanation or rationale for what I just said (or implied) in perhaps too crude, obscure, or blunt a fashion.*

   In other words, the ending -거든(요) also functions as a sort of politeness strategy or "grease on the skids" to keep conversational exchanges moving. It performs the latter function by inviting a response (notice that it usually has a rising, question-like intonation) from the person you are talking to (usually just an understanding 네 or a nod). Often the only way to approximate the flavor of this ending in English is with the tag *you see?* Here are some examples:

74. 나는 김치를 못 먹어요. 너무 맵거든요.
    I can't eat kimch'i. It's too hot.

75. 머리가 아파서 죽겠어요. 어제 술을 너무 많이 마셨거든요.
    I have an incredible headache. Last night I drank too much.

76. 요즘 연 선생님은 아주 기분이 좋으세요. 지난달에 건강한 아기를 낳았거든요.
    Mr. Yŏn is in a really good mood lately. Last month they gave birth to a healthy child.

77. 내일 다시 오세요. 준비가 아직 안 됐거든요.
    Please come again tomorrow. It's not ready yet.

78. 고객: [백화점에서 물건 값을 보고]: 와, 비싸다!
    Shopper: [looking at the price on an item]: *Wow, this is expensive!*
    점원: 물건이 튼튼하고 아주 좋거든요.
    Store employee: *It's because the merchandise is really nice and sturdy.*

79. A: 왜 그 차를 안 샀어요?
    Why didn't you buy the car?

    B: 돈이 없거든요.
    I don't have any money.

7. *You know [how]...?* with ...있잖아(요)?

You know how in English we sometimes start a conversation or jump-start an exchange by introducing a topic of conversation with *You know [how]...?* This is accomplished in Korean with TOPIC + 있잖아(요)? and a rising intonation. Another related meaning of 있잖아(요)? (often preceded by an interjection like 왜 or 저~) is ***You** know what I mean, right?* (when the speaker him- or herself can't remember!).

80. A: 제 동생 있잖아요?
    You know my little brother? [Well, guess what?]

    B: 응, 그런데 왜?
    Yeah—what about him?

This pattern can be extended to an entire clause by making the clause into a modifier phrase or a ... - 는 것 / ... - 는 거 phrase. Thus, *You know how we're supposed to get together tomorrow?* becomes 우리가 내일 만나는 거 있잖아요? Note that the noun (let's call it a "topic") which comes before the 있잖아(요)? almost never has a particle with it.

Now observe the following exchange from the example sentences for 말이 - in this lesson:

81. 어제 진호 씨를 만났는데 불고기를 사 주는 거 있지. 요즘 나는 다이어트 중인데 말이야.
    Yesterday I met Chinho, and you know, he treats me to pulgogi. And that's in spite of the fact that I'm on a diet.

While this last example doesn't translate very comfortably as *You know [how]...?*, it nevertheless behaves the same way in that it presents to the listener a new or newsworthy topic of conversation.

EXERCISES

Exercise 1: Reading Comprehension

Write out answers to the following questions.

1. 애니가 한국을 떠난 지 얼마나 되었습니까?
2. 모리와 애니는 한국에서 같이 무엇을 했습니까?
3. 모리는 애니가 떠난 지 오래 되었다고 생각하고 있습니까?
4. 모리가 애니한테 알려 준 소식은 무엇이었습니까?
5. 요즘 최 선생님은 어떠십니까?
6. 모리는 도봉산에 쉽게 올라갔습니까?
7. 내려올 때는 어땠습니까?
8. 모리는 요즘 애니가 어떻게 지내는지 잘 알고 있습니까?
9. 모리는 애니한테 편지를 받는 대로 어떻게 하라고 했습니까?

Exercise 2: Practice with -아 / -어 가-

Fill in the blanks with an appropriate form in - 아 / - 어 가 - .

1. A: 아직도 많이 기다려야 됩니까?
   B: 아니요, _____ 조금만 더 기다려 주십시오.
   [hint: "almost finished"]
2. A: 아직도 그 책을 다 못 읽었습니까?
   B: 거의 _____.
3. A: 저 부부는 남매 같지요?
   B: _____.
4. A: 힘드니까 좀 쉬었다 합시다.
   B: 좋습니다. 무리하지 말고 _____.
   [hint: "while resting / taking breaks"]
5. A: 준호 씨, 점심 먹고 와서 합시다.
   B: 저는 이 일 다 끝마치고 먹겠습니다.
   A: 일도 중요하지만 _____.
6. [음식점에서]
   A: 아줌마, 음식 나오려면 아직 멀었습니까?
   B: 아니요, _____.
   [hint: "almost done"]

Exercise 3: Practice with -(으)ㄴ / -는데(도) 말이-

Take each sentence below and recast it as a sentence followed by a fragment. In other words, take everything after the clause －(으)ㄴ／－는데도 as your initial sentence, then follow it up with the clause －(으)ㄴ／－는데도 as an afterthought and round it off with an appropriate interjection in "말이에요," "말입니다," etc. Here is an example to help you:

집에서 일찍 출발했는데도 오늘도 또 늦었어요. →
오늘도 또 늦었어요. 집에서 일찍 출발했는데도 말이에요.

1. 장마철인데도 친구들이 바닷가로 여행을 갔습니다.
   → _____.
2. 집에서 일찍 출발했는데도 길이 막혀서 늦고 말았습니다.
   → _____.
3. 그렇게 술을 끊으라고 얘기했는데도 남편이 아직도 매일 저녁 술에 취해 들어옵니다.
   → _____.
4. 내가 싫다고 그렇게 얘기하는데도 그 남자가 계속 쫓아다닙니다.
   → _____.
5. 정미는 키가 작은데도 굽이 낮은 구두만 신고 다닙니다.
   → _____.
6. 진수는 눈이 좋은데도 안경을 쓰고 다닙니다.
   → _____.

Exercise 4: Practice with -느라(고)

Use an appropriate verb in the －느라(고) form to complete the sentences below.

1. A: 어제 왜 안 왔어요?
   B: _____.
2. A: 요즘 상당히 바쁘신 것 같아요.
   B: _____.
3. A: 졸려요?
   B: _____.
4. A: 벌써 용돈을 다 썼어요?
   B: _____.
5. A: 어제 왜 전화도 안 했어요?
   B: _____.
6. A: 아이들이 굉장히 배가 고팠던 것 같네요.
   B: _____.
7. A: 어제 병원에 가서 주사를 맞았어요?
   B: _____.
8. _____ 느라고 신문도 읽지 못 했어요.

9. _____느라고 이렇게 늦었습니다.
10. _____느라고 그렇게 바빴습니다.
11. _____느라고 샤워도 못 하고 그냥 나왔어요.
12. _____느라고 일을 마치지 못 했습니다.
13. _____느라고 여행 준비도 못 했습니다.

Exercise 5: Practice with Retrospectives

Part One

A. "‑더라"를 이용해 _____에 알맞은 말을 넣으세요.

B. Rewrite each pair of sentences with Polite Style (해요) endings. Make sure the reply in each sentence uses a Polite Retrospective ending ‑던데요, ‑더라고요 or the like.

1.　A: 그 영화 재미있니?
　　B: _____.
2.　A: 진수 씨 좀 어때? 많이 좋아졌어?
　　B: _____.
3.　A: 수미야, 넌 무슨 꽃이 좋니?
　　B: _____.
4.　A: 영준이 지금 집에 있니?
　　B: _____.
5.　A: 아직도 극장에서 그 영화를 하니?
　　B: _____.
6.　A: 영민아, 형한테 그 사람에 대해서 좀 물어 봤어?
　　B: _____.
7.　A: 만호 씨를 못 봤니?
　　B: _____. ["he was on his way home"]
8.　할아버지 1: 그 회사의 제품이 어떻습니까?
　　할아버지 2: _____.
　　　　　　　[hint: "they break easily"—use Formal Style]
9.　할아버지 1: 만호는 어디 있습니까?
　　할아버지 2: _____.
　　　[hint: "When I came, he had already taken off"—use Formal Style]

Part Two

The following sentences either say *Someone does / did so-and-so* or ask *Does / Did someone do so-and-so?* Make each one Retrospective, and then translate the sentence into normal English.

1. 동생이 우체국에 혼자 가고 있었어요?
2. 제가 수미한테 연락을 하려고 했는데 진호가 벌써 했어요.
3. 베이커 선생님이 김 선생한테 한국말로 이야기하고 계셨어요.

4. 한국에서는 고등학교 때는 열심히 공부하지만, 대학교에서는 주로 놀아요.

5. 관객들이 모두 서서 오랫동안 박수를 쳤어요.

6. 그 교수의 강의는 지루했어요?

7. 지난 번 소풍 갈 때 날씨가 쌀쌀했어요?

8. 그 사람 집에 가니까 집에 있는 모든 귀중품을 다 팔았어요?

9. 장마철에는 우산을 들고 나가도 소용이 없어요.

Exercise 6: Practice with -(으)ㄴ / -는 대로

Part One

Fill in the blanks with an appropriate form or phrase using -는 대로.

1. A [전화를 받고]: 수미한테 어떻게 전할까요?

   B: _____.

2. A: 어디서 만나기로 했습니까?

   B: 아직 약속 장소는 결정하지 못했습니다.

   _____.

3. A: 오늘 수미 봤습니까?

   B: 아니요, 못 봤는데요.

   A: 급한 일이 있으니까, _____.

4. 요즘은 너무 피곤해서 _____.

5. 여보, 저녁에 집에 손님이 오신다고 했으니까 _____.

6. 잃어버린 아이를 찾고 있습니다. 이 아이를 _____.

Part Two

Each of the following items contains two sentences. Combine them so that the first sentence becomes a clause in -(으)ㄴ / -는 대로, meaning *as soon as* or *in accordance with*. For example, the first one would be: 선생님이 시키시는 대로 하세요. *Do as the teacher says.*

1. 선생님이 시키세요. 하세요.

2. 일을 끝내요. 갈 거예요.

3. 아버지가 한국에서 도착하세요. 바로 이사 갈 예정입니다.

4. 제가 불러요. 한 번 써 보세요.

5. 회의가 끝나요. 얼른 집에 와요.

6. 준비가 다 됩니다. 떠납시다.

7. 눈이 그쳐요. 출발할까요?

Exercise 7: Practice with -거든(요)

Each of the following items contains two sentences. Change the verb in the second sentence to the ‑ 거든 (요) ending, and then translate both sentences.

1. 어제 하나도 못 잤어요. 언니하고 밤늦게까지 이것저것에 대해서 이야기하고 있었어요.
2. 요즘 너무 바빠서 죽겠어요. 지난 주일에 개학을 했어요.
3. 손이 아파서 죽겠어요. 어제 다쳤어요.
4. 나는 바다에 가지 않고, 산에 갈래요. 수영을 못 해요.
5. A: 아니, 손이 왜 이렇게 차가워요?
   B: 밖이 추워요.
6. 거기 가지 마세요. 위험해요.
7. 요즘 매일 수영을 해요. 수영장이 우리 집에서 가까워요.
8. 따뜻한 옷을 가지고 가야 돼요. 산에서는 날씨가 잘 변해요.
9. 비옷을 가지고 가야지. 금방 비가 쏟아지는 일이 많아.
10. 한자를 열심히 공부하고 있어요. 재미있어요.

Exercise 8: Practice with... 있잖아(요)?

How would you translate the following sentences (all from the Internet) into English?

1. 있잖아요! 쉿~ 비밀인데요...
2. "왜 그거, 그거 있잖아" 등의 표현이 늘어납니다. 당신도 초기 치매환자군요.
3. 시력 있잖아요. 제가 근시가 있었는데 난시가 생겼거든요.
   [from a bulletin board for an online eye-care center]
4. 있잖아 비밀이야. [익명게시판]
5. 있잖아요... 제가 인터넷에서 봤는데...
6. 있잖아요, 나무는요... [from the beginning of a blog]
7. 저~ 있잖아요.
8. 입학 장학금 있잖아요~~ [경성대학교 게시판]
9. 왜 그럴 때가 있잖아요. 분위기가 한창 고조되는데 갑자기 남자의 어떤 말 때문에...

무슨 일이 있었길래 이렇게 되었습니까?

며칠 전 작은 오토바이를 타고 회사에 출근하는 길이었다. 집에서 회사까지 가는 길에는 차가 별로 다니지 않기 때문에 나는 아주 빨리 오토바이를 몰았다. 그런데 갑자기 큰 개 한 마리가 길 가운데로 뛰어들었다. 하마터면 그 개하고 부딪칠 뻔했다. 깜짝 놀란 나는 그 개를 피하기 위해 핸들을 오른쪽으로 확 돌렸다. 그 다음 순간 나는 오토바이에서 떨어져 길옆에 있는 웅덩이에 빠지고 말았다.

다시 집에 가서 옷을 갈아입고 올 만한 시간적 여유도 없었기 때문에 나는 옷에 온통 흙을 묻힌 채 출근할 수밖에 없었다. 회사에 갔더니 동료들이 내 모습을 보고 깜짝 놀라서 물었다.

"도대체 무슨 일이 있었길래 이렇게 되었어요?" 나는 출근 길에 있었던 일을 좀 과장해서 이야기해 주었다. 그랬더니 그 말을 들은 동료 한 사람이 다음과 같이 말했다.

"아니, 그 개가 그렇게 크면 개다리 사이로 빠져나오지 왜 피했습니까?"

NEW VOCABULARY

Vocabulary from the Main Text

오토바이	motorcycle	확	with a sudden, violent wrench
모 - 르 - (몰다)	drive sth; herd sth		
가운데	the middle, center; the midst of; between; among	돌리 -	turn it; make it turn
		웅덩이	puddle
뛰어드 - ㄹ - (- 들다)	run / dash in ("dash and enter")	빠지 -	fall into
		갈아입고 올 만한 시간	*time to* ["worthy of," "with the ability to," "sufficient / enough to"] *change and come.* (See Pattern 6 below for *worth doing* with - (으)ㄹ만 하 - .)
하마터면	nearly, almost (did sth). (This adverb often flags an upcoming *almost* pattern in - (으)ㄹ 뻔했 - . See Pattern 1 below.)		
		시간적 여유 (時間的 餘裕)	(timewise) leeway, margin, elbow room
부딪치 -	strike, collide with (the NOUN collided with is marked with 과, 하고, or (이)랑).	온통	all; wholly; entirely
		묻히 -	be / get smudged, smeared, stained
피(避)하 -	avoid; dodge; get away from; keep out of (the rain); refuse; shirk	출근할 수밖에 없었다	*I had no choice but to go to work.*
핸들	handlebars; steering wheel	과장(誇張)(을) 하 -	exaggerate

Vocabulary from the Example Sentences

화장(化粧)(을) 하 -	wear / apply/ put on make-up; make oneself up	홈스테이(를) 하 -	do a homestay (long-term, study-related)
자판기(自販機)← 자동판매기 (自動販賣機)	(automatic) vending machine	이래라, 저래라 명령 (命令)(을) 하 -	order, (saying) "Do this, do that!"
쏟 -	spill sth	하품(을) 하 -	yawn
신발	shoes; footwear	간장(~醬)	soy sauce
달려나가 -	run / dash out	깎 -	bargain, "cut" (the price)
장사가 안 되면	*if the business is not profit-able*	역사(歷史)	history
		훈민정음(訓民正音)	*Hunmin chŏngŭm; Correct Sounds for Instructing the People* (name of the native Korean script promulgated in 1446)
거절(拒絶)(을) 하 -	refuse; turn down		
입장(立場)	position, standpoint, stand (on an issue)		
꽉 차 -	be full up, chockablock, full to the brim, bursting, etc. (NB: processive)	고유 (固有)	indigenous; native; inherent; peculiar to
		문자(文字) [- 짜]	script; writing system
민박(民泊)(을) 하 -	do a (short) homestay on a vacation; stay as a paying guest in sb's home	획기적 (劃期的)	epoch-making
		문화(文化)	culture
		발명(發明)	invention

Vocabulary from the Exercises

붐비 -	be crowded, full of people (NB: processive)		hosts when you are leaving their house.)
있던 그대로	*just as it was (had been)*	방학(放學)	school holidays, school vacation
끼어드 - ㄹ - (-들다)	butt in, "insert and enter," cut in	스태프	staff
충혈(充血)(이) 되 -	get bloodshot	소설(小說)	fiction; work of fiction; novel
걔 = 그애	he; she	인물(人物)	person, personage, individual
경기(競技)(를) 하 -	compete in sports; have a match, contest, or sporting event	관점(觀點) [-쩜]	point of view; perspective
		연구(研究)	research
귀(貴)하 -	be noble, precious, esteemed, distinguished	해석(解釋)(을) 하 -	interpret
		화가(畫家)	painter
한잠도 못 잤다	*Couldn't sleep a wink.*	완전(完全)히	completely; totally
잘 놀다 갑니다	*I go now, having had a good time.* (This is the normal polite remark made to your	반응(反應)(을) 하 -	react

PATTERNS

1. *Almost did something* with -(으)ㄹ 뻔했-

The word 뻔 is closely tied to the words on either side of it: on the one hand it is a postmodifier that appears only after the prospective modifier -(으)ㄹ; on the other hand it is a descriptive verbal noun always followed by the auxiliary descriptive verb 하 - *is*. The expression -(으)ㄹ 뻔하 - means *almost [very nearly] do; barely escape doing; be on the verge of,* and most often it occurs in the past, with the implication that the thing that almost did or did not happen was avoided at the last minute. Here are some examples:

1. 나는 죽을 뻔했어요.
   I thought I'd die. ["I almost died."]

2. 화를 낼 뻔했지요.
   You see, I almost lost my temper.

3. 갈 뻔했습니다.
   He came very near to going. Or: *It's a wonder that he didn't go.*

4. 못 갈 뻔했다.
   He very nearly didn't go. Or: *It's a wonder that he went at all.*

5. 뛰어오다가 하마터면 넘어질 뻔했다.
   I came running over and almost fell.

6. 들고 오다가 하마터면 커피를 쏟을 뻔했습니다.
   I was carrying the coffee over here when I almost spilled it.

7. 조금만 늦었으면 차를 놓칠 뻔했습니다.
   If we had been just a little later, we would have missed the train.

8. 길이 막혀서 하마터면 약속 시간에 늦을 뻔했습니다.
   The roads were so congested that we were almost late for our appointment time.

9. 아까는 머리가 아파서 죽을 뻔했습니다.
   Just a little while ago my head hurt so much I practically died.

10. 집에 아무도 없었으면 큰일 날 뻔했습니다.
    If there hadn't been somebody at home, there could have been a disaster ["a disaster almost occurred"].

Usually this pattern occurs with processive verbs, but in contrary-to-fact wish conditions in -더라면, the *then* clause can consist of 좋을 뻔했다 or 좋았을 뻔했다:

11. 등산을 같이 갔더라면 좋았을 뻔했네요.
    Too bad you couldn't go hiking with us [It would "almost" have been good if...]!

12. 그 사람의 꾀에 넘어갈 뻔했어요.
    I was almost taken in by her ruse.

2. *Just as it is; as it stands; with no change* with -(으)ㄴ 채(로)

The postmodifier 채, meaning something like *the unaltered state*, usually occurs after the past modifier -(으)ㄴ only, and is optionally followed by the particle 로. The resulting pattern means *with the preceding action or activity just as it was* (or *wasn't*—the point is that there has been no change in the state of affairs). Here are some examples:

13. 신발도 신지 않은 채 달려 나갔습니다.
    I dashed out without even putting my shoes on.

14. 옷도 갈아입지 않은 채로 그냥 잠들어 버렸습니다.
    I just fell asleep with my clothes on [without even having changed my clothes].

15. 세수도 못한 채 출근했습니다.
    I went off to work without even washing my face.

16. 손도 씻지 않은 채로 밥을 먹고 있습니다.
    I'm eating my meal without even washing my hands first.

17. 바빠서 인사도 못한 채 왔습니다.
    I was so busy I left [lit.: came] without even having said good-bye ["paid my greetings"].

So far, all the examples have been negatives, but this is by no means always the case:

18. 안경을 쓴 채 목욕탕에 들어갔어요.
    I went in to the public bath with my glasses still on.

19. 화장을 한 채로 수영장에 들어갔어요.
    She got in the pool with her makeup on.

20. 신발도 신지 않은 채 밖에 나갔다.
    He went outside without even his shoes on.

21. 외투를 입은 채 방 안으로 들어왔다.
    She entered the room with her overcoat on.

22. 불을 컨 채로 자요.
    He sleeps with the light on.

23. 구두를 신은 채 들어오면 안 돼요.
    You mustn't enter the room with your shoes on.

Note that 채 can also function as a postnoun, with much the same meaning:

통 채로 삼킨다: swallows it whole
뿌리 채로 뽑아요: pulls it out, roots and all (뿌리 is "root")
뼈 채로 먹는다: eats it, bones and all (뼈 is "bone")

3. *Has no choice but to...* with -(으)ㄹ 수밖에 없-

You already know the little word 수 *way; means; occasion; possibility; likelihood* from the pattern -(으)ㄹ 수 없다 / 있다 *may [not], can [not] do.* Here this pattern is combined with another pattern you already know— 밖에 + NEGATIVE, meaning (literally) *Outside of..., does not...,* hence *only,* e.g., 영어밖에 모릅니다 *All she knows is English* (= *She only knows English*). (See also the example in number 24 just below). Here the combined meaning is *has no choice but to..., there is nothing for it but to...,* etc.

24. 자판기에서 음료수를 사고 싶은데 만 원짜리 지폐밖에 없었습니다.
    I wanted to buy a drink from the vending machine, but I only had [didn't have anything but] a 10,000-wŏn bill.

25. 다들 바쁘다고 하니 영주 씨를 보낼 수밖에 없겠습니다.
    Everybody else claims to be busy, so we'll have no choice but to send Yŏngju.

26. 계속 이렇게 장사가 안 되면 문을 닫을 수밖에 없겠습니다.
    If business continues to be as bad as this, we'll have no choice but to close.

27. 거절할 수밖에 없는 제 입장도 좀 생각해 주십시오.
    Please think of my position, too. I have no choice but to refuse.

28. 호텔이 꽉 차서 민박을 할 수밖에 없었습니다.
    The hotels were all full, so we had no choice but to do a homestay.

29. 2시간 기다렸는데도 안 와서 그냥 돌아올 수밖에 없었습니다.
    In spite of waiting for two hours, he didn't come, so we had no choice but to simply go back.

4. QUESTION WORD... -길래, ...?

The ending – 길래 can attach to any base and is always preceded by a question word. It is used to set up a question about something surprising, puzzling, or amazing to the asker. One way to get at the flavor of this ending in English is with *Just WH–...?* or by attaching *-ever* to the question word. Here are some examples:

30. 영진 씨는 어디에 갔길래 이렇게 안 보입니까?
    Where[ever] has Yŏngjin gone off to, that she should be so conspicuously absent?

31. 도대체 무엇을 했길래 옷이 이렇게 더러워졌습니까?
    What[ever] on earth have you done to get so dirty like this?

32. 다른 컴퓨터하고 뭐가 다르길래 이렇게 비쌉니까?
    Just what makes it so different from other computers, that it should be so expensive?

33. 야, 네가 뭐길래 나한테 이래라, 저래라 명령하니?
    Hey, just who do you think you are, ordering me to "Do this" and "Do that"?

34. 무슨 일이 있었길래 이렇게 술을 마시고 들어왔습니까?
    Just what [on earth] happened for you to come home drunk like this?

35. 어제 몇 시간 잤길래 그렇게 하품을 합니까?
    Just how many hours did you sleep yesterday that you are yawning like that?

5. *You should (have)...; Why didn't / don't you...?* with (a) -지(요)—REBUKE or (b) -지 그래(요)

The －지 of this pattern is the same －지 that, as you will recall, has as one of its meanings SUGGESTION—좀 앉으시지요. *Why don't you please take a seat?* The pattern here is a kind of fortified version of the meaning *Why don't you...?* or *Shouldn't you...?* that is latent in －지. It has one of two intonations:

(a) In mid-sentence, it has the suspensive, *I'm-not-finished-yet* intonation of the Imminent Elaboration pattern －(으)ㄴ데 / －는데.

(b) When used sentence-finally (e.g., Example 39 below), or rounded off with 그러－ (그래요, 그러세요, 그러시지요, etc.) (Examples 40 and 41 below), the intonation is not much different from the －지(요) pattern in which it originates, but here the intonation can sound rather reproachful.

36. 더 놀다 가지—벌써 갑니까?
    You should stay and visit a little longer—why are you leaving already?

37. 좀 참지—왜 싸웁니까?
    You should be a bit more patient—why do you argue?

38. 간장을 조금만 넣지—왜 이렇게 많이 넣었습니까?
    You should put in only a little soy sauce—why did you put so much?

39. 5분만 일찍 오지요. 금방 점심 먹으러 나갔는데.
    You should have come five minutes earlier—he just left for lunch.

40. 그럼 나한테 빌려 달라고 하지 그랬습니까?
    Then why didn't you ask to borrow some [money] from me?

41. 좀 깎지 그랬습니까?
    Why didn't you bargain a bit?

6. *Is worth doing* with -(으)ㄹ 만하-

Examine the following sentence:

42. 한국에는 볼 만한 것이 많나요?
    Are there many things worth seeing in Korea?

As you can see in the above sentence, the descriptive verbal noun expression 만하－ is used as a post-modifier expression after the prospective modifier form in －(으)ㄹ of a processive verb to give the meaning *is worth ... –ing* or *is good for ... –ing* etc. Here are more examples of this:

43. 김 선생님은 만날 만한 분이에요.
    Mr. Kim is a man worth meeting. Or: Mr. Kim is the man to see.

44. 이 공원이 쉴 만한 공원이에요.
    This park is a good park to relax in.

45. 그 오페라는 볼 만도 하고 들을 만도 해요.
    That opera is worth both seeing and hearing.

Similar expressions:

믿을 만하 -	trustworthy
먹을 만하 -	eatable; worth eating
읽을 만하 -	readable; worth reading
가질 만하 -	worth having or owning
살 만하 -	worth buying
입을 만하 -	worth wearing; wearable

The descriptive verbal noun 만 is always tied in two directions: to the preceding prospective modifier in - (으)ㄹ and to the following descriptive verb 하 - . In that respect, it is like the 뻔 of - (으)ㄹ 뻔하 - described in Pattern 1 above.

7. Using -적(-的)

The suffix - 적 (- 的) can be used to turn some Sino-Korean nouns into modifiers. When a Sino-Korean word + - 적 (- 的) modifies a following noun, - 적 (- 的) optionally takes the modifier form of the copula: - 인 (with no change in meaning). Thus, there are two modifier patterns with - 적 (- 的):

(a) Sino-Korean - 적 (- 的) NOUN, e.g., 문화적 차이 *cultural difference*
(b) Sino-Korean - 적 (- 的)인 NOUN, e.g., 문화적인 차이 *cultural difference*

These Sino-Korean modifiers - 적 (- 的) can be converted into adverbs by adding the particle - (으)로. Here are some examples:

46. 그것은 경제적인 문제다.
    That is an economic problem.

47. 한국은 경제적으로 발전했다.
    Korea has developed economically.

48. 그것은 역사적 사건이다.
    That is a historical event.

49. 중국은 역사적으로 아주 흥미 있는 나라입니다.

    China is a very interesting country, historically.

50. 일본은 문화적으로 한국과 다르다.

    Japan is culturally different than Korea.

51. 훈민정음은 한국의 고유문자로 획기적인 문화발명이었다.

    Hunmin chŏngŭm, Korea's indigenous script, was an epoch-making cultural invention.

EXERCISES

Exercise 1: Reading Comprehension

Write out answers to the following questions.

1. 이 일은 언제 생겼습니까?
2. 회사에 가는 길은 붐빕니까?
3. 나는 개하고 부딪쳤습니까?
4. 나는 개를 피하기 위해 어떻게 했습니까?
5. 나는 집에 다시 돌아가서 옷을 갈아입고 출근했습니까?
6. 회사에 갔더니 동료들이 뭐라고 말했습니까?
7. 나는 친구들에게 있던 그대로 설명해 주었습니까?
8. 내 설명을 듣고 동료가 뭐라고 말했습니까?

Exercise 2: Practice with -(으)ㄹ 뻔했-

Fill in the blanks with an appropriate form in - (으)ㄹ 뻔했 - .

1. A: 약속 시간에 안 늦었습니까?

   B: ＿＿＿＿＿＿＿＿＿＿＿＿＿ 다행히 길이 안 막혀서 안 늦었습니다.

2. A: 내가 부탁한 거 가지고 왔지?

   B: 응, 하마터면 ＿＿＿＿＿＿＿＿＿＿＿＿＿.

3. A: 어제 수미 만났습니까?

   B: 내가 좀 늦게 가서 하마터면 ＿＿＿＿＿＿＿＿＿＿＿.

4. A: 오늘은 웬일로 우산 안 잃어버리고 가지고 들어왔네.

   B: 오늘도 하마터면 ＿＿＿＿＿＿＿＿＿＿＿.

5. A: 어제 영화 봤습니까?

   B: 네, 그런데 ＿＿＿＿＿＿＿＿＿＿＿.

6. A: 안색이 안 좋은데, 무슨 일이 있었습니까?

   B: 학교에 오다가 갑자기 옆에 있는 차가 끼어드는 바람에

   ＿＿＿＿＿＿＿＿＿＿＿＿＿.

Exercise 3: Practice with -(으)ㄴ 채(로)

Fill in the blanks with an appropriate form in － (으) ㄴ 채 (로).

1. A: 머리가 왜 그렇습니까?

    B: 이상합니까? _____.

2. A: 우리 옆집 아저씨는 정말 이상합니다.

    B: 뭐가 이상합니까?

    A: _____밖에 나와서 돌아다닙니다.

3. A: 신발 벗고 들어오세요.

    B: 죄송합니다. 우리 나라에서는 _____.

4. A: 눈이 충혈됐네.

    B: 응, 어젯밤에 렌즈를 _____.

5. A: 민아 참 엉뚱하지?

    B: 응, 걔는 _____.

6. A: 어디서 지갑을 잃어 버렸습니까?

    B: 전화를 걸고 _____.

Exercise 4: Practice with -(으)ㄹ 수밖에 없-

Fill in the blanks with an appropriate phrase in － (으)ㄹ 수밖에 없 － .

1. A: 불편했을 텐데 왜 민박을 했습니까?

    B: _____.

2. A: 이 근처에 문을 닫은 집이 벌써 다섯 집이나 된답니다.

    B: 이렇게 장사가 안 되면 우리도 _____.

3. A: 비가 많이 오는데 경기할 수 있겠습니까?

    B: 힘들겠는데요. 다음으로 _____.

4. A: 이번 휴가에 어디 갔다 올 겁니까?

    B: 어디 좋은 데 가고 싶은데 돈이 없어서 _____.

5. A: 나한테 부탁했으면 도와주었을 텐데 왜 혼자 했습니까?

    B: 부탁하려고 전화했는데 안 계셔서 _____.

6. A: 그 가게는 비싼데 왜 거기서 샀습니까?

    B: 다른 가게가 다 문을 닫아서 _____.

Exercise 5: Practice with -길래

Compose appropriate questions for speaker "A" using a form in － 길래.

1. A: _____?

    B: 아까 저쪽에서 누구하고 얘기하는 것 같던데요.

2. A: _____?

    B: 얼굴이 많이 더럽습니까?

3. A: _____?

   B: 음식을 줄이고 운동을 했더니 이렇게 살이 빠졌습니다.

4. A: _____?

   B: 아주 귀한 손님이 오실 겁니다.

5. A: _____?

   B: 길이 막히는 시간을 피해서 6시 30분쯤 나옵니다.

6. A: _____?

   B: 친구랑 밤 새워 애기하느라고 한 잠도 못 잤습니다.

Exercise 6: Practice with -지 (그래(요))

Using the pattern - 지 (그래(요)), compose appropriate chiding remarks for speaker "B" below. Then translate the resulting exchanges into English.

1. A: 잘 놀다 갑니다. 안녕히 계십시오.

   B: _____.

2. A: 방학 내내 아무데도 안 가고 집에만 있었습니다.

   B: _____.

3. A: 찌개가 너무 맵지요.

   B: _____.

4. A: 여보세요. 수미 씨 좀 바꿔 주세요.

   B: _____.

5. A: 며칠 동안 아파서 꼼짝도 못하고 집에 있었습니다.

   B: _____.

6. A: 어제는 바빠서 혼났습니다.

   B: _____.

Exercise 7: Practice with -(으)ㄹ 만하-

Complete the speaker "B" responses using the pattern - (으)ㄹ 만하 - and following the hints in brackets.

1. A: 그 집 음식이 어떻습니까?

   B: _____. ["not bad," i.e., "worth eating"]

2. A: 날이 너무 덥지요?

   B: _____. ["Yes, but it's bearable." Use 참 - .]

3. A: 그 영화 어때요?

   B: _____. ["It's worth seeing once."]

4. A: 이거 다 버릴까요?

   B: _____. ["Don't throw out the usable ones."]

5. A: 선호 씨를 찾았습니까?

   B: _____. ["I looked in all the places he might likely be, but couldn't find him."]

6. A: 그 사람을 스태프로 뽑을까 생각 중인데, 어때요?

   B: _____. ["He's quite trustworthy." Use 믿 - .]

7. A: <태백산맥>이라는 소설을 읽어보셨습니까?

   B: _____. ["Yes, it's worth a read."]

Exercise 8: Practice with -적(-的)

Use this list of Sino-Korean nouns to fill in the blanks. Then translate the sentences into English:

역사(歷史)	history	부분(部分)	part; portion
주관(主觀)	subjectivity	논리(論理)	logic
객관(客觀)	objectivity	감정(感情)	emotion
구체(具體)	concrete object	극(劇)	drama
추상(抽象)	abstraction	세계(世界)	the world
보수(保守)	conservatism	정신(精神)	mentality

1. 한국의 _____ 인물은 누구누구 아십니까?
2. 세계를 보는 관점은 _____.
3. 연구를 할 때는 데이터를 _____ 해석해야 됩니다.
4. _____ 예를 하나 주시겠습니까?
5. 피카소는 _____ 유명한 화가입니다. 어떤 사람들은 피카소의 그림이 _____ 이라고 생각합니다.
6. 우리 한국어 선생님이 좀 _____ 것 같지 않아요?
7. A: 완전히 이해했습니까?

   B: 아니요, _____ 만 이해했습니다.
8. 너무 _____ 반응하지 말고 한 번 _____ 생각해 보세요.
9. 그분은 _____ 표현을 많이 쓰십니다.
10. 그 사람은 _____ 건강합니까?

주말치고는 유난히 바빴던 지난 일요일이었다

주말치고는 유난히 바빴던 일요일이었다. 낮에 가봐야 할 결혼식이 두 건이나 있었고, 월요일까지 잡지사에 써다 주어야 할 원고가 있었기 때문에 정신이 없었다. 그래서 집안일은 일단 다음으로 미루고 원고부터 썼다.

전날 밤에 두 시간밖에 자지 않고 일을 한 덕분에 오전 11시쯤 해서 일이 다 끝났다. 그다음 서둘러 준비를 하고 강남에 있는 결혼식장 두 군데를 들렀다가 집에 돌아왔다. 몸이 완전히 녹초가 되어 있었다.

그런데 그때 전화가 걸려왔다. 한 2년 동안 못 만난 대학 동창들한테서 였는데 우리 집에 쳐들어오겠다는 것이었다. 나는 그때부터 정신없이 집안을 치우기 시작했다. 며칠 전부터 집안 청소를 제대로 하지 않았기 때문에 집안은 엉망이었다. 방하고 거실은 그런 대로 치웠는데 설거지를 할 여유는 없었다. 그래서 나는 할 수 없이 더러운 그릇들을 오븐 속에다 처넣어 버렸다.

잠시 후 친구들이 도착했는데 친구들의 손에는 냉동피자가 들려 있었다.

NEW VOCABULARY

Vocabulary from the Main Text

유난히	particularly; especially; unusually	녹초(가) 되 -	get exhausted; become a tired wreck; be fatigued
건(件)	counter/classifier for events/happenings	전화(가) 걸려 왔다	*A call came in. (lit.: A telephone call was called in.)*
잡지사(雜誌社)	magazine company	쳐들어오 - , 쳐들어가 -	barge in on; invade
써다 주 -	write for sb (with emphasis on the shift in location when handing it over)	치우 -	clear it up / away; get rid of it
집안일 [- 닐]	housework	제대로	properly; as it should be done
일단(一旦) [- 딴]	first off; for starters; for the time being	엉망	mess
		거실(居室)	living room
다음으로 미루 -	postpone / put off until later	그런대로	more or less (*lit.*: "as they were")
원고부터 썼다	*The first thing I did was to write the manuscript; I started by writing the manuscript.*	설거지	the dishes; the washing up
		할 수 없이	had no choice but to (adv.)
		오븐	oven
일을 한 덕분(德分)에	*thanks to / owing to having done the work*	속에다	into the inside (with emphasis on the SHIFT in place / location)
11시쯤 해서	*when it got to about eleven o'clock*	처넣 -	jam in; shove in
서두르 - , 서둘러	rush; rush about	냉동(冷凍)(을) 하 - / 시키 -	freeze sth; make it freeze
강남(江南)	Kangnam (the area south of the Han River in Seoul)	들리 -	be / get held (up) in the hands
군데	counter / classifier for places	들려 있었다	*lit.: were in a state resulting from being held; were held*
완전(完全)히	completely; entirely; totally		

Vocabulary from the Example Sentences

서양(西洋)	the West		(some speakers treat this as 줏 - , but this is substandard)
동양(東洋)	the East; East Asia; "the Far East"		
썩	quite; rather	나 - ㄹ - (날다)	fly
벼락(이) 치 -	lightning strikes	날아가 -	fly away
벼락치기	last-minute cramming	전부(全部)	in its entirety; all of it / them; the whole thing
조숙(早熟)하 -	be precocious		
짐	luggage; baggage; burden	고래	whale
주w– (줍다)	pick a small object up between one's fingers	술고래	a boozer; someone who drinks a lot

반장 (班長)	the class leader; class president	좌우간 (左右間)	anyway; anyhow; in any case
옮기 -	move sth; shift sth; relocate it	부수 (部首)	radical (in Chinese characters)
움직이 -	move (both transitive and intransitive)	획 (劃)	stroke (in Chinese characters)
(사진을) 찍 -	take (a photo)	훨씬	much more so
제 생각대로	as one thinks; in the way one sees it	올려놓 -	place sth onto the top of sth (for future reference / use)
알아서 (하세요)	*(Do) as you think best.*	내려놓 -	put sth down (for future use / reference)
고집 (을) 부리 -	be stubborn (NB: processive)	걸리 -	get caught (on a nail, by the police)
고집쟁이	stubborn person	벌금 (罰金) (을) 내 -	pay a fine
현대 (現代)	contemporary; modern	수첩 (手帖)	pocket-size notepad
미술 (美術)	art; arts		
미술관 (美術館)	art gallery		

Vocabulary from the Exercises

놀러 오기로 되어 있었습니까?	*Had it been arranged to come over and visit?*	쟁반 (錚盤)	tray
깨끗이	cleanly, clean (adv)	갖다 놓 -	bring (and place) sth
알아듣기 힘듭니다	*It's difficult to understand / catch (the spoken word).*	접 -	fold sth
		사업 (事業)	business; enterprise
남 말하지 말고	*Don't talk of others* [do sth else!]	NOUN에 비해서	compared to NOUN
		발음 (發音)	pronunciation
술맛이 나 -	feel like drinking (*lit.:* "the alcohol's taste appears / comes out")	시 (詩)	poem; poetry
		시인 (詩人)	poet
		공기 (空氣)	air

PATTERNS

1. *For a NOUN; considering it's [just] a NOUN* with NOUN치고(는)

A noun followed by the particle-like sequence 치고는 translates as *for a NOUN, considering it's [just] a NOUN*, etc. The clause NOUN치고는 is usually followed by an observation that is somewhat unexpected for the speaker. Note that the NOUN in this pattern can be a verb or verb phrase modifying 것: *considering the fact that VERB / VERB phrase...* Look at the following examples.

1. 토마스 씨는 한국말을 1년 동안 배웠는데 잘 합니다.
   1년 배운 것치고는 한국말을 참 잘 합니다.
   Thomas has studied Korean for a year and yet he speaks well.
   Considering he has studied for [just] one year, he speaks really well.

2. 앨버트 씨는 키가 175센티미터입니다.
   서양 사람치고는 키가 크지 않은 편입니다.

   Albert is 175 centimeters tall.
   For a Westerner, he is on the not-very-tall side.

3. 시험을 썩 잘 보지는 않았습니다.
   그렇지만 벼락치기 한 것치고는 시험을 잘 보았습니다.

   I didn't do all that well on the test.
   But considering I crammed for it last minute, I did pretty well.

4. 진수는 경상도 사투리를 씁니다.
   그렇지만 1년 전에 서울에 온 사람치고는 사투리를 쓰지 않는 편입니다.

   Chinsu uses Kyŏngsang Province dialect.
   But for someone who came to Seoul [only] a year ago, he doesn't use dialect all that much.

5. 미선이는 대학생처럼 보입니다.
   고등학생치고는 좀 조숙한 편입니다.

   Misŏn looks like a college student.
   For a high school student, she is somewhat precocious.

6. 내 친구 용성이는 나보다 나이가 3살이나 많습니다.
   친구치고는 나이가 많습니다.

   My friend Yongsŏng is three years older than me.
   He's sort of old to be my friend.

2. Emphasizing Displacement with -아 / -어다 주-

As you may have learned already, the "transferentive" ending ‑다(가) implies some sort of shift or transfer in TIME or SPACE. All of the examples below involve just such a shift. Note also that all of the sentences involve a verb of motion or a pronoun of place (like 저쪽에 *over there*) to further highlight the change in location. The only difference with the normal transferentive pattern in ‑다(가) (i.e., verb base + ‑다(가)) is that here, the transferentive ending attaches to the infinitive ending (the ‑아 / ‑어 form), not to the verb base. Moreover, all our examples here use a compound verb, with 주‑ *give* in the favor-giving pattern.

7. 어머니, 사과 좀 사 주십시오. vs.
   어머니, 시장에 가는 길에 사과 좀 사다 주십시오.

   Mother, buy some apples on your way to the market.

8. 준영 씨, 책 좀 빌려 주십시오. vs.
   준영 씨, 학교에 가는 길에 도서관에서 책 좀 빌려다 주십시오.

   Chunyŏng, please borrow a book from the library for me on your way to school.

9. 수미 씨, 이 그릇 좀 씻어 주십시오. vs.
   수미 씨, 저쪽에 가서 이 그릇 좀 씻어다 주십시오.
   Sumi, could you please go over there and wash this dish for me?

10. 철민 씨, 잠깐만 이 짐 좀 들어 주십시오. vs.
    철민 씨, 택시를 타는 곳까지 이 짐 좀 들어다 주십시오.
    Ch'ŏlmin, please carry this bag for me to the taxi stand.

11. 앨버트 씨, 이것 좀 받아 주십시오. vs.
    앨버트 씨, 저것 좀 받아다 주십시오.
    Albert, would you please take that for a second and bring it to me?

12. 모리 씨, 이 밑에 떨어진 종이 좀 주워 주십시오. vs.
    모리 씨, 저쪽으로 날아간 종이 좀 주워다 주십시오.
    Mori, could you please pick up that piece of paper that flew over there and give it to me?

3. To start by VERB-ing and from NOUN on down, starting with NOUN with NOUN부터 [+ Verb]

You should already know the particle 부터 in its meaning *from; starting from*. Some of the examples here include the meaning you already know, while the other examples use extensions of this:

13. A: 야, 너 왜 매일 늦게 들어오니? 좀 일찍 들어와.
    Hey, why do you come home so late every day? You should come home earlier.
    B: 형부터 일찍 들어와 봐.
    You try coming home early first [older brother].

14. A: 영진이네 식구들은 모두 술을 잘 마시나 봅니다.
    Yŏngjin's family all seem to be good drinkers.
    B: 맞습니다. 아버지부터 전부 술고래입니다.
    That's right. They're all boozers, starting with the father.

15. 반장부터 지각하는 습관을 고치십시오.
    Change your habit of arriving late, starting with the class president.

16. 냉장고부터 옮겨야겠습니다.
    We'll have to move the fridge first.

17. 먼저 식사부터 하고 이야기합시다.
    Let's eat first, then talk.

18. A: 졸립니까?
    Are you sleepy?
    B: 네, 새벽 5시부터 전화가 와서 잠을 못 잤습니다.
    Yes, somebody called me at five in the morning, so I didn't sleep well.

4. *In accordance with* and *as soon as* with 대로

You have already seen in Lesson 7 that the two syllables 대로 function as either a postmodifier or as a postnoun in the patterns below. Here is another round of these patterns, with one new wrinkle: - (으) ㄴ 대로 in usage (b):

- (으) ㄴ 대로   (a) *in accordance with the way one did or was*
         (b) *as soon as; just as soon as one did it, then...*
- 는 대로   (a) *in accordance with the way one does it*
         (b) *just as soon as one does it, then...*

NOUN대로   *in accordance with NOUN*

Observe the following examples.

19. A: 움직이지 말고 그대로 계십시오. 찍겠습니다.
   Don't move—stay right where you are. I'm taking the picture now!

   B: 예쁘게 찍어 주십시오.
   Make it a good one!

20. A: 제 마음대로 해도 되겠습니까?
   Can I do as I please?

   B: 네, 수미 씨 마음대로 하십시오.
   Yes, do as you like, Sumi.

21. A: 이번에는 제 생각대로 하게 해 주십시오.
   This time please let me do it according to my ideas.

   B: 그럼 알아서 잘 해 보십시오.
   In that case, go ahead and do it your way.

22. A: 고집 부리지 말고 형이 시키는 대로 해.
   Stop being stubborn and do as your older brother tells you.

   B: 알았어요.
   Okay.

23. A: 어떻게 하면 되겠습니까?
   What should I do?

   B: 방금 내가 말한 대로 하면 될 것입니다.
   All you have to do is do as I told you just now.

24. 준호: 어제 현대 미술관에 잘 갔다 왔습니까?

    Did you have a nice outing to the Modern Art Gallery yesterday?

    진희: 네, 준호 씨가 가르쳐 준 대로 갔더니 찾아가기 쉬웠습니다.

    Yes, we went the way you told us to and had no troubles finding it.

25. 선생: 좌우간 여러 번 말씀드린 대로 한자의 부수들을 제대로 배워 놓으면, 한자 배우기가 훨씬 쉬워집니다.

    Teacher: *Anyway, like I've told you many times, if you learn the Chinese radicals properly, learning the characters becomes much easier.*

    학생: 네, 선생님. 알겠습니다.

    Student: *Yes, sir. I'll work on that.*

5. Transferentive Directionals in 에다(가): "Displacement" Again

As in Pattern 2 above, the transferentive -다(가) here adds an explicit nuance of shift, displacement, or transfer to the directional particle 에.

26. A: 어디에다가 놓을까요?

    Where shall I put it?

    B: 저쪽에다가 놓으십시오.

    Put it over there.

27. A: 책상 위에다 올려놓을까요?

    Shall I put it up on top of the desk?

    B: 아니요, 책상 밑에다 내려놓으십시오.

    No. Put it down beneath the desk.

28. A: 이 사진을 어디에다 걸까요?

    Where shall I hang this photo?

    B: 저쪽 벽에다가 걸어 주십시오.

    Please hang it over there on the wall.

29. 길에다 휴지를 버리다가 걸리면 벌금을 내야 합니다.

    If you get caught throwing paper on the road, you have to pay a fine.

30. 돈을 그냥 주머니에다 넣지 말고 지갑 안에다 넣어서 가지고 다니십시오.

    Don't just stick your money in your pocket—put it in your wallet and carry it around [that way].

31. 제 전화번호를 알려 드리겠습니다.
    잊어버리지 않도록 수첩에다 적어 놓으십시오.

    Let me give you my phone number.
    Please make a note of it in your diary so you don't forget.

6. *Is on the … –ing side* with -(으)ㄴ / -는 편이-

The basic meaning of the postmodifier 편 is *side*. Following a past-descriptive modifier in ‑(으)ㄴ, or following the processive modifier in ‑는, it forms a pattern meaning *does* or *is on the … –ing side*, i.e., *does* or *is somewhat ~ rather ~ quite* (well, poorly, or whatever). Observe the examples below (from Korea University's 한국어 2, Lesson 18).

32. A: 매운 음식을 좋아합니까?
     Do you like spicy food?

     B: 많이 먹지는 않습니다. 그렇지만 좋아하는 편입니다.
     I don't eat it a lot. But I like it pretty much ["I'm on the liking-it side"].

33. A: 수영하러 자주 가는 것 같습니다.
     Looks like you go swimming often.

     B: 네, 요즘은 자주 가는 편입니다.
     Yes, lately I'm going quite often ["I'm on the going-often side"].

34. A: 10시부터 잡니까?
     You go to bed at ten?

     B: 네, 저는 좀 일찍 자는 편입니다.
     Yes. I go to bed somewhat early ["on the early side"].

35. A: 영화가 재미없습니다.
     The movie is boring.

     B: 그래도 어제 본 영화보다는 재미있는 편입니다.
     Still, it's rather more interesting than the film we saw yesterday.

36. A: 철민 씨는 참 건강해 보입니다.
     Ch'ŏlmin, you look really healthy.

     B: 네, 건강한 편입니다.
     Yes, I'm pretty healthy ["on the healthy side"].

37. A: 수미 씨 집은 넓습니까?
     Sumi, is your house big?

     B: 네, 넓은 편입니다.
     Yes, it's pretty big ["on the big side"].

EXERCISES

Exercise 1: Reading Comprehension

Write out answers to the following questions.

1. 지난 일요일에 나는 왜 바빴습니까?
2. 집안일을 먼저 하고 원고를 썼습니까?
3. 무엇 덕분에 오전 11시쯤 일이 끝났습니까?
4. 결혼식장에 갔다가 돌아왔을 때는 몸이 어떻게 되어 있었습니까?
5. 저녁 때 친구들이 놀러 오기로 되어 있었습니까?
6. 친구들이 오기 전에 나는 집안을 깨끗이 치웠습니까?
7. 나는 닦지 않은 그릇들을 어떻게 하였습니까?
8. 친구들은 무엇을 사 가지고 우리 집에 왔습니까?

Exercise 2: Practice with 치고(는)

Complete the "B" responses below with a phrase using 치고(는).

1. A: 토마스 씨 한국말 참 잘하지요.
   B: 네, ＿＿＿＿＿＿＿＿＿＿＿＿＿ 한국말을 참 잘 합니다.
2. A: 선주는 키가 좀 작은 것 같습니다.
   B: ＿＿＿＿＿＿＿＿＿＿ 키가 작은 편입니다.
3. A: 진수 말은 사투리 때문에 가끔 알아듣기 힘듭니다.
   B: 그렇지만 ＿＿＿＿＿＿＿＿＿＿＿＿ 사투리를 쓰지 않는 편입니다.
4. A: 영호 씨 좀 어려 보이지 않니?
   B: 맞아. ＿＿＿＿＿＿＿＿＿＿ 어려 보이는 것 같아.
5. A: 너무 덥다.
   B: 그래도 ＿＿＿＿＿＿＿＿＿ 안 더운 편이잖아.
6. A: 찬구 씨는 좀 나이가 들어 보이지 않니?
   B: 아니요, ＿＿＿＿＿＿＿＿＿＿＿＿＿.

Exercise 3: Practice with -아 / -어(다) 주-

Complete the sentences below, using the patterns -아/-어 주- or -아/-어다 주- as appropriate.

1. 엄마, 저 빵 좀 ＿＿＿＿＿＿＿＿＿＿＿.
2. 준영 씨, 학교에 가는 길에 도서관에서 책 좀 ＿＿＿＿＿＿＿＿＿＿＿＿.
3. 수미 씨, 부엌에 가서 이 그릇 좀 ＿＿＿＿＿＿＿＿＿＿＿.
4. 철민 씨, 택시를 타는 곳까지 이 짐 좀 ＿＿＿＿＿＿＿＿＿＿.
5. 앨버트 씨, 저 의자 좀 이쪽으로 ＿＿＿＿＿＿＿＿＿＿＿.
6. 모리 씨, 이 밑에 떨어진 종이 좀 ＿＿＿＿＿＿＿＿＿＿＿.

7. 진영 씨, 은행에 가서 돈 좀＼＿＿＿＿＿＿＿＿＿＿＿＿＿.

8. 밤이라서 혼자 가기 무섭습니다. 택시 타는 데까지 ＿＿＿＿＿＿＿＿＿＿＿.

9. 여보, 오늘 퇴근하는 길에 책 한 권만＿＿＿＿＿＿＿＿＿＿＿＿.

10. 이 선물 좀 예쁘게 ＿＿＿＿＿＿＿＿＿＿＿＿.

Exercise 4: Practice with 부터

Complete the speaker "B" responses below using a phrase with 부터.

1. A: 야, 너 왜 매일 늦게 들어오니? 좀 일찍 들어와.
    B: 형은? 남 말하지 말고＿＿＿＿＿＿＿＿＿＿＿＿＿＿＿.

2. A: 졸립니까?
    B: 네, 친구가 ＿＿＿＿＿＿＿＿＿＿＿＿＿＿＿.

3. A: 준호네 식구들은 모두 키가 큰가 봅니다.
    B: 맞습니다. ＿＿＿＿＿＿＿＿＿＿＿＿＿＿＿.

4. A: 영민 씨네 회사 사람들은 아침 일찍 출근하나 봅니다.
    B: 네, ＿＿＿＿＿＿＿＿＿＿＿＿＿＿＿＿.

5. A: 할 일이 많은데 무엇을 먼저 할까요?
    B: ＿＿＿＿＿＿＿＿＿＿＿＿＿＿＿.

6. A: 식사를 하면서 일 이야기를 할까요?
    B: 아니요, ＿＿＿＿＿＿＿＿＿＿＿＿＿＿＿.

Exercise 5: Practice with 대로, -(으)ㄴ / -는 대로

Fill in the blanks below with a phrase in either NOUN대로 or -(으)ㄴ / -는 대로, as appropriate.

1. A: 이 쟁반 저쪽에 갖다 놓을까요?
    B: 아니요, 거기에 ＿＿＿＿＿＿＿＿＿＿ 두십시오.

2. A: 저는 이렇게 하고 싶은데 제 ＿＿＿＿＿＿＿＿＿ 해도 되겠습니까?
    B: 네, 수미 씨 ＿＿＿＿＿＿＿＿ 하십시오.

3. A: 고집 부리지 말고 내가 ＿＿＿＿＿＿＿＿＿.
    B: 알았어요.

4. A: 수미 씨, 종이접기를 가르쳐 주세요.
    B: 제가 ＿＿＿＿＿＿＿＿ 따라 접으세요.

5. A: 현수 씨, 사실대로 이야기하세요.
    B: 그게 바로 사실입니다. ＿＿＿＿＿＿＿＿＿.

6. A: 사업 잘 됩니까?
    B: ＿＿＿＿＿＿＿＿ 안 되는데요.

Exercise 6: Practice with 에다(가)

Complete the sentences below with appropriate phrases using 에다(가).

1. A: 이 우산 어디에다가 놓을까요?
   B: _____.
2. A: 책상 위에다 올려놓을까요?
   B: 아니요, _____.
3. A: 이 사진 어디다 걸까요?
   B: _____.
4. A: 엄마, 10만 원만 주세요.
   B: _____ 쓰려고?
5. _____ 벌금을 내야 합니다.
6. 책을 읽고 _____ 말고 꼭 _____.

Exercise 7: Practice with -(으)ㄴ / -는 편이-

Complete the following sentences using the pattern -(으)ㄴ / -는 편이- and following the hints in brackets. Then translate the sentences into English.

1. 우리 남편은 좀 _____. [키가 커요]
2. 한국말은 일본말에 비해서 _____. [발음이 어려워요]
3. 만원이면 _____. [꽤 비싸요]
4. 영미는 _____이라서 생각이 깊은 것 같아요. [시를 많이 읽어요]
5. _____이니까 아무거나 주세요. [아무거나 잘 먹어요]
6. 진호는 _____이에요? [공부를 잘 해요?]
7. 이 집 짬뽕은 _____이에요. [상당히 매워요]
8. 서울의 공기는 _____이에요. [깨끗하지 않아요.]
9. 열두 살밖에 안 됐지만 _____입니다. [좀 조숙해요]

제 10 과 복습 II

Review the example sentences below. Then, for each one, write a new sentence that uses the same pattern.

1. 속담

1. 호랑이도 제 말하면 온다.
2. 발 없는 말이 천리를 간다.
3. 서당 개 삼년이면 풍월 읊는다.
4. 종로에서 뺨 맞고 한강에 가서 화풀이 한다.
5. 백문이 불여일견.
6. 고생 끝에 낙이 온다.
7. 금강산도 식후경.
8. 콩 심은 데 콩 나고 팥 심은 데 팥 난다.

2. -고서 and -고도

9. 할아버지가 지팡이를 짚고서 왔다 갔다 하신다.
10. 대통령이 이야기를 다 듣고서 고개를 끄덕였어요.
11. 같은 일 하고도 여성 임금은 남성의 절반 밖에 못 된답니다.
12. 안경을 끼고도 안 보인다고요?

3. -(으)ㄴ / 는 법이-

13. 꼬리가 길면 밟히는 법이다.
14. 딸은 엄마를 닮는 법이다.
15. 작은 고추가 매운 법이다.

4. Warnings in -다가는

16. 잘못하다가는 다칠 수 있으니까, 조심하세요.
17. 일은 안 하고 놀기만 하다가는 부자가 못 돼요!

5. -(으)ㄴ / -는 김에

18. 쇠뿔도 단 김에 빼라.
19. 부엌을 청소하는 김에 화장실도 청소했어요.

6. -는 데에

20. 속담은 생활하는 데에 많은 교훈을 줍니다.
21. 이 지팡이는 등산을 하는 데에 사용하는 등산용 지팡이예요.
22. 고급스러운 한국말을 배우는 데에 가장 중요한 것은 한자 공부입니다.

7. NOUN에 의해서

23. 속담은 민족의 경험에 의해서 만들어진 지혜의 말입니다.
24. 이 건물은 유명한 영국 건축가에 의해서 설계되었다.
25. 심장 질환에 의한 사망률이 꽤 높답니다.

8. -는 수(가) 있-

26. 원숭이도 나무에서 떨어지는 수가 있다.
27. 운동하다가 다치는 수가 많아요.

9. -어지-

28. 소문은 입에서 입으로 전해지는 말입니다.
29. 우리 생활에 쓰여지는 석유는 모두 외국으로부터 수입됩니다.
30. 이 볼펜이 글씨가 잘 써지네요.

10. -아 / -어 가-

31. A: 아직도 할 일이 많이 남았습니까?
    B: 아니요, 다 끝나 갑니다.
32. A: 아직도 그 책을 다 못 읽었습니까?
    B: 거의 다 읽어 갑니다.
33. A: 전에는 몰랐는데 철민 씨하고 선영 씨는 많이 닮은 것 같습니다.
    B: 부부는 점점 닮아 간다고 하잖아요.

11. 말이-

34. 미안해요. 오늘도 또 늦었어요. 집에서 일찍 출발했는데도 말이에요.
35. 남편이 아직도 담배를 하루에 두 갑이나 피웁니다. 좀 줄이라고 그렇게 얘기했는데도 말입니다.
36. 얼굴이 많이 탔어. 그렇게 선크림을 발랐는데도 말이야.

12. -느라(고)

37. A: 일요일 날 무엇을 했습니까?

   B: 숙제 하느라고 꼼짝도 못했습니다.

38. A: 뭐 하느라고 매일 집에 늦게 들어갑니까?

   B: 친구들 만나서 술 마시느라고 늦습니다.

39. A: 요즘 뭐 하느라고 그렇게 바쁩니까?

   B: 취직 준비를 하느라고 바쁩니다.

13. -더라

40. A: 수미 씨 봤어?

   B: 응, 아까 저기서 영진이하고 얘기하고 있더라.

41. A: 어제 진호랑 같이 모임에 갔니?

   B: 아니, 같이 가려고 전화했는데 진호는 벌써 갔더라.

42. A: 너는 어떤 날씨가 좋니?

   B: 나는 좀 쌀쌀한 늦가을 날씨가 좋더라.

14. -는 대로

43. 수미한테 들어오는 대로 저희 집에 전화하라고 전해 주십시오.

44. 일이 끝나는 대로 바로 집으로 오십시오.

45. 영진 씨를 만나는 대로 즉시 전하겠습니다.

46. 약속 시간이 결정되는 대로 알려 드리겠습니다.

15. -거든(요)

47. 오늘 만날 수가 없어. 내일 한국어 시험 있거든?

48. 발이 아파서 죽겠어요. 운동을 하다가 다쳤거든요.

16. ...있잖아(요)?

49. A. "국민학교" 라는 말 있잖아?

   B. 응, 왜?

   A. 더 이상 쓰면 안 된대. "초등학교" 라는 말을 쓰래.

50. A. 그, 저기, 라식 수술 있잖아요?

   B. 그런데요?

   A. 한번 해 볼까 지금 고민 중이에요.

17. -(으)ㄹ 뻔했-

51. 뛰어오다가 하마터면 넘어질 뻔했습니다.

52. 조금만 늦었으면 차를 놓칠 뻔했습니다.

53. 길이 막혀서 하마터면 약속 시간에 늦을 뻔했습니다.
54. 아까는 머리가 아파서 죽을 뻔했습니다.

18. -(으)ㄴ 채(로)

55. 피곤해서 옷도 갈아입지 않은 채 그냥 잠들어 버렸습니다.
56. 아침에 늦게 일어나서 세수도 못한 채 출근했습니다.
57. 안경을 쓴 채 수영장에 들어갔습니다.

19. -(으)ㄹ 수밖에 없-

58. 자판기에서 음료수를 사고 싶은데 만 원짜리 지폐밖에 없었습니다.
59. 호텔이 꽉 차서 민박을 할 수밖에 없었습니다.
60. 2시간 기다렸는데도 안 와서 그냥 돌아올 수밖에 없었습니다.

20. -길래

61. A: 영진 씨는 어디에 갔길래 이렇게 안 보입니까?
    B: 아까 점심 때 밖에 나가는 것 같았습니다.
62. A: 야, 네가 뭐길래 나한테 이래라, 저래라 명령하니?
    B: 뭐기는? 친구지.
63. A: 무슨 일이 있었길래 이렇게 술을 마시고 들어왔습니까?
    B: 기분 나쁜 일이 있어서 좀 마셨습니다.

21. -지(요); -지 그래(요)

64. A: 잘 놀다 갑니다. 안녕히 계십시오.
    B: 더 놀다 가지 벌써 갑니까?
65. A: 속상해 죽겠어요. 영민 씨하고 싸웠어요.
    B: 화가 나도 좀 참지 왜 싸웠습니까?
66. A: 수미 씨는 벌써 갔습니까?
    B: 5분만 일찍 오지요. 금방 나갔는데.

22. -(으)ㄹ 만하-

67. 어땠어요? 현대미술관이 볼 만하던가요?
68. 제주도에 놀러 가면 민박을 할 만한 데가 있어요?

23. -적(-的)

69. 이야기를 너무 극적으로 과장하다가는 사람들이 믿어 주지 않을 겁니다.
70. 서울 88 올림픽은 역사적으로 획기적인 행사였습니다.

24. 치고는

71. 앨버트 씨는 키가 175센티미터입니다.
    서양 사람치고는 키가 크지 않은 편입니다.
72. A: 고등학생치고는 한자를 잘 아는 편이지.
    B: 삼천자나 쓸 수 있다고 그래.
73. 미선이는 대학생처럼 보입니다. 고등학생치고는 좀 조숙한 편입니다.
74. 시험을 썩 잘 보지는 않았습니다. 그렇지만 벼락치기 한 것 치고는 시험을 잘 보았습니다.

25. -아 / -어 주-, -아 / -어다 주-

75. 엄마, 맛있는 후식 좀 사 주십시오. 엄마, 시장에 가는 길에 맛있는 후식 좀 사다 주십시오.
76. 준영 씨, 책 좀 빌려 주십시오.
    준영 씨, 학교에 가는 길에 도서관에서 책 좀 빌려다 주십시오.
77. 철민 씨, 잠깐만 이 짐 좀 들어 주십시오.
    철민 씨, 택시를 타는 곳까지 이 짐 좀 들어다 주십시오.
78. 앨버트 씨, 이것 좀 받아 주십시오.
    앨버트 씨, 저것 좀 받아다 주십시오.

26. 부터

79. A: 야, 너 왜 매일 늦게 들어오나? 좀 일찍 들어와.
    B: 형은? 남 말하지 말고 형부터 일찍 들어와 봐.
80. A: 영진이네 식구들은 모두 술을 잘 마시나 봅니다.
    B: 맞습니다. 아버지부터 전부 술고래입니다.
81. 냉장고부터 옮겨야겠습니다.

27. 대로, -(으)ㄴ / -는 대로

82. A: 움직이지 말고 그대로 계십시오. 찍겠습니다.
    B: 예쁘게 찍어 주십시오.
83. A: 어떻게 하면 되겠습니까?
    B: 방금 내가 말한 대로 하면 될 것입니다.
84. 어머니: 고집 부리지 말고 형이 시키는 대로 해.
    아들: 알았어요.
85. 선생: 좌우간 여러 번 말씀드린 대로 한자의 부수들을 제대로 배워 놓으면, 한자 배우기가 훨씬 쉬워집니다.
    학생: 네, 선생님. 알겠습니다.

27. 에다(가)

86. A: 어디에다가 놓을까요?
    B: 저쪽에다가 놓으십시오.
87. A: 책상 위에다 올려놓을까요?
    B: 아니요, 책상 밑에다 내려놓으십시오.
88. 길에다 휴지를 버리다가 걸리면 벌금을 내야 합니다.

29. -(으)ㄴ / -는 편이-

89. A: 10시부터 잡니까?
    B: 네, 저는 좀 일찍 자는 편입니다.
90. A: 수미 씨 집은 넓습니까?
    B: 네, 넓은 편입니다.

그런 것쯤은 우리도 알고 있어요

한 인류학자가 아프리카 정글 속에 있는 한 마을을 조사하러 갔다. 그런데 그 학자가 도착했을 때 어린아이들이 앉았다 일어났다 하면서 독특한 놀이를 하고 있었다. 그 학자는 마침 잘 되었다 싶어서 사진을 찍으려고 하였다. 그랬더니 아이들이 마치 항의를 하는 듯이 소리를 지르면서 손가락질을 하는 것이었다.

좀 무안해진 인류학자는 아이들에게 다가가서 사진을 찍어도 혼이 빠져나가지 않는다고 설명하기 시작했다. 그리고 사진기에 대해서도 이것저것 말해 주었다. 아이들이 몇 번 그 사람의 말을 막고 뭔가 말하려 하였지만 학자는 아이들에게 말할 틈을 주지 않았다.

잠시 후 아이들이 자기가 한 말을 알아들었을 거라고 생각한 인류학자가 아이들에게 말할 기회를 주었다. 그러자 아이들은 이렇게 말했다.

"사진을 찍어도 혼이 나가지 않는다는 것쯤은 우리도 알고 있어요. 우리는 카메라 렌즈 덮개가 덮여 있다는 것을 말하고 싶었을 뿐이에요."

NEW VOCABULARY

Vocabulary from the Main Text

인류(人類)	humanity	도둑질← 도둑	stealing; theft
인류학(人類學)	anthropology	바느질← 바늘	needlework
인류학자(人學者)	anthropologist	톱질←톱	sawing
정글	jungle	무안(無顔)하 -	be "without face," i.e., lose face; feel embarrassed, ashamed
조사(調査)(를) 하 -	investigate		
독특(獨特)하 -	be peculiar, unique, original	다가가 -	approach; go up to
마침	just in time; at the right moment; in the nick of time; opportunely; luckily; as luck would have it	혼(魂)	soul; spirit
		빠져나가 -	lit.: fall and go out
		설명(說明)(을) 하 -	explain
		사진기(寫眞機)	camera (nowadays people also say 카메라)
마침 잘 되었다 싶어서	thought / felt this has turned out just fine		
마치...듯이	just like / as if... (The adverb 마치 means as; like; as if, and usually precedes a verbal pattern with the same meaning.)	틈	gap; crack; space; interval; time
		기회(機會)	opportunity
		기회주의자(機會主義者)	opportunist
		그러자	whereupon; no sooner had this happened, than... (from the as soon as pattern in - 자마자)
항의(抗議)(를) 하 -	object		
손가락 [- 까락]	finger		
손가락질(을) 하 -	point (The postnoun 질 comes after nouns to mean the act of ... –ing, sometimes with deprecatory meaning [when the preceding noun is a person (e.g., 선생질), as opposed to a thing (e.g., 부채질 'using a fan'), where the meaning is neutral].)	쯤은	as for (such an insignificant, paltry thing)
		덮개	lid; cover
		덮 -	cover sth
		덮이 -	be / get covered

Vocabulary from the Example Sentences

계단(階段)	stairs; staircase	동(使動) causative) (See Pattern 5 for a list of derived passives.)	
녹 -	melt (intransitive)		
가벼w– (가볍다)	be light (in weight)	묻 -	bury sth
낭비(浪費)	waste	주인공(主人公)	hero, heroine, main character, protagonist
~한테 속 -	be / get fooled, deceived, taken in by sb		
		식탁(食卓)	dining table
결석(缺席)(을) 하 -	be absent ("from one's seat") (NB: processive)	질기 -	be tough, chewy
		터 - ㄹ - (털다)	shake sth off or out
한번만 봐 주세요	Please give me a break just this one time.	오랫동안	for a long time
피동(被動)	passive (the opposite is 사	배신(背信)	betrayal, treachery

Vocabulary from the Exercises

가만히	quietly (often heard in 가만히 있어! 가만히 계세요. *Hang on a minute [let me think]; Keep quiet a moment, etc.*)	자기들끼리	amongst themselves (끼리 is a postnoun meaning *the separate group [of like people], among [by, between, to] ourselves [themselves, yourselves].*)
불안(不安)하 -	be uneasy; feel insecure, ill at ease, anxious	보기 흉(凶)하 -	be awful to see; the viewing of it is distasteful, bad
허리	waist; lower back		
숨	breath	형태(形態)	form; shape
숨(을) 들이쉬 -	breathe in	음료수(飲料水)	beverage
숨(을) 내쉬 -	breathe out	글씨	handwriting; penmanship; calligraphy
가라앉 -	sink down; go to the bottom; subside; abate; quiet down	신고(申告)(를) 하 -	report (sth, sb), notify, make a declaration
더 - ㄹ - (덜다)	subtract; deduct; lessen; mitigate	보물(寶物)	treasure, highly prized article
쓰러지 -	collapse; topple; sink to the ground; fall down	바위	rock, stone (usually quite large)
밤	chestnut	되 -	be thick, hard
밤색(~色)	chestnut color, i.e., brown		

PATTERNS

1. Alternating or Interrupting Actions with -았 / -었다... -았 / -었다 하-

Two transferentive - 다 (가) forms, of opposite or contrasting meaning (most commonly on a Past Base) and rounded off by a form of 하 - , mean that the two actions keep interrupting each other. For example:

1. 불을 켰다가 껐다가 하면 고장나요.
   If you keep turning the light on and off, it will break.

2. 달은 한 달마다 커지다가, 작아지다가 해요.
       - 졌다가   - 졌다가
   The moon waxes and wanes each month. Or: The moon gets bigger and smaller each month.

3. 엘리베이터가 고장이 나서 하루 종일 계단을 올라갔다 내려갔다 하느라고 피곤해 죽겠어.
   What with going up and down the stairs all day long because the elevator is broken, I'm so tired I could die.

4. 치과에 갔다, 상점에 들렀다, 친구네 집에 갔다 왔어요.
   I went to the dentist's, I dropped in at the store, and I went to a friend's house [and came home].

5. 냉장고 문을 자꾸 열었다 닫았다 하면 아이스크림이 녹습니다.
   If you keep opening and closing the fridge door, the ice cream will melt.

6. 어떤 때는 친절했다(가), 어떤 때는 불친절했다(가) 해요.
   He is sometimes kind and sometimes unkind.

See Lesson One for more discussion of the transferentive ‑ 다(가).

2. *One feels / it appears that QUOTE* with -다 싶-

The verb 싶 ‑ , in addition to its meaning of *want to do something*, can also mean *feel; think*. In this meaning, it combines with a Plain Style statement in ‑ 다, or with questions in ‑ 나, ‑ (으)ㄴ / 는 가, ‑ (으)냐 / ‑ 느냐, as if quoting the thing felt or thought. (But note that this pattern never occurs with the explicit quotation particle ‑ 고.)

7. A. 찌개 맛이 좀 이상한데요?
      This tchigae tastes funny, doesn't it?

   B: 그런 것 같아요. 물이 좀 적다 싶어서 나중에 더 넣었더니 맛이 이상해졌어요.
      Yeah, it seems so. I thought there wasn't enough water, so I put more in later, but [lo and behold—] it tastes funny now.

8. A: 늦을 것 같은데 전화하는 게 좋지 않을까요?
      Looks like we're going to be late; wouldn't it be good to call?

   B: 좀 늦겠다 싶어서 아까 늦게 간다고 전화를 했습니다.
      I thought we might be late, so I called just a minute ago to say we're running late.

9. 수미한테 할 말이 있었는데 길에서 우연히 수미를 만났습니다. 마침 잘 되었다 싶었습니다.
   I had something to say to Sumi, and happened to run into her on the street. I thought to myself, "This has turned out great."

10. 오늘 다 못 끝내겠다 싶었는데 다 됐네요.
    I was thinking we wouldn't be able to finish everything today, but we're all done!

11. 좀 위험하다 싶더니 역시 사고가 생겼네요.
    I was thinking it was a bit dangerous, and sure enough, there was an accident.

12. 많이 먹는다 싶더니 결국 배탈이 났나 봅니다.
    I thought he was eating a lot and, whadda ya know—looks like he's got a tummy ache.

3. *As if...; like* with Modifier + 듯(이), Base + -듯(이);
Seems... with Modifier + 듯하-, Base + -듯하-

These two patterns mean basically the same thing: *seems; as if; like.* The forms ‑이 are explicitly adverbial.

13.　A:　경진 씨, 오늘은 기분이 좋아 보이네요.
　　　　　Kyŏngjin, you look like you're in a good mood today.

　　　B:　네, 어제 푹 쉬었더니 몸이 날아갈 듯이 가볍습니다.
　　　　　Yes. I got a good night's sleep yesterday, and now I feel so light I could fly away.

14.　A:　정민 씨 낭비가 심하지요?
　　　　　Chŏngmin is terribly wasteful, isn't he?

　　　B:　네, 돈을 물 쓰듯이 씁니다.
　　　　　Yes. He spends money like water.

15.　A:　상호한테 또 속았습니다.
　　　　　I was duped again by Sangho.

　　　B:　상호처럼 거짓말을 밥 먹듯이 하는 애는 처음 보았습니다.
　　　　　I've never seen anybody lie so easily ["like eating rice"] as Sangho.

16.　A:　영미 씨 어디 갔습니까?
　　　　　Where did Yŏngmi go?

　　　B:　아프다고 하면서 집에 갔습니다. 머리가 많이 아픈 듯했습니다.
　　　　　She went home saying she was sick. It seemed like she had a headache.

17.　A:　영진 씨도 그 소문 알고 있습니까?
　　　　　Is Yŏngjin aware of that rumor, too?

　　　B:　아직은 모르는 듯합니다.
　　　　　It seems he doesn't know about it yet.

18.　A:　저 사람 어디선가 본 듯하지 않습니까?
　　　　　Doesn't it seem like we've seen her somewhere before?

　　　B:　글쎄요, 기억이 날 듯 하면서도 안 납니다.
　　　　　Hmm, it seems as if I might remember her, but then again, I can't.

4. *Even if...; even though...* with -아 / -어도

The infinitive form (‑아 / ‑어) of verbs can take the particle 도 *and; also; even* to produce a pattern meaning *even if...; even though...;* or *in spite of the fact that...* (See *Continuing Korean*, Section 18.2).

19. A: 내일 비가 와도 축구를 합니까?

    Are you playing soccer tomorrow even if it rains?

    B: 물론입니다. 비가 와도 합니다.

    Of course. We play even when it rains.

20. A: 초등학교 다닐 때 결석 많이 했습니까?

    Were you absent much when you were in elementary school?

    B: 아니요, 저는 어릴 때 몸이 많이 아파도 학교에 갔습니다.

    No. When I was little, I went to school even when I was really sick.

21. A: 영수야, 아무리 피곤해도 옷은 갈아입고 자.

    Hey, Yŏngsu—change out of your clothes before you sleep, however tired you may be.

    B: 엄마, 피곤해 죽겠으니까 한번만 봐 주세요.

    Mom—I'm dead tired. Give me a break this once.

22. A: 아이들 때문에 속상해 죽겠습니다.

    The kids are driving me nuts.

    B: 아직 어려서 그러니까 화가 나도 참으십시오.

    It's because they're still little. No matter how angry you might get, just grin and bear it.

23. A: 진우한테는 제가 전화할게요.

    I'll call Chinu.

    B: 전화해도 없을 겁니다. 여행 간다고 했거든요.

    Even if you do, he won't be there. You see, he told me he was going on a trip.

24. A: 뛰어갑시다. 뛰어가면 차를 탈 수 있을지도 모릅니다.

    Let's run. If we run, we might be able to catch the bus.

    B: 벌써 늦었습니다. 뛰어가도 못 타니까 천천히 갑시다.

    It's already too late. We won't make it even if we run, so let's take our time.

5. Derived Passives (피동어휘)

You have seen the following verb form: 보이 - *be / get seen; be visible*. This verb is derived from 보 - *look at; see*. Through this derivation (in this case, addition of - 이 - to the base 보 -), the new verb 보이 - acquires a **passive** meaning (as it happens, the same derivation also produces a **causative** meaning [*shows*], but let's ignore this for now).

A number of other verbs (though by no means all verbs) are also subject to this type of derivation. The derivation process changes the meaning of the original verb from a transitive verb into a passive one. Passive verbs can sometimes be translated to mean *it can be (done)*. For example: 바다가 보인다 can be translated literally as *The sea can be seen.*

You will notice that the passives (and causatives, too, as it turns out) are usually derived with the use of some suffix such as ‑이‑, ‑기‑, ‑히‑, or ‑리‑. When the suffix contains an "ㅣ" /i/ like this, in relaxed colloquial pronunciation the last vowel of the verb base may be fronted (graphically speaking, you can think of this as adding "ㅣ": ㅓ → ㅔ, etc.): colloquial 멕힌다 for standard and written 먹힌다, colloquial 잽힌다 for standard and written 잡힌다, etc. The shapes and meanings are largely unpredictable, so you would do best just to memorize each derived form as a separate, albeit related, verb.

Here is a list of some of the verbs you have learned, together with other verbs derived from them as passives (we will present a similar list of derived causatives in Lesson 14). They are given in the Plain Style present form (with King & Yeon‑style abstract base followed by the traditional Dictionary Form in parentheses for trickier verb types).

BASIC VERB	MEANING	DERIVED VERB	MEANING
건다 (거‑ㄹ‑; 걸다)	*hang sth*	걸린다	*be / get hung; be hanging*
끊는다	*snap sth; cut sth off*	끊긴다	*be / get cut off*
놓는다	*put*	놓인다	*be / get put*
닫는다	*close*	닫힌다 [다친다]	*sth closes; be / get closed*
담는다	*put sth in a vessel*	담긴다	*sth fills; be / get filled up*
덮는다	*cover sth*	덮인다	*be / get covered*
듣는다 (들‑; 듣다)	*listen to; hear*	들린다	*be / get heard; be audible*
뜬다	*open [eyes, ears]*	뜨인다	*[eyes, ears] open; be / get opened*
먹는다	*eat*	먹힌다	*be / get eaten*
문다 (무‑ㄹ‑; 물다)	*bite*	물린다	*be / get bitten*
묻는다	*stick to sth*	묻힌다 [무친다]	*be / get smeared, stained sth stains sth*
묻는다	*bury sth; conceal sth*	묻힌다 [무친다]	*be / get buried, concealed*
민다 (미‑ㄹ‑; 밀다)	*push*	밀린다	*be / get pushed; be backed up; sth accumulates*
밟는다	*step on*	밟힌다	*get stepped on*
본다	*see; look at*	보인다	*be / get seen; be visible*
뽑는다	*select sth*	뽑힌다	*be/ get picked, extracted, selected*
빼앗는다	*snatch away*	빼앗긴다	*be / get snatched away*
섞는다	*mix*	섞인다	*be / get mixed; sth mingles*
싼다	*wrap*	싸인다	*be / get wrapped, enveloped*
쌓는다	*pile sth; heap sth*	쌓인다	*sth piles up; be / get piled up*
쓴다	*write*	쓰인다	*sth "writes" [well]; be / get written*
씹는다	*chew*	씹힌다	*sth "chews"; be / get chewed*
안는다	*hug; embrace*	안긴다	*be / get embraced*
연다 (여‑ㄹ‑; 열다)	*open sth*	열린다	*be / get opened; sth opens*
잠근다	*immerse sth*	잠긴다	*be / get sunk, submerged; steep sth*
잠근다	*lock sth, fasten sth*	잠긴다	*sth locks; be / get fastened*
잡는다	*catch*	잡힌다	*be / get caught*
집는다	*pick up in fingers*	집힌다	*be / get picked up; "picks up"*
쫓는다	*chase*	쫓긴다	*be / get chased*
판다 (파‑ㄹ‑; 팔다)	*sell sth*	팔린다	*sth "sells" [well]; be / get sold*
푼다 (푸‑ㄹ‑; 풀다)	*solve / resolve*	풀린다	*be/get resolved, solved, cleared away*

Here are examples of some of these derived verbs in sentences:

25. 안개에 싸여서 바다가 잘 안 보이는데요.
    It's so covered by the fog you can't see the sea very well!

26. 침실에서도 라디오가 들린다는 말씀이에요?
    You mean the radio can be heard all the way from your bedroom?

27. 이 문이 잘 열리지 않는데, 고칠 수 있을까요?
    This window doesn't open properly; I wonder if it can be fixed?

28. 어제 밤에 우리 병원에 들어왔던 도둑놈이 잡혔대요.
    They say the thief that broke into our hospital last night was caught.

29. 이 볼펜은 잘 안 써집니다. 좀 바꾸어 주시겠어요?
    This pen doesn't write well. Will you exchange it for me?

30. 책상 위에 놓여 있는 신문 좀 갖다 주실래요?
    Would you mind bringing me the newspaper on the desk?

31. 문이 열려 있어요—들어오세요!
    The door is open—come in!

32. 주인공이 애인 품에 안겨서 자고 있어요.
    The protagonist is sleeping [embraced] in his lover's bosom.

33. 5시 45분에 상점에 달려갔더니 문이 벌써 닫혀 있었어요.
    I ran over to the store at 5:45, only to find that the doors were already closed.

34. 식탁 위에 놓여 있는 접시 위에 여러 가지 안주가 담겨 있어요.
    There are all kinds of bar snacks in the dish on top of the table.

35. 우리 동생은 어렸을 때 개한테 한번 물린 적이 있기 때문에, 개를 무서워해요.
    My little brother was once bitten by a dog when he was little, so he is afraid of dogs.

36. 고양이가 개한테 쫓기고 있어요.
    The cat is being chased by the dog.

37. 젓가락으로 잘 안 집히면 그냥 포크로 잡수세요.
    If you're having trouble picking it up with chopsticks, just eat it with a fork.

38. A: 어제 영화 봤습니까?

   Did you see the movie yesterday?

   B: 보러 갔는데 표가 다 팔려서 못 봤습니다.

   No. The tickets were all sold out, so we couldn't go.

39. 이 불고기는 너무 질겨서 잘 안 씹힙니다.

   This pulgogi is so tough it can't be chewed properly.

40. 이 문은 자동으로 잠기는 문이니까 잊지 말고 열쇠를 갖고 나가세요.

   This door locks automatically, so don't forget to take your key with you when you leave.

41. 산 위에 눈이 쌓여 있어요.

   There's snow on the mountain.

42. 전화가 고장 났나 봐요. 자주 끊기거든요.

   The telephone seems to be broken. I keep getting cut off, you see.

43. A: 수진아, 신발에 흙이 많이 묻었어. 좀 털어라.

   Sujin, there's all kinds of dirt on your shoe—wipe it off.

   B: 아까 지하철에서 옆에 있는 남자한테 발을 밟혀서 그래.

   It's because I got my foot stepped on by the guy next to me on the subway just now.

44. 저 사건은 오랫동안 묻혀 있었는데 한 신문기자가 그 사실을 발견했어요.

   That scandal remained unknown ["buried"] a long time before a newspaper reporter discovered it.

There is no simple way to use just any verb in a passive construction. The form ‐ 게 되 ‐ (cf. *Continuing Korean*, Section 17.5) usually means *get so that it does / is or get to do / be,* and the pattern descriptive verb + ‐ 어지 ‐ (*Elementary Korean*, Section 9.8) usually means *get so it is = become.*

In the case of many Verbal Noun + 하 ‐ collocations, you can replace 하 ‐ with 되 ‐ to create a passive. For example, see 미국이 발견됐어요 *America was / got discovered* in (44) just above, compared to something like 미국을 발견했어요 *discovered America.*

With certain other Verbal Noun + 하 ‐ collocations like 암살(을) 하 ‐ *assassinate,* 거절(을) 하 ‐ *refuse,* 협박(을) 하 ‐ *threaten,* etc., you make the passive by using the verbal noun as the object of another verb—당하 ‐ *suffer; undergo.* For example:

45. 그 여자에게 사귀자고 했는데 거절당했어요.

   He tried hooking up with that girl but was rejected [lit.: suffered rejection].

46. 옛 친구한테서 배신을 당했어요.

   He was betrayed by an old friend [lit.: suffered betrayal].

47. 길을 건너다가 교통사고를 당했어요.

   After crossing the street, he had a traffic accident [lit.: suffered a traffic accident].

EXERCISES

Exercise 1: Reading Comprehension

Write out answers to the following questions.

1. 인류학자가 마을에 왔을 때 아이들이 무엇을 하고 있었습니까?
2. 그것을 보고 학자는 어떻게 하려고 했습니까?
3. 그랬더니 아이들이 어떤 반응을 보였습니까?
4. 그래서 학자는 아이들에게 어떻게 했습니까?
5. 아이들은 학자의 말을 듣고만 있었습니까?
6. 학자는 아이들이 말하려고 할 때 아이들에게 말할 기회를 주었습니까?
7. 아이들이 사진을 찍으려고 할 때 소리를 지른 이유는 무엇이었습니까?

Exercise 2: Using ...-았 / -었다 ...-았 / -었다 하-

Complete the sentences below using phrases with the pattern - 았 / - 었다 ... - 았 / - 었다 하 - .

1. 엘리베이터가 고장이 나서 오늘은 계단을 열 번이나 _____.
2. 자꾸 _____ 가만히 앉아 계십시오.
3. 우리 형은 불안하면 자꾸 _____ - 는 버릇이 있습니다.
4. 정신이 _____ 보니 늙었나 봅니다.
5. 허리를 _____ 좋은 운동이 된다고 합니다.
6. 숨을 몇 번 _____. 그러면 마음이 좀 가라앉을 겁니다.

Exercise 3: Practice with -다 싶-

Fill in the blanks below with an appropriate phrase using the pattern - 다 싶 - .

1. 물이 좀 _____ 나중에 좀 덜었더니 밥이 되어졌습니다.
2. 친구가 집에 _____ 나가고 없었습니다.
3. _____ 제 시간이 도착해서 다행입니다.
4. 아이가 좀 _____ 걱정을 많이 했는데 오늘 운동을 하다가 쓰러졌대요?
5. _____ 미리 전화를 했습니다.
6. 진수가 하루 종일 아무 말도 안 하는 걸 보고 _____.

Exercise 4: Practice with -듯하- and -듯(이)

Write responses for "B" below using the patterns - 듯하 - and - 듯 (이).

1. A: 저 사람의 이름이 생각납니까?

   B: _____.

2. A: 일요일 날 몇 명쯤 산에 갈 것 같습니까?

   B: _____.

3. A: 영호 씨 지금 누구한테 전화하는 것입니까?

   B: _____.

4. A: 밤색 모자를 쓴 사람이 누구인지 압니까?

   B: _____.

5. A: 주경 씨, 오늘은 기분이 좋아 보이네요.

   B: _____.

7. A: 경민 씨, 머리가 많이 아픕니까?

   B: _____.

Exercise 5: Practice with -아 / -어도

Complete the "B" responses below using the pattern - 아 / - 어도.

1. A: 왜 영미를 안 만나고 그냥 왔습니까?

   B: _____.

2. A: 학교 다닐 때 결석 많이 했습니까?

   B: 한 번도 결석한 적이 없습니다. _____.

3. A: 아이들만 두고 시장에 가면 걱정되지 않습니까?

   B: _____. 자기들끼리 잘 놉니다.

4. A: 먹기 싫습니다.

   B: _____ 몸을 생각해서 좀 더 드십시오.

5. A: 정민이한테 부탁해 볼까요?

   B: _____.

   정민이도 요즘 아주 바쁘니까요.

6. A: 영준 씨, 옷에 뭐가 묻었습니다.

   B: 보기 흉합니까?

   며칠 전에 커피를 쏟았는데 _____.

Exercise 6: Practice with Derived Passives

Use an appropriate passive form of verbs from the list below to complete the sentences.

보이 - , 들리 - , 열리 - , 팔리 - , 닫히 - , 집히 - , 잡히 - ,
씹히 - , 밟히 - , 끊기 - , 잠기 - , 묻히 - , 덮이 - , 쌓이 -

1. A: 누가 문을 열어 주었습니까?

   B: 문이 _____ 그냥 들어왔습니다.

2. A: 장사 잘 됩니까?

   B: 네, 요즘은 더워서 음료수가 많이 _____.

3. A: 선생님, 글씨가 작아서 안 _____.

    B: 네, 좀 더 크게 써 줄게요.

4. A: 젓가락으로 음식을 먹습니까?

    B: 네, 먹기는 하는데, 젓가락으로 잘 안_____ 먹기가 힘듭니다.

5. A: 이게 무슨 소리입니까?

    B: 글쎄요, 바람 부는 소리처럼 _____.

6. A: 어디로 여행 갈 겁니까?

    B: 눈 _____ 설악산 쪽으로 갈까 합니다.

7. A: 너 나한테 _____ 죽어.

    B: 잡을 수 있으면 잡아 봐.

8. A: 고기가 질겨서 안 _____.

    B: 이쪽에 있는 걸로 드십시오.

9. A: 왜 집에 들어가지 않고 밖에 서 있습니까?

    B: 문이 _____ 못 들어갑니다.

10. A: 수미 씨, 내일은 일요일이니까 푹 쉬십시오.

    B: 집에 할 일이 너무 많이 _____ 쉴 수도 없습니다.

11. A: 전화가 왜 이러지요? 자꾸 _____.

    B: 고장났다고 신고해야겠습니다.

12. A: 롯데 백화점에 가서 샀습니까?

    B: 아니요, 롯데 백화점에 갔는데 문이 _____ 신세계 백화점에 가서 샀습니다.

13. A: 아, 아파.

    B: 왜 그럽니까?

    A: 옆 사람한테 발을 _____.

14. A: 보물이 어디에 있을까요?

    B: 저 바위 밑에 _____ 있을 겁니다.

물고기는 물에서 살아야 되잖아요

　아이를 기르다 보면 가끔 엉뚱한 일 때문에 놀라기도 하고 웃기도 한다.

　나는 아들 하나하고 딸 하나를 두었는데 딸은 비교적 얌전하게 말썽 없이 자란 편이다. 그런데 사내아이는 어찌나 장난이 심한지 기어 다니기 시작해서부터 나하고 아내를 힘들게 만들었다.

　한번은 이런 일이 있었다. 그 애가 네 살쯤 먹었을 때였다. 시장에 갔다 온 아내가 식탁 위에 놓아 둔 조기가 없어졌다고 하는 것이었다. 처음에 나는 별로 관심을 가지지 않았는데 아내가 자꾸 이상하다고 하면서 여기저기 찾고 있었기 때문에 나도 같이 찾기 시작했다.

　아내는 저녁 반찬을 만들려고 분명히 식탁 위에 올려놓았다고 말했다. 그런데 지갑을 가져다 놓으려고 잠깐 안방에 들어갔다 나온 사이에 조기가 없어졌다는 것이었다. 부엌을 샅샅이 뒤졌지만 조기는 보이지 않았다. 그래서 우리는 이웃집 고양이가 들어와서 물어 갔을 거라는 결론을 내리고 찾는 것을 포기했다. 아내는 몹시 속이 상한 듯했다. 그런데 잠시 후 목욕탕에 들어간 아내가 큰 소리로 나를 불렀다. 목욕탕에 가 보니 욕조 안에 조기 두 마리가 둥둥 떠 있었다. 그건 물어볼 것도 없이 아들 녀석의 짓이었다. 그런데 더욱 재미있는 것은 우리의 질문에 대한 아들 녀석의 대답이었다.

"물고기는 물에서 살아야 되잖아요. 그래서 내가 물에 넣어 주었어요."

NEW VOCABULARY

Vocabulary from the Main Text

물고기 [~꼬기]	fish (in its uncooked state)
기르 -	raise, rear (children); grow (a beard = 수염)
엉뚱하 -	be ridiculous, outrageous, preposterous
놀라 -	be surprised, astonished; be frightened
아들 / 딸 (을) 두었다	*has a son / daughter*
비교 (比較)	comparison
비교 (比較) (를) 하 -	compare
비교적 (比較的) (으로)	comparatively; relatively
얌전하 -	be gentle, charming, modest, well brought up
말썽 (을) 부리 -	create trouble; make a fuss
말썽꾸러기	troublemaker
NOUN 없이	without NOUN
자라 -	grow; grow up; be brought up
사내, 사나이	man; male
어찌나 장난이 심한지...	*He is such a little rascal that...* ("his tricks are so severe that...")
장난	game; play (공 장난: *a game of ball*); mischief; prank; fun; amusement (장난으로: *for fun*)
NOUN (을) 가지고 장난하 -	play with NOUN (e.g., 불을 가지고 장난 한다: *plays with fire*)
장난꾸러기	mischievous child
장난감 [- 깜]	toy, plaything
심 (甚) 하 -	be severe, intense
기 -	crawl
기어 다니 -	crawl around
기어 다니기 시작해서부터	*From the time when he began to crawl around; Ever since he started to crawl around*
힘들게 만들었다	*He gave (us) a hard time.*
네 살쯤 먹었을 때	*When he was about four years old*
놓아 두 -	put (sth) down (for a moment / for later use)
조기	(fish) a kind of croaker or sea bream
관심 (關心) 을 가지 -	have an interest in; be concerned about; be interested (NB: processive)
자꾸	continuously
자꾸 VERB	keep on VERBing
이상 (異常) 하 -	be strange
반찬 (飯饌)	side dishes to go with rice
분명 (分明) 히	clearly
분명 (分明) 하 -	be clear
올려 놓 -	place sth up on top of sth (*lit.*:"raise up and put")
가져다 놓 -	take sth and put it away (transferentive - 다 (가) on the infinitive of 가지 - *hold / take* + 놓 - *put / place*)

안방(~房)[- 빵]	the women's quarters; the room where the parents sleep	욕조(浴槽)	bathtub
		둥둥 / 동동	adv. for describing sth floating bouncingly on the surface of water
부엌	kitchen		
샅샅이	in every nook and cranny (adverb)	뜨 -	float
		떠 있어요	is (in a state resultant from) floating
뒤지 -	search; rummage; fumble		
이웃, 이웃집	neighbor; neighbor's house	물어볼 것도 없이	needless to say ("needless to ask")
무 - ㄹ - (물다)	bite		
물어 가 -	carry off in one's mouth	녀석	rascal; urchin
결론(結論)	conclusion	아들 녀석	my / our son (humble)
물어 갔을 거라는 결론(結論) =물어 갔을 것이라고 하는 결론	*conclusion to the effect that (QUOTE) [the cat] probably walked off with it*	짓	act, doing (often heard in: 그건 무슨 짓이야? *Just what the heck do you think you're doing?*)
결론(結論)을 내리 -	reach a conclusion; come to a conclusion	더욱	more; still more; all the more (*also:* 더욱이, 더욱 더, 더욱더욱, 더더욱)
포기(抛棄)(를) 하 -	give up; surrender		
몹시	terribly; awfully; very		
속(이) 상하 -	be upset, distressed, exasperated (NB: processive)		

Vocabulary from the Example Sentences

쭉 가 -	go straight; carry on straight	장미(꽃)	rose
		시드 - ㄹ - (시들다)	fade; wither
사업(事業)	business; enterprise; undertaking	아침까지만 해도	*(Why,) even / only just this morning (lit.: even if one considers the extent of until the morning)*
여러 번	several times		
고생(苦生)을 하 -	suffer		
여권(旅券)[- 꿘]	passport	싱싱하 -	be fresh (of produce)
죽이 -	kill	금방	any moment now
살리 -	save; let live	조금 전까지만 해도	*(Why,) even / only just a moment ago (lit.: even if one considers the extent of a little while previously)*
치우 -	clear up; clean up; tidy up; clear away		
한자(漢字)[- 짜]	Chinese character		
옥편(玉篇)	Chinese character dictionary for Koreans	맑 -	be clear, transparent
		눈(을) 뜨 -	open one's eyes
놓아 두세요	*Just leave it as it is (for later use / reference).*	환하 -	be bright
		산더미 [- 떠미]	a great mass; a huge amount; a mountain
이따가 제가 치울 테니...	*Since I'm going to clear it away in a little while...*	서울역 [- 력]	Seoul Station
누구누구?	*who all? (cf. also* 어디어디 *where all?,* 뭐뭐 *what all?)*	뜯 -	open (a letter); tear out; pick; pluck; tear apart; pull to pieces
(담배를) 끊 -	quit (smoking)		

| 신입생(新入生) | new student; "freshman" | 문신(文身) | tattoo |
| 가까이에서 | from up close | | |

Vocabulary from the Exercises

자식(子息)	one's children, sons and daughters; (vulgar) bastard (supposedly worse than 놈)	경비(警備) 아저씨	security guard at the entrance to a Korean apartment building entrance
행동(行動)	behavior; action; doings; conduct	체육(體育)	physical education; athletics
대한(大韓)	Korea, as in 대한민국(大韓民國): *Republic of Korea*	대회(大會)	large meeting, rally, tournament
빠 - ㄹ - (빨다)	launder, wash (clothes)	체육대회	athletics tournament / meet
열쇠 [- 쐬]	key		

PATTERNS

1. *If one does something over a period of time [and then steps back to reflect on it]...* with -다 보면

Like the fourth pattern in Lesson 1 of this course (- 다(가) 보니), this pattern uses the transferentive followed by the verb *to see*, only here the latter is in the conditional form - (으)면 rather than the sequential - (으)니. The meaning is basically the same: *if you do something for a while, then take a step back and reflect on it [what one finds is]...*

1. 쭉 가다 보면 오른 쪽에 있습니다.
   If you continue straight [for a while], it's on the right.

2. 자꾸 만나다 보면 알게 될 것입니다.
   If you meet him frequently [over a period of time], you'll come to realize it.

3. 아이를 기르다 보면 다 그렇지요, 뭐.
   Once you try raising children [for a while], you find everybody's like that, you know.

4. 사업을 하다 보면 그럴 때가 다 있습니다.
   If you try doing business for a while, there are plenty of times like that.

5. 여러 번 듣다 보면 내용이 무슨 소리인지 들을 수 있을 것입니다.
   If you listen to it several times, you'll be able to make out what the contents are all about.

6. 외국 여행을 자주 하다 보면 가끔 여권을 잃어버려서 고생을 할 때가 있습니다.
   If you try to travel abroad often, sometimes there are times when you suffer from losing your passport.

2. Does for future reference with -아 / -어 놓-, -아 / -어 두- (again)

You have already worked with these patterns in Lesson 3 of this course, but the pattern is important enough to bear reviewing. As you know by now, certain Korean verbs mean one thing when they are used by themselves, but mean something different when combined into phrases with infinitives. You have learned the following:

봐요	sees	→	해 봐요	tries out doing
주어요	gives	→	해 주어요	does for [sb]
드려요	gives [to sb esteemed]	→	해 드려요	does for [sb esteemed]

The two such combinations under review here are made by putting together an infinitive with a verb meaning originally to put, to place. Both resultant compound patterns mean something like does it for future reference or use; does it so as to get it out of the way for now.

놓아요 puts [often pronounced. 놔요]		→	해 놓아요	gets sth done; does sth now [in anticipation of a later need]; does sth for later
두어요 puts / leaves [somewhere] [often pronounced 둬요]		→	해 두어요	does sth and gets it out of the way, does sth and gets it over with; finishes up doing sth

Observe how each of these verbs is used by itself below:

7. 밥상에 포크 갖다 놓았어요?
    Did you put the forks on the table?

8. 한 사흘 두었다가 먹습니다.
    You leave it for about three days and then eat it.

Here are some more examples of their use in phrases with infinitives:

9. 우리가 채소를 사 놓으면, 아주머니가 김치를 만들어 주겠대요.
    Auntie says she'll make kimch'i if we buy the vegetables [in advance, ahead of time].

10. 음식을 잘 준비해 놓았어요.
    We've prepared the food well [ahead of time].

11. 젊었을 때 공부를 해 두어야 돼요.
    You must study while you are still young.

12. 지금 다 먹어 둬요.
    You'd better eat all of it now.

13. 한국 사람은 김치를 가을에 만들어 두었다가 겨울 동안 계속 먹어요.
    Koreans make kimch'i in the fall, and have it throughout the winter.

14. 그 위에 소금을 뿌려 둡니다.
    You sprinkle salt over them [and get that out of the way].

15. 숙제를 미리 해 놓는 게 좋겠다.
    It'd be best to do your homework in advance.

16. A: 방에 있던 모기를 죽였어?
    Did you kill the mosquito that was in the room?

    B: 응, 죽였어.
    Yup, I killed it.

17. A: 차는 어떻게 할까?
    What shall we do with the car?

    B: 여기 그냥 세워 두지, 뭐.
    Just park it here, I suppose.

18. 손님이 내일 오시니깐, 집을 빨리 좀 치워 놓아야겠어.
    We have guests coming tomorrow, so I'm going to have to get the house all cleaned up.

19. A: 이건 어디다 둘까요?
    Where shall I put this one?

    B: 당분간 그냥 놓아 두세요.
    Just leave it as it is for the time being.

20. 어젯밤 바람에 쓰러진 나무를 제가 다시 심어 놓았습니다.
    I replanted the tree that fell down last night in the wind.

21. 토마스: 우리 한국어 수업에서 한자를 배우기 시작했어.
    Thomas: We started learning Chinese characters in Korean class.
    철수: 그래? 그럼 옥편을 하나 사 둬야겠네.
    Ch'ŏlsu: Really? I guess you'd better buy yourself an okp'yŏn then.

22. 이따가 제가 치울테니 그대로 놓아두십시오.
    I'll clean up later, so just leave it as is.

3. **Remote Past with -았 / -었었-, -(이)었었-**

Although some Korean purist grammarians frown on it as a calque from the English "past perfect" (*had done*, etc.), Korean grammar allows you to double up on the past tense marker -았 / -었 -: -았었- / -었었-. With the copula, the resulting form is -이었었- (after a consonant) or -였었- (after a vowel). The effect on the meaning is to place the action (or state) in a more remote past time than just -았 / -었- by itself. With verbs of motion like 가- *go*, the effect is to emphasize that a round trip was made: 갔- *went [and is still gone]* vs. 갔었- *went [and is back]*. Here are some more examples:

23. A: 어제 어디 갔었습니까?
    Where'd you go last night?

    B: 친구를 만나러 시내에 갔었습니다.
    I went downtown to meet a friend.

24. A: 지난 번 모임에 누구누구 왔었지요?
    Who all came to the meeting last time?

    B: 우리 둘하고 수미 씨, 진영 씨가 왔었지요.
    The two of us, Sumi, and Chinyŏng came.

25. A: 영호 씨를 만났던 날이 언제였었지요?
    Now when was it again that we met Yŏngho?

    B: 수미 씨 생일날이었던 것 같은데요.
    It seems it was on Sumi's birthday.

26. A: 철민 씨, 담배 안 피웁니까?
    Ch'ŏlmin, don't you smoke?

    B: 네, 전에는 피웠었는데 끊었습니다.
    No. I used to smoke a long time ago, but I quit.

27. A: 장미가 벌써 시들었네요.
    The roses have already wilted.

    B: 어, 아침까지만 해도 성성했었는데.
    Oh? They were [had been] fine right up until this morning.

28. A: 하늘을 보니 금방 비가 올 것 같습니다.
    Judging by the sky, it looks like it'll rain any minute now.

    B: 조금 전까지만 해도 하늘이 맑았었는데 금방 흐려졌네요.
    The sky was [had been] clear until just a short while ago, but gee, it clouded over right away.

4. **When I ... –ed, [I discovered]... with -아 / -어 보니(까)**

This pattern should be mostly review for you, too. It combines the sequential -(으)니(까) ending in its meaning of *when...* with the exploratory meaning of the -아 / -어 보- pattern. Another way to interpret the pattern is to take 보- quite literally: *when I ... –ed, what did I discover but...* Here are some more examples:

29. 아침에 눈을 떠 보니 밖이 환했습니다.
   When I opened my eyes in the morning, [I discovered that] it was light outside.

30. 회사에 가 보니 할 일이 산더미처럼 쌓여 있었습니다.
   When I got to the office ["company"], there was a mountain of work waiting for me.

31. 밖에 나가 보니 눈이 오고 있었습니다.
   When I went outside, [I discovered that] it was snowing.

32. 서울역에 도착해 보니 기차는 벌써 떠나고 없었습니다.
   When we arrived at Seoul Station, [we found that] the train had already left.

33. 재미없는 책인 줄 알았는데 읽어 보니 재미있었습니다.
   I had assumed it was a boring book, but when I read it, it turned out to be interesting.

34. 편지를 뜯어 보니 그 안에 사진도 함께 들어 있었습니다.
   When I tore open the letter, I found there was a photograph inside, too.

35. A: 저기 저 잘 생긴 신입생 보이지?
   See that good-looking new student over there?

   B: 응, 왜?
   Yeah, why?

   A: 가까이에서 보니까 눈썹을 문신했더라.
   Seeing her up close, you can tell her eyebrows were tattooed.

EXERCISES

Exercise 1: Reading Comprehension

Write out answers to the following questions.

1. 나는 자식이 몇 명 있습니까?
2. 아이들이 모두 얌전합니까?
3. 아내는 조기를 사 와서 어디에 놓았습니까?

4. 언제 조기가 없어졌습니까?
5. 아내와 나는 어떻게 생각하면서 조기 찾는 것을 포기했습니까?
6. 없어진 조기는 어디에 있었습니까?
7. 우리는 아들한테서 얘기를 듣고 그것이 아들의 행동인지 알았습니까?
8. 아들은 왜 욕조 안에 물고기를 넣었습니까?
9. 여러분도 어릴 때 장난이 심했습니까?
   생각나는 것이 있으면 말해 보세요.

Exercise 2: Practice with -다 보면

Complete Speaker B's responses using the pattern ‐ 다 보면.

1. A: 대한극장이 어디에 있습니까?
    B: 이쪽으로 100미터쯤 _____ 오른쪽에 있습니다.
2. A: 서울에 산 지 얼마 안 돼서 어디가 어딘지 잘 모르겠습니다.
    B: _____ 알게 될 것입니다.
3. A: 요즘 한국말이 늘지 않아서 걱정입니다.
    B: 외국어를 _____ 그럴 때도 있지요.
4. A: 요즘은 일이 잘 안 되어서 고민입니다.
    B: _____ 그럴 때도 있지요.
5. A: 뉴스를 보는데 아나운서의 말이 너무 빨라서 무슨 소리인지 하나도 못 알아듣겠다.
    B: _____ 무슨 소리인지 들을 수 있을 거다.
6. A: 며칠 전에 산에 갔다가 길을 잃어버려서 고생을 했습니다.
    B: _____ 가끔 그럴 때가 있지요.

Exercise 3: Practice with -아 / -어 놓- and -아 / -어 두-

Use appropriate verb phrases with the patterns either ‐ 아 / ‐ 어 놓 ‐ or ‐ 아 / ‐ 어 두 ‐ to complete the sentences below.

1. 티셔츠가 더럽습니다.
    빨아야 되니까 저쪽에 _____.
2. 냉장고 안에 있는 사과는 _____.
    씻지 않고 그냥 먹어도 됩니다.
3. A: 이거 다 가지고 갈까요?
    B: 차는 조금 있다가 마실 것이니까 거기에 _____.
       과일만 가지고 오십시오.
4. A: 책상 위에 있는 물건들 제가 치울까요?
    B: 이따가 제가 치울 거니까 그대로 _____.
5. A: 엄마, 저 열쇠를 잃어버렸는데 어떻게 하지요?
    B: 내가 나가면서 경비 아저씨한테 _____.

6. 영수야, 엄마 잠깐 나갔다 올게.

식탁 위에 점심 _____ 배고프면 먹어.

Exercise 4: Practice with -았 / -었었-

Use an appropriate verb or verb phrase in the remote past pattern - 았 / - 었었 - to complete the responses below.

1. A: 어제 뭐 했습니까?

   B: _____.

2. A: 수미 씨는 요즘 수영을 배우러 고려 수영장에 다닌대요.

   B: 그래요? 나도 전에 _____.

3. A: 이번 체육 대회 때 무엇무엇 할까요?

   B: 지난번에 농구랑 배구를 _____ 이번에도 농구랑 배구를 합시다.

4. A: 철민 씨, 담배 안 피웁니까?

   B: 네, 전에는 _____ 끊었습니다.

5. A: 영호 키가 많이 컸네요.

   B: 글쎄 말이에요. 전에는 _____.

6. A: 베티 씨 요즘 한국말 참 잘하지요?

   B: 네, 처음 한국에 왔을 때는 _____ 이젠 아주 잘합니다.

Exercise 5: Practice -아 / -어 보니(까)

Complete the following sentences by describing what was discovered after completing the action in the first clause.

1. 아침에 눈을 떠 보니 _____.
2. 여행 갔다가 집에 와 보니 _____.
3. 친구한테서 온 편지를 뜯어 보니 _____.
4. 어릴 때 다녔던 초등학교에 가 보니 _____.
5. 맛이 없어 보였는데 먹어 보니 _____.
6. 길에서 주운 가방을 열어 보니 _____.

고맙기는요

　　나는 요즘 주차장에서 일하고 있다. 그런데 손님 중에는 가끔 열쇠를 차 안에 꽂아 두고 문을 잠가 버리는 분들이 있다. 그 때마다 나는 좀 굵은 철사를 이용해서 차 문을 열어 준다.

　　그런데 얼마 전에 웃지 못할 일이 있었다. 장마가 끝나서 그랬는지 날씨가 푹푹 쪘다. 나는 시원한 음료수라도 마실까 해서 슈퍼마켓에 갔다. 사이다를 한 병 사 가지고 막 가게를 나오는데 젊은 여자 두 명이 가게 앞에서 차 문을 열려고 애쓰는 것이 보였다. 나는 그냥 못 본 척하고 가려다가 걸음을 멈추고 서서 그 여자들이 하는 행동을 지켜보았다.

　　그 여자들은 문을 열려고 애를 썼지만 문은 열리지 않았다. 나는 도와주어야겠다는 생각이 들어서 뒷주머니에 있던 철사를 꺼내 차 옆으로 다가갔다. 문을 여는 데는 1분도 걸리지 않았다. 그 여자들은 나를 감탄스러운 표정으로 바라보면서 고맙다고 인사를 했다. 나는 기분이 아주 좋았다. 그런데 잘못 나온 말 한 마디가 그 여자들의 표정을 일그러지게 만들고 내 기분을 엉망으로 만들었다.

　　"고맙기는요. 저는 이걸로 먹고 사는데요, 뭐."

NEW VOCABULARY

Vocabulary from the Main Text

주차장 (駐車場)	parking lot
주차 (駐車) (를) 하 -	park the car (you can also make what seems like a redundant expression and say 차를 주차하 -)
꽂 -	insert sth, wedge sth in, stick sth in (to a rather narrow space)
잠그 - , 잠가요	lock it
굵 -	be thick; be burly; be sonorous (voice)
철사 (鐵絲)	wire
이용 (利用) (을) 하 -	use it
차 문 (車門)	car door
얼마 전에	not long ago
웃지 못할 일	sth which is no laughing matter; a rather serious matter
장마	the seasonal rains
장마가 끝나서 그랬는지	*perhaps it was because the seasonal rains had finished (I don't know for sure, but...)*
푹푹 찌 -	(the weather) be steaming hot (NB: processive verb) (the 푹푹 is a mimetic adverb, and the verb 찌 - means *steam sth*)
시원하 -	be refreshing, be cool
음료수 (飮料水)	beverage
시원한 음료수라도	*a refreshing beverage or the like*
사이다	fizzy Korean soft drink like Seven-Up or Sprite
막	just as (one was doing sth); just when
애 (를) 쓰 -	make efforts; try to do sth; strive
걸음	one's steps, pace (from the verb 걷다, 걸어요)
멈추 -	stop (sth); (sth) stops (i.e., functions as both transitive and intransitive)
행동 (行動)	action; behavior
지키 -	watch over; guard; defend; keep; observe; abide by
지켜보 -	watch sth closely; keep a watchful eye on
생각 (이) 드 - ㄹ - (들다)	a thought occurs to one
주머니	pocket
뒷주머니	back pocket
꺼내 -	pull / bring sth out; broach, bring up (a subject)
다가가 -	approach; go up to
문을 여는 데는	*(in) the course / process of opening the door*
감탄 (感歎) (을) 하 -	exclaim over; wonder at; marvel at
감탄스러w- (~스럽다)	be marvelous, impressive; induce wonder
~스러w- (~스럽다)	(This attaches to nouns to make descriptive verbs with the meaning: *be like, give the impression of, seem like, suggest, be suggestive of [the NOUN].*)
바라보 -	gaze at; stare at
말 한 마디	word; one word (also as in "I'd like to say a word")
일그러지 -	shrivel up; wither; wilt
이걸로←이것으로	by means of this
이걸로 먹고 사는데요, 뭐	Well, this is how I make my living, you know.

Vocabulary from the Example Sentences

회 (膾)	raw fish or meat for eating; sashimi	오락 (娛樂)	amusement; recreation; pastime
전 (全) 혀 (+ NEGATIVE)	(not) ... at all; (doesn't) ... at all	가까이	nearby; the vicinity
		가까이에서	from nearby; from up close
그만 + VERB	stop VERBing	멀리	far (adv); (from) afar; so that it is distant
식욕 (食慾)	appetite		
아까w- (아깝다)	be regrettable, pitiful; be precious, valuable	떨어지 -	fall down; drop; separate; be detached; be removed
- 기 (가) 아까w-	one regrets VERBing; VERBing would be a matter for regret	멀리 떨어져서	*dropping back to a distance*
		기분 (氣分) (이) 나쁘 -	be in a bad mood

Vocabulary from the Exercises

오해 (誤解) (를) 하 -	misunderstand; mistake (sth / sb for)	낚시 (를) 하 -	fish; go fishing
이불	blanket; cover; quilt	머리 (를) 자르 -	cut one's hair; get a haircut
생신 (生辰)	(elegant / honorific) birthday	행복 (幸福) 하 -	be happy
		활짝	wide (open)
생신날	(elegant / honorific) birthday	동의 (同意) (를) 하 -	agree; assent, consent, accede (to)
김밥 (을) 싸 - [~빱]	make kimpap (cold rice wrapped in seaweed which includes vegetables, seafood, or ham)	기타 (를) 치 -	play the guitar
		좋아 보이 -	look good; look like one is in a good mood

PATTERNS

1. ***Perhaps it is / was [so] because [I don't know, but]... with -아 / -어서 그런지, -아 / -어서 그랬는지***

You have already seen the pattern - 아 / - 어서 in its meaning of *because*. Thus, - 아 / - 어서 그래요 means *does so* (그러 -) or *is so* (그렇 -) *because...* When this collocation in - 어서 그래요 is put into the oblique question pattern - (으)ㄴ지 or - 었는지, the resulting pattern means *perhaps because*. You can interpret the pattern as having left out a following phrase ... 도 모르지만 *it may have been the case that [it was / did so] because... [I'm not sure / I don't know]*, i.e., *perhaps [it is / was] because...*

1. A: 영민 씨, 철민 씨 회 좋아합니까?
    Yŏngmin, does Ch'ŏlmin like raw fish?

    B: 네, 부산이 고향이라서 그런지 회를 아주 좋아합니다.
    Yes, a lot—probably because Pusan is his hometown.

2. A: 모리 씨는 전혀 외국 사람 같지 않지요.

    Mori doesn't seem like a foreigner at all, does he?

    B: 네, 한국말을 잘해서 그런지 전혀 외국 사람 같지 않습니다.

    No. Probably because he speaks Korean well, he doesn't seem like a foreigner at all.

3. A: 아까 수미 씨를 보았는데 살이 많이 빠진 것 같던데요.

    I just saw Sumi, and it seemed like she's lost a lot of weight.

    B: 요즘 일이 힘들어서 그런지 살이 많이 빠진 것 같습니다.

    Things must be tough for her lately; she seems to have lost a lot of weight.

4. A: 왜 그만 드세요? 더 드세요.

    Why aren't you eating any more? Eat some more.

    B: 날씨가 갑자기 더워져서 그런지 식욕이 없습니다.

    It's probably because the weather has suddenly turned hot, but I don't have any appetite.

5. A: 바닷가에 사람 많았지요?

    There were lots of people at the beach, weren't there?

    B: 아니요, 장마철이라서 그랬는지 별로 없었습니다.

    No. Maybe because it's the rainy season or something, but there was hardly anybody there.

6. A: 준섭 씨는 왜 같이 안 왔습니까?

    Why didn't Chunsŏp come with you?

    B: 여기에 오기 싫어서 그랬는지 다른 약속이 있다고 하던데요.

    He must not like coming here or something—he said something about having another commitment.

2. *NOUN or something; NOUN or the like* with NOUN-(이)라도

A noun followed by the pseudoparticle ‐(이)라도 means *NOUN or the like; NOUN or something; NOUN [for lack of anything better]; NOUN [at least]*. We call it a "pseudoparticle" because in its origin, it is just a form of the copula ‐이‐, ‐이에요—the same shape you see in forms like ‐(이)라고 (in quotations), ‐(이)라야 (same as ‐이어야), ‐(이)라서 (same as ‐이어서), etc. Literally, then, and in its origin, NOUN ‐(이)라도 means something like *even though it be NOUN; even if it is [just] NOUN*. However, the pattern is beginning to be used like a separate particle now. Here are some examples:

7. A: 만년필 좀 빌려 주십시오.

    Please lend me a fountain pen.

    B: 만년필은 없는데요.

    I don't have a fountain pen.

    A: 그러면 볼펜이라도 빌려 주십시오.

    Then lend me a ballpoint pen [at least].

8.　A:　돈 있으면 5만 원만 빌려 주십시오.

　　　If you have some money, can you please lend me 50,000 wŏn?

　　B:　저도 2만 원밖에 없는데, 이거라도 빌려 드릴까요?

　　　All I have is 20,000 wŏn myself; shall I lend you this [at least]?

9.　A:　시원한 주스 있습니까?

　　　Do you have any nice cold juice?

　　B:　주스가 없는데요.

　　　Sorry, I don't have any juice.

　　A:　그러면 물이라도 주십시오.

　　　Then please give me some water [for lack of anything better].

10.　A:　오늘 다 못 끝내겠는데 어떻게 하지요?

　　　I won't be able to finish it all today; what should we do?

　　B:　그럼 내일까지라도 끝내 주십시오.

　　　In that case please finish it by tomorrow [at least].

11.　A:　피곤하고 배가 고파서 일을 못하겠습니다.

　　　I'm so tired and hungry I don't think I can work.

　　B:　그럼 빵이라도 먹고 좀 쉬었다가 합시다.

　　　In that case, how about if we pick up again after eating a pastry or something and resting for a bit?

12.　이 옷 버리기 아까우니까 집에서라도 입어야겠습니다.

　　I am loath to throw away these clothes, so I'll have to wear them around the house or something.

3.　*Was just going to ... but / when ...* with -(으)려다(가)

You have already learned the intentional pattern ‑(으)려(고) 하‑ (often pronounced ‑(으)르려고 하‑), which is the historical source for the "wanna" pattern ‑(으)ㄹ래(요). You can combine this with the transferentive pattern ‑다(가) to render a pattern that means *I was going to [do something]*, *but [then—SHIFT—I changed my mind, or something else happened, etc.]*. The shape of the pattern is ‑(으)려다(가) from ‑(으)려[고 하‑]다(가). In colloquial Korean, this combined pattern is often built on the "wanna" form, so you will often hear ‑(으)ㄹ래다(가) alongside the more proper ‑(으)려다(가). Here are some examples:

13.　처음에는 혼자만 가려다가, 친구 한 명도 초대했어요.

　　　At first, I was just going to go alone, but then I invited a friend, too.

14.　팩스로 보내 드리려다가, 급하지 않으니깐 그냥 편지로 보냈어요.

　　　I was going to send it to you by fax, but since it wasn't urgent, I just sent it as a letter.

15. 커피를 또 한 잔 마실래다가 유자차를 마셨어.
    I was going to drink a cup of coffee, but had citron tea instead.

16. 때리려다가 나보다 훨씬 큰 것 같아서, 말았지.
    I was going to hit him, but he seemed so much bigger than me that I thought better of it.

17. 축구 시합을 좀 볼래다가, 졸려서 그냥 잤지요.
    I was going to watch a bit of the soccer match, but I was sleepy, so I just went to bed.

18. 한국말로 발표를 하려다가, 준비할 시간이 없어서, 영어로 할 수밖에 없게 됐어요.
    I was going to give my presentation in Korean, but I had no time to prepare, so I ended up with no choice but to do it in English.

19. 일본학을 전공하려다가, 한국말 선생님이 어찌나 잘 가르치시던지 한국학으로 바꿨어요.
    I was going to major in Japanese studies, but the Korean language teacher taught so well that I changed to Korean studies.

4. Causatives with -게 하- and -게 만드-ㄹ-

Any verb in Korean can be turned into a causative by plugging it into the pattern -게 하- / 만드-ㄹ-. Given that the basic meaning of the adverbative -게 is *in such a way that*, the literal meaning of the pattern is *does [to] / makes [somebody] in such a way that [something happens]*. The resulting pattern has a range of meanings, from *lets somebody do it* to *has somebody do it*, *makes somebody do it*, *forces somebody to do it*, etc. The exact nuances are dictated to a certain extent by the particles you put on the Causee, but usually it is by context. Thus, if a standard causative construction is:

Causer makes Causee do something

Korean allows the following options for Causee-marking:

Causer가 **Causee**를 **do something** -게 한다
Causer가 **Causee**한테 **do something** -게 한다

The option with **Causee**를 tends to be interpreted more as *force; make*, while the option with **Causee**한테 tends to be interpreted as *let; allow*. Here are some examples:

20. A: 수미가 요즘 너무 늦게 들어오는 것 같지요?
    It seems Sumi is coming home too late these days, doesn't it?

    B: 좀 일찍 들어오게 해야겠습니다.
    I'll have to have her come home a bit earlier.

21. A: 아이들이 요즘 오락을 자주 하는 것 같습니다.

    Seems like the kids are playing video games often lately.

    B: 하지 못하게 해야겠습니다.

    We'll have to stop them from doing so ("make them so they can't do [it]").

22. A: 진수가 텔레비전을 가까이에서 봐서 눈이 많이 나빠졌습니다.

    Chinsu's eyes have gotten really bad because he watches television from up close.

    B: 멀리 떨어져서 보게 하십시오.

    Please have him watch from a distance.

23. A: 요즘 수미한테 무슨 일이 있습니까? 웃는 걸 못 보았습니다.

    Is something wrong with Sumi lately? I haven't seen her smile.

    B: 나도 잘 모르겠습니다. 좀 웃게 만들어 보십시오.

    I'm wondering the same thing. Try to make her laugh.

24. A: 철민 씨, 화났어?

    Ch'ŏlmin, are you angry?

    B: 나 지금 기분이 나쁘니까 화나게 만들지 말고 가만히 있어.

    I'm in a bad mood right now, so be quiet and don't piss me off.

25. A: 이 시계 고장났습니까?

    Is this watch broken?

    B: 아까 정미가 밟아서 못 쓰게 만들어 버렸습니다.

    Chŏngmi stepped on it just now and ruined it ["made it so that one can't use it"].

5. *Whadda ya mean, VERB?* with VERB-기는(요)

A Plain Base followed by ‑기는(요) is a snappy way of contradicting something just said, asked of, or suggested to you. It is the equivalent of the English *Whadda ya mean...?* [*That is emphatically not the case*], or *Are you kidding?* [*The situation is / was quite different from what you are assuming*], but it doesn't have the same cheeky effect as the English equivalents—in fact, it is often used in Korean as a modest way to decline a compliment.

26. A: 요새 바쁘시지요?

    You're quite busy lately, aren't you?

    B: 바쁘기는요. 어디 좀 놀러 갈까요?

    Busy? Far from it. Shall we go out somewhere?

27. A: 백화점에 사람이 많지요?

    There were lots of people in the department store, weren't there?

    B: 많기는요. 아무도 없었어요.

    Nothing of the sort. There wasn't a soul.

28. A: 새로 들어온 부장님은 잘 생겼지요?

   The new section chief is good-looking, don't you think?

   B: 잘 생기기는요. 별로던데요.

   Good-looking? Hardly, as I recall.

29. A: 어제 본 영화가 재미있었지요?

   The film we saw yesterday was interesting, wasn't it?

   B: 재미있기는요. 지루해서 도중에 졸았어요.

   Interesting? Surely not—it was so boring I dozed off in the middle.

30. A: 시험 공부는 다 했니?

   Have you finished all your test preparations?

   B: 다 하기는. 하나도 안 했지.

   Are you kidding? I haven't done a thing.

31. A: 우리말 잘 하시네요.

   My, you speak Korean well!

   B: 잘 하기는요. 어려워서 죽겠어요.

   Are you kidding? It's so difficult I think I'm going to die.

EXERCISES

Exercise 1: Reading Comprehension

Write out answers to the following questions.

1. 나는 어디에서 일을 하고 있습니까?
2. 나는 손님들이 어떻게 했을 때 철사를 이용해서 차 문을 열어줍니까?
3. 요즘 날씨가 어떻습니까?
4. 며칠 전에 나는 무엇을 하러 슈퍼마켓에 갔습니까?
5. 젊은 여자들은 왜 슈퍼마켓 앞에서 고생하고 있었습니까?
6. 나는 그 여자들을 못 본 척하고 그냥 갔습니까?
7. 문을 여는 데 시간이 얼마나 걸렸습니까?
8. 그 여자들은 나를 무엇을 하는 사람으로 오해했습니까?

Exercise 2: Using -아 / -어서 그런지, -아 / -어서 그랬는지

Complete the following sentences to reveal what led to the *perhaps because* statement in the first clause.

1. 철민 씨는 시골이 고향이라서 그런지 _____.
2. 앨버트 씨는 요즘 바빠서 그런지 _____.

3. 우리 집이 불편해서 그랬는지 _____.
4. 어제 밤에 이불을 안 덮고 자서 그런지 _____.
5. 미영이는 요즘 살이 쪄서 그런지 _____.
6. 기다려도 안 와서 그랬는지 _____.

Exercise 3: Practice with -(이)라도

Complete the sentences below using an appropriate phrase with - (이) 라도.

1. 주스를 마시고 싶은데 주스가 없으니까 _____.
2. 오래간만에 오셨는데 그냥 가지 말고 _____.
3. 박 선생님이 요즘 바쁘신 것 같으니까 _____ 도와 드립시다.
4. 지금 빵밖에 없는데 _____.
5. 오백원짜리 동전이 없으면 _____.
6. 아버님 생신날인데 _____ 초대해야 되지 않겠습니까?

Exercise 4: Practice with -(으)려다가

Complete the "B" responses below using an appropriate phrase with - (으) 려다가.

1. A: 일요일 날 수미 만났습니까?
   B: _____.
2. A: 어제 친구 만나서 영화를 봤습니까?
   B: _____.
3. A: 김밥 싸 가지고 놀러갔다 왔습니까?
   B: _____.
4. 4. A: 주말에 낚시하러 갔다 왔습니다.
   B: _____.
5. A: 아직도 머리를 안 잘랐네요.
   B: _____.
6. A: 어, 비가 오잖아요.
   B: 창문을 활짝 열어 놓고 나왔는데 큰일이네요. _____.

Exercise 5: Practice with -게 하- / 만드-ㄹ-

Complete the "B" responses below using the causative pattern either - 게 하 - or - 게 만드 - ㄹ -.

1. A: 요즘 수미한테 무슨 일이 있습니까? 웃는 걸 못 보았습니다.
   B: 나도 잘 모르겠습니다. _____.
2. A: 철민 씨, 화났어?
   B: 나 지금 기분이 나쁘니까 _____.
3. A: 진우 씨, 아까 어머니를 만났는데 아주 행복해 보이시던데요.
   B: 오늘이 어머니 생신이거든요. 우리가 어머니를 _____.

4. A: 성민이가 요즘 술을 너무 많이 마시는 것 같습니다.

   B: _____.

5. A: 축구하다가 다쳤어요.

   B: 누가 _____.

   A: 민수가 저를 밀었거든요.

6. A: 남편이 담배를 많이 피워서 걱정입니다.

   B: 저도 남편한테 담배 _____고생 많이 했습니다.

Exercise 6: Practice with -기는(요)

Speaker B disagrees with what Speaker A has just said. Craft the responses using the pattern - 기는(요).

1. A: 토마스 씨는 언제나 열심히 공부하는 것 같습니다.

   B: _____.

2. A: 너무 많이 산 게 아닐까요?

   B: _____.

3. A: 기타 참 잘 치시네요.

   B: _____.

4. A: 아드님이 참 잘 생겼네요.

   B: _____.

5. A: 선영 씨, 요즘 아주 좋아 보이는데 무슨 좋은 일 있습니까?

   B: _____.

6. A: 날씨가 많이 좋아졌지요?

   B: _____.

사랑하는 나의 아내에게

사랑하늘 ...

　　오늘은 아내의 생일이다. 나는 며칠 전부터 아내에게 무슨 선물을 주면 좋을까 하고 고민해 왔다. 벌써 아내와 30년 가까이 살았다. 나이를 먹어 갈수록 아내가 소중하게 느껴진다. 그래서 이번에는 내 정성이 담긴 선물을 주어서 아내를 놀라게 해야겠다고 마음먹었다. 그런데 아무리 생각해도 좋은 생각이 떠오르지 않았다. 그래서 나는 할 수 없이 어제 백화점에 가서 목걸이를 하나 샀다.

　　그렇지만 그 선물이 썩 마음에 들지 않았기 때문에 아내의 생일날 새벽인 지금까지도 이불 속에 누워서 생각을 하고 있다. 이런저런 생각 끝에 50년 전에 있었던 일이 떠올랐다.

　　내가 열한 살 때였다. 우리 집에서는 농사를 짓고 있었기 때문에 부모님은 쉴 새 없이 일을 하셨다. 나는 맏아들이었기 때문에 부모님을 도와 드려야 했다. 나는 새벽에 일찍 일어나 소에게 밥을 주는 일이 제일 싫었다. 아버지는 매일 아침 우리 방에 들어와 일어나기 싫어하는 나를 흔들어 깨우셨다.

아버지의 생일이 얼마 남지 않았을 때였다. 나는 언제나 우리를 위해 고생을 하시는 아버지를 기쁘게 해 드리고 싶었다. 그렇지만 나에게는 돈이 없었다. 그 때 아주 멋진 생각이 떠올랐다.

아버지의 생일날 나는 아버지가 나를 깨우는 시간보다 한 시간 반쯤 일찍 일어나서 밖으로 나갔다. 그리고 부모님이 깨시지 않게 조용조용 소죽을 끓여서 소에게 주고 방으로 들어왔다. "아버지가 그걸 보시면 어떤 얼굴을 하실까?" 나는 이불 속에 누워서 행복한 생각에 빠졌다.

잠시 후 안방 문이 열리는 소리와 함께 나를 부르는 아버지의 목소리가 들렸다. 나는 아버지가 부르는 소리를 들었으면서도 처음에는 못 들은 척 가만히 있었다. 그러다가 아버지가 서너 번 부른 다음에 일어나 밖으로 나갔다. 아버지는 외양간 앞을 지나다가 소가 벌써 밥을 먹고 있는 것을 보았다. 그리고는 깜짝 놀라 내 쪽을 쳐다보았다. 나는 말없이 씩 웃었다.

그 생각을 하니까 그때의 감동이 그대로 되살아나 코끝이 찡했다. 그리고 아내에게 어떤 선물을 주면 좋을까 하는 생각이 떠올랐다. 나는 얼른 일어나서 서재로 건너가서 아내에게 편지를 쓰기 시작했다.

"사랑하는 나의 아내에게......"

NEW VOCABULARY

Vocabulary from the Main Text

고민(苦悶)(을) 하 -	agonize; be in anguish	담기 -	be / get contained; be filled with
30년(年) 가까이	for close to thirty years; nearly thirty years	마음(을) 먹 -	make up one's mind
나이를 먹어 갈수록	*the more I age, the more...; the older I get, the more...*	생각(이) 떠오르 -	a thought occurs ("floats up") to one
소중(所重)하 -	be important, weighty; be precious, dear	목걸이	necklace
		귀걸이	earring
느끼 -	feel; sense; experience; be conscious of; realize; be deeply moved	썩	quite; rather; greatly; very much
느껴지 -	get so that it is realized; come to feel / sense	농사(農事)를 지(ㅅ) - (짓다, 지어)	engage in farming / agriculture
		쉴 새 없이	without a(ny) chance / moment to rest
정성(精誠)	sincerity and devoted affection	맏아들	oldest son

흔드 - ㄹ - (흔들다)	shake, sway, disturb, agitate sth	내 쪽	toward me; in my direction
얼마 남지 않았어요	*Not much (time) is left / remaining.*	쳐다보 -	stare at; gaze at
소죽	boiled fodder	씩 웃 -	smile sheepishly; give a quick (sheepish) smile
끓이 -	boil sth; make sth boil	감동 (感動)	being moved / touched; deep emotion
빠지 -	fall into	되살아나 -	revive; come back to life; rekindle; burn up again
안방문 [- 빵]	the door to the 안방 [안빵], or parents' bedroom	코끝이 찡하 -	(the end of one's nose) get itchy (because one feels like crying)
목소리	voice		
못 들은 척	*pretending not to have heard*	얼른	immediately, right away
그러다가	after (doing sth for) a while, then (suddenly / unexpectedly)	서재 (書齋)	study (a studying room or a library)
서너 번 (番)	three or four times; a few times	건너 -	cross over, go over (e.g., 길을 건너다)
외양간 [- 깐]	stable; cowshed	건너가 - , 건너오 -	go across; come across

Vocabulary from the Example Sentences

태어나서 지금까지 쭉	*ever since I was born until now, uninterruptedly*		language ability); expand; lengthen
태어나 -	be born; come into the world	사동어휘 (使動語彙)	causative vocabulary
말리지 마십시오	*Don't stop / dissuade me; Don't get in my way (of doing sth).*	연필 (을) 돌리 -	flip one's pencil round and round between the thumb and third finger (a favorite trick of Korean students)
더 이상 (以上)	anymore; more; further	넓히 -	widen sth
이어져 온 것	*something which has been passed down over time; something handed down; something inherited*	인원 (人員)	the number of persons; staff, personnel
		인원수 (~數)	the number of personnel
민속 (民俗)	folkways, folk customs	늘리 -	increase sth; augment sth; stretch sth; enlarge sth; expand sth
민속학 (民俗學)	the study of folklore		
민속놀이	folk game; traditional game	맡기 -	entrust sth; leave a person with; trust a person with; leave in a person's charge
윷놀이	the game of *yut*		
널뛰기	the game of seesaw, teeter-totter	책임 (責任) (을) 지 -	take ("bear") responsibility
널	board, plank	책임자 (責任者)	the person in charge; the person responsible
뛰 -	jump; leap; run		
비누	soap	남기 -	leave sth left over; leave sth undone (cf. 인상을 남기 - *leave an impression*)
수질 (水質)	water quality		
오염 (汚染)	contamination; pollution		
비누로 바꿨습니다	*I switched over to soap.*	무리 (無理)이 -	be over the top, too much, a strain, unreasonable
느 - ㄹ - (늘다)	increase; accrue; make progress; improve (one's	퇴출 (退出) 시키 -	throw out, weed out, kick out

소리를 지르 –	shout, yell, cry (out)	옷이 다 젖었어요.	*Your clothes are all wet.*
자명종(自鳴鐘)	alarm clock	남	others; people from one's "out-group"; outsiders
합격(合格)(을) 하 –	pass (the test); make the grade; come up to the standard	도w–(돕다)	help; assist
		품질(品質)	the quality (of goods)
갑자기 내린 소나기	*a sudden downpour / cloudburst*	멍청하 –	be dim-witted, stupid
		비상(非常)하 –	(mind, brain) be brilliant, extraordinary
몽땅	in total; totally; in one big lump		
		비상상태(非常狀態)	emergency; emergency situation
젖 –	get / become wet; get soaked / moistened		

Vocabulary from the Exercises

만족(滿足)하 –	feel satisfied (NB: processive)	만우절(萬愚節)	April Fools' Day
		우울(憂鬱)하 –	be depressed, blue
직업(職業)	occupation; career	실컷	to one's heart's content
몇 번째?	how-many-th?	껍질	(banana, apple, etc.) peel; (tree) bark
결국(結局)	at the end of the day; ultimately		
		돼지 저금통(貯金桶)	piggybank
입장(立場)	position; situation	가득 or 가뜩	to the top; full; chocka-block; brimming; to the brim
철(이) 없 – / 있 –	lack / have maturity, sense		
보름	fortnight [two weeks]		
훼방(毁謗)(을) 놓 –	slander; defame; interfere with; thwart	따라가지를 못하겠다	*can't keep up; can't follow*
		튼튼하 –	be strong, sturdy
채우 –	fill sth up; complete (a number); make up; satisfy; fill; fulfill	성적표(成績表)	report card
		도장(刀匠)	seal, handstamp, chop
		도장(刀匠)(을) 찍 –	stamp / affix one's name chop
무언가←무엇인가	sth (or other)		
하루만에	in just one day	멍하 –	be spaced-out, glazed over
한 푼도	*not even a penny*	눈(이) 부시 –	be blinded, dazzled
봄이라서 그런지	*perhaps because it is spring (I don't know, but...)*	불(을) 끄 –	put out a fire; extinguish a light
입맛(을) 돋우 –	stimulate the appetite		
꼭	be sure to...; without fail; definitely		

PATTERNS

1. Moving Toward the Speaker (in time) with -아 / -어 오-

A main verb in the infinitive ‑ 아 / ‑ 어 form followed by 오‑ *come* used as an auxiliary verb has the various meanings *gradually [comes in doing]; comes up [along]; starts [has started becoming / doing]; has / had been doing [up until now]*. In general, the effect is to say that whatever the main verb is, it has been happening from some point in the past all the way up to the present. The 오‑ is used to emphasize the perspective that something is coming toward the speaker (in this case, from a point in time rather than a place). See Lesson Seven for the parallel pattern in ‑ 아 / ‑ 어 가 ‑.

1. A: 수미 씨는 고향이 서울이지요? 다른 곳에서 살아 본 적은 없습니까?
   Sumi, you're originally from Seoul, right? Haven't you ever lived anywhere else?

   B: 없습니다. 태어나서 지금까지 쭉 서울에서만 살아 왔습니다.
   No. I've only lived in Seoul from the time I was born until now.

2. A: 영진 씨, 참으십시오.
   Yŏngjin, hold your temper.

   B: 말리지 마십시오. 지금까지는 제가 참아 왔지만 이제는 더 이상 못 참겠습니다.
   Don't try to stop me. I've held my temper until now, but I can't stand it any longer.

3. A: 선호 씨는 부모님한테 용돈을 타서 씁니까?
   Sŏnho, do you get your pocket money from your parents?

   B: 지금까지는 부모님한테서 용돈을 받아서 써 왔지만 이제부터는 제가 벌어서 써야겠습니다.
   I've been getting spending money from my parents up until now, but from now on I should earn it myself.

4. A: 옛날부터 이어져 온 민속놀이에는 어떤 것이 있습니까?
   What are some of the kind of folk games that have been passed down from the olden days?

   B: 윷놀이하고 널뛰기가 옛날부터 이어져 온 민속놀이입니다.
   Yut and nŏlttwigi are folk games that have come down from the old days.

5. A: 아니 선영 씨, 머리를 비누로 감으십니까?
   Say, Sŏnyŏng, do you wash your hair with soap?

   B: 네, 수질 오염이 심하답니다. 그래서 샴푸를 써 오다가 얼마 전부터 비누로 바꿨습니다.
   Yes. They say that the water pollution is quite bad. So after using shampoo, I recently changed over to soap.

6. A: 저 가게는 물건 값이 비싸답니다.
   I'm told that store's prices are expensive.

   B: 그래요? 저는 지금까지 저 가게에서 사 왔는데요.
   Really? I've always done my shopping there until now...

2. *The more... the more...* with (-(으)면)... -(으)ㄹ수록

The pattern for Korean sentences meaning *the more... the more...* is to repeat the initial verb—first using it in the conditional form with －(으)면, then again as a prospective modifier －(으)ㄹ followed by the postmodifier 수록. This takes care of both parts of the English expression; a regular statement (or question) will complete the sentence. Note that the initial clause in －(으)면 is optional. Here are some examples:

7. 외국말은 하면 할수록 느는 것이 아닙니까?
   Isn't it true that the more you speak a foreign language the better you get at it?

8. 사귀면 사귈수록 좋은 점이 많은 것 같아.
   The more I get to know [him], the more good points he has!

9. 그런 책을 읽으면 읽을수록 한국을 더 잘 이해하게 될 거예요.
   The more you read books like that, the better you'll [more you'll come to] understand Korea.

10. 크면 클수록 좋아요.
    The bigger the better.

11. 작으면 작을수록 맛이 있어요.
    The smaller they are, the more flavor they have.

12. 그 이야기는 들으면 들을수록 재미있어요.
    The more you hear that story, the more interesting it is.

13. 돈은 있으면 있을수록 쓰는 것이에요.
    The more money you have, the more you spend. [lit.: Money is a thing that the more you have the more you spend of it.]

14. 그 자동차는 보면 볼수록 사고 싶어요.
    The more I look at that car, the more I want to buy it.

3. Derived Causatives (사동어휘)

By now you should know these two common verb forms:

보이 -   *be / get seen, be visible; show, cause to see*
죽이 -   *kill; cause to die*

These are derived, respectively, from 보 - *look at; see* and 죽 - *die*. Through this derivation, 보이 - acquires a **causative** meaning (*show*) as well as a **passive** meaning (*can be seen; be visible*) while 죽이 - acquires only the causative meaning (*kill; make die*).

A number of other verbs (though by no means all of them) are also subject to this type of derivation. The derivation process changes the meaning of the original verb either from intransitive (that is, not able to have an object—e.g., 끝나 - *sth stop, come to an end*) to transitive (able to have an object, e.g., 끝내 - make *sth stop; stop sth; bring sth to an end*), or else the derivation changes a transitive verb into a causative or passive one (or in some cases, both, like the verb derived from 보 -).

Causative verbs are sometimes translated as *has someone do it*, sometimes *makes someone do it*, sometimes *lets someone do it*, and sometimes *gets someone to do it*. The Korean form itself does not make it clear whether the "causative" is by coercion, persuasion, or permission. You will recall from Lesson 13, Section 4, on causatives in - 게 하 -, that the usual way to make a causative construction out of any verb is to put the verb into its adverbative form - 게 and add some form of 하 - *do*, so that 먹게 하 - *make / let eat* means much the same thing as 먹이 - *feed*. As you have seen, some of the causative nuances are conveyed through the differential use of case particles:

Causer 가 *Causee* 를 *do something-CAUSE*
Causer 가 *Causee* 한테 *do something-CAUSE*

The option with **Causee** 를 tends to be interpreted more as *force; make*, while the option with **Causee** 한테 tends to be interpreted as *let; allow*.

Back to the shape of the derived causatives themselves, you will notice that the causative (or passive) is usually formed using some suffix such as - 이 -, - 기 -, - 히 -, - 리 - (either passive or causative, depending on the base) and - 우 -, - 구 -, - 추 - (causatives), etc. When the suffix contains an "ㅣ" /i/, in relaxed pronunciation (but not in spelling!), the last vowel of the verb base may be fronted (i.e., acquire the graphic "ㅣ," as in ㅓ→ㅔ): 멕인다 for 먹인다, 잽힌다 for 잡힌다, etc. The shapes and meanings are largely unpredictable, so you would do best just to learn each derived form as a separate, though related, verb.

Here is a list of some common verbs, together with other verbs derived from them as causatives. They are given in the Plain Style present form (with King & Yeon–style abstract base followed by the traditional Dictionary Form in parentheses for trickier verb types).

BASIC VERB	MEANING	DERIVED VERB	MEANING
감는다	*bathe; wash*	감긴다	*have sb bathe or wash*
걷는다 (걸 -; 걷다)	*walk*	걸린다	*have sb walk*
굶는다	*starve, be hungry*	굶긴다	*starve sb; make go hungry*
굽다	*be bent*	굽힌다	*bend sth*

BASIC VERB	MEANING	DERIVED VERB	MEANING
깬다	*wake up*	깨운다	*wake sb up*
끝난다	*sth stops*	끝낸다	*stop sth; finish sth*
난다	*exit*	낸다	*put / take out; pay*
난다 (나 – ㄹ – ; 날다)	*sth flies*	날린다	*fly sth; make / let sth fly*
남는다	*remain; be left*	남긴다	*leave sth [behind]*
넓다	*be wide, broad*	넓힌다	*widen, broaden sth*
논다 (노 – ㄹ – ; 놀다)	*play; goof off*	놀린다	*let sb play; give sb a day off*
높다	*be high*	높인다	*raise [up]; elevate*
는다 (느 – ㄹ – ; 늘다)	*increase*	늘린다	*increase sth, make sth increase*
늦다	*be late; be loose*	늦춘다	*postpone sth; loosen sth*
덥다 (더w–; 덥다)	*be hot, warm*	데운다	*heat sth; warm sth up*
덥다 (더w–; 덥다)	*be hot, warm*	덥힌다	*heat sth; warm sth up*
돈다 (도 – ㄹ – ; 돌다)	*sth turns*	돌린다	*turn sth; make / let sth go around; pass sth around*
돋는다	*stick up / out, protrude*	돋운다	*raise, lift (up); stimulate, heighten*
듣는다 (들 – ; 듣다)	*listen to; hear*	들린다	*let / make sb hear*
마른다	*get dry*	말린다	*dry sth; make sth dry*
만다 (마 – ㄹ – ; 말다)	*cease; desist*	말린다	*prevent sb from doing; stop / dissuade sb*
맡는다	*take responsibility*	맡긴다	*entrust to, put in the care of, take charge of*
먹는다	*eat*	먹인다	*feed; let sb eat*
벗는다	*get undressed*	벗긴다	*undress sb; take [sb's clothes] off*
본다	*see; look at*	보인다	*show; let sb see*
부른다	*call*	불린다	*have sb call*
빗는다	*comb (one's hair)*	빗긴다	*comb (sb's hair)*
산다 (사 – ㄹ – ; 살다)	*live*	살린다	*make / let live; save; revive*
선다	*stand*	세운다	*erect sth; stop (a car)*
신는다	*wear (on feet)*	신긴다	*put sth on (sb's feet)*
안다 (아 – ㄹ – ; 알다)	*know*	알린다	*let sb know; inform*
앉는다	*sit*	앉힌다	*seat sb*
없다	*be lacking*	없앤다	*eliminate; get rid of*
오른다	*rise; ascend*	올린다	*raise; lift; present; give*
입는다	*get dressed*	입힌다	*dress sb*
잡는다	*catch*	잡힌다	*have sth caught; have sb catch*
젖는다	*get wet*	적신다	*wet sth; make sth wet (irregular derivation)*
좁다	*be narrow*	좁힌다	*make narrow; narrow sth*
죽는다	*die*	죽인다	*kill*
탄다	*sth burns*	태운다	*burn sth*
탄다	*ride sth*	태운다	*give a ride (to sb)*

Here are examples of some of these derived verbs in sentences:

15. 사무원을 놀리고 싶지 않아서 할 일이 많다고 핑계를 댔지.

    You see, I didn't want to give the office workers the day off, so I made up the excuse that there was a lot of work to do.

16. 아기를 혼자 걸려 봤지만 아직 잘 못 걸어.

    I tried having the baby walk by himself, but he still isn't able to walk very well.

17. 그 외과 의사는 환자를 살려 주고 싶었기 때문에 수술했답니다.

    The surgeon said he operated because he wanted to save the patient.

18. 이 헌 다리를 없애지 않으면 위험해요.

    If they don't get rid of this old bridge, it will be dangerous.

19. 개가 배탈이 나서, 굶겨야겠어요.

    The dog has stomach trouble so we'll have to keep him off his food.

20. 한국 학생들은 공부를 하면서 손가락으로 연필을 돌리는 버릇이 있습니다.

    Korean students have the habit of twirling their pencil around with their fingers while they study.

21. 대문 앞의 길을 넓히겠다고 시청에서 누가 왔었어요.

    Somebody came from City Hall to say they are going to widen the street in front of our gate.

22. 그 회사에서는 인원이 좀 모자라서, 인원수를 좀 늘려야겠답니다.

    They say that company is short of staff, so they'll have to increase their personnel.

23. 사장님은 이 사업에 대한 모든 책임을 김 과장한테 맡기기로 하셨습니다.

    The company president decided to entrust Manager Kim with all of the responsibility for this project.

24. 새벽 4시에 출발하는 것은 무리입니다. 시간을 좀 늦출 수는 없나요?

    Departing at 4:00 AM is a bit overdoing it. Can't we move the time back a bit?

25. 음식을 남기지 말고 다 먹어라!

    Clean your plate! ["Don't leave any food remaining—eat it all up!"]

26. 국을 데워서 먹을까요?

    Shall we heat the soup and eat it?

27. 아이들을 저기에 앉히시면 어떻습니까?

    How about having the children sit over there?

28. 아이 (의) 옷을 벗겨 드릴까요?
    Shall I undress the child for you?

29. 잔을 좀 돌립시다.
    Let's exchange [booze] glasses.

30. 회장님께 알려야겠어요.
    We ought to tell the president of the society.

31. 말씀 높이세요.
    Elevate your speech a bit [= Speak more politely].

32. 말씀 낮추세요.
    Lower your speech [= Speak less formally].

To make a Verbal Noun expression causative, ordinarily you change 하 - to 시키 - (where you would expect 하게 하 - , see *Continuing Korean*, Section 22.10). For example: 학생한테 공부(를) 시킨다 *causes the student to study = makes / lets the student study*. Here is another example:

33. 한국에 있는 일본계 회사를 퇴출시켰다.
    Japanese companies in Korea were kicked out.

But sometimes a more roundabout expression is used, as in the following:

34. 다른 사람을 시켜서 물건을 만들었답니다.
    [They say] he ordered somebody else to make the product.

    (Note the verb 시키 - by itself means *order [people or food]*.)

4. Particle 에 for Causes: *[be surprised, happy, angry, etc.] at, upon, on account of*

The particle 에 has a great many functions. The function under review here is that of "cause" or "agent," and the function corresponds to that of the English words *by* (as in *hit by a bullet*), *with* (as in *gets wet with rain*), *from* (as in *numb from the cold*), etc.

35. A: 왜 그렇게 놀라십니까?
       Why are you so startled?
    B: 저는 전화벨 소리에 잘 놀랍니다.
       I often get startled at the sound of the phone ringing.

36. A: 수미 씨는 갔습니까?
   Did Sumi leave?

   B: 네, 아까 내가 한 말에 화가 나서 갔습니다.
   Yes. Just now she got angry at something I said and left.

37. A: 진영이 화를 내면 언제나 그렇게 소리를 지르니?
   Does Chinyŏng always yell that way when he's angry?

   B: 아냐, 나도 어제 개 행동에 얼마나 놀랐는지 몰라.
   No. I was incredibly surprised at his behavior yesterday, too.

38. 자다가 자명종 소리에 깼다.
   I was awoken from my sleep by the sound of the alarm clock.

39. 준호가 대학에 합격했다는 소식에 모두들 기뻐했다.
   Everybody was delighted at the news that Chunho had been accepted to a university.

40. 갑자기 내린 소나기에 옷이 몽땅 젖었다.
   My clothes got soaking wet because of the sudden downpour.

5. *While; even while / though...* with -(으)면서(도)

The basic meaning of both the Korean - (으)면서 and the English *while* is simultaneity: *at the same that*. And just as the English *while* can sometimes have the concessive meaning of *even though* (a meaning that is more dominant in the related, if now somewhat old-fashioned *whilst*), the Korean - (으)면서 can mean *even though; even while*, in which case it is typically strengthened by adding the particle 도: - (으)면서도.

41. 철민 씨는 자기 일이 바쁘면서도 남의 일을 잘 돕습니다.
   Even when he's busy with his own work, Ch'ŏlmin is quick to help others.

42. 영주는 그 일에 대해 잘 알지 못하면서도 아는 척한다.
   Even though she knows little about that, Yŏngju pretends like she knows it all.

43. 저 가게 물건은 값이 싸면서도 품질이 좋다.
   The prices of things in that store are cheap, and yet the quality is good.

44. 준희는 머리가 비상한 것 같으면서도 가끔 멍청한 소리를 해요.
   Even though she has an extraordinary mind, Chunhŭi sometimes says stupid things.

45. 성호 씨는 오늘 하루 종일 놀았으면서 열심히 일한 척한다.

    Even though he goofed off all day today, Sŏngho is pretending that he worked.

46. 내 동생은 오늘 아침 일찍 일어났으면서도 학교에 늦었다.

    Even though she got up early this morning, my little sister was late to school.

EXERCISES

Exercise 1: Reading Comprehension

Write out answers to the following questions.

1. 지금은 몇 시쯤 되었을까요?
2. 나는 결혼한 지 얼마나 되었습니까?
3. 나는 아내의 생일 선물로 무엇을 준비했습니까?
4. 나는 그 목걸이를 사고 아주 만족했습니까?
5. 우리 아버지의 직업은 무엇이었습니까?
6. 나는 몇 번째 아들이었습니까?
7. 어릴 때 나는 어떤 일이 제일 하기 싫었습니까?
8. 아버지가 나를 불러 깨우면 나는 금방 일어났습니까?
9. 나는 아버지의 생일날 어떻게 했습니까?
10. 그 날 나는 아버지가 부르는 소리를 못 들었습니까?
11. 결국 나는 아내에게 줄 멋진 선물을 생각해 냈습니까?
12. 여러분이 이 남편의 입장이 되어서 아내에게 줄 편지를 써 보십시오. 뭐라고 쓰겠습니까?

Exercise 2: Practice with -아 / -어 오- and -아 / -어 가-

Using the patterns －아 / －어 오－ and －아 / －어 가－ as appropriate, fill in the blanks below.

1. A: 현주 씨, 진성이가 철이 없어서 그런 것이니까 참으십시오.

   B: 지금까지는 제가 _____이제는 더 이상 못 참겠습니다.

2. A: 영호 씨는 용돈을 벌어서 씁니까?

   B: 지금까지는 부모님한테서 용돈을 _____ 이제부터는
   제가 벌어서 써야겠습니다.

3. A: 앨버트 씨, 한자 쓸 줄 압니까?

   B: 아니요, 그래서 지금까지는 한글만 _____앞으로는
   한자도 배우고 싶습니다.

4. A: 아직도 멀었습니까?

   B: 아니요, _____.

5. A: 한국에 온 지 얼마나 되었습니까?

   B: 작년 10월 16일에 왔으니까 _____.

6. A: 이 선생님, 요즘 담배 피우시는 걸 못 보았는데 끊으셨습니까?

   B: 21살 때부터 30년간 _____ 보름 전부터 끊었습니다.

Exercise 3: Practice with (-(으)면) -(으)ㄹ수록

Complete the second half of each sentence below.

1. A: 그 책이 그렇게 재미있습니까?

   B: 네, 읽으면 읽을수록 _____.

2. A: 수미 씨가 그렇게 좋습니까?

   B: 네, 만나면 만날수록 _____.

3. A: 한국말 쉽지요?

   B: 쉽기는요. 공부할수록 _____.

4. 남쪽으로 갈수록 _____.

5. 시골 사람일수록 _____.

6. 나이를 먹을수록 _____.

7. 날씨가 추워질수록 _____.

Exercise 4: Practice with Derived Causatives

Complete each of the sentences using an appropriate form of one of the causative verbs listed in the 보기 below.

먹이 -, 보이 -, 죽이 -, 속이 -, 줄이 -, 넓히 -,
알리 -, 돌리 -, 놀리 -, 늘리 -, 맡기 -, 웃기 -,
숨기 -, 남기 -, 벗기 -, 깨우 -, 채우 -, 낮추 -,
늦추 -, 돋우 -

1. 새벽까지 책을 읽다가 잤으니까 지금 _____ 마십시오.

2. 오빠가 무언가를 보고 있다가 내가 방에 들어갔더니 얼른 _____.

3. 1달 동안 써야 될 용돈을 하루 만에 한 푼도 _____ 다 써 버렸습니다.

4. 요즘 봄이라서 그런지 입맛이 없으니까 입맛 _____ 음식 좀 해 주세요.

5. 엄마, 우리 반 애들이 자꾸 나를 돼지라고 _____.

6. 수미 씨, 결혼할 때 꼭 _____.

7. 내일은 만우절이니까 친구들을 좀 _____.

8. "보물찾기" 란 안 보이는 곳에 _____ 물건을 찾는 게임입니다.

9. 선영 씨, 음악 소리가 너무 큽니다. 소리 좀 _____.

10. 매일 한 시간만 공부해서는 한국어를 잘 할 수 없습니다. 공부하는 시간을 좀 _____
    _____.
11. 요즘 좀 우울해. 어디 가서_____영화 보고 실컷 웃었으면
    좋겠다.
12. 원숭이들도 바나나 먹을 때 껍질을 _____먹습니까?
13. 돼지 저금통에 동전을 가득 _____.
14. 길이 좁아서 길이 많이 막히네요. 좀 _____.
15. 진수는 벌레를 무서워해서 그런지 바퀴벌레도 못 _____.
16. 영진아, 너는 수준이 너무 높아서 우리가 따라가지를 못하겠다.
    수준 좀 _____.
17. 정윤이가 전에도 비슷한 일을 많이 했으니까 이 일은 정윤이한테 _____
    _____.
18. 아기한테 뭘 _____아기가 이렇게 튼튼합니까?
19. 8시에 출발하는 것은 무리입니다. 시간을 좀 _____.
20. 이 성적표 집에 가서 어머니게_____여기에다 도장 받아 오십시오.

Exercise 5: Practice with 에

Fill in the blanks with an appropriate phrase using the particle 에 for causes.

1. A: 아니, 무슨 죄 지었습니까? 왜 그렇게 놀라십니까?
   B: 멍하게 앉아 있다가 _____.
2. A: 수미는 벌써 갔습니까?
   B: 네, _____. 기분이 나빴나 봅니다.
3. A: 선호야, _____눈이 부셔서 잠을 못 자겠으니까 불 좀 꺼줘.
   B: 알았어. 5분만 있으면 끝나니까 조금만 참아.
4. A: 준섭 씨, 옷이 왜 그렇게 다 젖었습니까?
   B: 갑자기 내린 _____.
5. 아기가 _____놀라 웁니다.
6. 교통사고가 심하게 났다고 합니다. _____
   어제 여행간 친구가 걱정이 되었습니다.

Exercise 6: Practice with -(으)면서(도)

Complete each of the sentences below.

1. 영민 씨는 자기 일이 바쁘면서도 _____.
2. 영주는 성철이가 좋으면서도 _____.
3. 민수는 미국에서 오랫동안 살았으면서도_____.
4. 진영이는 경상도 사람이면서도 _____.
5. 우리 언니는 돈이 많으면서도 _____.
6. 내 동생은 매일 일찍 일어나면서도 _____.

제 **15** 과 복습 III

Review the example sentences below. Then, for each one, write a new sentence that uses the same pattern.

1. -았 / -었다 -았 / -었다 하-

1. 자꾸 들어왔다 나갔다 하지 말고 가만히 앉아 있어.
2. 자꾸 뚜껑을 열었다 닫았다 하면 감자가 잘 안 익습니다.
3. 냉장고 문을 자꾸 열었다 닫았다 하면 아이스크림이 녹습니다.

2. -다 싶-

4. 많이 먹는다 싶더니 결국 배탈이 났나 봅니다.
5. A: 늦을 것 같은데 전화하는 게 좋지 않을까요?
   B: 좀 늦겠다 싶어서 아까 늦게 간다고 전화를 했습니다.
6. 좀 위험하다 싶더니 역시 사고가 생겼네요.
7. 수미한테 할 말이 있었는데 길에서 우연히 수미를 만났습니다. 마침 잘 되었다 싶었습니다.

3. -듯하-, -듯(이)

8. A: 영미 씨 어디 갔습니까?
   B: 아프다고 하면서 집에 갔습니다.
      머리가 많이 아픈 듯했습니다.
9. A: 영진 씨도 그 소문 알고 있습니까?
   B: 아직은 모르는 듯합니다.
10. A: 영미 씨, 오늘은 기분이 좋아 보이는데요?
    B: 그래요, 몸이 날아갈 듯이 가벼워요.
11. A: 진호 씨 낭비가 심하지요?
    B: 네, 돈을 물 쓰듯이 씁니다.

12. A: 저 사람 어디선가 본 듯하지 않습니까?

　　B: 글쎄요, 기억이 날 듯하면서도 안 납니다.

4. -아 / -어도

13. A: 내일 비가 와도 축구를 합니까?

　　B: 물론입니다. 비가 와도 합니다.

14. A: 초등학교 다닐 때 결석 많이 했습니까?

　　B: 아니요, 저는 어릴 때 몸이 많이 아파도 학교에 갔습니다.

15. A: 뛰어갑시다. 뛰어가면 차를 탈 수 있을지도 모릅니다.

　　B: 벌써 늦었습니다. 뛰어가도 못 타니까 천천히 갑시다.

5. 피동어휘

보이 - , 들리 - , 열리 - , 팔리 - , 닫히 - , 집히 - , 잡히 - ,
씹히 - , 끊기 - , 담기 - , 잠기 - , 묻히 - , 덮이 - , 쌓이 -

16. A: 어제 영화 봤습니까?

　　B: 보러 갔는데 표가 다 팔려서 못 봤습니다.

17. A: 왜 집에 들어가지 않고 밖에 서 있습니까?

　　B: 문이 잠겨 있어서 못 들어갑니다.

18. A: 수미 씨, 내일은 일요일이니까 푹 쉬십시오.

　　B: 집에 빨래거리가 잔뜩 쌓여 있어서 쉴 수도 없습니다.

19. 어제 밤에 우리 병원에 들어왔던 도둑놈이 잡혔대요.

20. 주인공이 애인 품에 안겨서 자고 있어요.

21. A: 수진아, 양말에 흙이 많이 묻었어. 좀 털어라.

　　B: 아까 지하철에서 옆에 있는 남자한테 발을 밟혀서 그래.

6. -다 보면

22. A: 교보문고가 어디에 있습니까?

　　B: 이쪽으로 쪽 가다 보면 오른쪽에 있습니다.

23. A: 그 사람 어디가 좋은지 모르겠습니다.

　　B: 자꾸 만나다 보면 알게 될 것입니다.

24. A: 요즘은 아이 때문에 걱정이 많습니다.

　　B: 아이를 기르다 보면 다 그렇지요, 뭐.

7. -아 / -어 놓-, -아 / -어 두-

25. 와이셔츠를 갈아 입어야 되니까 좀 다려 놓으십시오.

26. 손님들이 오실 거니까 방 좀 깨끗하게 치워 놓으십시오.

27. 사다리를 치우지 말고 그쪽에 그대로 세워 두십시오.
28. 이따가 제가 치울 테니 그대로 놓아 두십시오.

8. -았 / -었었-, -(이)었었-

29. A: 어제 어디 갔었습니까?
    B: 친구를 만나러 시내에 갔었습니다.
30. A: 영호 씨를 만났던 날이 언제였었지요?
    B: 수미 씨 생일날이었던 것 같은데요?
31. A: 철민 씨, 담배 안 피웁니까?
    B: 네, 전에는 피웠었는데 끊었습니다.

9. -아 / -어 보니(까)

32. 아침에 눈을 떠 보니 밖이 환했습니다.
33. 회사에 가 보니 할 일이 산더미처럼 쌓여 있었습니다.
34. 밖에 나가 보니 눈이 오고 있었습니다.
35. 편지를 뜯어 보니 그 안에 사진도 함께 들어 있었습니다.

10. -아 / -어서 그런지, -아 / -어서 그랬는지

36. A: 영민 씨, 철민 씨 회 좋아합니까?
    B: 네, 부산이 고향이라서 그런지 회를 아주 좋아합니다.
37. A: 아까 수미 씨를 보았는데 살이 많이 빠진 것 같던데요.
    B: 요즘 일이 힘들어서 그런지 살이 많이 빠진 것 같습니다.
38. A: 바닷가에 사람 많았지요?
    B: 아니요, 장마철이라서 그랬는지 별로 없었습니다.

11. -(이)라도

39. A: 만년필 좀 빌려 주십시오.
    B: 만년필은 없는데요. 볼펜이라도 빌려 드릴까요?
40. A: 돈 있으면 5만 원만 빌려 주십시오.
    B: 저도 2만 원밖에 없는데, 이거라도 빌려 드릴까요?
41. A: 오늘 다 못 끝내겠는데 어떻게 하지요?
    B: 그럼 내일까지라도 끝내 주십시오.

12. -(으)려다가

42. A: 어제 산에 갔다 왔습니까?
    B: 아니요, 가려다가 너무 피곤해서 안 갔습니다.
43. A: 운동을 해야 하는데 왜 치마를 입고 왔습니까?
    B: 바지를 입고 오려다가 운동화가 없어서 치마를 입고 왔습니다.

44. A: 진경이한테 텐트 빌려 주었어?
    B: 아니, 빌려 주려다가 너무 얄미워서 안 빌려 주었어.

13. -게 하-, -게 만드-ㄹ-

45. A: 수미가 요즘 너무 늦게 들어오는 것 같지요?
    B: 좀 일찍 들어오게 해야겠습니다.
46. A: 진수가 텔레비전을 가까이에서 봐서 눈이 많이 나빠졌습니다.
    B: 멀리 떨어져서 보게 하십시오.
47. A: 요즘 수미한테 무슨 일이 있습니까? 웃는 걸 못 보았습니다.
    B: 나도 잘 모르겠습니다. 좀 웃게 만들어 보십시오.
48. A: 철민 씨, 화났어?
    B: 나 지금 기분이 나쁘니까 화나게 만들지 말고 가만히 있어.

14. -기는(요)

49. A: 꽃이 좀 시든 것 같습니다.
    B: 시들기는요. 오늘 가지고 온 건데요.
50. A: 좀 비싼 것 같습니다.
    B: 비싸기는요. 백화점에 가면 10만 원은 주어야 살 수 있는데요.
51. A: 이서방 요즘 일찍 들어오지?
    B: 일찍 들어오기는요. 매일 12시에 들어오는데요.

15. -아 / -어 오-

52. A: 수미 씨는 서울 말고 다른 곳에서 살아 본 적이 있습니까?
    B: 없습니다. 태어나서 지금까지 쭉 서울에서만 살아 왔습니다.
53. A: 영진 씨, 화가 나도 참으십시오.
    B: 지금까지는 제가 참아 왔지만 이제는 더 이상 못 참겠습니다.
54. A: 아니 선영 씨, 머리를 비누로 감으십니까?
    B: 네, 수질 오염이 심하답니다.
    그래서 샴푸를 써 오다가 얼마 전부터 비누로 바꿨습니다.

16. ...-(으)면) ...-(으)ㄹ수록

55. 내 조카는 보면 볼수록 귀엽다.
56. 밤이 깊어 갈수록 정신이 맑아졌다.
57. 시골일수록 인심이 좋다.
58. 이럴수록 (이런 때일수록) 기운을 내야 됩니다.

17. 사동어휘

먹이 -, 보이 -, 죽이 -, 속이 -, 줄이 -, 넓히 -, 알리 -,
돌리 -, 놀리 -, 늘리 -, 맡기 -, 웃기 -, 숨기 -, 남기 -,
벗기 -, 깨우 -, 채우 -, 낮추 -, 늦추 -, 돋우 -

59. 저도 다 알고 있으니까 속일 생각은 하지 마십시오.
60. 선영 씨, 라디오 소리 좀 줄여 주십시오.
61. 방을 한 개 줄이고 마루를 넓혔습니다.
62. 결혼할 때 꼭 알려 주십시오.
63. 성준아, 연필 좀 돌리지 마.
64. 이 일을 한 사람한테 맡겨서 책임지고 하게 합시다.
65. 진규 씨, 등 뒤에 숨긴 게 뭐예요?
66. 목이 마르니까 한 잔 가득 채워 주십시오.
67. 해 뜨는 걸 보러 갈 거니까 내일 새벽 5시에 꼭 깨워 주십시오.
68. 아침 8시에 출발하는 것은 무리입니다. 시간을 좀 늦춥시다.
69. 화 돋우지 말고 가만히 있어.

18. 에

70. A: 왜 그렇게 놀라십니까?
    B: 저는 전화벨 소리에 잘 놀랍니다.
71. A: 수미 씨는 갔습니까?
    B: 네, 내가 아까 한 말에 화가 나서 갔습니다.
72. A: 진영이가 화를 내면 언제나 그렇게 소리를 지르니?
    B: 아냐, 나도 어제 개 행동에 얼마나 놀랐는지 몰라.

19. -(으)면서(도)

73. 철민 씨는 자기 일이 바쁘면서도 남의 일을 잘 돕는다.
74. 영주는 그 일에 대해 잘 알지 못하면서도 아는 척한다.
75. 저 가게 물건은 값이 싸면서도 품질이 좋다.
76. 준희는 고등학생이면서도 대학생인 척한다.

내가 요즘 좀 바쁘니?

- 선영이니? 나 수민데, 뭐 하니?
- 그럼 나랑 좀 얘기해도 되겠구나. 아휴, 속상해.
- 요즘 우리 과 애들이랑 오전에 모여서 공부하거든. 그런데 그 중에 시간을 잘 안 지키는 애가 있어. 30분 늦게 오면 일찍 오는 거고 보통 1시간씩 늦게 오는 거 있지. 내가 요즘 좀 바쁘니? 그래서 시간 좀 지켜 달라고 전에도 얘기했거든. 그런데도 전혀 소용이 없는 거 있지. 오늘도 한 시간이나 늦게 왔길래 한바탕 했어. 그런데 오히려 자기가 화를 내더라고.
- 야, 내가 뭐 한두 번 말했는지 아니? 그동안 몇 번이나 얘기했다고.
- 아무튼 걔한테는 아무리 얘기해도 소귀에 경 읽기야. 난 정말 그런 애는 처음 봤어. 내가 앞으로 걔랑 같이 뭘 하면 사람이 아니다.
- 그래도 너랑 얘기하고 나니까 마음이 좀 풀린다. 아까는 너무 기분 나빴어. 야, 그런데 우리 너무 오랫동안 통화했네. 이제 전화 끊어야겠다.
- 미안해, 나만 혼자 얘기해서. 그럼 또 전화할게. 안녕.

NEW VOCABULARY

Vocabulary from the Main Text

속상하 –	be upset
과 (科)	department (at a university)
오전 (午前)	a.m.
모이 –	gather, assemble (intransitive)
시간 (을) 지키 –	be timely; be on time (NB: processive)
소용 (所用) (이) 없 –	be useless
한바탕 (을) 하 –	go a round (of fighting); have a go
오히려	contrary to what one might think / expect
자기	he himself / she herself
화 (火) (를) 내 –	get angry
아무튼	anyhow; anyway
걔←그애	he / she
소귀에 경 (經) 읽기	*reading sutras to a cow's ear, i.e., talking to a brick wall (proverb)*

너랑 얘기하고 나니까	*(Now that) I have spoken with you, (I feel / discover that)...* This is the Sequential – (으)니 (까) in its meaning of *when* on another pattern, namely – 고 나 – *finish doing sth*, e.g., – 고 나서 *after VERBing*, – 고 나면 *after VERBing*. This pattern rarely occurs sentence-finally, i.e., * – 고 났어요 seems not to occur.)
마음 (이) 풀리 –	feel better; feel reassured, relieved
기분 (이) 나쁘 –	be in a bad mood
전화할 데 (가) 있 –	needs to make a phone call ("has a place to call to")
끊 –	hang up (the phone)

Vocabulary from the Example Sentences

대리 (代理)	job title for lowest ladder position in a company: representative (the ranking goes: 대리 → 과장 → 차장 → 부장)
알뜰하 –	be frugal, thrifty; be earnest, assiduous
생선회	raw fish; sashimi
온몸	the whole body
난리 (亂離)	disturbance; war; rebellion
물난리 (亂離) (가) 나 –	water disaster occurs; flooding happens
난리 (가) 났어요	*There was a tumult / uproar; All hell broke loose.*
그제 = 그저께	day before yesterday
웬 = 무슨	what sort of? *here:* 웬 우산은 들고 다니니? *Why the umbrella? Why are you*

	carrying an umbrella around?
다니 –	go around
(음식이) 상하 –	(food) go bad, go off, spoil
수영복 (水泳服)	swimming suit; swimming costume
벌	counter for outfits / suits / pieces of clothing
집들이	housewarming (party / celebration)
세제 (洗劑)	detergent, cleanser
화장지 (化粧紙)	toilet tissue; toilet paper
무릎	knee
길눈 (이) 어두w– (어둡다)	*one's street eyes are dark =* be poor at navigation, have poor orientation sense
피로 (疲勞)	fatigue, tiredness, exhaustion

피로(疲勞)(가) 쌓이 -	fatigue accumulates; tiredness piles up
최고 (最高)	the best; the greatest
언제 = 언젠가는	at some point; sometime; at some time or other
못되 -	be awful, bad (as a person; always past tense)

줄(을) 쪽 서 -	stand in a long (= 쪽) line
경상도(慶尚道) 쪽에는	(down) Kyŏngsang Province way; in the direction of Kyŏngsang Province
떠내려가 -	float away (in a downward direction away from the speaker)

Vocabulary from the Exercises

효과(效果)	effect (many Koreans pronounce as [효꽈])
자연(自然)스러w– (- 스럽다)	be natural
자연(自然)스럽게	naturally
비(를) 쫄딱 맞 -	get sopping (= 쫄딱) wet / soaked in the rain
계산(計算)(을) 하 -	calculate; reckon; pay the bill (in a restaurant)
짐	bag(s), luggage
짐(을) 싸 -	pack one's bags
그치 = 그렇지	*Of course; It is so, isn't it?*
원래(原來 / 元來)	originally; primarily; from the first; to start with; actually
설악산(雪嶽山)	Mount Sŏrak; Sŏrak Mountains
무척	incredibly; very much
당일치기	one-day affair (outing / trip); doing something on one day / the same day
왜 이렇게 먼 데다 집을 샀어요?	*Why have you bought a house in such a faraway place?*
딱 맞았어요	*It fit perfectly / just right.*
장난감 [- 깜]	toy, plaything
요 앞 = 이 앞	in the front (of here, where we are)
거 - ㄹ - (걸다)	hang (up), hang on
걸려 있었어요	*was (in a state resulting from) hanging*

화해(和解)(를) 하 -	make up with; become reconciled; reach an amicable settlement
잘못했다고 비 - ㄹ - (빌다)	apologize, beg sb's pardon, (saying) "I was wrong"
용서(容恕)(를) 하 -	forgive
부부싸움	quarrel between husband and wife
부부싸움은 칼로 물 베기	*A quarrel between husband and wife is like cutting water with a knife (i.e., they make up again right away) (proverb).*
부부싸움은 칼로 물 베기라니까	This is a new pattern that involves combining a quotation [here a reported copular statement from 베기+ - (이) -] with the sequential - (으)니까(요). It means something like: *I'm telling you (insistently): A quarrel between husband and wife is like...; I'm trying to tell you (you dolt), that... QUOTE.* (You can do this with commands, too: *I just told you to shut the door (so why are sitting there doing nothing?)* would be 문을 닫으라니까!)
베 -	cut (e.g., one's finger)

PATTERNS

1. **Sudden Realization with -(는)군(요), -(는)구먼(요), -(는)구나!**

The Main Text contains the following sentence:

그럼 나랑 좀 얘기해도 되겠구나
So, [I see now suddenly] that it's OK for you to talk to me!

Forms － (는) 군 (요) , － (는) 구나 and － (는) 구먼 (요) are called "apperceptives" by S. E. Martin and are a "first realization" or "eureka" surprise form. The form － (는) 구나 functions as Plain Style.

These markers attach as endings (without 는) to the bases of descriptive verbs (and of 있 － , 없 －) as well as to all Past and Future Bases:

On a Descriptive Base:
참 그렇군요 ~ 그렇구먼요 ~ 그렇구나!
Why, that's true!

On 있 － and － 없 － :
있군요 ~ 있구먼요 ~ 있구나!
Why, there's...!

없군요 ~ 없구먼요 ~ 없구나!
Well, there isn't...!

On a Past Base:
했군요 ~ 했구먼요 ~ 했구나!
Why, he did...!

On a Future Base:
하겠군요 ~ 하겠구먼요 ~ 하겠구나 !
Well! He's going to...!

With processive verb bases, the marker is not used as an ending. Rather, it comes after the processive modifier form as a postmodifier.

1. 달을 보는구먼요! or 보는군요!
    What do you know! They're looking at the moon!

This marker adds a feeling of surprise to the sentences where it occurs, and shows a sudden realization. Typical English equivalents are *Well, I'll be...!* or *Well, what do you know...! Oh, [now] I see!, Now I realize...,* or simply *Why!* (as an exclamation). Here are some more examples:

2. 오늘밤 별이 참 많군요!
    My, there are so many stars out tonight!

3. 이 유리창이 깨졌구먼요!
    Well, what do you know! This window's broken!

4. 아! 숟가락을 떨어뜨렸구나!
    Oh, I've dropped my spoon!

5. 빵이 부서지는군!
    I see! The bread crumbles!

6. 실을 끊으시겠군요!
    I see, you're going to snap the thread!

7. 새집이 나무에서 떨어졌군!
    The birdhouse has fallen from the tree, I see!

8. 옷이 어린애한테 작아졌구먼요!
    I see, the child has outgrown his clothes!

9. 그 구두가 복동이한테 너무 크군요!
    Why, those shoes are too big for Poktong-i!

2. *You know how...? And, you know...* with -(으)ㄴ / -는 것 ~ 거 있지(요)

Literally, this patterns means something like: *[And,] as for the fact* (것) *of...—it exists, you know?* It is rather difficult to render in English, and is highly colloquial and casual. Possible equivalents are: *Wouldn't you know it—...; You know how...? And, you know...* This pattern, by virtue of its ‑지, draws the person you are speaking to into the conversation and elicits some sort of response, if only a grunt to reassure the speaker that one is following the story.

10. 나 어제 남대문 시장에 옷 사러 갔었다.
    그런데 옷이 아주 싼 것 있지.
    I went to Namdaemun Market yesterday to buy clothes.
    But you know how clothes are so cheap there?

11. 어제 영화 보러 갔다가 못 보고 그냥 왔어.
    표가 다 팔린 거 있지.
    I went to see a movie yesterday, but ended up coming back without seeing it.
    Wouldn't you know it—the tickets were all sold out.

12. 나 며칠 전에 선주 남자 친구 만났어.
    그런데 그 사람 너무 웃기는 거 있지.

    I met Sŏnju's boyfriend a few days ago.
    You wouldn't believe how funny that guy is.

13. 너 요즘 토마스 씨 한국말 하는 거 들어봤니?
    난 어제 만나서 얘기했는데 한국말이 너무 많이 는 것 있지.

    Have you heard Thomas speak Korean lately?
    I met him yesterday and talked with him, and oh my God, his Korean has improved so much!

14. 비가 자꾸 와서 걱정이에요.
    등산을 못 가게 되는 거 있죠.

    It keeps on raining so much it's getting to be worrisome.
    I mean, it's making it so we can't go hiking.

3.   Colloquial -(으)ㄴ / -는지 for -(으)ㄴ / -는 줄

The Main Text contains the following sentence:

15. 야, 내가 뭐 한두 번 말했는지 아니?

    Do you think [erroneously] that I said something [just] once or twice? [in fact, I said something dozens of times!].

In Lesson Four, you learned the pattern with postmodifier 줄 plus verb 아 - ㄹ - (알다) *to know* meaning *to think or presume [erroneously, often] that...* In colloquial Korean, this 줄 can be replaced by 지. Here is another example:

16. 어제 선 본 남자 키가 엄청 큰 거 있지. 그래서 운동선수인지 알았어.

    You know how the guy I met yesterday for "sŏn" was so incredibly tall? I thought he was a jock or something.

4.   Rhetorical 좀

By now, you have learned that the little word 좀 meaning *a little* also functions somewhat like English *please* when making polite requests. The examples below, however, demonstrate a different function of 좀. All of the questions here retain (somewhat) the literal meaning of 좀, but are rhetorical and somewhat sarcastic. They ask, *Is such-and-such only a little?*, to which the expected answer is *No way!*

17. A: 어제 진수가 와서 많이 도와주었다면서요?

    Is it true that Chinsu came yesterday and helped you a lot?

    B: 네, 진수가 일을 좀 잘합니까? 진수 덕분에 이사가 빨리 끝났습니다.

    Yes. And is Chinsu a good worker or what? Thanks to Chinsu we finished moving quickly.

18. A: 음식이 남을 줄 알았는데 모자라네요.

   I thought there would be food left over but we're short.

   B: 사람이 좀 많이 왔습니까?

   Are there a lot of people here or what?

19. A: 이 대리네는 벌써 집을 샀답니다.

   I hear that Deputy Director Lee has already bought a house.

   B: 이 대리 부인이 좀 알뜰합니까?

   Is his wife just a little bit thrifty or what?

20. A: 부산에 가서 생선 많이 먹고 왔습니까?

   Did you eat lots of fish down in Pusan?

   B: 제가 생선회를 좀 좋아합니까? 부산에 간 김에 잔뜩 먹고 왔지요.

   Do I like sashimi or what? You bet I ate my fill while I was down there.

21. A: 갑자기 운동을 해서 그런지 온몸이 다 아픕니다.

   Maybe it's because I started exercising all of a sudden, but my whole body aches.

   B: 어제 좀 무리했습니까?

   Don't you think you overdid it yesterday just a little bit?

22. A: 남쪽에는 물난리가 났다는데요.

   Apparently there's a huge problem with flooding in the south.

   B: 어제하고 그제 비가 좀 왔습니까?

   Did you think that was just a passing shower we got yesterday and the day before?

5. *Because* with -길래

You have already seen this ending used in a pattern where it pairs up with a question word in Lesson Eight. However, in colloquial Korean this ending can also function like －기 때문에 to mean *because*. It usually attaches to a Plain Base mid-sentence and picks up any past or future tense reference from the verb at the end of the sentence.

23. A: 수미 만나고 왔어?

   Did you meet Sumi?

   B: 아니, 30분 기다려도 안 오길래 그냥 왔어.

   Nope. She didn't come so I just came back after thirty minutes.

24. A: 이렇게 맑은 날 웬 우산은 들고 다니니?

   Why are you carrying around an umbrella on such a clear day?

   B: 아침에 비가 올 것 같길래 가지고 나왔는데 비가 안 오네.

   It looked like it might rain in the morning, so I brought it with me, but there's no rain!

25. A: 영진이는 어디 갔어?

   Where did Yŏngjin go?

   B: 피곤해 보이길래 집에 가서 쉬라고 했어.

   She looked tired, so I told her to go home and rest.

26. A: 엄마, 아침에 먹던 생선 없어요?

   Mom, is there any leftover fish from what what we ate this morning?

   B: 좀 상한 것 같길래 버렸어.

   It looked like it had gone bad, so I threw it away.

27. A: 웬 음식을 이렇게 많이 해요?

   What are you making all this food for?

   B: 서울에서 진수 친구들이 온다길래 이것저것 만들어 봤어요. 한번 맛 좀 보세요.

   Chinsu said his friends were coming from Seoul, so I whipped up a bit of this and that. Here, try some.

28. A: 웬 아이들 수영복입니까?

   What's with the children's swimming suits?

   B: 아까 남대문 시장에 갔다가 싸길래 조카들 주려고 몇 벌 사 왔습니다.

   I was at Namdaemun Market just now and they were cheap, so I bought a few to give to my nieces and nephews.

6. Retrospectives with -더라고(요) (again)

In Lesson Seven, you learned how to use Plain and Intimate Style retrospectives -더라 with the general meaning of *I recall that...* or *I have vague personal evidence for the fact that...* (without wanting to commit oneself to a categorical factual statement). Technically speaking, there are separate retrospective forms for the Formal and Polite Styles: 합디다 and 하데요, respectively. But the endings -(스)ㅂ디다 and -데요 are not used all that much, as the former can sound presumptuous when used by somebody younger to somebody older, and the latter sometimes sounds too confusingly close to contracted quotations in -대(요). So, as a kind of gap-filler to come up with a Polite Style equivalent to -더라, Korean speakers have innovated a new form by quoting -더라 and rounding it off with the polite 요: -더라고요.

29. A: 수미한테 빌리지 왜 샀습니까?

   You should have borrowed one from Sumi—why'd you buy one?

   B: 빌려 달라고 얘기했는데 안 빌려 주더라고요. 그래서 그냥 샀습니다.

   I asked her to lend me one, but she wouldn't. So I just bought one.

30. A: 나는 독일어를 못하는데 토마스 씨하고 어떻게 얘기하지요?

   I can't speak German so how will I talk to Thomas?

   B: 걱정하지 마세요. 토마스 씨가 한국말을 아주 잘하더라고요.

   Don't worry. Thomas speaks Korean really well [as I recall].

31. A: 집들이 가는데 뭐 사 가지고 가는 게 좋을까?
    I'm going to a housewarming party; what should I buy?

    B: 세제나 화장지 사 가는 게 어때?
    요즘은 그런 거 많이 사 가지고 가더라고.
    How about taking some detergent or toilet paper?
    Lately that's what everybody seems to be buying [as I recall].

32. A: 술을 얼마나 준비하면 될까요?
    How much alcohol should I prepare?

    B: 맥주나 몇 병 준비해 둬요. 사람들이 별로 술을 안 마시더라고요.
    Stock up on a few bottles of beer. They don't drink much [as I recall].

33. A: 아니, 무릎이 왜 그래? 넘어졌어?
    Say, what's wrong with your knee? Did you fall down?

    B: 응, 며칠 전에 계단에서 넘어졌어. 갑자기 어지럽더라고.
    Yeah. I fell down the stairs a few days ago. I suddenly got dizzy [that's all I remember].

34. A: 우리 집 찾기 어려울 텐데 찾아올 수 있겠습니까?
    Our place is likely difficult to find; do you think you can find your way?

    B: 저는 길눈이 어둡지만 진아하고 같이 가니까 괜찮습니다.
    진아가 집을 잘 찾더라고요.
    I get lost pretty easily, but I'll be going with Jina, so it's OK.
    I remember she's good at finding places.

35. A: 시험 잘 봤어요?
    Did you do well on the test?

    B: 아니요, 잘 못 봤어요. 문제가 어렵더라고요.
    No, not at all. The questions were hard.

36. A: 어제 많이 피곤했지? 잘 잤니?
    You were really tired yesterday, weren't you? Did you sleep well?

    B: 응. 피로가 그렇게 많이 쌓이면 푹 자는 게 최고더라고.
    Yeah. When you get so tired like that, having a good sleep is the best.

7. *It was <u>so</u>... [let me tell you]* with WH–... (이)나... -다고(요)

This pattern takes the exclamatory pattern QUESTION WORD + ‐(이)나 (as in 얼마나, 몇 번이나, etc.) followed by a verb in interrogative form, and then quotes it for emphatic effect. In other words, if you start with a sentence like 한국말을 얼마나 잘 합니까! *My, how well he speaks Korean!*, with this pattern it becomes 한국말을 얼마나 잘 한다고요. *Let me tell you—boy does he speak Korean well!* or *I'm tellin' ya, he speaks Korean incredibly well!*

37. A: 진호가 그렇게 노래를 잘한다면서요?
    Is it true that Chinho is such a good singer?

    B: 네, 얼마나 잘한다고요.
    Yes, he's incredibly good.

    A: 나도 언제 들어 봐야겠네요.
    I'll have to listen to him once myself.

38. A: 민정이 성격 어때요? 친구들이 별로 안 좋아하는 것 같던데.
    What's Minjŏng's personality like? It seems her friends don't like her that much.

    B: 얼마나 못됐다고요. 언제나 자기밖에 몰라요.
    Oh my, she's so awful! All she cares about is herself.

39. A: 아까 대한극장 앞을 지나왔는데 사람들이 극장 앞에 줄을 쭉 서 있던데요. 그 영화가 그렇게 재미있어요?
    I was passing by the Taehan Cinema just now, and there was a long lineup in front of the theater. Is the film that good?

    B: 그럼요, 얼마나 재미있다고요.
    수미 씨도 가서 보세요.
    You bet—it's incredibly interesting.
    You should go see it, too, Sumi.

40. A: 뉴스 봤더니 경상도 쪽에는 비가 꽤 많이 온 것 같더라.
    I was watching the news and it looks like there is quite a bit of rain down in Kyŏngsang Province.

    B: 내가 지난주에 거기 있었잖아. 비가 얼마나 많이 왔다고. 떠내려가는 줄 알았다.
    I was down there last week, you know. You wouldn't believe how much rain there was. I thought I was going to be swept away.

41. A: 이 집에 웬 바퀴벌레가 이렇게 많니?
    What's with all the cockroaches in this place?

    B: 글쎄 말이야. 나도 몇 마리나 잡았다고.
    I know what you mean. I've killed a lot myself.

42. A: 그 책이 그렇게 재미있다면서요?
   Is it true that book is so interesting?

   B: 네, 나는 몇 번이나 읽었다고요.
   Yes—I've read it several times over.

EXERCISES

Exercise 1: Reading Comprehension

Write out answers to the following questions.

1. 누가 누구한테 전화했습니까?
2. 수미는 오늘 왜 속이 상했습니까?
3. 수미 친구는 보통 얼마나 늦게 옵니까?
4. 수미는 요즘 바쁩니까?
5. 수미는 전에도 친구한테 시간 좀 지켜 달라고 부탁했습니까?
6. 그 부탁이 효과가 있었습니까?
7. 수미 친구는 수미한테 왜 화를 냈습니까?
8. 수미는 왜 전화를 끊어야 된다고 말했습니까?

Exercise 2: Practice with -(으)ㄴ / -는 것 ~ 거 있지

Change the underlined forms into the pattern -(으)ㄴ / 는 것 ~ 거 있지. Then translate the sentences into English.

1. 나 어제 남대문 시장에 옷 사러 갔었다. 그런데 옷이 아주 <u>싸더라</u>.
2. 어제 영화 보러 갔다가 못 보고 그냥 왔어.
   표가 다 팔려서 <u>못 보고 왔어</u>.
3. 나 어제 야구 구경하러 갔다가 <u>비를 쫄딱 맞았어</u>.
4. 며칠 전에 길에서 우연히 희수 봤다.
   그런데 걔가 나를 못 본 척하고 <u>가더라</u>.
5. 아침에 일찍 일어나려고 하는데도 <u>잘 안 돼요</u>.
6. 그 집 음식 값이 <u>너무 비쌌어요</u>.
   계산하려고 값을 물어 보고 깜짝 놀랐어.

Exercise 3: Practice with 좀 . . . ?

Change the underlined phrases into rhetorical questions in 좀 …?. Then translate the dialogues into English.

1. A: 진수가 제일 먼저 왔다면서요?
    B: 네, 개가 부지런하잖아요.
       새벽부터 와서 짐 싸는 것부터 다 했어요.
2. A: 어디가 어딘지 하나도 모르겠습니다.
    B: 서울이 너무 많이 달라졌습니다.
3. A: 지난 번 노래방에 갔을 때 철민 씨가 그렇게 인기 있었다면서요?
    B: 노래를 아주 잘하잖아요.
4. A: 어릴 때 언니랑 나랑 참 많이 싸웠다, 그치?
    B: 그래, 참 많이 싸웠지.
5. A: 정민이 때문에 기분 나빠 죽겠어요. 말하고 싶지 않은데 계속 이것저것 묻는 거예요.
    B: 개가 원래 못됐잖아요.
6. A: 일요일 날 설악산에 갔다 왔더니 힘들어 죽겠습니다.
    B: 무척 멀잖아요. 그런데 당일치기로 갔다 왔습니까?

Exercise 4: Practice with -길래

Write responses using the ending – 길래 to express a reason.

6. A: 이렇게 맑은 날 웬 우산은 들고 다니니?
    B: _____.
7. A: 영진이는 어디 갔어?
    B: _____.
8. A: 어제 민주한테 연락했어?
    B: _____.
9. A: 왜 이렇게 먼 데다 집을 샀어요?
    B: _____.
10. A: 선민이랑 내일 만나기로 했어요?
    B: _____.
11. A: 소문 들었어요? 수미 씨랑 진수 씨랑 곧 결혼한대요.
    B: 정말 잘 됐네요. _____.

Exercise 5: Practice with -더라고(요)

Change the underlined forms into the pattern – 더라고 (요). Then translate the dialogues into English.

6. A: 수미한테 빌리지 왜 샀습니까?
    B: 빌려 달라고 얘기했는데 안 빌려 주었어요. 그래서 그냥 샀습니다.
7. A: 영민이가 우리가 준 선물 보고 기뻐했어요?

B: 네, 아주 좋아했어요. 그리고 몸에 딱 맞았어요.

8. A: 토마스 씨, 대학에서 공부하는 게 어때요? 말은 다 알아들어요?

    B: 아니요, 말이 빠르고 모르는 단어가 많아서 <u>못 알아듣겠어요</u>.

9. A: 친구 아기 돌이라는데 뭘 사 가지고 가면 좋을까요?

    B: 옷이나 장난감 같은 게 어때요? 내 친구들 보니까 그런 거 많이 <u>사 가지고 가던데요</u>.

10. A: 어머, 선주야. 너 그 옷 어디서 샀니? 참 예쁘다.

    B: 며칠 전에 요 앞 옷가게를 지나가는데 이게 밖에 <u>걸려 있었어</u>. 마음에 들어서 샀어.

11. A: 선영아, 너 기분 좋은 것 보니까 남편이랑 화해한 모양이구나.

    B: 응, 철민 씨가 잘못했다고 빌었어. 그래서 용서해 줬지, 뭐.

    A: 그래서 부부싸움은 칼로 물 <u>베기라니까</u>.

Exercise 6: Practice with WH– ...(이)나... -다고(요)

Complete the responses below by using the pattern WH– ...(이)나... – 다고(요).

1. A: 진호가 그렇게 웃긴다면서요?

    B: _____.

2. A: 민정이 성격 어때요? 친구들한테 인기가 많은 것 같던데.

    B: _____.

3. A: 그 책 그렇게 재미있어요?

    B: 그럼요, _____.

    수미 씨도 제가 빌려 드릴 테니 읽어 보세요.

4. A: 왜 철민 씨한테 연락 안 했니?

    B: 연락을 안 하긴. _____.

    그런데 할 때마다 없더라고.

5. A: 어제 못 주무셨어요? 왜 그렇게 자꾸 하품을 하세요?

    B: _____.

    그런데 이상하게 자꾸 하품이 나네.

6. A: 이 집에 웬 바퀴벌레가 이렇게 많니?

    B: 글쎄 말이야. _____.

도망을 쳐 보았자
근처에서 잡힐 것이 뻔했다

모두들 휴가를 떠나 도시는 텅 빈 듯했다. 푹푹 찌는 날씨에 도시 한가운데에 있으니 차라리 고생을 해도 도시를 떠나는 게 낫겠다고 생각한 모양이다.

특히 부자들이 많이 사는 평창동은 더 그랬다. 군데군데 가로등이 켜져 있을 뿐이었다. 그런데 어둠 속에서 한 여자가 나타나더니 재빠른 동작으로 어느 집으로 들어갔다.

그 여자는 곧바로 2층 서재로 올라가서 능숙한 솜씨로 그림을 떼어 냈다. 그리고 그 뒤에 있는 비밀 금고를 여는 순간 벨이 울리기 시작했다. 그 여자는 그 순간 너무나 당황했다. 아마 3분쯤 뒤면 경찰이 달려올 것이다. 도망을 쳐 보았자 근처에서 잡힐 것이 뻔했다.

예상했던 대로 몇 분 뒤 초인종이 울렸다. 벨소리가 점점 요란스러워졌다. 경찰이 막 현관문을 부수고 들어오려는 순간 머리에 목욕 캡을 쓰고 얼굴에는 마사지 크림을 잔뜩 바른 여자가 현관문을 열었다. 방금 목욕을 마친 듯했다. 당황한 것은 경찰들이었다.

"누가 와 주었으면 했는데 와 주셨군요. 갑자기 비상벨이 울려 당황했어요."

"아니, 아가씨는 누구십니까?"

"저는 이 집 주인의 조카예요. 며칠 동안 집을 봐 주러 왔어요. 빨리 들어와서 저 벨소리 좀 안 나게 해주세요."

경찰들은 들어와서 벨소리를 멈추게 하고 그 아가씨에게 친절하게 설명까지 해 주고 돌아갔다. 그리고 10분쯤 후, 아까 그 집의 조카라고 말했던 아가씨는 자기가 원했던 것을 가지고 그 집을 나왔다.

NEW VOCABULARY

Vocabulary from the Main Text

모두들	everybody
휴가 (休暇)	leave; holiday; break
휴가(를) 떠나 -	leave on one's holiday / vacation
도시 (都市)	city
도시 한가운데	*right (smack) in the middle of the city*
도시에 있느니 (차라리) 도시를 떠나는 게 낫겠다	*Rather than staying in the city, it would be better to leave the city.*
비 -	be empty, vacant, hollow (Always used with past tense: 비었어요. Note that this cannot contract to *볐어요 and is processive.)
텅 비었어요	*is totally empty*
빈 병	an empty bottle
찌 -	(weather) be steaming hot (NB: processive)
푹푹 찌 -	(weather) be brutally steaming hot
모양 (模樣)	appearance(s); shape; form
생각한 모양이다	*It seems they thought...; They seem to have thought...*
특 (特)히	especially; in particular
평창동	P'yŏngch'angdong (area in Seoul)
군데군데	here and there (in various places)
가로등 (街路燈)	streetlights
켜지 -	be / get turned on
어둠	darkness
나타나 -	show up; appear
재빠르 -	be skillful and fast, nimble, agile
동작 (動作)	movement (of parts of the body); motion; carriage; bearing; action; act
곧바로	directly; straightaway; right away
서재 (書齋)	a study
능숙 (能熟)하 -	be skillful, expert, adept
솜씨	(manual / domestic) skill, dexterity, knack
그림	picture
떼 -	remove; take away; subtract; take off; separate; get rid of
떼어내 -	take away, remove (and put away)
금고 (金庫)	safe, strongbox, coffer
순간 (瞬間)	moment; instant
금고를 여는 순간	*the instant she opened the safe*

벨	bell
울리 -	ring (intransitive); sound
당황(唐況)하 -	be flustered, at a loss
경찰(警察)	police; policeman
달려오 -	come running
도망(逃亡)(을)치 -	flee; run away; beat a retreat
근처(近處)	vicinity
근처에서 잡힐 것이 뻔했다	*It was clear / obvious she would be apprehended nearby.*
뻔하 -	be clear, obvious, plain to see
예상(豫想)(을)하 -	expect; foresee; anticipate
예상했던 대로	*as she had anticipated*
초인종(招人鐘)	doorbell; call bell; buzzer
점점(漸漸)	gradually; by degrees
요란(搖亂)스러w– (~스럽다)	be noisy, loud, clamorous, boisterous
막	just about to (with - (으)려고 하 -)
현관(玄關)	entrance hall, vestibule

현관문(~門)	door to the vestibule / entrance hall
부수 -	smash sth; break sth
목욕 캡	bathing cap
마사지 크림	massage cream
잔뜩	full; to the max; all the way
바르 -	apply, put on (makeup, ointment, etc.)
마치 -	finish sth
비상(非常)	emergency; contingency
비상벨	emergency bell, alarm
주인(主人)	owner; proprietor
조카	nephew; niece
친절(親切)하 -	be kind
멈추 -	sth stops; stop sth (functions as both transitive and intransitive)
자기(自己)	self; oneself
원(願)하 -	want; desire

Vocabulary from the Example Sentences

타자기(打字機)	typewriter
수상(殊常)하 -	be suspicious, doubtful-looking, "fishy"
불행(不幸)하 -	be unfortunate
불행(不幸)하게도	unfortunately
그만 갑시다	*Let's just go.*
들어 주 -	listen to (and acquiesce) a person's request for a favor; do sb the favor of listening

겨우	barely; scarcely
VERB는 것은 물론이고, ...까지 한다	*Not only does one VERB (it is a matter of course), but one even...*
손짓 [- 찟]	gesture with a hand or hands
발짓 [- 찟]	gesture with a foot or feet
사모님	one's teacher's wife; Madam, ma'am

Vocabulary from the Exercises

위기(危機)	crisis
모면(謀免)(을)하 -	shirk; evade; elude; escape
목적(目的)	goal, objective
목적을 달성(達成)하 -	achieve one's objective
동생한테 시키세요	*Have / make your younger sibling do it.*

여보!	*Honey!* (term of address between spouses)
이거 5만 원짜리라는데 어때?	*They say this costs 50,000 wŏn—what do you think?*
후덥(텁)지근하 -	be muggy, humid
얼굴(이)타 -	get a tanned face
정중(鄭重)하 -	be earnest, grave; be courteous, respectful

몸살(이) 나-	suffer from general fatigue and miseries (from overwork)		lacking alternatives; at the worst; at the least; at the extreme; finally; at last
지저분하-	be dirty, filthy	어린이날	Children's Day
하다못해	go so far as to; be driven by dire necessity to (do);	서울대공원(서울大公園)	Seoul Grand Park

PATTERNS

1. *Rather than... one ought to...; it would be best to...* with -느니 (차라리)... -겠-

The one-shape ending - 느니 attaches only to processive verbs, and the 차라리 is optional but strengthens or makes explicit the notion of *the option I am about to suggest is preferable*. This pattern should remind you of the pattern - 는 게 좋겠 - *It would be best to...* —another pattern that can also be preceded by the adverb 차라리. Notice that all of the second clauses in the examples below contain a verb form with the tentative - 겠 - :

1. 철민이랑 같이 가느니 차라리 혼자 가겠다.
   I would rather go alone than go with Ch'ŏlmin.

2. 영수에게 시키느니 차라리 내가 하겠다.
   I would rather do it myself than have Yŏngsu do it.

3. 그런 영화를 보느니 차라리 낮잠을 자겠다.
   I would rather take a nap than see a film like that.

4. 그런 사람하고 결혼하느니 차라리 혼자 살겠다.
   I would rather live alone than marry a person like that.

5. 오래 된 타자기를 가지고 있느니 차라리 버리는 게 낫지 않겠습니까?
   Wouldn't it be better to throw out rather than keep that old typewriter?

6. 앓느니 죽겠다.
   I'd rather die than be ill.

2. Modifiers with 모양: -(으)ㄴ / -는 / -(으)ㄹ 모양이-

When the noun 모양 *appearance* is used with a modifier preceding it and the copula after, it expresses the meaning *seem; appear*.

쉬는 모양이에요	*seems to be resting*
자는 모양이에요	*seems to be sleeping*

축구를 한 모양이에요	seems to have played soccer
숙제를 한 모양이에요	seems to have done [her] homework
소나기가 올 모양이에요	looks as if it will rain
바람이 불 모양이에요	looks as if the wind will blow
바람이 불 모양이었어요	looked as if the wind would blow

In this construction, both the modifier form and the copula can shift tense to express specific time meanings, as shown in the following:

PRESENT COPULA

- 는	[비가 오]는 모양이에요	it seems to be [rain]ing
- (으)ㄴ	[비가 오]ㄴ 모양이에요	it seems to have [rain]ed
	[좋]은 모양이에요	it seems [to be] [good]
- (으)ㄹ	[비가 오]ㄹ 모양이에요	it seems to be going to [rain]
	[날이 좋]을 모양이에요	it seems as if [the weather] will be [good]

PAST COPULA

- 는	[비가 오]는 모양이었어요	it seemed to be [rain]ing
- (으)ㄴ	[비가 오]ㄴ 모양이었어요	it seemed to have [rain]ed
	[좋]은 모양이었어요	it seemed [to be] [good]
- (으)ㄹ	[비가 오]ㄹ 모양이었어요	it seemed as if it would [rain]
	[날이 좋]을 모양이었어요	it seemed as if [the weather] would be [good]

FUTURE-PRESUMPTIVE COPULA (UNLIKELY TO OCCUR OFTEN)

- 는	[비가 오]는 모양이겠어요	it will seem to be [rain]ing or
		it must seem to be [rain]ing
- (으)ㄴ	[비가 오]ㄴ 모양이겠어요	it will seem to have [rain]ed or
		it must seem to have [rain]ed
	[좋]은 모양이겠어요	it will seem [to be] [good] or
		it must seem [to be] [good]
- (으)ㄹ	[비가 오]ㄹ 모양이겠어요	it will seem to be going to [rain] or
		it must seem to be going to [rain]
	[좋]을 모양이겠어요	it will seem to be going to be [good] or
		it must seem to be going to be [good]

Here are some more examples:

7.   A: 영준 씨, 진호 씨 요즘 어떻게 지냅니까?
       Yŏngjun, how is Chinho doing these days?

    B: 아르바이트 하느라고 바쁜 모양입니다.
       He seems busy working part-time jobs.

8.   A: 영재 씨하고 경미 씨 사이가 요즘 수상하지 않습니까?

        Doesn't the relationship between Yŏngjae and Kyŏngmi seem suspicious lately?

     B: 네, 요즘 자주 만나는 모양입니다.

        Yes, they seem to be meeting often these days.

9.   A: 영준 씨는 내일 산에 안 간답니까?

        Does Yŏngjun say he's not going to the mountains tomorrow?

     B: 네, 아쉽게도 안 갈 모양입니다.

        Yes—unfortunately it looks like he won't be going.

10. 교실에 미국 사람이 있는 모양이지요?

    It looks like there are some Americans in the classroom, doesn't it?

11. A: 선주가 요즘 우울해 보입니다.

       Sŏnju looks depressed lately.

    B: 남자 친구하고 헤어진 모양입니다.

       Seems she broke up with her boyfriend.

12. 박 선생님 사모님께서 내일 오실 모양이에요.

    It looks as if Mrs. Pak will get here tomorrow.

13. 여자는 나이가 아직 많지 않은 모양인데 아이가 셋이나 있대요.

    While she still seems young, they say she has three or so kids.

14. 돈이 없는 모양이라서 돈을 빌리지 못 했어요.

    He seemed to have no money, so we couldn't borrow any from him.

15. 학교에서 소풍을 가기로 한 것을 보니 내일 비가 오지 않을 모양입니다.

    Seeing that we decided to go on a school picnic, it seems there won't be any rain tomorrow.

16. A: 왜 아직까지 연락이 없지요?

       Why do you suppose she hasn't contacted us yet?

    B: 지금까지 전화가 없는 것을 보니 시험에 떨어진 모양입니다.

       Judging by the fact she still hasn't called, it seems she failed the exam.

17. 누님은 아직 결혼하고 싶지 않은 모양인지 지금도 일을 하고 계시지요.

    My older sister is now working, apparently not wanting to get married yet, you see.

18. 이것을 그것으로 바꾸지 못할 모양이야.

    It looks as though we won't be able to trade this for that.

3. *Even supposing one VERBs... [the outcome will be negative / all the same]* with -아 / -어 보았자

This is the Exploratory Pattern – 아 / – 어 보 – (*give it a try; do it and see what it's like / see what happens*) in the past tense, followed by – 자. It is not immediately obvious how this ending comes to get the meaning that it does, but you probably already know that the ending – 자 can mean *as soon as; when* (recall also – 자마자 *as soon as*), and that one extension of this function occurs with하 – in its meaning of *say* in the past tense ("BLAH-BLAH" (이)라고 했자 *once we say BLAH-BLAH / once one says that BLAH-BLAH*) which leads to *even supposing we say that*, etc. From the latter it is only a short hop, skip, and a jump to – 아 / – 어 봤자 *even supposing one does it (and sees what it's like)*.

19. 말을 안 들으니까 애기를 해 보았자 소용이 없습니다.
    He doesn't listen, so even if you try talking to him it's no use.

20. 더 기다려 보았자 안 올 것 같으니까 그만 갑시다.
    It looks like she won't come even if we wait longer, so let's just go.

21. 대학을 졸업해 봤자 취직하기도 힘듭니다.
    Even if you graduate from college, it's still difficult to get a job.

22. 영준 씨한테 부탁해 봤자 들어주지도 않을 겁니다.
    Even supposing you ask Yŏngjun to do it for you, he probably won't even listen.

23. 그런 사람을 도와줘 봤자 좋은 소리도 못 들을 겁니다.
    Even if you help out a person like that, you're unlikely ever to hear a nice word [in return].

24. 벌써 퇴근하셨을 겁니다. 지금 가 보았자 만나지도 못할 거니까 내일 가십시오.
    He must have gone home already. Even if you do go now, you won't be able to meet him, so go tomorrow.

4. *Would you mind... –ing [for me]? I [rather stiffly and formally]* request you to... for me with -았 / -었으면 하-

This pattern was introduced in *Continuing Korean*, Lesson 21, where it was introduced as 해 주셨으면 합니다 with the 해 주 – favor pattern. It is related to the similar pattern found in the following sentence:

25. 아침에 일찍 좀 깨워 주시면 고맙겠어요.
    I'd be grateful if you would wake me early in the morning.

In the pattern here, 합니다 means *wish* or the like, and the desired action is expressed as a Past Base, which helps make the request more tentative, and thus more stiff / formal, more polite:

26. 아침에 일찍 깨워 주셨으면 합니다.
    I should be grateful if you would wake me early in the morning.

Here are some more examples:

27. 바쁘지 않으시면 꼭 와 주셨으면 합니다.
    If you're not busy, I'd very much appreciate if you would be sure to come.

28. 저쪽에서 잠깐만 기다려 주셨으면 합니다.
    Would you mind waiting over there for a moment, please?

29. 오늘은 좀 일찍 나갔으면 합니다.
    I'd like you to leave a little early today, please.

30. 꼭 같이 갔으면 했는데 같이 못 가서 섭섭합니다.
    I was really wanting to go with you, so I feel sorry we can't go together.

31. 내일은 집에서 쉬었으면 합니다.
    I'd like to rest at home tomorrow.

32. 내일 아침 일찍 사무실로 전화 좀 해 주셨으면 한다고 전해주세요.
    Please tell him I would be grateful if he could call me tomorrow at the office.

5. *Even NOUN* with *NOUN*까지

This is simply an extension of the meaning you already know for this particle: *up to, as far as, including; even.*

33. 우리 저 아이 좀 도와줍시다.
    이제 겨우 12살인데 밥하고 빨래하는 것은 물론이고 밖에 나가서 돈 버는 일까지 한답니다.
    Let's help that girl out a bit.
    Not only does she prepare meals and do the laundry on her own, she even goes out and earns money.

34. 정민 씨, 일하면서 노래까지 하는 걸 보니 기분이 좋은가 봅니다.
    Chŏngmin, judging by the fact that you're even singing while working, you seem to be in a good mood.

35. 수미 씨까지 가 버리면 저 혼자 어떻게 합니까?
    If even you take off, Sumi, how am I going to manage on my own?

36. 정호 씨네 집은 아주 커서 집에 수영장까지 있다.
    Chŏngho's place is so huge they even have a swimming pool.

37. 말이 통하지 않아서 손짓 발짓까지 했지만 소용이 없었다.
    We couldn't communicate, we even gestured with our hands and feet, but it was no use.

38. 며칠 전에 지리산에 갔었는데 산 아래 계곡은 물론이고 산 꼭대기까지 쓰레기가 가득했다.

    I went to Mount Chiri a few days ago, and the place was full of garbage; in the valley at the bottom of the mountain to be sure, but [also] right up to the summit.

Note that numbers 33 and 38 above are concealing another useful sub-pattern:

...은 물론이고... 까지 한다.

Not only does one do the one thing [i.e., one's doing the one thing is a matter of course], but they even...

EXERCISES

Exercise 1: Reading Comprehension

Write out answers to the following questions.

1. 서울이 왜 텅 비었습니까?
2. 사람들은 여름에 밖에 나가는 것과 집에서 쉬는 것 중에 어느 것을 더 좋아합니까?
3. 젊은 여자는 그 집에 왜 들어갔습니까?
4. 언제 비상벨이 울리기 시작했습니까?
5. 그 여자는 비상벨 소리를 듣고 어떻게 했습니까?
6. 왜 도망가지 않았습니까?
7. 비상벨 소리를 들은 경찰은 어떻게 했습니까?
8. 그 여자는 그 위기를 어떻게 모면했습니까?
9. 결국 그 여자는 그 집에 들어간 목적을 달성했습니까?

Exercise 2: Using ...-느니 (차라리) ...-겠-

Use the pattern ... - 느니 (차라리) ... - 겠 - to complete the responses below.

1. A: 혼자 가지 말고 철민이랑 같이 가세요.
   B: _____.
2. A: 수미 씨, 몸도 안 좋은데 직접 하지 말고 동생한테 시키세요.
   B: _____.
3. A: 여보, 날씨도 좋은데 이렇게 집에만 있을 거예요?
   B: _____.
4. A: 미선아, 준영 씨 어때?
   B: _____.
5. A: 이 옷이 5만 원짜리라는데 어때?
   B: 5만 원 주고 이걸 _____.

6. A: 생일파티를 집에서 할 생각이에요?

 B: 집에서 하면 준비할 게 많으니까 _____.

Exercise 3: Practice with -(으)ㄴ / -는 / -(으)ㄹ 모양이-

Use the seem pattern − (으)ㄴ / − 는 / − (으)ㄹ 모양이 − to complete the responses below.

1. A: 영준 씨, 진호 씨 요즘 어떻게 지냅니까?

 B: _____.

2. A: 승미가 요즘 우울해 보입니다. 무슨 일 있습니까?

 B: _____.

3. A: 날씨가 후텁지근하지요?

 B: _____.

4. A: 정민이 아직도 잡니까?

 B: _____.

5. A: 앨버트 씨는 방학에 뭘 했길래 얼굴이 그렇게 탔답니까?

 B: _____.

6. A: 세준 씨한테 요즘 좋은 일이 있나 봅니다. 매일 싱글벙글 하고 다닙니다.

 B: _____.

Exercise 4: Practice with -아 / -어 봤자

Use the pattern − 아 / − 어 봤자 to complete the responses below.

1. A: 이 선생님 지금 댁에 계시는지 전화 좀 해 봐야겠습니다.

 B: _____.

2. A: 왜 대학에 가지 않고 취직했습니까?

 B: _____.

3. A: 동창회 가지 않고 왜 일찍 들어왔습니까?

 B: _____.

4. A: 커피 한 잔 마실까요?

 B: _____.

5. A: 연우 씨한테 부탁해 보면 어떨까요?

 B: _____.

6. A: 지금 출발하면 결혼식이 끝나기 전에 도착할 수 있지 않을까요?

 B: _____.

Exercise 5: Practice with -았 / -었으면 하-

Use the pattern − 았 / − 었으면 합니다 to change the direct commands in − (으)십시오 into indirect requests or wishes.

1. 다음 주 일요일에 결혼을 합니다. 바빠도 꼭 와 주십시오.
2. 일이 다 끝나 가니까 저쪽에서 잠깐만 기다려 주십시오.

3. 돈 좀 빌려 주십시오.
4. 여보세요, 과장님이십니까?
   저 이영진인데요, 몸살이 나서 오늘 집에서 쉬고 싶습니다.
5. 작년 휴가 때는 바다로 갔으니까 이번에는 산으로 가는 게 좋겠습니다.
6. 들어오는 대로 저희 집에 전화 좀 해 달라고 전해 주십시오.

Exercise 6: Practice with NOUN까지

Use an appropriate phrase with 까지 to complete the following.

1. 수미 씨는 오늘 기분이 좋은 모양입니다.
   일하면서 ______________________________.
2. 영호야, 넌 좀 더 도와주고 가. ______________________________.
3. 그 식당은 너무 지저분해서 가기 싫습니다.
   가끔 밥에서 ______________________________.
4. 진우네 집에는 외국 물건이 참 많습니다.
   하다못해 ______________________________.
5. 어린이날에 서울대공원에 갔는데 주차장이 꽉 차서 ______________
   ______________________________.
6. 수미가 너무 슬프게 우는 거 있지.
   그래서 ______________________________.

설마 곰이 사람이 됐을까

"아빠, 우리나라는 언제부터 있었어요? 누가 만들었어요?"

이제 막 여섯 살이 된 딸아이가 궁금한 게 많은지 나를 자꾸 귀찮게 했다. 그래서 나는 단군신화를 알아듣기 쉽게 설명해 주었다.

"지금부터 아빠가 이야기해 줄 테니까 잘 들어. 옛날 옛날 호랑이가 담배 피우던 시절에 있었던 이야기야. 하늘에 환인이라고 하는 하느님이 살고 계셨거든. 그분에게는 환웅이라는 아들이 있었는데 환웅은 인간 세계에 내려와서 살고 싶어 했어. 그래서 아버지한테 땅에 내려가서 살게 해 달라고 부탁했어. 그랬더니 아버지는 바람, 비, 구름을 다스리는 신하와 3,000명의 사람들을 주면서 내려가 살라고 했어.

환웅이 태백산에 내려와서 살고 있는데 어느 날 곰하고 호랑이가 찾아와서 사람이 되고 싶다고 말하는 거야. 그래서 환웅은 쑥하고 마늘을 먹으면서 100일 동안 햇빛을 보지 않으면 사람이 될 수 있다고 했어. 그랬더니 곰하고 호랑이는 마늘하고 쑥 한 다발씩을 가지고 동굴 속으로 들어갔어. 그런데 곰은 끝까지 참아 냈지만 호랑이는 참지 못하고 며칠 만에 동굴에서 뛰쳐나왔어."

"곰은 미련하고 둔하니까 잘 참았나 봐요."

"아무튼 100일이 지났을 때 곰은 아주 예쁜 여자가 되었어. 그리고 환웅하고 결혼을 했어. 그래서 낳은 자식이 우리의 조상인 단군 할아버지야. 단군 할아버지는 커서 고조선이라고 하는 나라를 세웠는데 그게 지금부터 5,000년 전의 일이란다."

"에이, 설마 곰이 사람이 됐을까? 그리고 또 이상한 게 있어요. 지금 우리나라 사람들은 호랑이를 아주 좋아하잖아요. 그런데 왜 우리 조상이 호랑이가 아니라 곰이에요? 호랑이면 더 좋을 텐데,"

"글쎄, 왜 그랬을까? 그건 아빠도 잘 모르겠는데?"

NEW VOCABULARY

Vocabulary from the Main Text

궁금한 게 많은지	*Perhaps because there were many things she was curious about...*	곰	bear
		쑥	mugwort
나를 자꾸 귀찮게 했다	*She kept pestering me / being a nuisance to me.*	마늘	garlic
		햇빛 ← 해 + 빛	sunlight
단군 (檀君)	Tan'gun, mythical founder of the Korean race	다발	bundle, bunch, sheaf
		동굴 (洞窟)	cave; cavern
신화 (神話)	myth	며칠 만에	after a few days, within a few days
알아듣기 쉽게	*in such a way that it was easy to understand*	뛰쳐나오 -	come running out
		미련하 -	be clumsy, awkward, foolish, stupid
호랑이	tiger		
시절 (時節)	time; era; occasion (cf. 청년 시절에, 젊은 시절에 *in one's youth, while young*)	둔 (鈍) 하 -	be thickheaded, dull, slow-witted, dense, "thick"
		아무튼	anyway; anyhow
하느님 ← 하늘 + 님	god; God	자식 (子息)	children; sons and daughters
환인이라고 하는 하느님이 살고 계셨거든	*There lived a god named Hwanin, see?*	고조선 (古朝鮮)	Ancient Chosŏn
		세우 -	set up, establish
인간 (人間)	human being	설마 곰이 사람이 됐을까?	*Surely the bear didn't become / couldn't have become a human?*
다스리 -	rule over; reign over; govern; manage; administer		
신하 (臣下)	minister; statesman; subject	조상 (祖上)	ancestor(s)
태백산 (太白山)	Mount T'aebaek		

Vocabulary from the Example Sentences

진로(進路)	course (to advance); the way ahead; one's path in life
상담(相談)	counseling; advising
진로상담(進路相談)	career advising
상담비(相談費)	counseling fees; advising fees
상담소(相談所)	counseling agency; counseling office
학생생활(學生生活)	student life
역(役)	(dramatic) role
로미오 역(役)	the role of Romeo
염려(念慮)(를) 하 -	worry; be concerned
번역(飜譯)	translation
번역(을) 하 -	translate
통역(通譯)	interpretation
동시통역(同時通譯)	simultaneous interpretation
군대(軍隊)	army; armed forces
수면제(睡眠劑)	sleeping pill (cf. also 소화 (消化), 소화제 *digestion, digestive medicine*)
복용(服用)(을) 하 -	take / ingest (medicine)
운전면허(運轉免許)	driver's license
금방 땄지요?	*You got it right away, right?*
범인(犯人)	criminal; culprit
자신(自信)	confidence
자신감(自信感)	(feeling of) confidence
자신감을 가지고	confidently; with confidence
도전(挑戰)(을) 하 -	challenge; make a challenge; defy
작품(作品)	work, opus, production (of art, literature, etc.)
완성(完成)(을) 하 -	complete sth
이기 -	win over; overcome; beat
갚 -	pay back; repay; settle one's account; give (sth) in return
탈	trouble; a hitch; a problem
... - 아 / - 어서 탈이 -	be... so it's a problem
순진(純眞)하 -	be naive, genuine, pure
잠실	Chamsil (place name in Seoul)
올림픽이 열렸어요	*The Olympics were held ("opened").*
중학교(中學校)	middle school
깨 -	break sth
일부러	on purpose, deliberately, intentionally
작가(作家)	author; creative writer
낙천적(樂天的)	optimistic
천생(天生)	by nature (adv.)
그는 천생 학자다.	*He is a scholar by nature (a born scholar).*
자살(自殺)(을) 하 -	commit suicide

Vocabulary from the Exercises

사랑니	wisdom tooth
빼 -	pull out; take out; extract; leave out; omit
사랑니 빼는 데 시간 많이 걸립니까?	*Does it take a long time to pull a wisdom tooth?*
딸기	strawberry
산딸기	wild strawberry (cf. 돼지, 산돼지 *pig; wild boar*); wild raspberry (산딸기 is actually a kind of raspberry)
관객(觀客)	spectator(s); onlooker(s); the audience; viewer(s)
상영(上映)(을) 하 -	show (a film); project; screen
방이 어찌나 더러운지...	*The room was so dirty, that...*
뭔가	something (or other)
의지(意志)	will; volition; intention
살겠다는 의지	*the will to live*
구두쇠	miser; tightwad; pinch-penny
불우(不遇)	misfortune; bad luck; bad fortune (*as modifier*: unfortunate, less fortunate) (*here*: "unfortunate neighbors")

성금(誠金)	donation, contribution	구멍	hole
상대방(相對方)	one's opposite, counter-part; opponent; adversary	뚫리 -	be / get pierced, drilled, bored, penetrated
부드러w– (부드럽다)	be soft	구멍이 뚫린 것	sth with a hole ("bored") in it
삼촌(三寸)	uncle (on the father's side) ("uncle on the mother's side" is 외삼촌)	대드 - ㄹ - (대들다)	defy; turn against; stand up to; go at; attack; tackle
전기(電氣)	electricity; electric (as modifier)	혹시(나)…?	Do/does sth/sb per-chance/possibly…?
전기(電氣) 다리미	electric iron	다음 기회가 있으니까	("Since") there is always next time...
동그랗 - (동그래, 동그란)	be round, circular, spherical		

PATTERNS

1. *Since it is the expectation / intention that...* with -(으)ㄹ 테니(까) (again)

This is a combination of two patterns. The first is - (으)ㄹ 테(이) - where the postmodifier 테 means *intention; expectation*. You saw this in Lesson Two of this book. The second is the Sequential - (으)니(까) in its meaning of *since; as; because*, etc. This pattern tends to occur mostly in the first person (*I, we*) and sets up a following command, request, or suggestion. The combined effect of this pattern is *Since I / we intend to do something...* [*followed by a command, request, or suggestion*].

1. 진로상담비는 내가 낼 테니까 학생생활상담소 한 번 다녀 봐라.
   I'll pay the career counseling fee, so why don't you try going to the student life counseling center once.

2. 일이 끝나는 대로 내려갈 테니 지하 커피숍에서 기다려 주십시오.
   I'm planning on going down as soon as work finishes, so please wait for me in the coffee shop in the basement.

3. 내가 로미오 역을 할 테니 수미 씨는 줄리엣 역을 하십시오.
   I'm going to play the role of Romeo, so Sumi, you play Juliet.

4. 저녁 6시쯤 갈 테니 저녁 준비 좀 해 주십시오.
   I'm going to leave around 6:00 PM, so please prepare supper.

5. 제가 다시 한 번 부탁해 볼 테니 너무 염려하지 마십시오.
   I'm going to try asking him again, so please don't worry too much.

6. 진호 씨 생일 선물로 제가 지갑을 살 테니 수미 씨는 다른 걸 사십시오.
   I'm going to buy a wallet for Chinho's birthday present, so Sumi, you buy something else.

2. *[Did it] in the space of...; after an interval of...; within* with Time Expression + 만에

The particle sequence 만에 after a time expression means *[finally] after [the interval]; only after / within*, and you will probably recognize it in the stock phrase 오래간만에 뵙겠습니다 *Long time no see* (but literally: *I am seeing you for the first time after a long interval*). The time interval preceding 만에 can be a simple noun (두 달 만에 *in / within two months*) or a *time-since* pattern in -(으)ㄴ 지 (떠난 지 사흘 만에 *within three days of leaving*). Here are some more examples.

7.　A:　번역하는 데 오래 걸렸습니까?
　　　　Did it take a long time to do the translation?

　　B:　아니요, 하루 만에 다 했습니다.
　　　　No, I finished it within a day.

8.　A:　성진이 어머니, 뭐가 그렇게 좋으세요?
　　　　Say, Sŏngjin's mother—what are you so happy about?

　　B:　우리 아들놈이 군대에 간 지 두 달 만에 편지를 보냈어.
　　　　Our son sent a letter for the first time since entering the army two months ago.

9.　A:　종호한테는 책이 수면제야.
　　　　Books are sleeping pills for Chongho.

　　B:　책을 읽기 시작한 지 5분 만에 잠들었어.
　　　　He fell asleep within five minutes of starting to read the book.

10.　A:　결혼하기 전에 오랫동안 사귀었습니까?
　　　　Did you date each other for a long time before marrying?

　　B:　아니요, 만난 지 삼개 월 만에 결혼했습니다.
　　　　No. We got married within three months of meeting each other.

11.　A:　선생님, 아이가 학교에 간 지 2시간 만에 집에 돌아왔는데 학교에서 무슨 일이 있었습니까?
　　　　[to the teacher] Our child came back home today only two hours after leaving; was there some problem at school?

　　B:　아닙니다. 오늘 학교에 일이 있어서 수업이 일찍 끝났습니다.
　　　　No. Today there was something going on at school so classes finished early.

12.　A:　성진 씨, 속상해요. 운전면허 시험에 또 떨어졌어요.성진 씨는 금방 땄지요?
　　　　Sŏngjin, I'm upset. I failed my driver's license test again. You passed it right away, didn't you?

　　B:　아니요, 저도 두 번 떨어지고 세 번 만에 땄습니다.
　　　　No. I, too, failed twice before passing the third time.

3. **Does it all the way [to the end / thoroughly / through and through]** with -아 /
-어 내-

As an independent verb, the verb 내 - has the basic meanings *bring out; produce; put forth;* but as an auxiliary verb in combination with the infinitive - 아 / - 어, it means *does all the way [to the very end / thoroughly / through and through],* and adds a note of once-and-for-all finality and accomplishment to the expression. Notice that some of the example sentences combine this pattern with the pattern - 고 말겠 -,
which has the similar and compatible meaning of *will do it without fail; will do it come hell or high water;* etc.

13. 힘든 일들을 잘 참아 내 주셔서 대단히 고맙습니다.
    Thanks so much for enduring so well through these difficult matters.

14. 제가 범인을 꼭 잡아 내고 말겠습니다.
    I am determined to catch the culprit once and for all.

15. 영준 씨, 해낼 수 있다는 자신감을 가지고 도전해 보십시오.
    Yŏngjun, pluck up your courage to do it and give it your best shot.

16. 이번 주말까지 이 작품을 다 완성해 내야 합니다.
    I have to finish off this work by this weekend.

17. 가난을 이겨내고 열심히 공부해서 좋은 대학에 합격했습니다.
    Having overcome poverty and studied hard, [she] entered a good university.

18. 그 사람이 돈을 갚지 않겠다고 해도 제가 꼭 받아 내고 말겠습니다.
    Even if he says he won't pay me the money back, I am determined to get it back.

4. **Let me tell ya; They say...** with -(ㄴ / 는)단다, -(이)란다

In origin, this pattern is an abbreviated / contracted quotation in the Plain Style from - (ㄴ / 는)다고
한다, - 다고 한다, - (이)라고 한다. However, as the example sentences below demonstrate, this
contracted form is used for a soft, caring explanation. The tone is slightly avuncular (when used by an adult
to a child), and sometimes a bit boastful or bragging. Thus, the original quotative sense has been attenuated,
and instead we have an ending that implies: *I hereby put you on notice that...; I'm telling you [in a somewhat
lively way] that...* Note the implied contexts of the example sentences:

19. A: 너는 아이들을 가르치니까 더 잘 알겠지만, 요즘 애들은 너무 아는 게 많아서
       탈이야.
       *You probably know better, since you teach children, but kids nowadays know too much that it's a
       problem.*

    B: 다 그런 건 아니야. 순진한 애들도 많단다.
       They're not all like that. There are plenty of innocent kids, too, I can say.

20. A: 이 아파트 언제 지은 거예요?

        When was this apartment block built?

    B: 한 칠팔 년 되었을 거야. 그 전에는 아무것도 없었단다.

        It must be around seven or eight years now. Before that there was nothing here [let me tell ya—I remember].

21. A: 여기가 잠실 운동장이에요?

        Is this the Chamsil Stadium?

    B: 그래, 20년 전에 여기서 올림픽이 열렸단다.

        Yes, twenty years ago the Olympics were held here, you know.

22. A: 아빠가 다닌 중학교는 아빠네 동네에서 멀었지요?

        Daddy, was the middle school you attended far from home?

    B: 응, 한 시간 이상을 걸어다녔단다.

        Yeah, so I walked more than an hour every day to school, you know.

23. A: 아빠, "사시" 라는 말이 무슨 뜻이에요?

        Daddy, what does the word "사시" mean?

    B: 사시라고 하는 것은 춘하추동이라는 사계절이란다. 그러니까 봄, 여름, 가을, 겨울이지.

        "사시" is the four seasons of "춘하추동." In other words, it's spring, summer, fall, winter.

24. A: 이 사진에서 아버지 옆에 계신 분은 누구세요?

        Who's that next to dad in this photo?

    B: 아버지 사촌이란다.

        That's dad's cousin, see?

5. *Surely... not...? Surely... wouldn't?* with 설마

The adverb 설마 sets up a (negative) rhetorical question: *Surely it isn't / wouldn't be the case that...?* The tone is incredulous, and while the English equivalents for this pattern have to take a negative, the Korean is almost always an affirmative rhetorical question that can optionally take a negative marker with no change in meaning.

25. A: 영진 씨가 오늘도 늦게 오지 않을까요?

        You don't suppose Yŏngjin will come late today, too?

    B: 설마 자기 결혼식 날 늦겠습니까?

        Surely she wouldn't be late on her own wedding day?

26. A: 준섭 씨가 경선이 안경을 깼답니다.

        They say Chunsŏp broke Kyŏngsŏn's glasses.

    B: 설마 일부러 그렇게 했겠습니까?

        Surely he wouldn't have done it on purpose?

27. A: 영호가 왜 이렇게 늦지요? 무슨 일이 생겼을까요?
    Why do you suppose Yŏngho is so late? Do you suppose something might have happened?

    B: 설마 무슨 일이 생겼겠습니까? 걱정하지 말고 기다리십시오.
    Surely nothing could have happened. Just wait, and don't worry.

28. A: 준호 씨가 어제 모임에 안 갔다 온 것 같습니다.
    It seems Chunho didn't go to yesterday's meeting.

    B: 설마 안 갔다 왔으면서 갔다 왔다고 했을까요?
    Surely he wouldn't have said he went, even when he hadn't?

29. 설마 설마 했는데 결국 이런 일이 생기고 말았네요.
    I said to myself "surely not, surely not," but in the end, this sort of thing has happened.

30. 설마 국어사전 한 권도 없이 번역 작가의 길에 들어서려고 하는 건 아니시겠죠?
    Surely you do not intend to embark on the path of the creative translator without so much as one Korean-Korean dictionary?

31. 설마 그렇게 천생 낙천적인 사람이 자살을 했을까?
    Surely such an innately optimistic person wouldn't have committed suicide?

32. 설마가 사람 잡는다.
    [Saying / Proverb] *"Surely not" kills people.*

EXERCISES

Exercise 1: Reading Comprehension

Write out answers to the following questions.

1. 나는 왜 아이에게 단군 신화를 이야기해 주었습니까?
2. 나는 "아주 오래 전에"를 어떻게 표현했습니까?
3. 환웅은 왜 태백산에 내려왔습니까?
4. 누구와 내려왔습니까?
5. 곰하고 호랑이는 왜 환웅을 찾아왔습니까?
6. 환웅은 곰하고 호랑이한테 뭐라고 말했습니까?
7. 곰하고 호랑이는 끝까지 잘 참았습니까?
8. 환웅은 누구하고 결혼했습니까?
9. 단군 할아버지는 누구입니까?
10. 딸아이는 내 애기를 듣고 어떤 반응을 보였습니까?

11. 여러분 나라에도 건국신화가 있습니까?

있으면 친구들에게 이야기해 보십시오.

Exercise 2: Practice with -(으)ㄹ 테니(까)

Complete the following sentences and translate the results into English.

1. 이 일은 내가 할 테니까 _____.
2. 제가 집을 볼 테니까 _____.
3. 우리가 먼저 가서 기다릴 테니 _____.
4. 일이 끝나는 대로 _____.
5. 청소는 내가 _____.
6. 내가 돈을 _____.

Exercise 3: Practice with 만에

Use an appropriate phrase with 만에 to complete the "B" responses.

1. A: 사랑니 빼는 데 시간이 많이 걸립니까?
   B: 아니요, _____.
2. A: 세진 씨, <산딸기> 영화 보러 갑시다.
   B: 그 영화 지금 안 합니다.
      관객이 없어서 상영한 지 _____.
3. A: 청소하느라고 힘들었지요?
   B: 네, 방이 어찌나 더러운지 _____.
4. A: 진경 씨, 오래간만입니다.
   B: 우리가 _____.
5. A: 진경 씨는 면허 시험에 한 번도 안 떨어졌습니까?
   B: 아니요, _____.
6. A: 병원에 입원해 있었다고 들었습니다. 오래 계셨습니까?
   B: 아니요, _____.

Exercise 4: Practice with -(ㄴ / 는)단다, -(이)란다

Use the pattern - (ㄴ / 는) 단다, - (이) 란다 to write friendly and caring explanatory replies.

1. A: 저쪽에서 삼촌하고 얘기하시는 분 누구세요?
   B: _____.
2. A: 할머니, 학교가 집에서 먼데도 버스나 지하철에 없을 때에는 어떻게 학교에 다녔어요?
   B: _____.
3. A: 아저씨, 여기가 잠실 운동장이에요?
   B: _____.

4. A: 아버지, 저기 있는 게 뭡니까?

    B: 동그랗고 가운데 구멍이 뚫린 것 말이지?

    _____.

5. A: 선생님, 10년 전에도 서울에 사람이 이렇게 많았습니까?

    B: _____.

6. A: 할아버지는 어릴 때 무엇을 하면서 친구들과 노셨습니까?

    B: _____.

Exercise 5: Practice with -아 / -어 내-

Use an appropriate phrase with - 아 / - 어 내 - to complete the sentences.

1. 힘든 일들을 잘 _____ 대단히 고맙습니다.
2. 제가 범인을 꼭 _____.
3. 아무도 도와주지 않아도 꼭 _____.
4. 뭔가 우리에게 숨기는 것이 있는 것 같습니다.
    그게 뭔지 제가 꼭 _____.
5. 꼭 합격하겠다는 마음으로 시험을_____.
6. 그 구두쇠한테서 불우 이웃 돕기 성금을 꼭 _____.

Exercise 6: Practice with 설마

Use appropriate phrases or sentences with the special adverb 설마 to complete the following.

1. A: 영진 씨가 오늘도 늦게 오지 않을까요?

    B: _____?

2. A: 진영이가 어제 최 선생님한테 막 대든 거 있지요.

    B: _____?

3. A: 영호가 왜 이렇게 늦지요?

    혹시 무슨 일이 생긴 게 아닐까요?

    B: _____?

    걱정하지 말고 기다리십시오.

4. A: 김 선생님이 왜 안 오시지요? 지각하는 분이 아닌데.

    B: _____?

    아무튼 조금만 더 기다려 봅시다.

5. A: _____ 결국 떨어지고 말았어요.

    B: 다음 기회가 있으니까 너무 걱정하지 마십시오.

6. A: 친구들이 1시까지 오기로 했는데 왜 안 오지요?

    B: _____?

외출하기가 겁납니다

병원에 있다 보면 별별 환자들이 다 찾아온다.

서너 달 전에는 어떤 여자가 찾아와서 이런 이야기를 했다.

"살이 쪄서 고민인데 어떻게 살을 빼는 방법이 없을까요?"

그래서 나는 농담 삼아,

"살을 빼는 비결 같은 것은 원래 없는걸요."

그런데 여자는 살이 쪄서 입고 싶은 옷도 마음대로 입을 수 없고 나이도 더 들어 보인다며 남편이랑 같이 외출하기도 겁이 난다고 계속 불평을 했다.

나는 알고 있는 방법을 이것저것 말해 주었다. 그렇지만 그 여자는 다른 방법은 없느냐고 물었다. 내가 말한 방법은 벌써 써 보았지만 하나 마나였다는 것이었다.

나는 또 농담처럼 전에 어디선가 읽은 적이 있는 우스갯소리를 했다. 냉장고 안에 수영복을 입고 있는 날씬한 여자의 사진을 붙여 놓아 살을 빼는 방법이었다. 냉장고 문을 열 때마다 그 사진을 보게 될 것이고, 그 사진을 보면 먹고 싶은 것을 참게 될 거라는 이야기였다.

그 환자가 돌아가고 나서 나는 그 일을 까마득하게 잊었다. 그런데 오늘, 환자도 없고 해서 점심이나 먹으러 가야겠다고 생각하고 막 진찰실을 나가려는데 날씬한 아가씨 하나가 들어왔다.

"저를 기억하시겠어요?"

"누구시더라. 죄송합니다, 기억이 안 나는데요."

"지난번에 살 빼는 방법을 물으러 왔던 사람이에요."

그 말을 듣고 보니 생각이 났다. 그 여자는 정말 몰라볼 정도로 날씬해져 있었다.

"선생님, 그 방법은 정말 효과가 있었어요. 어때요, 놀라셨지요?"

내가 감탄을 하며 신기해하니까 그 여자는 새로 생긴 고민을 이야기했다.

"남편 몸무게가 10kg이나 늘었는데 어떻게 뺄 방법이 없을까요?"

NEW VOCABULARY

Vocabulary from the Main Text

별별 NOUN	all kinds of NOUN, all sorts of NOUN (implying that some of them are strange)
환자 (患者)	patient; sick person
찾아오 -	come calling; pay a visit to
서너	three or four; a few
살 (이) 찌 -	get fat
고민 (苦悶)	worry; sth that vexes you
살 (을) 빼 -	lose weight
방법 (方法)	a method, way, means
농담 (弄談)	joke
농담 삼아	as a joke; jokingly
- (으)ㄴ걸요, - 는걸요, - (으)ㄹ걸요	*contrary to what you might think or expect* (see Pattern 6 below)
비결 (秘訣)	a secret (way to do sth), "trick"
원래 (元來)	originally; to start with; actually
마음대로	as one pleases; as one likes (*lit.:* "in accordance with one's mind")
나이 (가) 드 - ㄹ - (들다)	be old (*lit.:* "age enters"), e.g., 나이 들었어요. *Is old.*
외출 (外出) (을) 하 -	go out
겁 (怯)	fear
겁 (이) 나 -	be afraid (NB: processive)
어디선가	somewhere or other
우스갯소리	joke; anecdote; funny story (cf. 웃다)
냉장고	fridge
수영복 (水泳服)	swimming suit
날씬하 -	be slim
붙이 -	stick sth to; make sth stick to
참 -	bear; suffer; put up with
까마득하게 잊 -	forget sth completely
기억 (記憶)	memory
(NOUN의) 기억 (이) 나 -	remember (sth)

기억력(記憶力)	one's (power of) memory	알아보 -	recognize sb
기억력(이) 좋 -	have a good memory	효과(效果) [- 꽈]	effect
환자도 없고 해서	*because there were no patients or anything* (- 고 해서, - 고 그래서)	놀라 -	be surprised, startled (NB: processive)
막 ... - 는데	*just as I was about to; just as I was in the process of...*	감탄(感歎)(을) 하 -	exclaim; express one's surprise
진찰실(診察室)	examining room	신기(神奇)하 -	be strange, amazing, wondrous
(NOUN의) 생각(이) 나 -	think of (sth); recall (sth)	무게	weight
몰라보 -	not recognize sb	몸무게	one's body weight

Vocabulary from the Example Sentences

뜻	meaning	신경(神經)(을) 쓰 -	worry about; be concerned about
전시회(展示會)	exhibition; show	시집(을) 가 -	(woman) get married
오래	for a long time	형편(形便)	circumstances, situation (often in a personal sense)
병원(病院)	hospital		
20세기(世紀) 초(初)	beginning of the twentieth century	생기 -	come about; appear
개원(開院)	open a hospital (or anything ending in - 원 [院])	상(床)(을) 차리 -	set the table
		봉투(封套)	envelope
		60세(歲)	sixty years of age
이래(以來)	ever since	넘 -	exceed; go over
개원(開院)한 이래	ever since opening (the hospital)	염색(染色)(을) 하 -	dye
		친절운동(親切運動)	kindness movement
세계적(世界的)으로 유명(有名)하 -	be world famous	노인(老人)	elderly person; senior citizen
폐원(閉院)(을) 하 -	close a hospital (or anything ending in - 원)	문제(問題)	problem
		등(等)	etc.; and the like
위기(危機)에 처(處) 하 -	face a crisis	당면(當面)하 -	to face; be pressing / imminent
상의(相議)(를) 하 -	consult with	사회(社會)	society
만나 뵈 - ~ 만나 뵙 -	(humbly) meet sb esteemed. Use 뵈 - before vowel endings and 뵙 - before consonant endings. (Once upon a time this was just 뵈w– but younger speakers have altered the usage.)	한꺼번에	in one fell swoop; all at once
		해결(解決)(을) 하 -	solve; resolve
		헛소리	nonsense; hot air
		소형차(小形車)	small-size car
		경제적(經濟的)	economical

Vocabulary from the Exercises

실제(實際) [- 쩨]	actuality	내키 -	feel like (doing sth); feel an inclination (subject can be 마음)
실제 NOUN	actual NOUN		

말(을) 꺼내 -	bring up sth, bring up a subject (to talk about)	환영(歡迎)(을) 하 - 환영회(歡迎會)	welcome welcome party
꼬박	without sleeping a wink; straight through	돌려주 - 자상(仔詳)하 -	return sth; give sth back be attentive to detail, considerate of others
눈(을) 붙이 -	*lit.*: "make one's eyes stick together / adhere," i.e., get some shut-eye, sleep	어울리 -	suit sb; becomes sb; go well with
부츠	boots	입히 -	dress sb; make sb wear
계획(計劃)(을) 세우 -	set up / make a plan		

PATTERNS

1. *Does / is... (all right), but...* with -기는 하-

A Plain Base -기 form with particle 는 followed by either the same base or 하 - means *does / is... (all right), but...* Note that the question arises as to whether auxiliary 하 - is descriptive (하다) or processive (한다). The answer is simple: 하 - assumes the properties of the verb base in the -기 form. So, we get 읽기는 하는데 *I am reading it, all right, but...* (processive) versus 예쁘기는 한데 *she's pretty, all right, but...* (descriptive).

1. 이 책을 읽기는 하지만 뜻을 몰라요. or
   이 책을 읽기는 읽지만 뜻을 몰라요.
   *I **am** reading this book, but I don't understand it.*

2. 공책에 그 말을 쓰기는 했지만 잘못 썼어요. or
   공책에 그 말을 쓰기는 썼지만 잘못 썼어요.
   *I **did** write the words in my notebook; but I didn't write them properly.*

3. A: 실크 내의를 샀다면서?
   Is it true you bought some silk underwear?

   B: 응. 돈은 다소 과용한 면이 있기는 하지만 어쨌든 감이 좋거든?
   Yep. I sort of went overboard a bit with the money, but anyhow, they feel great, so...

4. A: 어제 전시회에 들렀어?
   Did you stop in at the exhibition yesterday?

   B: 들르기는 했는데 오래 있을 수는 없었어.
   I did, but I wasn't able to be there long.

Notice that the past or future markers attach only to the -지만 form in this construction—not to the -기 form—which remains constant.

1.1. More Related Patterns: -기도 하다 ~ 한다 (I)

A Plain Base ‑기 form with... 도 하‑ after it means *really does/is, sure does/is,* or *does/is indeed.* This form usually goes with the mild exclamation pattern ‑네(요).

5. 무겁기도 하네요.
   It sure is heavy!

6. 많이 오기도 했네요.
   There sure are a lot of them [that have come] here!

7. 비싸기도 하네요.
   It is expensive indeed!

8. 부지런하기도 하네요.
   He's really hard-working.

Note that the past and future elements, as usual, attach to the auxiliary verb 하‑. The honorific ‑(으)시‑, also usually attaches to the final auxiliary:

9. 참 자주 가기도 하시네요.
   He really goes [there] frequently.

1.2. More Related Patterns: -기도 하다 ~ 한다 (II)

If there are two instances of ‑기도 하‑ right together (either descriptive or processive), the meaning is *does / is **both** x and y.* Sometimes the second or parallel instance is merely implied (as in Example 14 below). Here are some more examples:

10. 잘 치기도 하고, 못 치기도 해요.
    Some [exams] I get through, some I don't.

11. 좋기도 하고, 나쁘기도 해요.
    It's both good and bad. Or: *It has its good points and its bad points.*

12. 춥기도 하고, 덥기도 해요.
    It [e.g., a country] is both cold and hot. Or: *There are cold parts and hot parts.*

13. 춥기도 하고, 바람도 불어요.
    It's both cold and windy.

14. 그 병원은 20세기 초에 개원을 한 이래 세계적으로 유명한 병원이 되었지만 폐원의 위기에 여러 번 처하기도 했다.
    Ever since opening at the beginning of the twentieth century, that hospital has been a world famous one, though it has also faced closure crises several times, too.

Notice that this construction is used for comparing actions or descriptions that are expressed by verbs. For comparing actions expressed by Verbal Nouns (as well as other nouns), it is the *nouns* which have 도 after them, as below:

> 15. 운동도 하고, 산책도 해요.
> *He both engages in sports and takes walks.*

But it is somewhat more natural to use 하기 (도 해요) after *descriptive* verbal nouns, as shown below:

> 16. 바쁘기도 하고, 피곤(하기)도 해요.
> *We're both busy and tired.*

You can have a verbal noun in one part of the construction and a verb in the other part, as in this example:

> 17. 공부도 하고, 놀기도 해요.
> *He both studies and plays around.*

1.3. More Related Patterns: -기만 하다 ~ 한다

The construction … - 기만 하 - means *does nothing but… or only…–s (does only…)*:

> 18. 자기만 해요.
> *I do nothing but sleep.*

> 19. 먹기만 해요.
> *Only eats. [Does nothing but eat.]*

> 20. 놀기만 해요.
> *Fools around all the time. [Does nothing but play.]*

Notice that technically, the English sentences *I read only books* and *I only read books* are different; similarly, in Korean 책만 읽어요 *Books are all I read* is theoretically different from 책을 읽기만 해요 *All I do is read books*. But in both languages, this distinction is often ignored.

With verbal nouns, you can omit 하기: 공부(하기)만 해요 *I do nothing but study*. Somewhat similar are cognate objects, as in 잠을 자요 *sleep [a sleep]* and 춤(을) 춰요 *dance [a dance]*, etc.: you can say either 잠을 자기만 해요 or 잠만 자요 for *does nothing but sleep [one's sleep]*.

2. **It's all the same whether one does it or not; whether one does it or not, it makes no difference with -(으)나 마나**

Aside from the somewhat idiomatic expression 보나 마나 *one doesn't even have to ask; it is obvious that…*, this pattern is usually followed by the copula.

21. A: 철호하고 상의해 보아야겠어.

     I'll have to consult with Ch'ŏrho.

     B: 철호 이야기는 들으나 마나니까 다른 사람하고 상의해.

     It's pointless listening to what Ch'ŏrho says; get your advice from somebody else.

22. A: 지금 가면 박 사장님을 만나 뵐 수 있겠습니까?

     If I go now will I be able to meet Company President Pak?

     B: 지금은 가도 안 계실 거야. 가보나 마나니까 다음에 가.

     [Even] If you go now, he won't be there. There's no point in going, so go another time.

23. A: 이 약 효과가 있습니까?

     Is this medicine effective?

     B: 전혀 없습니다. 먹으나 마나입니다.

     Not at all. Taking it makes no difference at all.

24. A: 준호 씨한테 부탁하면 들어 주지 않겠습니까?

     If I ask Chunho, won't he oblige?

     B: 제 생각에는 부탁해 보나 마나일 것 같은데요.

     To my mind, I reckon there's no point in asking him.

25. A: 영진 씨가 오늘은 일찍 올까요?

     Do you suppose Yŏngjin might come early today?

     B: 보나 마나 오늘도 늦게 올 겁니다.

     It's obvious that she'll come late today, too.

26. A: 아주 좋은 사람이니까 꼭 한 번 만나 보십시오.

     She's a really nice person—please try meeting her once.

     B: 명호 씨가 소개해 주는 사람이니까 보나 마나 좋은 사람이겠지요, 뭐.

     Since you're introducing her, Myŏngho, she's obviously a really nice person!

3. *NOUN or something; NOUN or the like* with NOUN(이)나

Attaching – (이)나 to a NOUN implies that there is a choice in the matter, but either (a) one doesn't really care either way (the choice is not an important one), or (b) one will choose the NOUN but doesn't think much of that particular choice or option. In other words, it somewhat downplays or even deprecates the NOUN to which it attaches. Thus, it is more or less equivalent to – (이)라도.

27. 이번 일요일에는 어디 가지 말고 집에서 잠이나 자야겠다.

     This Sunday, instead of going somewhere, I think I'll just stay at home and sleep or something.

28. 점심에는 라면이나 끓여서 먹어야겠다.

     For lunch I think I'll just make some ramen or something.

29. 남의 일에 신경 쓰지 말고 네 일이나 잘 해.
    Don't worry about other people's business, and just mind your own.

30. 나는 먹기 싫으니까 너나 먹어.
    I don't want to eat it, so you eat it [if nobody else will].

31. 심심한데 테니스나 치자.
    I'm bored; let's play tennis or something.

32. 쓸데없는 얘기하지 말고 식사나 합시다.
    Enough of the useless chatter. Let's eat.

4. **Now let me think—WH[what, who, when, etc.] was it? with (무엇, 누구, 언제, 어디, 왜, 어떻게) -더라?**

This is simply the Plain Style Retrospective ending －더라 coupled with a "WH–question" word: *who, where, what, when, why*. The pattern has the effect of an almost rhetorical question (hence the otherwise bizarre use of a statement ending in a question) asked to oneself. In other words, it is acceptable to use this form in conversation with somebody you normally use 합니다 or 해요 forms to, since you are not really addressing the question to anybody but yourself. The retrospective suffix －더－ provides the nuance of *Now let me think back in time...* Here are some examples:

33. A: 저 모르겠어요?
    Don't you recognize me?
    B: 누구시더라. 기억이 잘 안 나는데요.
    Now who were you again? I'm afraid I can't remember.

34. A: 저 사람 이름이 뭐지?
    What's that person's name?
    B: 이름이 뭐더라. 전에 알았었는데.
    Now what was her name again? I used to know...

35. A: 수미 생일이 언제더라.
    When's Sumi's birthday again?
    B: 음력 5월 23일이잖아.
    May 23 by the lunar calendar—don't you remember?

36. A: 너 지난 일요일 날 뭐 했니?
    What did you do last Sunday?
    B: 그날 내가 뭐를 했더라. 생각이 안 나.
    Let me see, what did I do that day? I can't recall.

37. A: 내가 여행 가방을 어디에 뒀더라.
    Now where did I put my travel bag?

    B: 잘 찾아 봐.
    Have a good look around.

38. A: 너 전에 서울대공원에 가 봤지? 어떻게 가면 되니?
    Have you ever been to Seoul Grand Park? How do you get there?

    B: 어떻게 갔더라. 가보기는 했는데 어떻게 갔는지 생각이 안 나.
    Hmm, how did we get there? I've been there before all right, but I can't recall how we got there.

39. A: 수학시험 점수가 잘 나왔어?
    Did you get a good grade on your math exam?

    B: 음, 몇 점 나왔더라?
    Hmm, what was my score again?

5. *Now that one has done it...; once one did it...* with -고 보니

This pattern is a fairly straightforward combination of its constituent parts:

(a) - 고: *having done it, ...; after doing it, then...*
(b) 보 - : *check it out; take a look and see*
(c) - (으)니 (까): *the in-your-face when or "discovery" when*

(a) + (b) + (c) = *having done it, I took a look back on it, and discover that...*

40. 처음엔 이해하지 못 했습니다.
    그런데 선생님 설명을 듣고 보니 이해가 갑니다.
    At first I didn't understand.
    But now that I've heard the teacher's explanation, I get it.

41. 나 지난 주에 소개팅했어.
    그런데 만나고 보니 아는 사람인 거 있지.
    I went on a blind date last week.
    But wouldn't you know it—when we got together it was somebody I know.

42. 나 지금까지는 형편이 어려운 사람들한테 관심이 없었거든. 그런데 그 사람들 얘기를 듣고 보니 도와주고 싶은 마음이 생기더라.
    Actually, until now, I've never been interested in less fortunate people. But after hearing their stories, I started to feel like I wanted to help them.

43. 뭘 많이 만든 것 같은데 상을 차려 놓고 보니 양이 적네.
    I thought I had prepared a lot, but now that I set the table, I see there's too little.

44. 편지를 보내 놓고 보니 빈 봉투만 보낸 것 있지.

Wouldn't you know it—after mailing the letter, I realized I had sent just an empty envelope.

45. 내가 쓴 글 좀 읽어 봐.
생각할 때는 괜찮은 것 같았는데 써 놓고 보니 이상하다.

Read what I wrote.
When I thought about it, it seemed OK, but now that I write it down, it's strange.

6. *Contrary to what you might expect...* with -(으)ㄴ / -는 / -(으)ㄹ걸(요)?

The Main Text to this lesson contains the following line:

"살을 빼는 비결 같은 것은 원래 없는걸요."

Actually, [contrary to your assumption], there is no secret to losing weight.

The particle 을 / 를 has, in addition to its other meanings, an antithetical use: *but; although; even though; contrary to prevailing conditions or assumptions.* There are basically two patterns that incorporate this "antithetical" 을 / 를:

(a) In the middle of a sentence, 을 / 를 (often reduced to just ㄹ) means *but; although; in spite of the fact that...* and is commonly used in such contexts as *When A did so-and-so, B countered with something else* or *When A happened, then B (of an opposite or contrary nature) resulted.* Some examples:

46. 싫다고 하는 것을 부모가 결혼하게 했지요.

You see, his parents made him get married in spite of his objections.

47. 어제 밤에 집에서 공부할 걸 (or 것을) 극장에 가서 오늘 그 시험을 잘못 봤어.

I was going to study at home last night but [instead] I went to the theater, so I didn't do very well on that test today.

(b) At the end of a sentence, ...것을 or (more usually) ...걸 may mean *contrary to what one might expect; but* or *after all* or *but... so there!* In this usage, the intonation is rising—just like it sometimes goes up for the sentence-final ... ‑ 거든(요) and yes-no questions. Moreover, the ...것을 or ...걸 can attach to the modifiers ‑(으)ㄴ (in both its descriptive and past tense functions), ‑는, and ‑(으)ㄹ, but note that Korean orthography insists that the 걸 be written flush with the modifier. Here are some more examples:

48. A: 저 할머니가 60세 밖에 안 돼 보이는데 알고 보니 70세 넘으셨다고 하네.

That old lady doesn't look older than sixty, but I just learned that apparently she is over seventy.

B: 머리를 염색을 하는걸요.

I'll bet you she dyes her hair.

49. 그 돈은 다 써 버린걸.

    [I'm sorry, but contrary to your expectation] I have spent all the money.

50. A: "친절 운동" 하는 사람들은 친절하기만 하면 노인문제, 교통문제 등 당면한 사회문제를 한꺼번에 해결할 수 있다는데…

    The people involved in the "kindness movement" claim that if only we are kind, we can solve in one fell swoop the pressing social problems of the day like aging, traffic, etc.

    B: 다 헛소리인걸.

    Ah, it's all a bunch of hot air (contrary to what they say).

When paired with a prospective modifier ‑(으)ㄹ, this pattern has the effect of *But [I wonder if…]?* or *But don't you think…?*

51. A: 나 SUV 하나 살까 봐.

    I think I'll buy an SUV.

    B: 소형차가 더 경제적일걸.

    Don't you think a small-size car would be more economical?

52. 그 여자가 아직도 저기서 살고 있을걸?

    But don't you suppose she is still living there?

53. 거긴 참 비쌀걸.

    But that place would / might be very expensive.

54. 그 영화는 우리 인천에도 들어올걸.

    I'll bet that movie will come to us in Inch'ŏn after all.

55. 그 모자는 나한테 좀 클걸.

    But I reckon that hat will be a bit too big for me…

In this meaning, and this meaning only, the 걸 can be preceded by the restricted modifiers ‑었는 and ‑겠는 (optionally used instead of ‑(으)ㄴ and ‑(으)ㄹ):

56. 손님이 벌써 왔는걸.

    But [contrary to what you think] the guests are already here!

57. 생각을 잘못 했는걸.

    But you've got the wrong idea.

58. 인제 가야 하겠는걸.

    But I'll have to leave now…

In the sentence-final use, you can always add the polite particle 요 to make the sentence polite, but before 요, the construction always appears in its abbreviated form …걸(요) and is pronounced [걸료].

59. 아마 모르실걸요?
     But I'll bet you probably don't know.

EXERCISES

Exercise 1: Reading Comprehension

Write out answers to the following questions.

1. 서너 달 전에 나를 찾아온 환자는 왜 온 것입니까?
2. 그 여자는 살이 쪄서 뭐가 나쁘다고 말했습니까?
3. 그 여자는 실제 나이보다 젊어 보였습니까?
4. 살을 빼기 위해 병원을 찾은 것은 그 때가 처음이었습니까?
5. 내가 그 여자에게 가르쳐 준 새로운 방법은 어떤 것이었습니까?
6. 나는 그 환자에 대해 가끔 생각했습니까?
7. 오늘 언제 그 여자가 진찰실에 들어왔습니까?
8. 나는 그 여자를 금방 알아보았습니까?
9. 오늘은 무엇 때문에 나를 찾아왔습니까?

Exercise 2: Practice with -기는 하-

Use the pattern -기는 하- to complete the responses.

1. A: 저걸 사는 게 어떻겠습니까?
   B: 글쎄요, 저게 _____.
2. A: 진우 씨, 아프다면서 왜 나왔습니까?
   B: _____ 참을 만합니다.
3. A: 어떻습니까? 이번 시합에 이길 자신 있습니까?
   B: 글쎄요, _____.
4. A: 진아가 왜 이렇게 늦지요?
   B: 글쎄요, 늦게 들어올 거라고_____ 너무
   늦는 것 같은데요.
5. A: 저녁 때 승현 씨 집에 갈 거지요?
   B: 글쎄요, _____ 별로 내
   키지가 않습니다.
6. A: 아니, 웬 음식을 이렇게 많이 차렸습니까?
   B: _____맛이 어떨지 모르겠습니다.

Exercise 3: Practice with -(으)나 마나

Use an appropriate phrase with -(으)나 마나 to fill in the blanks below. Then translate the dialogues into English.

1. A: 성준 씨한테 부탁해 봐야겠습니다.
    B: 성준 씨가 그런 부탁 들어주는 것 봤습니까?
    _____ 말도 꺼내지 마십시오.
2. A: 밤을 꼬박 새우면 낮에 피곤해서 안 됩니다.
        한 시간이라도 눈을 붙이십시오.
    B: 그 정도는 _____.
3. A: 그 부츠 아주 따뜻해 보이는데요.
    B: 그래요? 그렇지만 _____.
4. A: 진우 지금 집에 있을까요?
    B: _____ 집에서 자고 있을 겁니다.
5. A: 웬 바람이 이렇게 불지요?
    B: 글쎄 말이에요. 우산을 _____.
6. A: 무슨 날씨가 이렇게 덥지요?
    B: 찬 물로 샤워 좀 하십시오. 그러면 좀 나아질 겁니다.
    A: 날씨가 너무 더우니까 _____.
        오늘 벌써 5번이나 했는걸요.

Exercise 4: Practice with -(이)나 and -(이)라도

Fill in the blanks below with phrases using either -(이)나 or -(이)라도, as appropriate.

1. A: 일요일 날 산에 같이 가실래요?
    B: 혼자 갔다 오십시오. 저는 집에서 _____.
2. A: 철민아, 심심한데 우리 나가서 _____.
    B: 구두 신고 해도 될까?
3. A: 꼭 까만 볼펜으로 써야 됩니까?
    B: 까만색이 없으면 _____.
4. A: 정미야, 괜찮은 사람 있는데 소개해 줄까?
    B: 난 필요 없으니까 _____.
5. A: 수미야, 아침 먹어야지.
    B: 밥 먹기 싫어요.
    A: 그럼 _____.
6. A: 여기를 이렇게 하면 안 되잖아. 좀 잘 해.
    B: 내 일은 내가 알아서 할 테니까 _____.
7. A: 휴가 계획 세웠습니까?
    B: 네, 애들도 방학을 해서 집에 있으니까 어디 _____.

8. A: 오래간만에 오셨는데 저희랑 같이 식사하고 가십시오.

    B: 일찍 가야 되니까 _____.

Exercise 5: Practice with WH[*what, who, when*, etc.] + ...-더라?

Use the "rack your brains" pattern in WH[*what, who, when*, etc.] + ... ‑ 더라? to fill in the blanks below.

1. A: 우리가 언제 처음 만났지?

    B: _____.

    아, 생각났다. 신입생 환영회 때 네가 내 옆에 앉았었잖아.

2. A: _____.

    B: 너는 아버지 생신도 모르니?

3. A: 수미야, 저 사람이 너를 자꾸 쳐다보는데 너 저 사람 아니?

    B: 어디서 본 것 같아. 그런데 내가 저 사람을 _____.

4. A: 아까 나한테 할 말 있다고 했잖아. 무슨 말 하려고 했어?

    B: 내가 너한테 _____.

    생각이 안 나.

    A: 나중에 생각나면 얘기해 줘.

5. A: 진성아, 고등학교 때 우리 심하게 싸운 거 기억나니?

    B: 응, 기억나.

    그런데 그 때 _____.

6. A: _____.

    B: 그저께 빌렸으니까 다음 주 월요일까지 돌려주면 돼.

Exercise 6: Practice with -고 보니

Complete the sentences below to reveal the unexpected turn of events that you personally witnessed or experienced.

1. 나 지난주에 선 봤어.

    그런데 만나고 보니 _____.

2. 결혼하기 전에는 승훈 씨가 그렇게 자상한지 몰랐습니다.

    그런데 결혼하고 보니 _____.

3. 경민 씨 이사 간 거 알지요?

    그런데 알고 보니 _____.

4. 정아네 집에 전화하려고 했습니다.

    그런데 전화를 걸고 보니 _____.

5. 이 옷이 주경이한테 잘 어울릴 것 같았습니다.

    그런데 입혀 놓고 보니까 _____.

6. 영준이가 현수보다 더 큰 줄 알았습니다.

    그런데 두 사람을 세워 놓고 보니 _____.

Exercise 7: Practice with -(으)ㄴ / -는 / -(으)ㄹ걸(요)

Following the 보기 below, convert the responses into an appropriate form in -(으)ㄴ / -는 / -(으)ㄹ걸(요) so as to imply *contrary to what you might be expecting*...

보기:　A. 지리산에 눈이 많이 내렸겠어요.
　　　B. 설악산에도 눈이 많이 내렸어요.
　　　→ 설악산에도 눈이 많이 내렸을걸요.

1. A. 오늘 오후에 영풍문고에 가볼까?
   B. 오늘은 거기까지 갈 시간이 없어요.
   → _____.

2. A. 이 옷을 선영이한테 사 줄까?
   B. 걔한테는 잘 안 어울릴 것 같은데.
   → _____.

3. A. 이번 패션 전시회에 사람이 안 오면 큰일 날 텐데요.
   B. 표를 사는 사람이 생각보다 많은데요.
   → _____.

4. A. 모리 씨도 농담을 잘 하지요?
   B. 농담을 잘 안 해요.
   → _____.

5. A. 언제 시집을 갈 거예요?
   B. 벌써 갔어요.
   → _____.

6. A. 내일도 만날까요?
   B. 내일부터 휴가인데요.
   → _____.

7. A. 살을 빼는 방법이나 약이 없을까요?
   B. 살을 빼는 비결 같은 것은 원래 없어요.
   → _____.

8. A. 나의 옛 남자친구가 나를 아직까지도 기억하고 있을까?
   B. 벌써 까마득하게 잊어버렸어요.
   → _____.

제20과 복습 IV

Review the example sentences below. Then, for each one, write a new sentence that uses the same pattern.

1. -(는)군(요), -(는)구먼(요), -(는)구나!

1. 아기를 그렇게 입히니까 잘 어울리는군요!
2. "만나 뵈다" 하고 "만나 뵙다"의 차이를 설명하기가 어렵구나!
3. 들어도 자꾸 잊어버리는구먼!

2. -(으)ㄴ / -는 것 ~ 거 있지(요)

4. 나 어제 남대문 시장에 옷 사러 갔었다.
   그런데 옷이 아주 싼 것 있지.
5. 어제 영화 보러 갔다가 못 보고 그냥 왔어.
   표가 다 팔린 거 있지.
6. 어제 선 본 남자 키가 엄청 큰 거 있지.
   그래서 운동선수인지 알았어.

3. -(으)ㄴ / -는지

7. 네가 벌써 운전면허를 땄지 알았는데 아직 못 땄구나!
8. 학교에서 진로상담을 하는데 상담비를 그렇게 비싸게 받는지 몰랐어.
9. 한국인들의 조상이 곰인지 몰랐네.

4. 좀...?

10. A: 음식이 남을 줄 알았는데 모자라네요.
    B: 사람이 좀 많이 왔습니까?
11. A: 이 대리네는 벌써 집을 샀답니다.
    B: 이 대리 부인이 좀 알뜰합니까?

12. A: 부산에 출장 가서 생선 많이 먹고 왔습니까?

    B: 제가 생선회를 좀 좋아합니까? 간 김에 잔뜩 먹고 왔지요.

5. -길래

13. A: 수미 만나고 왔어?

    B: 아니, 30분 기다려도 안 오길래 그냥 왔어.

14. A: 웬 음식을 이렇게 많이 해요?

    B: 서울에서 진수 친구들이 온다길래 이것저것 만들어 봤어요. 한 번 맛 좀 보세요.

15. A: 엄마, 아침에 먹던 생선 없어요?

    B: 좀 상한 것 같길래 버렸어.

6. -더라고(요)

16. A: 수미한테 빌리지 왜 샀습니까?

    B: 빌려 달라고 얘기했는데 안 빌려 주더라고요. 그래서 그냥 샀습니다.

17. A: 집들이 가는데 뭐 사가지고 가는 게 좋을까?

    B: 세제나 화장지를 사가는 게 어때? 요즘은 그런 거 많이 사가지고 가더라고.

18. A: 아니, 무릎이 왜 그래? 넘어졌어?

    B: 응, 며칠 전에 계단에서 넘어졌어. 갑자기 어지럽더라고.

7. WH– ...(이)나... -다고(요)

19. A: 진호가 그렇게 노래를 잘한다면서요?

    B: 네, 얼마나 잘한다고요.

    A: 나도 언제 들어 봐야겠네요.

20. A: 민정이 성격 어때요? 친구들이 별로 안 좋아하는 것 같던데.

    B: 얼마나 못됐다고요. 언제나 자기 밖에 몰라요.

21. A: 피로가 쌓였을 때는 목욕하고 자는 게 최고야.

    B: 어제 몇 시간이나 잤다고. 그런데도 전혀 소용이 없어.

8. -느니 (차라리)... -겠-

22. 타자기 사느니 차라리 컴퓨터를 사는 게 낫지 않겠습니까?

23. 영수에게 시키느니 차라리 내가 하겠다.

24. 그런 영화를 보느니 차라리 낮잠을 자겠다.

25. 그런 사람하고 결혼하느니 차라리 혼자 살겠다.

9. -(으)ㄴ / -는 / -(으)ㄹ 모양이-

26. A: 영재 씨하고 경미 씨 사이가 요즘 수상하지 않습니까?

    B: 네, 요즘 자주 만나는 모양입니다.

27. A: 선주가 요즘 우울해 보입니다.

   B: 남자 친구하고 헤어진 모양입니다.

28. A: 왜 아직까지 연락이 없지요?

   B: 지금까지 전화가 없는 것을 보니 시험에 떨어진 모양입니다.

29. 이것을 그것으로 바꾸지 못할 모양이야.

10. -아 / -어 보았자

30. 말을 안 들으니까 얘기를 해 보았자 소용이 없습니다.

31. 벌써 퇴근하셨을 겁니다. 지금 가 보았자 만나지도 못할 거니까 내일 가십시오.

32. 대학을 졸업해 봤자 취직하기도 힘듭니다.

33. 영준 씨한테 부탁해 봤자 들어 주지도 않을 겁니다.

11. -았 / -었으면 하-

34. 바쁘지 않으시면 꼭 와 주셨으면 합니다.

35. 저쪽에서 잠깐만 기다려 주셨으면 합니다.

36. 내일 아침 일찍 사무실로 전화 좀 해 주셨으면 한다고 전해주세요.

37. 내일은 집에서 쉬었으면 합니다.

12. NOUN까지

38. 정민 씨, 일하면서 노래까지 하는 걸 보니 기분이 좋은가 봅니다.

39. 며칠 전에 지리산에 갔다 왔는데 산 아래 계곡은 물론이고 산꼭대기까지 쓰레기가 가득했다.

40. 정호 씨네 집은 아주 커서 집에 수영장까지 있다.

41. 말이 통하지 않아서 손짓 발짓까지 했지만 소용이 없었다.

13. -(으)ㄹ 테니(까)

42. 진로상담비는 내가 낼 테니까 학생생활상담소 한번 다녀 봐라.

43. 일이 끝나는 대로 내려갈 테니 커피숍에서 기다려 주십시오.

44. 내가 로미오 역을 할 테니 수미 씨는 줄리엣 역을 하십시오.

45. 진호 씨 생일 선물로 제가 지갑을 살 테니 수미 씨는 다른 걸 사십시오.

14. Time Expression + 만에

46. A: 성진 씨, 속상해요. 운전면허 시험에 또 떨어졌어요. 성진 씨는 금방 땄지요?

   B: 아니요, 저도 두 번 떨어지고 세 번 만에 땄습니다.

47. A: 종호한테는 책이 수면제야.

   B: 책을 읽기 시작한 지 5분 만에 잠들었어.

48. A: 선생님, 아이가 학교에 간 지 2시간 만에 집에 돌아왔는데 학교에서 무슨 일이 있었습니까?
    B: 아닙니다. 오늘 학교에 일이 있어서 수업이 일찍 끝났습니다.

15. -아 / -어 내-

49. 제가 범인을 꼭 잡아 내고 말겠습니다.
50. 영준 씨, 해 낼 수 있다는 자신감을 가지고 도전해 보십시오.
51. 이번 주말까지 이 작품을 다 완성해 내야 합니다.
52. 매서운 추위와 바람을 이겨 내고 북극점을 정복해 냈습니다.

16. -(ㄴ / 는)단다, -(이)란다

53. A: 여기가 잠실 운동장이에요?
    B: 그래, 30년 전에 여기서 올림픽이 열렸단다.
54. A: 아빠, "사시"라는 말이 무슨 뜻이에요?
    B: 사시라고 하는 것은 춘하추동이라는 사계절이란다. 그러니까 봄, 여름, 가을, 겨울이지.
55. A: 이 사진에서 아버지 옆에 계신 분은 누구세요?
    B: 아버지 사촌이란다.

17. 설마

56. A: 영진 씨가 오늘도 늦게 오지 않을까요?
    B: 설마 자기 결혼식 날 늦겠습니까?
57. A: 영호가 왜 이렇게 늦지요? 혹시 무슨 일이 생긴 게 아닐까요?
    B: 설마 무슨 일이 생겼겠습니까? 걱정하지 말고 기다리십시오.
58. 설마 그렇게 천생 낙천적인 사람이 자살을 했을까?

18. -기는 하-

59. 이것이 좋기는 한데 좀 비싼 것 같습니다.
60. 열심히 하기는 하는데 잘 안 됩니다.
61. 시골에서 사는 것이 심심하기는 하지만 여유가 있어서 좋습니다.
62. 늦을 거라고 얘기하고 오기는 했지만 다시 전화를 해야겠습니다.

19. -(으)나 마나

63. A: 철호하고 상의해 보아야겠어.
    B: 철호 이야기는 들으나 마나니까 다른 사람하고 상의해.
64. A: 지금 가면 박 사장님을 만나 뵐 수 있겠습니까?
    B: 지금은 가도 안 계실 거야. 가보나 마나니까 다음에 가.

65. A: 영진 씨가 오늘은 일찍 올까요?

    B: 보나 마나 오늘도 늦게 올 겁니다.

20. NOUN(이)나

66. 이번 일요일에는 어디 가지 말고 집에서 잠이나 자야겠다.

67. 나는 그런 거 필요 없으니까 너나 가져.

68. 영진이는 오늘 안 올 것 같으니까 우리끼리 바둑이나 두자.

69. 여자가 무슨 일을 한다고 그럽니까? 시집이나 가십시오.

21. (무엇, 누구, 언제, 어디, 왜, 어떻게) -더라?

70. A: 저 모르시겠어요?

    B: 누구시더라. 기억이 잘 안 나는데요.

71. A: 수미 생일이 언제더라.

    B: 음력 5월 23일이잖아.

72. A: 너 전에 서울대공원에 가 봤지? 어떻게 가면 되니?

    B: 어떻게 갔더라. 어떻게 갔는지 생각이 안 난다.

22. -고 보니

73. 처음엔 이해하지 못 했습니다.

    그런데 선생님 설명을 듣고 보니 이해가 갑니다.

74. 나 지난주에 선 봤어.

    그런데 만나고 보니 아는 사람인 거 있지.

75. 편지를 보내 놓고 보니 알맹이는 빼놓고 껍데기만 보낸 것 있지.

23. -(으)ㄴ / -는 / -(으)ㄹ걸(요)?

76. 싫다고 하는 것을 부모가 결혼하게 했지요.

77. 어제 밤에 집에서 공부할 걸 극장에 가서 오늘 그 시험을 잘못 봤어.

78. A: 살을 빼는 방법이나 약이 없을까요?

    B: 살을 빼는 비결 같은 것은 원래 없는걸요.

79. A: 나의 옛 남자친구가 나를 아직까지도 기억하고 있을까?

    B: 벌써 까마득하게 잊어버렸을걸.

KOREAN-ENGLISH NEW VOCABULARY GLOSSARY

ㄱ

가 버리- leave; take off; up and go (1)

가까이 (30년 ~) for close to (thirty years); nigh on (thirty years) (14)

가까이 nearby; the vicinity (13)

가까이에서 from nearby; from up close (12, 13)

가득 / 가뜩 to the top; full; chockablock; brimming; to the brim (14)

가라앉- sink down; go to the bottom; subside; abate; quiet down (11)

가로등(街路燈) street lights (17)

가루 powder (16)

가루비누 powdered soap (16)

가만히 있어! Keep quiet a moment (11)

가만히 quietly (11, 12)

가벼w– (가볍다) be light (in weight) (11)

가불(假拂)(을) 하– get paid in advance (17)

가운데 the middle, center; the midst of; between; among (8)

가을 학기(學期) fall semester; autumn term (5)

가져다 놓- take sth and put it away (12)

가출(家出)(을) 하– move out; leave the home (2)

간식(間食) snack (5)

간장(~醬) soy sauce (8)

갈아입- change (apparel) (6)

감- bathe; wash (14)

감기- have sb bathe or wash (14)

감동(感動) being moved / touched; deep emotion (14)

감염(感染)(이) 되- be / get infected (6)

감정(感情) emotion (8)

감탄(感歎)(을) 하– exclaim; express one's surprise (12, 19)

감탄스러w– (~스럽다) be marvelous, impressive; induce wonder (13)

갑(匣) (cigarette, match) case, box (7)

갑자기 suddenly (1)

강(强)하– be strong (6)

강남(江南) Kangnam (the area south of the Han River in Seoul) (9)

강아지 puppy; doggie (2)

갖다 놓- bring (and place) sth (9)

갖다 주- bring to / for (2)

갖추- have a thing ready, in stock; to equip, furnish (7)

갚- repay sth (6)

갚- pay back; repay; settle one's account; give (sth) in return (18)

개- (weather) clear up (1)

객관(客觀) objectivity (8)

걔 ← 그애 he; she (8)

거-ㄹ- (걸다) hang (up), hang on (11)

거실(居室) living room (9)

거울 mirror (18)

거의 virtually, nearly (all, etc.) (3)

거절(拒絶)(을) 하– refuse; turn down (8)

격정거리 [-꺼리] matter for concern (7)

건(件) counter/classifier for events/happenings (9)

건강(健康)하– be healthy (7)

건너 오- come across (14)

건너- cross over; go over (e.g., 길을 건너다) (14)

건너가- go across (14)

건축가(建築家) architect (6)

걸- (걷다) walk (14)

걸리- get caught (on a nail, by the police) (9)

걸리- be / get hung up (11)

걸리- have sb walk (14)

걸어다니- go about / attend on foot (1)

걸음 pace; step; gait; walking; one's steps; one's pace (1)

겁(怯) fear (19)

겁(怯)(이) 많- be timid; "have much fear"; be cowardly, timid (14)

겁(이) 나- be afraid (19)

겁쟁이 coward, chicken, "fraidycat" (14)

게시판(揭示板) bulletin board (6)

게으르- be lazy (1)

게으름(을) 피우- act like a lazy bum; be lazy (6)

겨우 barely; scarcely (17)

격침(擊沈) attacking and sinking sth (14)

겪- suffer, experience, undergo (6)

견문(見聞) one's personal experience (things "seen and heard") (6)

견문(이) 생기- gain / acquire experience; broaden one's horizons (6)

결과(結果) result (6)

결국(結局) at the end of the day, ultimately; in the end (2, 14)

결론(結論) conclusion

결론(結論)을 내리- reach a conclusion, come to a conclusion (12)

결석(缺席)(을) 하– be absent ("from one's seat") (NB: processive) (11)

결심(決心)(을) 하– resolve (to do), make a resolution (to do); make up one's mind (to do) (3)

결정(決定)(이) 되- be / get decided, determined (6)

경기 대회(競技大會) athletic meet; competition (2)

경기(競技)(를) 하– compete in sports; have a match / contest / sporting event (8)

경기장(競技場) stadium, track and field (2)

경부 고속도로 the Seoul-Pusan Highway (4)

경비(警備) 아저씨 security guard / porter at the entrance to

a Korean apartment building entrance (12)

경상도(慶尙道) 쪽에는　(down) Kyŏngsang Province-way; "in the direction of Kyŏngsang Province" (16)

경제적(經濟的)　economical (1)

경제형편(經濟形便)　economic situation / circumstances (4)

경찰(警察)　police; policeman (2, 17)

경찰관(警察官)　police officer (2)

경찰국가(警察國家)　police state (2)

경찰서(警察署)　police station (2)

경험(經驗)　experience (6)

계단(階段)　stairs; staircase (11)

계산(計算)(을) 하–　calculate; reckon; pay the bill (in a restaurant) (16)

계속(繼續)　continuously (1)

계획(計劃)(을) 세우+　set up / make a plan (19)

고w–　(곱다, 고와) be pretty, beautiful (6)

고급(高級)스러w–　(~스럽다) high-class; refined (6)

고래　whale (9)

고민(苦悶)　anguish, worry, mental agony; sth that vexes you (1, 19)

고민(苦悶)(을) 하–　agonize; be in anguish (14)

고생(苦生)　suffering (6)

고생(苦生)(을) 하–　suffer (12)

고속(高速)　"high speed" (4)

고속버스　highway bus; coach (4)

고유　indigenous; native; inherent; peculiar (8)

고장(故障)(이) 나–　break; break down (1)

고조(高潮)(가) 되–　be / get heightened; reach a high point / climax (7)

고조선(古朝鮮)　Ancient Chosŏn (18)

고집(을) 부리–　be stubborn (NB: processive) (9)

고집쟁이　stubborn person (9)

고춧가루　red hot pepper powder (2)

고혈압(高血壓)　high blood pressure (6)

곤란(困難)하–　be awkward, embarrassing; feel ill at ease; be complicated, vexing, problematic (3)

곧바로　directly; straight away; right away (17)

곰　bear (18)

공기(空氣)　air (9)

공대(工大)　engineering faculty / college (5)

공약(公約)(을) 하–　make a public pledge or promise (6)

공장(工場)　factory (5)

공장난　game of ball (12)

공통적(共通的)　common; in common (6)

과(科)　department (at a university) (16)

과목(科目)　subject, course (4)

과장(課長)　section chief; section head; manager (2)

과장(誇張)(을) 하–　exaggerate (8)

과태료(過怠料)　negligence fee / fine (2)

관객(觀客)　spectator(s); onlooker(s); the audience; viewer(s) (18)

관리자(管理者)　manager; webmaster (6)

관심(關心)을 가지–　be concerned about; have an interest in; be interested (NB: processive) (12)

관점(觀點) [–쩜]　point of view; perspective (8)

괴로w–　(괴롭다) be tormenting, onerous; feel tormented, out of sorts (6)

교통법규(交通法規)　traffic rules / regulations / legislation (2)

교황(敎皇)　the Pope (2)

교황청(敎皇廳)　the Vatican (2)

교훈(敎訓)　moral (to a story) (6)

구두쇠　miser; tightwad; pinchpenny (18)

구멍　hole (18)

구성(構成)(이) 되–　be / get composed of, made up of (6)

구체(具體)　concrete object (8)

국가(國家)　nation, nation-state (6)

국거리　makings for soup (7)

국민(國民)　the people of a nation (6)

국민(國民)의 단결(團結)　unity / solidarity of the populace (6)

국민투표(國民投票)　popular vote (6)

군대(軍隊)　army; armed forces; military (5, 18)

군데　counter / classifier for places (9)

군데군데　here and there (in various places) (17)

굳–　be hard, solid, firm (functions both as processive and descriptive) (6)

굵–　be thick; be burly; be sonorous (voice) (13)

굶–　starve, be hungry; skip (a meal) (2, 14)

굶기–　starve sb; make go hungry (14)

굽　heel; hoof (7)

굽–　be bent (14)

굽히–　bend sth (14)

궁금하–　it causes concern, is worrisome; I am curious to know about (7)

귀　ear (12)

귀(貴)하–　be noble, precious, esteemed, distinguished (8)

귀걸이　earring (14)

그녀　she (formal / written) (1)

그대로　just as it is / was; intact; just as you are (1)

그랬더니　whereupon (first person) (4)

그러다가　after (doing this for) a while, then (suddenly / unexpectedly) (14)

그러더니　whereupon (non-first person) (4)

그러자　whereupon; no sooner had this happened, than (11)

그런 식으로　in such a way, manner (3)

그런대로　more or less (lit.: as it is / as they are ~ were) (9)

그리고는　and then; after that; after which (1)

그림　picture (17)

그만 + **VERB**　stop VERBing (13)

그제 = 그저께　day before yesterday (16)

그치 = 그렇지　Of course; It is so, isn't it? (16)

극(劇)　drama (8)

근시(近視) nearsightedness (7)

근처(近處) vicinity (17)

글(을) 잘하– be good in studies (NB: processive) (6)

글씨 handwriting; penmanship; calligraphy (6, 11)

금강산(金剛山) the Diamond Mountains (6)

금고(金庫) safe, strongbox, coffer (17)

금방(今方) any moment now (12)

급(急)하– be urgent (3)

급하게 urgently; hurriedly; in a rush (3)

기– crawl (12)

기능(機能) function (8)

기르– raise, rear (children); grow (a beard = 수염) (12)

기분(氣分)(이) 나쁘– be in a bad mood (13)

기어 다니– crawl around (12)

기억(記憶) memory (19)

기억(記憶)(을) 하– remember (19)

기억(記憶)(이) 나– remember (sth) (19)

기억력(記憶力) one's memory (power) (19)

기억력(記憶力)(이) 좋– have a good memory (19)

기운(을) 내– put on a brave face; screw up one's courage; buck up; pull oneself together; rally one's strength, etc. (14)

기일(期日) designated date, deadline (2)

기절(氣絶)(을) 하– faint; pass out; swoon (16)

기차(汽車) train (4)

기차사고(汽車事故) train accident (4)

기초(基礎) fundament; basis; foundation (7)

기초반(班) basic course; basic class; elementary class (7)

기침(을) 하– cough (1)

기타(를) 치– play the guitar (13)

기회(機會) opportunity (11)

길(을) 잃어버리– get lost; lose one's way (6)

길(이) 막히– road is blocked, jammed (with traffic) (1)

길눈(이) 어두w– (어둡다) "one's street-eyes are dark" = be poor at navigation, have poor orientation sense (16)

길이 length (16)

김밥(을) 싸– [-빱] make ("wrap") *kimpap* (13)

깊– be deep (6)

까마귀 crow (19)

까마득하게 잊– forget sth completely (19)

까매 ← 까맣다 be black (7)

깎– bargain, "cut" (the price) (8)

깜짝 놀라– be / get gobsmacked, utterly surprised, amazed (3)

깨– break sth (18)

깨– wake up (14)

깨끗이 cleanly, clean (adv.) (9)

깨뜨리– break sth (2)

깨우– wake sb up (14)

꺼내– take out, produce (from your pocket, a bag, etc.) (4); bring up (a subject) (6)

껍질 (banana, apple, etc.) peel; (tree) bark (14)

꼬리 tail (6)

꼬박 without sleeping a wink; straight through (19)

꼭 exactly (one year) (3)

꼭 (chew) firmly, thoroughly; be sure to...; without fail; definitely (14)

꼭대기 the peak, summit, tip (1)

꼴 a (pitiful / derogatory) shape, form, appearance, sight (6)

꼼짝도 못하– can't even budge; can't move an inch (2)

꽂다 insert sth; wedge sth in, stick sth in (to a rather narrow space) (14)

꽉 차– be full up, chockablock, full to the brim, etc. (8)

꽤 quite; rather (6)

꾸준하– be consistently persistent, steadfast, unflagging (6)

꿈 속에서 in one's dreams (3)

끊– snap sth; cut sth off; sever (3, 11); (담배를 ~) quit (smoking) (12); hang up (the phone) (16)

끊기– be / get cut off (11)

끊어지– get cut off (6)

끓이– boil sth; make it boil (14)

끔찍하– be disgusting (in a horrific, scary way); give one the creeps; be horrid, horrible (4)

끝 end; tip; "the end" (6)

끝나– sth stops (14)

끝내– finish sth; stop sth (2, 14)

끝마치– finish sth (7)

끼– put on (glasses) (6)

끼어드–ㄹ– (끼어들다) butt in; "insert and enter"; cut in (8)

ㄴ

나 말고는 except for me; other than me; besides me (1)

나– exit (14)

나(ㅅ)– (낫다) be preferable, be better than (6)

나누– divide, share it (4)

나누어 주– share it with sb (4)

나–ㄹ– (날다) fly; sth flies (9, 14)

나라(를) 발전(發展)시키– develop the country (6)

나이(가) 드–ㄹ– (들다) get old (*lit.*: "age enters") (19)

나타나– show up; appear (1, 17)

낙(樂) joy, pleasure (6)

낙천적(樂天的) optimistic (18)

낚시(를) 하– fish; go fishing (13)

난리(가) 나– there is a tumult, uproar; all hell breaks loose (16)

난리(亂離) disturbance; war; rebellion (16)

난시(亂視) astigmatism (7)

날리– fly sth; make / let sth fly (14)

날씬하– be slim, slender (4)

날아가– fly away (9)

낡– be old (of things) (1)

남 others; other people (3)

남 others; outsiders; people from one's "out-group" (14)

남- remain; be left (14)

남기- leave sth left over; leave sth undone (14)

남녀평등(男女平等) equality of the sexes (5)

남들처럼 like the others (2)

남성(男性) men; the male gender (6)

낫 a Korean sickle (6)

낭비(浪費) waste (11)

낮 daytime (6)

낯 face (11)

낯(이) 익- (be ~) familiar (face) (11)

내- put / take out; pay (14)

내 쪽 toward me; in my direction (14)

내내 continuously; all throughout (3)

내려놓- put sth down (for future use / reference) (9)

내버리- leave alone; "leave be'"; "let be" (3)

내쉬- (숨(을) ~) breathe out (11)

내용(內容) contents (1)

내키- feel like (doing sth); feel an inclination (19)

냉동(冷凍)하- / ~시키- freeze sth (9)

너무나 ever so (much) (3)

널 board, plank (14)

널뛰기 the game of seesaw, teeter-totter (14)

널리 far and wide (6)

널어 놓- hang out (the laundry) (1)

넓히- widen, broaden sth (14)

넘기- get past, through or over sth unpleasant; "weather" (a trying moment) (3)

넘어지- fall over; fall down (1)

넘치- overflow; go beyond; be more than can be handled (4)

녀석 rascal; urchin (12)

노-ㄹ- (놀다) play; goof off (14)

노력(努力 / 努力) effort(s); trouble (6)

노력(努力)(을) 하- make effort(s); exert oneself (6)

노망(老妄)기 [-끼] touch of dementia; hints of dementia (11)

녹- melt (intransitive) (11)

녹초(가) 되- become a tired wreck (9)

논 rice paddy (18)

논리(論理) logic (8)

논문(論文) thesis; scholarly paper (4)

놀라- be surprised, astonished; be frightened, startled (NB: processive) (11, 19)

놀라w- (놀랍다) be surprising, amazing (4)

놀리- let sb play; give sb a day off (14)

농담 삼아 as a joke; jokingly (19)

농담(弄談) joke (19)

농사(農事)를 지(ㅅ)- (짓다) engage in farming / agriculture (14)

높- be high (14)

높이- raise [up]; elevate (14)

놓아 두- put (sth) down (for a moment / for later use) (12)

놓이- be / get put (11)

누구누구? who all? (12)

누군가 sb or other (2)

눈(을) 뜨- open one's eyes (4)

눈에 선하- be fresh / vivid "before one's eyes"; be fresh in one's mind / memory (7)

눈을 뜨고 보- watch with one's eyes wide open (4)

느껴지- get so that it is realized; come to feel / sense (14)

느끼- feel; sense; experience; be conscious of; realize; be deeply moved (1, 14)

느-ㄹ- (늘다) increase; accrue; make progress; improve; expand; lengthen (14)

늘 always; constantly (6)

늘리- increase sth; augment sth; stretch sth; enlarge sth; expand sth (14)

늘어나- increase; be on the increase (7)

능력(能力) ability (2)

능숙(能熟)하- be skillful, expert, adept (17)

늦- be late; be loose (14)

늦가을 late autumn (7)

늦잠(을) 자- sleep late; sleep in (1)

늦추- postpone; loosen sth (14)

ㄷ

다가 오- approach; come near (2)

다가가- approach; go up to (11)

다니- go around (16)

다-ㄹ- (달다) get heated, become very hot (6)

다루- handle; take care of; deal with (6)

다른 날 같았으면 if it had been ("like") any other day (2)

다리- iron, press sth (12)

다리미 iron (12)

다리에 쥐(가) 나- get a cramp in the leg (2)

다발 bundle, bunch, sheaf (18)

다스리- rule over; reign over; govern; manage; administer (18)

다음으로 미루- postpone / put off until later (9)

다이어트(를) 하- diet; go on a diet (1)

다치- hurt oneself (1)

다행(多幸)이- it is a great fortune; it is fortunate (1)

다행히(多幸)히 fortunately; luckily (8)

닦- wipe sth (3)

단골집 one's regular or favorite restaurant / bar (4)

단군(檀君) Tan'gun, mythical founder of the Korean race (18)

단지(但只) just; only; merely; simply (2)

닫히- be / get closed/shut (6, 11)

달려나가- run / dash out (8)

달려오- come running (17)

달리- run; race along (2)

달성(達成)(을) 하- achieve (one's objective) (17)

닮- take after; resemble (6)

담– put sth in a vessel; hold in; keep in (6, 11)

담그–, 담가요 soak; steep; prepare, pickle (kimch'i) (3)

담기– be / get contained; be filled with (11)

답장(答狀) a reply letter (7)

당일치기 one-day affair (outing / trip); doing sth on one and the same day (16)

당첨(當籤)(이) 되– get selected in a drawing (4)

당황(唐慌 / 唐惶)하– be confused; feel at a loss as to what to do (NB: processive) (1)

닿– it reaches, goes as far as (4)

대단한 미인(美人) an incredible beauty (5)

대드–ㄹ– (대들다) defy; turn against; stand up to; go at; attack; tackle (18)

대리(代理) job title for lowest ladder position in a company: representative (16)

대통령(大統領) president (of a country) (4)

대한(大韓) Korea, as in 대한민국(大韓民國) Republic of Korea (12)

대회(大會) large meeting, rally, tournament (12)

더 이상(以上) anymore; more; further (14)

더–ㄹ– (덜다) subtract; deduct; lessen; mitigate (11)

더러w– (더럽다) be dirty, filthy, unkempt (1)

더욱 more; still more; all the more (12)

덕분(德分) indebtedness; favor; grace (4)

던지– throw (4)

덥히– heat sth; warm sth up (14)

덮– cover with; put on (11, 13)

덮개 lid; cover (11)

덮이– be / get covered (11, 13)

데우– heat sth; warm sth up (14)

데이터 data (6)

도w– (돕다) help; assist (14)

도끼 axe (6)

도둑 thief (6)

도둑질←도둑 stealing; theft (11)

도–ㄹ– (돌다) sth turns (14)

도망(逃亡)(을) 가– flee; head for the hills; run away; escape (16, 17)

도망(逃亡)(을) 치– flee; run away; beat a retreat (17)

도시 한가운데 right (smack) in the middle of the city (17)

도시(都市) city (17)

도장(刀匠) seal, handstamp, chop (14)

도장(刀匠)(을) 찍– stamp / affix one's name chop (14)

도전(挑戰)(을) 하– challenge; make a challenge; bid defiance to (18)

도착(到着)(을) 하– arrive at; reach (1)

독자(讀者) reader (6)

독특(獨特)하– be peculiar, unique, original (11)

돋– stick up / out, protrude(14)

돋보기 spectacles; magnifying glass (11)

돋우– raise, lift (up); stimulate, heighten; (화(火)를 ~) provoke / incite sb's anger (14); (입맛(을) ~) stimulate the appetite) (14)

돌 anniversary; first anniversary (1)

돌 잔치 ceremony in honor of baby's first birthday (1)

돌려 주– return sth; give sth back (19)

돌리– turn sth; make sth turn; let sth go around; pass sth around (2, 14)

돌아다보– turn around and look; look back; look behind oneself (1)

돌아보– look back; turn around and look (4)

동굴(洞窟) cave; cavern (18)

동그랗– (동그래, 동그란) be round, circular, spherical (18)

동방예의지국(東方禮義之國) Eastern Country of Propriety (i.e., Korea) (6)

동시통역(同時通譯) simultaneous interpretation (18)

동양(東洋) the East; East Asia; the Far East (9)

동의(同意)(를) 하다 agree; assent, consent, accede (to) (13)

동작(動作) movement (of members of the body); motion; carriage; bearing; action; act (17)

동전(銅錢) coins; change; silver (2)

동창회(同窓會) alumni / alumnae society (5)

돼지 pig (18)

돼지 저금통(貯金桶) piggy bank (14)

되살아나– revive; come back to life; rekindle; burn up again (14)

두고 오– leave sth behind by accident (1)

두어 two or three; a few (4)

둔(鈍)하– be thickheaded, dull, slow-witted, dense, "thick" (18)

둥둥 / 동동 adverb for describing sth floating bouncingly on the surface of water (12)

뒤떨어지– fall behind (6)

뒤지– search; rummage; fumble (12)

뒷모습 one's appearance from behind (4)

뒷주머니 back pocket (13)

드라이브 (computer) drive (6)

들고 다니– carry around (e.g., an umbrella) (2, 7)

들렀다 가– drop in, stop by, drop by (and then be on one's way again) (3)

들르– stop in; drop by (3)

들리– be heard, audible (NB: processive) (11)

들리– be / get held (up) in the hands (9)

들리– let / make sb hear (14)

들어 주– listen to (and acquiesce) sb's request for a favor; do sb the favor of listening (17)

들어주– give in to; accede to (6)

들이쉬– (숨(을) ~) breathe in (11)

들키– be / get caught (6)

등 the back (14)

등(等) and so on; and so forth; and the like; etc. (7)

등산(登山)(을) 하- hike; go hiking (6)

따- get (a license) (2)

따르-, 따라 follow (2)

따르-, 따라 pour (4)

딱 맞- fit perfectly / just right (16)

딱지(를) 떼이- get a ticket (2)

딸기 strawberry (18)

떠내려가- float away (in a downward direction away from the speaker) (16)

떠드-ㄹ- (떠들다) make a ruckus; horse around (2)

떨리- shake, tremble (intransitive) (7)

떨어지- fall down; drop; separate; be detached; be removed (13)

떼- remove; take away; subtract; take off; spearate; get rid of (17)

떼어내- take away; remove (and put away) (17)

똑같은 (which is) exactly the same (8)

뚜껑 lid; cover (11)

뚫리- be / get pierced, drilled, bored, penetrated (18)

뚱뚱하- be fat, chubby (3)

뛰- jump; leap; run (14)

뛰어드-ㄹ- (뛰어들다) run / dash in ("dash and enter") (8)

뛰쳐나오- come running out (18)

뜨- (눈을 ~)open (one's eyes) (11)

뜨- float; rise up (3, 12)

뜨이- (eyes, ears ~) open; be / get opened (11)

뜯- open (a letter); tear out; pick; pluck; tear apart; pull to pieces (12)

뜻 meaning (19)

뜻대로 as one intends; in accord with one's wishes (3)

ㄹ

러시아 Russia (4)

러시아인 Russian (person) (4)

레이저 laser (6)

로마법(法) [-뻡] the ways ("law") of Rome (2)

로미오 역(役) the role of Romeo (18)

리(里) li, ri—measure of length (about 1/3 mile) (18)

ㅁ

마누라 "old lady"(pejorative or jocular term for one's wife) (7)

마늘 garlic (18)

마당 courtyard inside a traditional Korean house (1)

마-ㄹ- (말다) cease; desist (14)

마루 the living room (14)

마르- lose weight; be thin, skinny (NB: processive) (2)

마르- get dry (14)

마사지 크림 massage cream (17)

마음 놓고 with peace of mind; without anxiety; free from care (4)

마음(을) 먹- make up one's mind (14)

마음(이) 약(弱)하- be weak-willed; have a weak stomach (14)

마음(이) 잘 통(通)하- (two people's minds / hearts) communicate well; understand each other (2)

마음(이) 풀리- feel better; feel reassured; relieved (16)

마음대로 as one pleases; as one likes (19)

마치- finish sth (17)

마치...듯이 just like / as if... (11)

마침 just in time; at the right moment; in the nick of time; opportunely; luckily; as luck would have it (11)

막- stop; block (6)

막 just about to (with -(으)려고 하 -); just as (one was doing sth); just when (13)

막내 youngest child; youngest (son, daughter) (3)

만나 뵈- ~ 뵙- (humbly) meet sb honorific (19)

만들어지- get made (6)

만우절(萬愚節) April Fools' Day (14)

만족(滿足)하- be satisfied (14)

맏아들 oldest son (14)

말 한 마디 word; one word (13)

말라리아 malaria (6)

말리- dry sth; make sth dry (14)

말썽(을) 부리- create trouble; make a fuss (12)

말썽꾸러기 troublemaker (12)

맑- be clear, transparent (12)

맞- get hit, smacked (6)

맡- take responsibility for, take charge of (14)

맡기- entrust sth; leave a person with; trust sb with; leave in sb's charge (14)

매번(每番) every time; all the time (6)

매서w- (매섭다) (a person) be severe, strict, fierce, violent (18)

매우 awfully; terribly; very (9)

매표소(賣票所) ticket office, booth (1)

머리(를) 자르- cut one's hair; get a haircut (13)

머릿속으로 in one's mind ("inside one's head") (3)

먹이- feed; let sb eat (14)

먹히- be / get eaten (11)

멀리 떨어져서 dropping back to a distance (13)

멀리 far (adverb); (from) afar; so that it is distant (13)

멈추- sth stop; stop sth (functions as both transitive and intransitive) (13, 17)

멍청하- be dim-witted, stupid (14)

멍하- be spaced-out, glazed over (14)

며칠 a few days; several days; also: how many days? (3)

며칠 만에 after a few days; within a few days (18)

명답(名答)(을) 하- give a brilliant answer (5)

명령(命令) order; command (6)

명령(命令)(을) 하- order; command (2)

몇 번째? how-many-eth? (14)

모금 a mouthful, a sip (4)

모기 mosquito (6)

모두 all; everyone; in all cases (6)

모두들 everybody (17)

모-ㄹ- (몰다) drive it; herd it (8)

모면(謀免)(을) 하- shirk; evade; elude; escape (17)

모양(模樣) appearance(s); shape; form (2, 17)

모이- gather; assemble (intransitive) (16)

모임 meeting; gathering; get-together (2)

모자라- be not enough; be insufficient ; lack; be deficient, short of; be dull, stupid (NB: processive) (1, 14)

목(이) 마르- be thirsty ("throat is dry") (14)

목(이) 쉬- get a hoarse throat (6)

목걸이 necklace (14)

목소리 voice (14)

목욕 캡 bathing cap (17)

목적(目的) objective; goal (17)

몰라보- not recognize sb (19)

몸무게 one's body weight (19)

몸살(이) 나- suffer from general fatigue and miseries (from overwork) (17)

몸조리(~調理)(를) 하- take good care of oneself (usually after sickness or childbirth) (4)

몹시 terribly; awfully; very (12)

못되- be awful, bad (as a person; always past tense) (16)

몽땅 in total; totally; in one big lump (14)

무게 weight (19)

무-ㄹ- (물다) bite (11)

무릎 knee (16)

무리(無理)이- be over the top, too much, a strain, unreasonable (14)

무리(無理)하- overdo it; go over the top in one's efforts; exert oneself unreasonably (7)

무사(無事)히 safely; without incident (14)

무식(無識)하- be ignorant (6)

무심(無心)코 inadvertently; without realizing it (5)

무안(無顔)하- be "without face"; i.e., lose face, feel embarrassed, ashamed (11)

무언가 something or other (2)

무언가 ← 무엇인가 sth (or other) (14)

무지무지 incredibly; very (16)

무척 very much (so); terribly; awfully; incredibly (2, 16)

묵- spend the night; lodge; put up at (2)

묵 jelly (made from acorns or peas / beans) (11)

문신 (文身) tattoo (12)

문자(文字) [-짜] script; writing system (8)

문화(文化) culture (8)

묻- bury sth (11); stick to sth; stain sth (11)

묻히- be / get smudged, smeared, stained; be / get buried, concealed (8, 11)

물건(物件) thing; item; goods (6)

물고기 [물꼬기] fish (in its uncooked state) (12)

물난리(亂離)(가) 나- water disaster occurs; flooding happens (16)

물리- be / get bitten (11)

물어 가- carry off in one's mouth (12)

물어볼 것도 없이 needless to say ("needless to ask") (12)

뭐뭐 what all? (12)

뭔가 sth (or other) (18)

미w- (밉다) be hateful, odious, repulsive (13)

미국인(美國人) American (person) (4)

미-ㄹ- (밀다) push (11)

미련하- be clumsy, awkward, foolish, stupid (18)

미리 beforehand; in advance; ahead of time (2)

미성년(未成年) minor, underage person (3)

미술(美術) art; arts (9)

미술관(美術館) art gallery (9)

민박(民泊)(을) 하- do a (short) homestay on a vacation; stay as a paying guest in sb's home (8)

민속(民俗) folkways, folk customs (14)

민속놀이 folk games; traditional games (14)

민속학(民俗學) the study of folklore (14)

민족(民族) people, race, nation, ethnos (6)

믿- believe in; rely on (6)

밀리- *lit.:* be pushed (get backed up, jammed, clogged [traffic]); back up; accumulate (2, 11)

ㅂ

바구니 basket; hamper (11)

바느질 ← 바늘 needlework (11)

바늘 needle (6)

바닷가 the seaside (1)

바둑(을) 두- play *paduk* (Korean version of go) (19)

바라보- gaze at; stare at (13)

바람(을) 쐬- take some fresh air; get some fresh air (3)

바르- apply, put on (makeup, ointment, etc.) (17)

바위 rock, stone (usually quite large) (11)

반드시 for sure; certainly; without fail (2)

반말 Intimate or Plain Style speech (1)

반복(反復)(을) 하- repeat; reiterate (6)

반영(反影 / 反映)(이) 되- be / get reflected (6)

반응(反應)(을) 보이- give ("show / evince") a reaction (3)

반응(反應)(을) 하- react (8)

반장(班長) the class leader; class president (9)

반찬(飯饌) side dishes to accompany rice (6, 12)

받는 대로 as soon as you receive it (7)

발등 [-뜽] top of the foot (6)

발명(發明) invention (8)

발음(發音) pronunciation (9)

발전(發展)시키-(나라를 ~) develop (the country) (6)

발짓 [-찟] gesture with the foot or feet (17)

밟- tread on; step on (6, 11)

밟히- get stepped / trodden on (11)

밤 chestnut (11)

밤(을) 새우- stay up all night; take an all-nighter (2)

밤색(~色) chestnut color, i.e., brown (11)

방법(方法) method; means (6)

방송국(放送局) broadcasting station (6)

방학 내내 right / all the way through the school holidays (8)

배탈(이) 나- have tummy troubles; get a stomach upset (1)

뱁새 crow tit; parrotbill (tiny bird) (6)

버릇(이) 없- be badly behaved; have poor/bad habits/manners (2)

버리- discard; throw away (1)

번거로w- (번거롭다) feel burdened (NB: descriptive) (17)

번역(飜譯) translation (18)

번역(飜譯)(을) 하- translate (18)

번쩍 (lifts sth) briskly (4)

번호(番號) number (2)

벌 counter for outfits / suits / pieces of clothing (16)

벌(罰)(을) 받- be / get punished (6)

벌금(罰金)(을) 내- pay a fine (9)

벌떡 (stands up) abruptly, suddenly (4)

벌어지- (sth) happens; (an event) develops, unfolds (3)

범인(犯人) criminal; culprit (18)

법규(法規) law(s); rule(s); regulation(s) (2)

법규에 따라 according to the law (2)

벗기- remove, [make] take off (clothing); unclothe, undress, strip (sb / sth); strip off; peel; pare; remove (a covering); take off (a cover) (6, 14)

베- cut (e.g., one's finger) (16)

벨 bell (17)

벼락(이) 치- lightning strikes (9)

벼락치기 last-minute cramming (9)

변소(便所) toilet (not an elegant word) (5)

변호사(辯護士) lawyer (4)

별별 **NOUN** all kinds of NOUN, all sorts of NOUN (implying that some of them are strange) (19)

병(病)(이) 나- get sick (not to be confused with 병(이) 나(ㅅ)- *sickness gets better*) (1)

보고서(報告書) written report (1)

보기 흉(凶)하- be awful to see; the viewing of it is distasteful, bad (11)

보름 fortnight (14)

보물(寶物) treasure, highly prized article (11)

보수(保守) conservatism (8)

보약(補藥) tonic, restorative (6)

보이- be visible, seen (NB: processive) (11)

보이- show; let sb see (14)

복(福)(을) 받- be blessed / fortunate (lit. "receive blessings") (NB: processive) (6)

복권(福券) lottery ticket (4)

복권에 당첨(이) 되- win the lottery; win on a lottery ticket (4)

복숭아 peach (11)

복용(服用)(을) 하- take / ingest (medicine) (18)

복학(復學)(을) 하- resume one's studies after a leave (5)

봉투(封套) envelope (19)

봐 주세요 *Please give me a break.* (11)

부(ㅅ)- (붓다) (sth) swells (1)

부드러w- (부드럽다) be soft (18)

부딪치- strike; collide with (8)

부부(夫婦) married couple; husband and wife (2)

부부(夫婦)싸움 a quarrel between husband and wife (16)

부분(部分) part; portion (8)

부상(負傷) injury (11)

부수 (部首) radical (in Chinese characters) (9)

부수- smash sth, break sth (17)

부시-(눈이 ~) be blinded, dazzled (14)

부엌 kitchen (6)

부자(富者) rich person (6)

부장(部長) chief of section / department / division (6)

부츠 boots (19)

부탁(을) 들어 주- (듣다) do the favor that sb asks (2)

북극점(北極点) the North Pole (18)

분교(分校) branch campus (5)

분명(分明)하- be clear, obvious (6)

분수(分數) one's station in life (6)

분위기(雰圍氣) atmosphere (3)

불(을) 끄- put out a fire; extinguish a light (14)

불리- have sb call

불안(不安)하- be uneasy; feel insecure, ill at ease, anxious (11)

불우(不遇) misfortune; ill luck; ill fortune (18)

불행(不幸)하- be unfortunate (17)

불행(不幸)하게도 unfortunately (17)

붐비- be crowded, full of people (NB: processive) (8)

붙이- (눈을 ~) lit.: make one's eyes stick together / adhere, i.e., get some shut-eye, sleep (19)

붙이- stick sth to; make sth stick to (19)

비- (비었어요) become empty, vacant, hollow (always used with past tense) (17, 19)

비(를) 맞- get rained on (4)

비(를) 쫄딱 맞- get sopping (= 쫄딱) wet in the rain (16)

비결(祕訣) the secret, key, or knack to sth (1)

비교(比較) comparison (12)

비교(比較)(를) 하- compare (12)

비교적(比較的)(으로) comparatively; relatively (12)

비누 soap (14, 16)

비-ㄹ- (빌다) (잘못했다고 ~) apologize; beg sb's pardon (16)

비밀(祕密) secret you might tell sb (1)

비상(非常) emergency; contingency (17)

비상(非常)하- (mind, brain) be brilliant, extraordinary (14)

비상벨 emergency bell, alarm (17)
비상상태(非常狀態) emergency; emergency situation (14)
비슷하- be similar (3)
빗- comb [one's hair] (14)
빗기- comb [sb's hair] (14)
빚(을) 지- incur debt; go into debt (6)
빨-ㄹ- (빨다) launder, wash (clothes) (12)
빠져나가- lit.: fall and go out (11)
빠지- fall into (8); be absent; fail to turn up (4)
빨래 the laundry (1)
빨래 washing; laundry (11)
빨래(를) 하- do the laundry (1)
빨래거리 [-꺼리] things to be washed, laundered (11)
빼- pull out; take out; extract; leave out; omit; take off (glasses); remove (6, 18)
빼놓- remove (19)
빼앗- snatch away (11)
빼앗기- be / get snatched away (11)
뺨 cheek (6)
뻔하- be clear, obvious, plain to see (17)
뽑- select sth; extract sth; choose; hire (6, 11)
뽑히- be / get picked, extracted, [s]elected (11)
뾰로통하- be sulky; pout (14)
뿌옇-, 뿌애요 be a pearly, misty color (8)

ㅅ

사과(謝過)(를) 하- apologize (6)
사내, 사나이 man; male (12)
사다리 ladder (15)
사동(使動) causative (in grammar) (11)
사동어휘(使動語彙) causative vocabulary (14)
사랑니 wisdom tooth (18)
사망률(死亡率) death rate (6)
사망자(死亡者) casualty, victim, dead person (6)
사살(射殺) death by shooting (11)
사업(事業) business; enterprise; undertaking (9, 12)
사이 "the space between"; relationship (2)
사이다 fizzy Korean soft drink like Seven-Up or Sprite (13)
사정(事情) (extenuating) circumstance (6)
사진(寫眞) photo (9)
사진기(寫眞機) camera (nowadays people also say 카메라) (11)
사촌동생(四寸同生) younger cousin (5)
사치(奢侈) luxury, extravagance (6)
사치(奢侈)스러w- (~스럽다) be luxurious, extravagant (6)
사투리 dialect; brogue (4)
삭제(削除)(를) 하- delete (6)
산더미 [-떠미] a great mass; a huge amount; a mountain (12)
산돼지 [-뙈지] wild boar (18)
산딸기 wild strawberry (18)

산소(山所) family or clan burial site (3)
살(을) 빼- lose weight (intentional) (4)
살(이) 빠지- lose weight (unintentional) (1)
살(이) 찌- get fat (19)
살리- save; let live (12)
살피- examine; check out; observe (12)
삼촌(三寸) uncle (on father's side) (5, 18)
상(床)(을) 차리- set the table (19)
상담(相談) counseling; advising (18)
상담비(相談費) counseling fees; advising fees (18)
상담소(相談所) counseling agency; a counseling office (18)
상당(相當)히 quite; rather (7)
상대방(相對方) one's opposite, counterpart; one's opponent, adversary (18)
상영(上映)(을) 하- show (a film); project; screen (18)
상의(相議)(를) 하- consult with (19)
상징(象徵) symbol (3)
상하- (음식이 ~) (food) go bad, go off, spoil (16)
샅샅이 (adv.) in every nook and cranny (1)
새벽 dawn; daybreak (1)
새우- (밤(을) ~) stay up all night, take an all-nighter (4)
색동옷 colorful Korean traditional costume (2)
생각(이) 나- think of; recall (1, 19)
생각(이) 들- a thought occurs to one (13)
생각(이) 떠오르- a thought occurs to (me); a thought "floats up" (into my head) (3)
생겨나- come about; come into being (6)
생기- turn out a certain way; "look" a certain way; come about; appear (3, 19)
생선회 raw fish; sashimi (16)
생신(生辰), 생신날 birthday (honorific equivalent of 생일) (3, 13)
생전(生前) 처음 for the first time in one's life (5)
생활(生活) life (6)
생활(生活)(을) 하- "do living" i.e., conduct one's day-to-day life (3)
서- stand (14)
서너 번(番) three or four times; a few times (14)
서너 three or four; a few (19)
서당(書堂) traditional village schoolhouse for learning the Chinese classics (6)
서두르- rush; rush about (1)
서방(書房) (Folksy) one's husband, one's master; [Familiar Style] title for Mr., title used within the family for an unmarried male (13)
서양(西洋) the West (9)
서울대공원(大公園) Seoul Grand Park (17)
서울역 [-력] Seoul Station (12)
서재(書齋) study (14)
서적(書籍) books; publications (12)
석유(石油) gasoline (6)

섞– mix (11)

섞이– be / get mixed; sth mingles (11)

선(을) 보– have a preliminary meeting with a prospective spouse; have a sort of matchmaking date, often set up by the parents (4)

선배(先輩) one's senior from school (3)

선언(宣言)(을) 하– declare (4)

선조(先祖) ancestor (6)

선진국(先進國) advanced country (6)

선하– be fresh / vivid (before one's eyes), be fresh (in one's mind / memory) (7)

설 Korean New Year; New Year's Day (3)

설거지 the dishes; the washing up (9)

설계(設計)(가) 되– be / get designed (6)

설날 Korean New Year's Day (3)

설득(說得)(을) 시키– persuade (2)

설명(說明)(을) 하– explain (11)

설악산(雪嶽山) Mount Sŏrak (16)

설치– do a slipshod or half-assed job of sth; do sth in a less than satisfactory manner (9); 잠(을) ~ have an unsatisfactory sleep (9)

섭섭하– feel *Abschiedsschmerzen*; be sad that someone is leaving; be disappointed; be regrettable (2)

섭섭하게도 to one's regret / disappointment (2)

성공(成功)(을) 하– succeed (2)

성금(誠金) donation, contribution (18)

성실(誠實)하– be trustworthy, earnest, honest (6)

성적표(成績表) report card (14)

성품(性品) personal character (2)

성형수술(成形手術) cosmetic surgery; plastic surgery (5)

세– count (4)

세계(世界) world (8)

세련(洗練)(이) 되– be refined (in the social sense) (9)

세우– stop (a car); park (a car) (2); set up; establish (6)

세우– set up; establish; stand sth up; make sth stand; stop sth (e.g., a car) (12)

세월(歲月) time (as in "time flies") (7)

세탁(洗濯)(을) 하– do the laundry (3)

세탁기(洗濯機) laundry machine; washing machine (3)

세탁소(洗濯所) laundromat; launderette (3)

소귀에 경(經) 읽기 "reading sutras to a cow's ear," i.e., talking to a brick wall (16)

소나기 downpour / cloudburst (14)

소련(蘇聯) Soviet Union (9)

소련인(蘇聯人) Soviet (person) (9)

소문(所聞) rumor (6)

소설(小說) fiction; work of fiction; novel (8)

소수(小數) minority (2)

소식(消息) news; tidings; word (7)

소양댐 Soyang Dam (1)

소용(所用)(이) 없– be useless (16)

소죽 boiled fodder (14)

소중(所重)하– be important, weighty; be precious, dear (14)

소화(消化) digestion (18)

소화제(消化劑) digestive medicine (18)

속– be / get cheated, fooled, deceived (6)

속(이) 상하– be distressed, annoyed, exasperated, upset (NB: processive) (8, 12)

속담(俗談) proverb (6)

속상하– be upset (16)

속이– cheat; fool; deceive (6)

손가락 [–까락] finger (11)

손가락질 하– point (11)

손상(損傷)(이) 되– be / get damaged, injured (6)

손짓 [–찟] gesture with the hands (17)

솜씨 skill or dexterity, usually involving the hands (1, 17)

쇠뿔 cow's horn; ox horn (6)

수면제(睡眠劑) sleeping medicine (18)

수박 watermelon (3)

수박 한 통 one watermelon (3)

수상(殊常)하– be suspicious, doubtful-looking, "fishy" (17)

수영(水泳)(을) 하– swim (3)

수영복(水泳服) swimming suit, swimming costume (16)

수영장(水泳場) swimming pool (3)

수입(輸入)(을) 하– import (6)

수질(水質) water quality (5, 14)

수첩(手帖) pocket-size notepad (9)

순간(瞬間) moment (3)

순간(瞬間) moment; instant (17)

순간적으로 momentarily (3)

순진(純眞)하– be naive, genuine and pure (18)

술고래 boozer; someone who drinks a lot (9)

술맛이 나– feel like drinking ("the alcohol's taste appears / comes out") (9)

술에 취(醉)하– be / get drunk with alcohol (7)

숨 breath (11)

숨(을) 내쉬– breathe out (11)

숨(을) 들이쉬– breathe in (11)

숨기– hide sth; conceal; keep secret (14)

쉴 새 없이 without a[ny] chance / moment to rest (14)

스태프 staff (8)

습관(習慣) custom; habit (2)

습관(이) 되– get used to it (2)

승객(乘客) passenger (1)

시(詩) poem; poetry (9)

시가 cigar (4)

시간(을) 지키– be timely; be on time (NB: processive) (16)

시간적 여유(時間的 餘裕) time-wise leeway, margin, elbow-room (8)

시골 the countryside (7)

시골집 [–찝] one's home/house in the countryside/provinces (7)

시드-ㄹ- (시들다) fade; wither (12)
시력(視力) one's eyesight (7)
시멘트 cement (6)
시원하- be refreshing (13)
시인(詩人) poet (9)
시장 hunger (6)
시절(時節) time; era; occasion (18)
시집(을) 가- (woman) get married (3, 19)
시집(을) 보내- marry off (one's daughter) (3)
시키- order sth (as in a restaurant); order to do sth; make sb do sth (3, 9)
시험(試驗)에 붙- "stick to," i.e., pass an exam (1)
시험에 떨어지- fail an exam (1)
시험지(試驗紙) test; test paper (6)
식- (food) goes cold (3)
식사(食事) meal (fancy) (2)
식욕(食慾) appetite (13)
식은 땀 cold sweat (3)
식탁(食卓) dining table (11)
신- wear [on feet] (14)
신경(神經)(을) 쓰- worry about; be concerned about; get worked up about; stress about (expend nerves on) (2, 19)
신고(申告)(를) 하- report (sth, sb); notify; make a declaration (11)
신기- put sth on [sb's feet] (14)
신기(神奇)하- be strange, amazing, wondrous (19)
신발 shoes; footwear (8)
신입생(新入生) new student (12)
신장(腎臟) kidneys (6)
신하(臣下) minister; statesman; subject (18)
신화(神話) myth (18)
실망(失望)(을) 하- become disappointed (2)
실수(失手)(를) 하- make an error, mistake; commit an indiscretion (4)
실제 **NOUN** actual NOUN (19)
실제(實際) actuality (19)
실제(實際)로 in actual fact; in real life (6)
실천(實踐) putting into practice; practice (as opposed to theory) (2)
실컷 one's heart's content (14)
심- plant (6)
심(甚)하게 in a grave / serious way; terribly; (uses dialect) "something terrible" (4); extremely; severely (6)
심부름 (가-) (go on) an errand (7)
심부름꾼 errand boy (7)
싱글벙글하- be all smiles (NB: processive) (7)
싱싱하- be fresh (of produce) (12)
싸- (짐을 ~) pack one's bags (16)
싸- wrap (11); (김밥을 ~) make ("wrap") (kimpap) (13)
싸이- be / get wrapped, enveloped (11)
쌀 rice grain; uncooked rice (2)

쌀쌀하- be chilly (7)
쌓- pile sth; heap sth (11)
쌓이- (피로가 ~) fatigue accumulates; tiredness piles up (16)
쌓이- be / get piled up (hence, accumulate, get accumulated) (11, 12)
써다 주- write for sb (9)
썩 quite; rather; greatly; very much (9, 14)
쏟- spill sth (8)
쑥 mugwort (18)
쓰고 다니- wear around (7)
쓰러지- collapse; topple; sink to the ground; fall down (11)
쓰이- be / get used (6)
쓰이- sth "writes" [well]; be / get written (11)
씩 웃- smile sheepishly; give a quick (sheepish) smile (14)
씹- chew (11)
씹히- be / get chewed (11)

ㅇ

아까w- (아깝다) be regrettable, pitiful; is precious, valuable (4, 13)
아니면 or (if that is not the case, then) (3)
아들 녀석 my / our son [humble] (12)
아르바이트(를) 하- do part-time work on the side (usually said of students) (3)
아무렇게나 any old which way (1)
아무렇지도 않- be cool as a cucumber, unaffected by events (3)
아무튼 anyway; anyhow (16)
안- hug; embrace (11)
안기- be / get embraced (11)
안방(~房) [안빵] the women's quarters; the room where the parents sleep (12)
안색(顔色) one's complexion; the color of one's face (1)
안심(安心)하- be / feel at ease; feel unworried (2)
안전(安全)하- be safe (1)
앉히- seat sb (14)
알뜰하- be frugal, thrifty; earnest, assiduous (16)
알리- inform; let know (7, 14)
알맹이 substance; matter; content (19)
알아들- (알아듣다) understand, catch (sth said) (1)
알아보- recognize sb (19)
알아서 하세요 Do as you think best. (9)
암(癌) cancer (18)
앞서 in advance of; ahead of (1)
앞서 가- go ahead of; precede (1)
애(가) 타- be anxious; worry oneself sick (7)
애(를) 쓰- make efforts; try hard (3, 13)
애인(愛人) 사이 a dating relationship (2)
애인(愛人) boyfriend / girlfriend (2)

야구경기(野球競技) baseball game (2)

야구중계(野球中繼) baseball (re-)broadcast (6)

약(을) 올리– provoke sb, get up sb's nose (on purpose); exasperate sb (16)

약간(若干) a bit; a little; somewhat (2, 11)

약속(約束)(을) 지키– keep an appointment or promise (4)

얄미w– (얄밉다) slightly more hateful, odious, and repulsive than just 미w– (밉다) (13)

얌전하– be gentle, charming, modest, well behaved, well brought up (4, 12)

양품점(洋品店) a foreign-goods shop, haberdashery (16)

어둠 darkness (17)

어디선가 somewhere or other (2, 19)

어디어디 where all? (12)

어떨 때는 sometimes; on some occasions (4)

어른 elder or adult (6)

어린이날 Children's Day (17)

어머니날 Mother's Day (3)

어버이날 Parents' Day (3)

어울리– match; suit; be appropriate for; (people) get along with, go well together; (clothes) go well with, match, look good on (1, 19)

어지러w– (어지럽다) be / feel dizzy (NB: descriptive) (2)

억울하– feel pent-up frustration; feel frustrated or wronged (NB: descriptive) (2)

억지로 by force; against one's will; under compulsion / coercion, duress (14)

언제 = 언젠가는 at some point; sometime; at some time or other (16)

언젠가(는) once, sometime or other (I don't remember) (2)

얻어 먹– get free meals; freeload (6)

얼굴 face; features (6)

얼른 immediately; right away (14)

얼마 전에 not long ago (13)

얼마 전에는 not too long ago (7)

없애– eliminate; get rid of (14)

없이 (NOUN ~) without NOUN (12)

엉뚱하– be ridiculous, outrageous, preposterous (6, 12)

엉뚱한 실수(失手) stupid mistake; silly gaffe (4)

엉망 mess (9)

엊그제 a few days ago (7)

–에 비해서 compared to (NOUN) (9)

여권(旅券) [-꿘] passport (12)

여기저기 here and there (3)

여러 번 several times (12)

여러분 ladies and gentlemen! (3)

여보! Honey! (term of address between spouses) (17)

여성(女性) woman; the female gender (6)

여유(餘裕) (extra) space; (extra) room; (extra) time; leeway; elbowroom (19)

여전(如前)하– be the same as ever (2)

여행(旅行) traveling; a journey, trip (1)

여행객(旅行客) traveler (1)

역(役) (dramatic) role (18)

역사(歷史) history (8)

연구(研究) research (8)

연락(連絡)하– connect; get in touch with (1)

연습경기(練習競技) practice game (2)

연필(을) 돌리– flip one's pencil round and round between the thumb and third finger (a favorite trick of Korean students) (14)

열리– be / get opened (11)

열쇠 [-쐬] key (12)

염려(念慮)(를) [하지] 마세요 *Don't worry.* (2)

염려(念慮)(를) 하– worry; be concerned (18)

영악하– be smart, sharp, shrewd; have gumption (18)

예(例) example (6)

예(例)를 들어(서) for example; for instance (6)

예상(豫想)(을) 하– expect; foresee; anticipate (3, 17)

예의(禮儀) courtesy; decorum; propriety (6)

예절(禮節) etiquette; politeness (2)

오늘로 as of today (3)

오락(娛樂) amusement; recreation; pastime (13)

오락실(娛樂室) amusement room (usually with video games) (13)

오래 for a long time (6, 19)

오랫동안 for a long time (11)

오븐 oven (9)

오염(汚染) contamination; pollution (14)

오염(汚染)(이) 되– be / get polluted (9)

오이 cucumber (7)

오전(午前) AM (16)

오토바이 motorcycle (8)

오해(誤解)(를) 받– be / get misunderstand (6)

오해(誤解)(를) 하– misunderstand; mistake (sth / sb for) (13)

오히려 contrary to expectations; contrary to what one might think / expect (6)

옥편(玉篇) Chinese character dictionary (for Koreans) (12)

온 몸 whole body (16)

온통 all; wholly; entirely (8)

올려 놓– place sth onto the top of sth (9, 12)

올리– raise; lift; present; give (14)

옮기– move sth; shift sth; relocate sth (9)

와이셔츠 dress shirt (12)

완성(完成)(을) 하– complete sth (18)

완전히(完全-) completely; entirely; totally (8)

왠지 for some reason or other (5)

외삼촌 uncle (on mother's side) (18)

외양간 [-깐] stable; cow shed (14)

외우– memorize; recite from memory (3)

외출(外出)(을) 하– go out (19)

요 앞 = 이 앞   in the front (of here, where we are) (16)

요구(要求) a demand (6)

요구조건(要求條件) one's conditions and demands (6)

요란(搖亂)스러w– (~스럽다) be noisy, loud, clamorous, boisterous (17)

요리(料理) cooking; cuisine (1)

요즘 lately (1)

욕(辱) humiliation, abuse; swearing, "cussing" (6)

욕(을) 당하– suffer humiliation, be humiliated (6)

욕조(浴槽) bathtub (12)

용기(를) 주– encourage (6)

용기(勇氣) courage (6)

용돈 [-똔] spending money; pocket money (2)

용서(容恕)(를) 하– forgive (16)

우스갯소리 joke; anecdote; funny story (cf. 웃다) (19)

우연히(偶然-) coincidentally; by chance (3)

우울(憂鬱)하– be depressed, blue (14)

우정(友情) friendship; bonds of friendship (6)

운동화(運動靴) sneakers; sports shoes (13)

운전면허(運轉免許) driving license (18)

운전면허증(運轉免許證) [-쯩] driver's license (2)

울리– ring (intransitive); sound (17)

움직이– move (both transitive and intransitive) (6, 9)

웃기– be funny; make people laugh (14)

웃음거리 laughingstock; butt of ridicule (7)

웃지 못할 일 *sth which is no laughing matter; a rather serious matter* (13)

웅덩이 puddle (8)

원(願)하– want; desire (17)

원래(原來 / 元來) originally; primarily; from the first; to start with; actually; as a matter of fact (4, 16)

원숭이 monkey (6)

원시(遠視) farsightedness (7)

웬 = 무슨 what sort of? (what's with the...?) (16)

웬일로 Why? What for? "On account of what thing?" For what reason? (2)

웬일이세요? What's the matter (with you)? (2, 4)

위기(危機) crisis (17)

위반(違反) (을) 하– violate; infringe; break (2)

유난히 particularly; especially; unusually (9)

유명(有名)하– be famous (1)

유전(遺傳) genetics; heredity (6)

유전자(遺傳子) gene (6)

유턴 U-turn (2)

윷놀이 the game of *yut* (14)

읊– recite (poetry) (6)

음료수(飮料水) beverage (11, 13)

음주운전(飮酒運轉) drunk driving (2)

의견(意見) opinion (2)

의견에 찬성(을) 하– agree with an opinion (2)

의문(疑問) doubt; question (1)

의지(意志) will; volition; intention (18)

이걸로← 이것으로 by means of this (13)

이기– win; beat sb (use 을 / 를); overcome (18, 19)

이따가 in a while; a little while later (3)

이불 blanket; cover; quilt (13)

이상(異常)하– be strange, odd (7, 12)

이상(異常)하게 strangely, oddly (7)

이야기(를) 꺼내– bring up / raise a subject (6)

이야깃거리 subject of talk, topic (7)

이웃 neighbor (12)

이웃집 neighbor's house; neighboring house (12)

이유(理由) reason (2)

이해(理解)(가) 되– "get it"; understand (1)

이해(理解)(를) 하– understand (1)

이혼(離婚)(을) 하– get divorced (2)

익– get used to; be familiar with; get cooked; be done; ripen; mature (11)

익명(匿名) anonymous; anonymity (7)

익명으로 anonymously (7)

익명의 **NOUN** anonymous NOUN (7)

익숙해지– get accustomed / used to (2)

인간(人間) human being (18)

인구(人口) population (5)

인기(人氣) (가) 있– be popular (of people) (1)

인류(人類) mankind; human race; humanity (6, 11)

인류학(人類學) anthropology (11)

인류학자(人類學者) anthropologist (11)

인물(人物) a person, personage, individual (8)

인상(印象)을 남기– leave an impression (14)

인심(人心)(이) 좋– be good-hearted, genial (14)

인원(人員) the number of persons; staff; personnel (14)

인원수(-數) [-쑤] the number of personnel (14)

인질(人質) hostage (14)

인형(人形) doll (5)

일거리 [-꺼리] a piece of work; a job (7)

일그러지– shrivel up; wither; wilt (13)

일기예보(日氣豫報) weather forecast (6)

일단(一旦) first off; for starters; for the time being (9)

일등(一等) first class (2)

일등(一等)(을) 하– get first place / prize (2)

일본(日本) 말들 Japanese words (5)

일부러 on purpose; deliberately; intentionally (18)

일상생활(日常生活) daily life (6)

일어(日語) Japanese language (5)

잃어버리– lose sth (1)

임금(賃金) wage(s) (6)

입고 다니– wear around (7)

입맛 appetite (14)

입맛(을) 돋우– stimulate the appetite (14)

입맛(을) 잃어버리– lose one's appetite (2)

입맛에 맞– suit one's tastes (7)

입장(立場) position, situation, standpoint, stand (on an issue) (8, 14)

입히- dress sb; make sb wear (14)

있던 그대로 just as it was (had been) (8)

ㅈ

자기 뜻대로 as one envisions / intends (3)

자기(自己) self; oneself (3, 17); he himself / she herself (16)

자기들끼리 among themselves (11)

자꾸 continually; all the time; keep on... –ing (1)

자꾸 **VERB** keep on VERBing; continuously (12)

자녀(子女)분 children (honorific) (5)

자라- grow; grow up; be brought up (12)

자명종(自鳴鐘) alarm clock (14)

자살(自殺)(을) 하- commit suicide (18)

자상(仔詳)하- be attentive to detail, considerate of others (19)

자식(子息) one's children, sons and daughters; (vulgar) bastard (supposedly worse than 놈) (12)

자신(自信) confidence (18)

자신감(自信感) (feeling of) confidence (18)

자신감(自信感)을 가지고 confidently; with confidence (18)

자연(自然) nature; naturally, as a matter of course (6)

자연(自然)스러w- (-스럽다) be natural (16)

자연(自然)스럽게 naturally (16)

작가(作家) author; creative writer (18)

작문(作文) (을) 하- write a composition; compose a sentence (3)

작품(作品) work, opus, production (of art, literature, etc.) (18)

잔뜩 full; to the brim; to the max; all the way (11)

잔치 ceremonial feast; banquet (1)

잘 놀다 갑니다 a polite remark made to one's hosts when one is leaving their house: "I go now, having had a good time" (8)

잘 봐 주- give sb a break (2)

잘 생겼어요 is handsome (3)

잘나- be handsome, good-looking; be distinguished, great (3)

잘난 척하- put on airs; pretend to be sth great (3)

잘못 타- get on the wrong conveyance ("ride in error") (2)

잘못 (1) an error, mistake, as in 내 잘못이에요 *it's my mistake*, or (2) (adv.) mistakenly, in error (2)

잘못했다고 비-ㄹ (빌다) apologize, beg sb's pardon (16)

잠(을) 설치- sleep poorly, have an unsatisfactory sleep (9)

잠(이) 드-ㄹ (들다) fall asleep (1)

잠그- immerse sth; steep sth (11); lock sth, fasten sth(11)

잠기- be/get submersed/submerged in (11); sth locks; be / get fastened (11)

잠실 Chamsil (place name in Seoul) (18)

잠에 취하다 be drunk / woozy with sleep (NB: processive) (7)

잡- catch (14)

잡지사(雜誌社) magazine company (9)

잡히- be / get caught (11)

잡히- have [sth] caught; have sb catch (14)

장가(를) 가- (man) get married (4)

장난 game, play; mischief, prank; fun, amusement (12)

장난감 [-깜] toy, plaything (12, 16)

장난꾸러기 mischievous child (12)

장난으로 for fun (12)

장난하- play (play with: NOUN(을) 가지고) (12)

장마 the seasonal rains, monsoons (7)

장마철 the rainy season (7)

장만(을) 하- get sth ready; provide oneself with; buy (7)

장미(꽃) rose (12)

장소(場所) place (1)

장어 eel (6)

재빠르- be skillful and fast, nimble, agile (17)

재주 talent(s); skill(s) (2)

재촉(을) 하- urge on (sb); press on, importune (sb) (1)

쟁반(錚盤) tray (9)

저장(貯藏)(을) 하- save (a computer file) (6)

적- write down; take note of; jot down (3)

적당(適當)하- be appropriate (2)

적시- wet sth; make sth wet (14)

적자(赤字) financial deficit; (with the copula) be in the red (3)

전(傳)하- pass (a message) on (7)

전(全)혀 (+ **Negative**) [not]... at all; [doesn't]... at all (13)

전기(電氣) 다리미 electric iron (18)

전기(電氣) electricity; electric (as modifier) (18)

전날(前~) the previous day (1)

전부(全部) in its entirety; all of it / them; the whole thing (9)

전부터(前~) from the very beginning (4)

전시회(展示會) exhibition; show (19)

전화(電話)(가) 걸려 오- a call comes in (*lit.*: a telephone call is called in) (9)

전화(電話)할 데 있- need to make a phone call ("have a place to call to") (16)

절반(折半) half (6)

점(點) birthmark (6)

점점(漸漸) gradually; bit by bit; by degrees (7, 17)

접- fold sth (9)

접시 plate, dish (4)

정(情)(이) 드-ㄹ- (들다) "affection enters" = grow fond of, attached to; come to love sb (but not necessarily romantically) (1)

정글 jungle (11)

정력(精力) virility (6)

정력(精力)(을) 돋우- boost virility (6)

정문(正門) front gate; main entrance (5)

정복(征服)(을) 하– conquer (18)

정부(政府) government (2)

정성(精誠) sincerity and devoted affection (14)

정신(情神) mentality; one's mental state, state of mind, senses (8, 11)

정중(鄭重)하– be earnest, grave; be courteous, respectful (17)

젖– get / become wet; get soaked / moistened (14)

제 one's own, self's (6)

제 마음대로 as one pleases (9)

제 생각대로 as I think; in the way I think (9)

제 시간에 on time (2)

제거(除去)(를) 하– remove, get rid of (6)

제대로 properly; as it should be done (9)

제사(祭祀)(를) 지내– conduct a ritual ceremony (6)

제주도(濟州道) Cheju Island (2)

제출(提出)(을) 하– hand in; submit (4)

조건(條件) [ˉ껀] condition (6)

조그맣– (조그매, 조그만) be little, small (12)

조기 (fish) a kind of croaker (12)

조사(調査)(를) 하– investigate (11)

조상(祖上) ancestor(s) (18)

조선시대(朝鮮時代) the Chosŏn era (6)

조숙(早熟)하– be precocious (9)

조언(助言) advice (6)

조용히 quietly (2)

조카 nephew; niece (17)

존댓말 Polite or Formal Style speech (1)

졸리– be / feel sleepy (7)

좁– be narrow (14)

좁히– make narrow; narrow (sth) (14)

종로 (鍾路) Chongno ["Bell Road"], a main boulevard in downtown Seoul (3, 6)

좌우간 (左右間) anyway; anyhow; in any case (9)

죄(罪)(를) 지(ㅅ)– (짓다) commit a crime / sin (6)

주(主)로 for the most part; in the main; mainly (6)

주w– (줍다) pick up (sth small) with one's fingers (9)

주관(主觀) subjectivity (8)

주머니 pocket (13)

주의(注意)(를) 하– pay attention; be cautious of (6)

주인(主人) owner; proprietor (17)

주인공(主人公) the hero, heroine, main character, protagonist (11)

주정(酒酊)(을) 하– act in a drunken and disorderly way; be a bad drunk (14)

주차(駐車)(를) 하– park a car; park a vehicle (5, 13)

주차장(駐車場) parking lot (13)

죽이– kill (12)

줄(을) 쭉 서– stand in a long (쭉) line (16)

줄이– cut down on (cigarettes, booze); reduce; diminish; lessen (7)

중단(中斷) (이) 되– be / get suspended, broken off, interrupted (2)

중지(中止)(를) 하– discontinue; suspend; interrupt (5)

중학교(中學校) middle school (18)

즉(卽) namely; to wit; that is to say (6)

즐거w– (즐겁다) be enjoyable, fun (1)

증조(曾祖) 할아버지 great-grandfather (18)

지–(빚(을) ~) incur debt; go into debt (6)

지(ㅅ)–(짓다)(죄(를) ~) commit a crime / sin (6)

지각(遲刻)(을) 하– arrive late (3)

지갑(紙匣) wallet, purse (where people keep their money); pocketbook (1)

지나– it passes; *recall:* 지난 주일 last ("past") week (3)

지내– (제사(를) ~) conduct a ritual ceremony (6)

지–ㄹ– (질다) be slushy, watery; muddy (11)

지루하– be boring (1)

지우– erase (6)

지저분하– be dirty, filthy (17)

지치– get exhausted, tired, worn out (4)

지켜 나가– maintain (into the future) (6)

지켜보– watch sth closely; keep a watchful eye on (13)

지키– watch over; guard; defend; keep; observe; abide by (13)

지팡이 cane (6)

지혜(智慧 / 知慧) wisdom (6)

지휘(指揮) command, supervision, direction(s) (14)

직업(職業) occupation; career (14)

진로(進路) course (to advance); the way ahead; one's path in life (18)

진로상담(進路相談) career advising (18)

진리(眞理) truth (6)

진찰실(診察室) examining room (19)

질기– be tough, chewy (11)

질병(疾病) disease; affliction; ailment (6)

짐 luggage; baggage; burden (9, 16)

짐(을) 싸– pack one's bags (16)

집– pick up, take up (with the fingers) (2, 11)

집들이 housewarming celebration (16)

집안일 housework (9)

집히– be / get picked up in a tweezer-like fashion (11)

짓 act; doing (12)

짖– bark (6)

짚– feel (pulse); carry (a cane) (6)

짜– be [too] salty (8)

쩔쩔매– be flustered; be at a complete loss as to what to do; be at one's wits' end (NB: processive) (3)

쫓– chase (11)

쫓기– be / get chased (11)

쫓아다니– follow (sb) around (7)

쭉 가– go straight, carry on straight (12)

쯤은 as for (such an insignificant, paltry thing) (11)

찌– (weather) be steaming hot (17)

찌개 stew (2)

찍- take (a photo) (9)
찍히- be / get chopped (6)

ㅊ

차- be cold (to the touch) (13)
차가w- (차갑다) be cold (to the touch) (13)
차리- prepare; make ready (13)
차문(車門) car door (13)
착하- be good (at heart); often used of dogs and children
  ("Good boy!"), or of anybody who is a good-hearted,
  honest person (3)
찬밥 cold rice (13)
찬성(贊成)(을) 하- agree with (2)
참- grin and bear it; suffer it; be patient (4)
창(窓) window (3)
찾아오- come calling; pay a visit on (19)
채우- fill sth up; complete (a number); make up; satisfy;
  fill; fulfill (14)
책임(責任)(을) 지- take ("bear") responsibility (14)
책임자(責任者) the person in charge; the person responsible
  (14)
처넣- jam in; shove in (9)
처벌(處罰)(을) 하- punish (2)
천리(千里) one thousand *li* (6)
천생(天生) by nature (adv.) (18)
천장 ceiling (4)
천장(天障)에 닿- reach the ceiling (4)
철(이) 없- / 있- lacks / has maturity, sense (14)
철사(鐵絲) wire (13)
첫눈에 반하- fall in love at first sight ("at first eye") (1)
첫배 the first boat (1)
-청(廳) administrative headquarters, as in 시청(市廳) city
  hall, etc. (2)
청평사(淸平寺) Ch'ŏngp'yŏng Temple (1)
체육(體育) physical education; athletics (12)
체육대회(體育大會) an athletics tournament / meet (12)
체질(體質) one's physical constitution (6)
체질에 맞- fit / match one's physical constitution (6)
체하- have a bad effect on one's stomach; feel heavy on the
  stomach (2)
쳐다보- stare at; gaze at (14)
쳐들어오-, 쳐들어가- barge in on; invade (9)
초기(初期) first stage(s); early stage(s); initial period (7)
초대(招待)(를) 하- invite (2)
초상집(初喪~) family / house in mourning (2)
초인종(招人鐘) doorbell; call bell; buzzer (17)
촌(村) village (9)

촌스러w- (~스럽다) a bit rustic, hick; country bumpkin-ish
  (9)
최고(最高) the best; the greatest (16)

추돌(追突) (rear-end) collision (2)
추상(抽象) abstraction (8)
춘천(春川) Ch'unch'ŏn (place name) (1)
출발(出發)(을) 하- set off; depart (7)
출장(出張) (을) 가- go away on an official trip; go away on
  business (1)
출장(出張) official trip; business trip (1)
충혈(充血)(이) 되- be / become bloodshot (8)
취(醉)하- get drunk (NB: processive) (2)
취소(取消)(를) 하- cancel; annul (6)
취직(就職) getting / landing a job; finding employment (1)
취직(就職)(을) 하- get / find a job (1)
치료(治療)(를) 하- heal, cure, treat (medically) (3)
치매(癡呆) senile dementia (7)
치매환자(癡呆患者) senile dementia sufferer; senile person
  (7)
치우- clear sth up / away; get rid of sth; clean up (9, 12)
친구(親舊) 사이 "just friends" relationship (2)
친절(親切)하- be kind (17)
침략(侵掠) invasion (11)

ㅋ

칸 space, column (2)
켜지- be / get turned on (17)
코끝이 찡하- (the end of one's nose) get itchy (because one
  feels like crying) (14)
콩 black beans (6)

ㅌ

타- sth burn; ride something (14)
타고 나- be / get born with / naturally endowed with (2)
타자기(打字機) typewriter (17)
탈 trouble; a hitch; a problem (18)
태백산(太白山) Mount T'aebaek (18)
태어나- come into the world; be born (14)
태어나서 지금까지 쭉 *ever since I was born until now; uninter-
  ruptedly* (14)
태연(泰然)하- be / remain as if nothing happened; remain
  unaffected (NB: descriptive) (3)
태우- burn sth; give a ride to sb (14)
터-ㄹ- (털다) shake sth off or out (11)
테이프 tape (12)
텐트 tent (13)
토질(土質) soil quality (5)
톱질 ← 톱 sawing (11)
통(通)하- "(one's words) get through" = communicate
  with, get through to (2)
통역(通譯) interpretation (18)
퇴근(退勤)(을) 하- leave work for home (3)
특(特)히 especially; in particular (17)
특별(特別)하- be special, particular (2)
특성(特性) special characteristics (6)

튼튼하– be strong, sturdy (14)

틈 gap; crack; space; interval; time (11)

티 mote; particle; grit; foreign particle; flaw; speck (11)

ㅍ

파산(破産) bankruptcy; insolvency (4)

팔리– be / get sold (11)

팥 red beans (6)

패션 전시회(展示會) fashion show; fashion exhibition (19)

패션 fashion (19)

팽이(를) 돌리– spin a top (14)

퍼지– spread (6)

펴– open (a book); lay out; spread open (3)

평방(平方) 몇 미터? how many square meters? (5)

평소(平素)에 normally; during normal times; usually (5)

평일(平日) working day, weekday (1)

평일(平日)에 on weekdays (1)

평창동 P'yŏngch'angdong (area in Seoul) (17)

포기(抛棄)(를) 하– give up; surrender (12)

포로(捕虜) prisoner of war; captive (12)

표정(表情) expression (facial rather than verbal, which is 표현) (3)

표정(表情)(을) 지(ㅅ)-, (짓다) make a face (3)

표현(表現) (verbal) expression (3)

푸-ㄹ (풀다) solve / resolve (11)

푹 쉬– have a good / thorough rest (4)

푹푹 찌– (weather) be brutally steaming hot (NB: processive) (13, 17)

풀려나– be released, let go (NB: processive) (14)

풀리– be / get resolved, solved, cleared away; (one's doubts) are dispelled, removed, cleared away (NB: processive) (1, 11)

품질(品質) the quality (of goods) (14)

풍월(風月) "wind and moon"; poetry (6)

피(避)하– avoid; dodge; get away from; keep out of (rain); shirk (8)

피동(被動) passive (in grammar) (11)

피로(疲勞) fatigue, tiredness, exhaustion (16)

피로(疲勞)(가) 쌓이– fatigue accumulates; tiredness piles up (16)

ㅎ

하느님 ← 하늘 + 님 god, God (18)

하다못해 go so far as to; be driven by dire necessity to (do); faute de mieux; lacking alternatives; at the worst; at the least; at the extreme; finally; at last (17)

하도 so (much so that) (7)

하루만에 in just one day (14)

하마터면 nearly, almost (did sth) (8)

하숙비(下宿費) boarding expenses; lodging fees (4)

하품(을) 하– yawn (8)

학(鶴) crane (9)

학생생활(學生生活) student life (18)

학자(學者) scholar (4)

한 번만 봐 주세요 *Please give me a break just this one time* (11)

한 푼도 (not) even a penny (14)

한가(閒暇 / 閑暇)하– be at leisure, free of commitments; have spare time (16)

한국식(韓國式)으로 in the Korean way; Korean style (3)

한꺼번에 all at once; in one go; in one breath (1)

한바탕(을) 하– go a round (of fighting); have a go (16)

한방(韓方) Korean traditional medicine (5)

한술 one spoonful (6)

한자(漢字) [-짜] Chinese character (12)

한참 for quite a while (4)

한창 in full swing; in full bloom; at its peak (7)

할 수 없이 had no choice but to (adv.) (9)

할퀴– scratch; claw (13)

합(合)하– combine; join (9)

합격(合格)(을) 하– pass (a test); make the grade; come up to the standard (14)

항의(抗議)(를) 하– object (11)

해(害)(가) 되– be injurious, harmful (NB: processive) (6)

해(서) 오– do sth before one comes; do sth and then come; come having done sth (2)

해삼(海蔘) sea cucumber (11)

해석(解釋)(을) 하– interpret (8)

핸들 steering wheel (← English "handle") (8)

햇빛 ← 해 + 빛 sunlight (18)

행동(行動) behavior; action; doings; conduct (12)

행복(幸福)하– be happy (13)

허락(許諾) permission (2)

허리 waist; lower back (11)

현관(玄關) entrance hall; vestibule (17)

현관문(玄關門) door to the vestibule / entrance hall (17)

현대(現代) contemporary; modern (9)

현실(現實) reality (6)

형성(形成)(이) 되– be / get formed (6)

형태(形態) form; shape (11)

형편(形便) the situation, state of affairs (often in a personal sense) (4, 19)

형편(形便) 없– be a mess; be in a sorry state (said of a country's economy, for example) (4)

호기심(好奇心) curiosity (1)

호랑이 tiger (6, 18)

혹시(나)...? Do/does perchance/possibly...? (18)

혼(魂) soul; spirit (11)

혼(魂)(이) 나– have a hard time of it (6, 7)

홈스테이(를) 하– do a (long-term, study-related) homestay (8)

화(火)(가) 나– get angry (1)

화(火)(를) 내– get angry (16)

화(火)(를) 돋우– provoke / incite sb's anger (14)

화가(畫家) painter (8)

화산(火山) volcano (5)

화장지(化粧紙) toilet tissue; toilet paper (16)

화풀이(를) 하– vent one's anger; take out one's anger (6)

화해(和解)(를) 하– make up with; become reconciled; reach an amicable settlement (16)

확 with a sudden, violent wrench (8)

환갑(還甲) sixty-first birthday; celebration of completion of a traditional sixty-year cycle (17)

환갑잔치 sixty-first birthday party (17)

환경(環境) environment (6)

환영(歡迎)(을) 하– welcome (19)

환영회(歡迎會) welcome party (19)

환자(患者) patient; sick person (7, 19)

환하– be bright (12)

황새 stork (6)

회(膾) raw fish or meat (13)

획(劃) stroke (in Chinese characters) (9)

획기적(劃期的) epoch-making (8)

효과(效果) effect (16)

후덥지근하– be muggy (17)

후들후들 (shaking, trembling) terribly, like a leaf (7)

후배(後輩) one's junior from school (3)

후식(後食) dessert (5)

후추 black pepper (2)

후회(後悔)(를) 하– regret (6)

훈민정음(訓民正音) *Correct Sounds for Instructing the People* (name of the native Korean script and of the book that promulgated it in 1446) (8)

훨씬 much more so (9)

훼방(毀謗)(을) 놓– slander; defame; interfere with; thwart (14)

휴가(를) 떠나– leave on one's holiday / vacation (17)

휴가(休暇) leave of absence; holiday; vacation (4)

휴가(休暇) leave (of absence); holiday from work (as opposed to holiday from school, which is 방학) (17, 19)

흉(을) 보– speak ill of; disparage; criticize; run down (1)

흑자(黑字) financial surplus; (with the copula) be in the black (3)

흔드–ㄹ– (흔들다) shake, sway, disturb, agitate sth (14)

흔하– be common (4)

흔히 frequently; usually (6)

흥(興) merriment, mirth (6)

흥(이) 나– feel merry / excited (6)

ENGLISH-KOREAN NEW VOCABULARY GLOSSARY

A

abate 가라앉 - (11)

abide by 지키 - (13)

ability 능력(能力) (2)

abruptly (stand up ~) 벌떡 (4)

Abschiedsschmerzen (feel ~) 섭섭하 - (2)

absence (leave of ~) 휴가(休暇) (4)

absent (be ~)결석(缺席)(을) 하 - (11)

absent oneself 빠지 - (4)

abstraction 추상(抽象) (8)

abuse 욕(辱) (6)

accede (to) 동의(同意)(를) 하 - (13)

accede to 들어 주 - (6)

accident (leave sth behind by ~) 두고 오 - (1)

accord with one's wishes (in ~) 뜻대로 (3)

according to the law 법규에 따라 (2)

accrue 느 - ㄹ - (늘다) (14)

accumulate (intransitive) 쌓이 - (11, 12); 밀리 - (11)

accustomed to (get ~) 익숙해지 - (2)

achieve (one's objective) 달성(達成)(을) 하 - (17)

acorn jelly 묵 (11)

acquiesce 들어 주 - (17)

acquire experience 견문(이) 생기 - (6)

act drunken and disorderly 주정(酒酊)(을) 하 - (14)

act lazy 게으름(을) 피우 - (6)

act 동작(動作) (17); 짓 (12)

action 동작(動作) (17); 행동 (行動) (12)

actual fact (in ~) 실제(實際)로 (6)

actual NOUN 실제 NOUN (19)

actuality 실제(實際) (19)

actually 원래(原來 / 元來) (16)

actually 원래(原來 / 元來) (4)

adept (be ~) 능숙(能熟)하 - (17)

administer 다스리 - (18)

administrative headquarters– 청(廳) (2)

adult 어른 (6)

advance (get paid in ~) 가불(假拂)(을) 하 - (17)

advance of (in ~) 앞서 (1)

advance (in ~) 미리 (2)

advanced country 선진국(先進國) (6)

adversary 상대방(相對方) (18)

advice 조언(助言) (6)

advising fees 상담비(相談費) (18)

advising 상담(相談) (18)

affairs (state of ~) 형편(形便) (4)

affection enters (grow fond of) 정(情)(이) 드 - ㄹ - (들다) (1)

affix one's name chop 도장(刀匠)(을) 찍 - (14)

affliction 질병(疾病) (6)

afraid (be ~) 겁(이) 나 - (19)

after a few days 며칠 만에 (18)

after a while, then... 그러다가 (14)

after that / which 그리고는 (1)

against one's will 억지로 (14)

agile (be ~) 재빠르 - (17)

agitate 흔드 - ㄹ - (흔들다) (14)

ago (a few days ~) 엊그제 (7)

ago (not too long ~) 얼마 전에는 (7)

agonize 고민(苦悶)(을) 하 - (14)

agony (mental ~) 고민(苦悶) (1)

agree with an opinion 의견에 찬성(贊成)(을) 하 - (2)

agree 동의(同意)(를) 하 - (13)

agriculture (engage in ~) 농사(農事)를 지(ㅅ) - (짓다) (14)

ahead of time 미리 (2)

ahead of (go ~) 앞서 가 - (1)

ahead of 앞서 (1)

ailment 질병(疾病) (6)

air (take / get some fresh ~) 바람(을) 쐬 - (3)

air 공기(空氣) (9)

airs (put on ~) 잘난 척하 - (3)

alarm clock 자명종(自鳴鐘) (14)

alarm 비상벨 (17)

alcohol's taste comes out 술맛이 나 - (9)

alcohol (be / get drunk with ~) 술에 취(醉)하 - (7)

alike (look ~) 닮았다 (6,7)

all-nighter (take an ~) 밤(을) 새우 - (4)

all at once 한꺼번에 (1)

all hell breaks loose 난리(가) 나 - (16)

all kinds of NOUN 별별 NOUN (19)

all night (stay up ~)밤(을) 새우 - (4)

all of it / them 전부(全部) (9)

all smiles (be ~) 싱글벙글하 - (NB: processive) (7)

all the more 더욱 (12)

all the time 자꾸 (1); 매번(每番) (6)

all the way 잔뜩 (11)

all throughout 내내 (3)

all 모두 (6)

all 온통 (8)

almost (did sth) 하마터면 (8)

along well with (go ~) 어울리 - (1)

along with (get ~) 어울리 - (1)

alumni / alumnae society 동창회(同窓會) (5)

always 늘 (6)

AM 오전(午前) (16)

amazed (be ~) 깜짝 놀라 - (3)

amazing　(be ~) 신기(神奇)하－(19)

amazing　(be ~) 놀라w－(놀랍다)(4)

American　(an ~) 미국인(美國人)(4)

amicable settlement　(reach an ~) 화해(和解)(를) 하－(16)

among　가운데 (8)

amongst themselves　자기들끼리 (11)

amusement　오락(娛樂)(13); 장난 (12)

ancestor　선조(先祖)(6)

ancestor(s)　조상(祖上)(18)

Ancient Chosŏn　고조선(古朝鮮)(18)

and so on; and so forth　등(等)(7)

and the like　등(等)(7)

and then　그리고는 (1)

anecdote　우스갯소리 (19)

anger　(vent / take out one's ~) 화풀이(를) 하－(6)

angry　(be / get ~) 화(火)(를) 내－(16)

angry　(get ~) 화가 나－(1)

anguish　(be in ~) 고민(苦悶)(을) 하－(14)

anguish　고민(苦悶)(1)

anniversary (first)　돌 (1)

annoyed　(be / feel ~) 속(이) 상하－(8)

annul　취소(取消)(를) 하－(6)

anonymity　익명(匿名)(7)

anonymous　익명(匿名), 익명의 NOUN (7)

anonymously　익명으로 (7)

anthropologist　인류학자(人類學者)(11)

anthropology　인류학(人類學)(11)

anticipate　예상(豫想)(을) 하－(17)

anxiety　(without ~) 마음 놓고 (4)

anxious　(be ~) 궁금하－(7)

anxious　(be / feel ~) 불안(不安)하－(11)

anxious　(be ~) 애(가) 타－(NB: processive)(7)

any moment now　금방(今方)(12)

any more　더 이상(以上)(14)

any old which way　아무렇게나 (1)

anyhow　좌우간(左右間)(9)

anyhow　아무튼 (16)

anyway　아무튼 (16)

anyway　좌우간(左右間)(9)

apologize　사과(謝過)(를) 하－(6)

apologize　잘못했다고 비－ㄹ－(빌다)(16)

appear　나타나－(1)

appear　나타나－(17); 생기－(19)

appearance from behind　(one's ~) 뒷모습 (4)

appearance　(pitiful / derogatory ~) 꼴 (6)

appearance　모양(模樣)(2)

appearance(s)　모양(模樣)(17)

appetite　(lose one's ~) 입맛(을) 잃어버리－(2)

appetite　(stimulate the ~) 입맛(을) 돋우－(14)

appetite　식욕(食慾)(13); 입맛 (14)

apply (makeup, etc.)　바르－(17)

appointment　(keep an ~) 약속(을) 지키－(4)

approach　다가 오－(2)

approach　다가가－(13)

appropriate for / to　(be ~) 어울리－(NB: processive)(1)

appropriate　(be ~) 적당하－(2)

April Fools' Day　만우절(萬愚節)(14)

arcade　오락실(娛樂室)(13)

architect　건축가(建築家)(6)

armed forces　군대(軍隊)(18)

army　군대(軍隊)(18)

army　군대(軍隊)(5)

arrive at　도착(到着)(을) 하－

arrive late　지각(遲刻)(을) 하－(3)

art gallery　미술관(美術館)(9)

art / arts　미술(美術)(9)

as a joke　농담 삼아 (19)

as if...　마치...듯이 (11)

as it should be done　제대로 (9)

as luck would have it　마침 (11)

as one intends　뜻대로 (3)

as one likes / pleases　마음대로 (19)

as one pleases　제 마음대로 (9)

as soon as you receive it　받는 대로 (7)

as they were　그런대로 (9)

ashamed　(be ~) 무안(無顏)하－(11)

Asia　(East ~) 동양(東洋)(9)

asleep　(fall ~) 잠(이) 드－ㄹ－(들다)(1)

assemble (intransitive)　모이－(16)

assent　동의(同意)(를) 하－(13)

assiduous　(be ~) 알뜰하－(16)

assist　도w－(돕다)(14)

astigmatism　난시(亂視)(7)

astonished　(be ~) 놀라－(NB: processive)(11,19)

at all　(not ~) 전(全)혀 (+ NEGATIVE)(13)

at its peak　한창 (7)

at last　하다못해 (17)

at some point　언제 ← 언젠가는 (16)

at the end of the day　결국(結局)(14)

at the extreme / least　하다못해 (17)

at the right moment　마침 (11)

at the worst　하다못해 (17)

athletic meet　경기대회(競技大會)(2)

athletics tournament　체육대회(體育大會)(12)

athletics　체육(體育)(12)

atmosphere　분위기(雰圍氣)(3)

attached to　(feel ~) 정(情)(이) 드－ㄹ－(들다)(1)

attack　대드－ㄹ－(대들다)(18)

attacking and sinking sth　격침(擊沈)(14)

attend on foot　걸어다니－(1)

attention　(pay ~) 주의(注意)(를) 하－(6)

attentive to detail (be ~) 자상(仔詳)하 - (19)
audible (be ~)들리 - (11)
audience 관객(觀客) (18)
augment it 늘리 - (14)
author 작가(作家) (18)
autumn term 가을 학기(學期) (5)
autumn (late ~) 늦가을 (7)
avoid 피(避)하 - (8)
away from (get ~) 피(避)하 - (8)
away on an official trip (go ~) 출장(出張)(을) 가 - (1)
away on business (go ~) 출장(出張)(을) 가 - (1)
away (fly ~) 날아가 - (9)
awful to see 보기 흉(凶)하 - (11)
awful 못되 - (as a person; always past tense) (16)
awfully 몹시 (12)
awfully 무척 (3); 매우 (9)
awkward (be ~) 미련하 - (18)
awkward (be ~) 곤란(困難)하 - (3)
axe 도끼 (6)

B

baby (ceremony in honor of ~'s first birthday) 돌 잔치 (1)
back pocket 뒷주머니 (13)
back up 밀리 - (11)
back 등 (14)
backed up (get ~) 밀리 - (2)
bad drunk (be a ~) 주정(酒酊)(을) 하 - (14)
bad effect on one's stomach (have a ~) 체하 - (2)
bad habits (have ~) 버릇(이) 없 - (2)
bad mood (be in a ~) 기분(氣分)(이) 나쁘 - (13)
bad 못되 - (as a person; always past tense) (16)
badly behaved (be ~) 버릇(이) 없 - (2)
bag(s) 짐 (16)
baggage 짐 (9)
ball game 공 장난 (12)
bankruptcy 파산(破産) (4)
banquet 잔치 (1)
bar (one's regular or favorite ~) 단골집 (4)
barely 겨우 (17)
bargain 깎 - (8)
barge in on 쳐들어 오 - , 쳐들어 가 - (9)
bark 껍질 (14)
bark 짖 - (6)
baseball (re-)broadcast 야구중계(野球中繼) (6)
baseball game 야구경기(野球競技) (2)
basic course / class 기초반(基礎班) (7)
basis 기초(基礎) (7)
basket 바구니 (11)
bastard (vulgar) 자식(子息) (12)
bathe 감 - (14)
bathing cap 목욕 캡 (17)

bathtub 욕조(浴槽) (12)
beans (black ~) 콩 (6)
beans (red ~) 팥 (6)
bear sth 참 - (4)
bear 곰 (18)
bearing 동작(動作) (17)
beat (in sth) 이기 - (18,19)
beat a retreat 도망(逃亡)(을) 치 - (17)
beautiful (be ~) 고w– (곱다, 고와) (6)
become a tired wreck 녹초(가) 되 - (9)
become disappointed 실망(失望)(을) 하 - (2)
become someone 어울리 - (19)
before one's eyes (be fresh / vivid ~) 눈에 선하 - (7)
beforehand 미리 (2)
beg sb's pardon 잘못했다고 비 - ㄹ - (빌다) (16)
beginning (from the very ~) 전(前)부터 (4)
behaved (be badly ~) 버릇(이) 없 - (2)
behavior 행동(行動) (12)
behind oneself (look ~) 돌아다 보 - (1)
behind (fall ~) 뒤떨어지 - (6)
behind (leave sth ~ by accident) 두고 오 - (1)
behind (one's appearance from ~) 뒷모습 (4)
being moved / touched 감동(感動) (14)
being (for the time ~) 일단 [일딴] (9)
believe in 믿 - (6)
bell 벨 (17)
bend sth 굽히 - (14)
bent (be ~) 굽 - (14)
besides me 나 말고는 (1)
best (Do as you think ~) 알아서 하세요. (9)
best 최고(最高) (16)
better (feel ~) 마음(이) 풀리 - (16)
better than (be ~) 나(ㅅ) - (낫다, 나아) (6)
between (the space ~) 사이 (2)
between 가운데 (8)
beverage 음료수(飮料水) (11,13)
bewildered (be ~) 당황(唐慌)하 - (NB: processive) (1)
beyond (go ~) 넘치 - (4)
bid defiance to 도전(挑戰)(을) 하 - (18)
bird (tiny ~) 뱁새 (6)
birth mark 점(點) (6)
birthday (honorific) 생신, 생신날 (生辰) (13)
birthday (ceremony in honor of baby's first ~) 돌 잔치 (1)
birthday (honorific equivalent of 생일) 생신(生辰) (3)
bit by bit 점점(漸漸) (7)
bit (a ~) 약간(若干) (2)
bite 무 - ㄹ - (물다) (11)
bitten (be / get ~) 물리 - (11)
black beans 콩 (6)
black pepper 후추 (2)
black (be ~) 까맣 - , 까매 (7)

black (be in the ~) 흑자(黑字) (3)
blanket 이불 (13)
blessed (be ~) 복(福)(을) 받 - (6)
blinded (be ~)부시 - (눈이 ~) (14)
block 막 - (6)
blocked (road is ~) 길(이) 막히 - (1)
blood pressure (high ~) 고혈압(高血壓) (6)
bloodshot (be ~) 충혈(充血)(이) 되 - (8)
blue (be ~) 우울(憂鬱)하 - (14)
board 널 (14)
boarding expenses 하숙비(下宿費) (4)
boat (the first ~) 첫배 (1)
bobbingly 동동; 둥둥 (12)
body weight (one's ~) 몸무게 - (19)
boil sth 끓이 - (14)
boiled fodder 소죽 (14)
boisterous (be ~) 요란(搖亂)스러w- (~스럽다) (17)
bonds of friendship 우정(友情) (6)
books 서적(書籍) (12)
boost virility 정력(精力)(을) 돋우 - (6)
booth (ticket ~) 매표소(賣票所) (1)
boots 부츠 (19)
boozer (a ~) 술고래 (9)
bored (be / get ~) 뚫리 - (18)
boring (be ~) 지루하 - (1)
born (be ~) 태어나 - (14)
born with (be ~) 타고나 - (NB: processive) (2)
box (counter for a ~ of cigarettes, matches) 갑(匣) (7)
boyfriend 애인(愛人) (2)
branch campus 분교(分校) (5)
break (Give me a ~) 봐 주세요. (11)
break (a rule) 위반(違反)(을) 하 - (2)
break (down) 고장(故障)(이) 나 - (1)
break (sth) 깨 - (18); 부수 - (17)
break sth 깨뜨리 - (2)
break (give sb a ~) 잘 봐 주 - (2)
breath 숨 (11)
breathe in 숨(을) 들이쉬 - (11)
breathe out 숨(을) 내쉬 - (11)
bright (be ~) 환하 - (12)
brilliant answer (give a ~) 명답(名答)(을) 하 - (5)
brilliant 비상(非常)하 - (14)
brim (to the ~) 잔뜩 (11)
brimming 가득 / 가뜩 (14)
bring (and place) sth 갖다 놓 - (9)
bring to / for 갖다 주 - (2)
bring up (a subject) 꺼내 - (4)
briskly (lift sth ~) 번쩍 (4)
broad (be ~) 넓 - (14)
broadcasting station 방송국(放送局) (6)
broaden one's horizons 견문(이) 생기 - (6)

broaden sth 넓히 - (14)
brogue 사투리 (4)
broken off (be / get ~) 중단(中斷)(이) 되 - (2)
brought up (be ~) 자라 - (12)
brown 밤색(~色) (11)
brutally steaming hot (be ~)푹푹 찌 - (13,17)
buck up 기운(을) 내 - (14)
budge (can't even ~) 꼼짝도 못 하 - (2)
bulletin board 게시판(揭示板) (6)
bumpkin-ish (country ~) 촌스러w- (~스럽다) (9)
bunch 다발 (18)
burden 짐 (9)
burial site (family or clan ~) 산소(山所) (3)
buried (be / get ~) 묻히 - (11)
burly (be ~) 굵 - (13)
burn (intransitive) 타 - (14)
burn sth 태우 - (14)
burn up again 되살아나 - (14)
bursting full 꽉 차 - (8)
bury sth 묻 - (11)
bus (highway ~) 고속(高速)버스 (4)
business (~ trip) 출장(出張) (1)
business (go away on ~) 출장(出張)(을) 가 - (1)
business 사업(事業) (12)
business 사업(事業) (9)
butt in 끼어드 - ㄹ - (끼어들다) (8)
butt of ridicule 웃음거리 [- 꺼리] (7)
buy 장만(을) 하 - (7)
buzzer 초인종(招人鐘) (17)
by chance 우연(偶然)히 (3)
by degrees 점점(漸漸) (17)
by force 억지로 (14)
by means of this 이걸로 (13)
by nature (adv.) 천생 (天生) (18)

C

calculate 계산(計算)(을) 하 - (16)
call bell 초인종(招人鐘) (17)
call comes in (a ~) 전화(電話)가 걸려 오 - (9)
call (have sb ~) 불리 - (14)
calligraphy 글씨 (11)
camera 사진기(寫眞機); 카메라 (11)
can't budge / move an inch 꼼짝도 못 하 - (2)
cancel 취소(取消)(를) 하 - (6)
cancer 암(癌) (18)
cane 지팡이 (6)
captive 포로(捕虜) (12)
car door 차문(車門) (13)
care (free from ~) 마음 놓고 (4)
care (take good ~ of oneself) 몸조리(~調理) (를) 하 - (4)
career advising 진로상담(進路相談) (18)

career 직업(職業) (14)

carriage 동작(動作) (17)

carry (a cane) 짚- (6)

carry around (e.g., an umbrella) 들고 다니- (2,7)

carry off in one's mouth 물어 가- (12)

carry on straight 쭉 가- (12)

case (counter for a ~ of cigarettes, matches) 갑(匣) (7)

casualty; (dead) victim 사망자(死亡者) (6)

catch 잡- (14)

catch (sth said) 알아들- (알아듣다) (1)

caught (be / get ~) 잡히- (11)

caught (be / get ~) 들키- (6)

caught (get ~ [on a nail, by the police]) 걸리- (9)

causative (in grammar) 사동(使動) (11)

causative vocabulary 사동어휘(使動語彙) (14)

causes concern (it ~) 궁금하- (7)

cautious of (be ~) 주의(注意)(를) 하- (NB: processive) (6)

cave 동굴(洞窟) (18)

cease 마-ㄹ- (말다) (14)

ceiling 천장 (4)

cement 시멘트 (6)

center 가운데 (8)

ceremonial feast 잔치 (1)

ceremony for baby's 1st birthday 돌잔치 (1)

certain way (turn out a / look a ~) 생기- (3)

certainly (will do) 반드시 (2)

Ch'ŏngp'yŏng Temple 청평사(淸平寺) (1)

Ch'unch'ŏn (place name) 춘천(春川) (1)

challenge 도전(挑戰)(을) 하- (18)

Chamsil 잠실 (18)

chance (by ~) 우연(偶然)히 (3)

change (apparel) 갈아입- (6)

change 동전(銅錢) (2)

character (personal ~) 성품(性品) (2)

characteristics (special ~) 특성(特性) (6)

charming (be ~) 얌전하- (12)

chase 쫓- (11)

chased (be / get ~) 쫓기- (11)

cheat 속이- (6)

cheated (be / get ~) 속- (6)

check out 살피- (12)

cheek 뺨 (6)

Cheju Island 제주도(濟州道) (2)

chestnut color 밤색(~色) (11)

chestnut 밤 (11)

chew 씹- (11)

chewed (be / get ~) 씹히- (11)

chewy (be ~) 질기- (11)

chicken 겁쟁이 (14)

chief of division 부장(部長) (6)

chief (section ~) 과장(課長) (2)

Children's Day 어린이날 (17)

children (one's ~) 자식(子息) (12)

children (honorific) 자녀(子女)분 (5)

chilly (be ~) 쌀쌀하- (7)

Chinese character dictionary 옥편(玉篇) (12)

Chinese character 한자(漢字) [-짜] (12)

chockablock 가득 / 가뜩 (14)

chockablock 꽉 차- (8)

choice (have no ~ but to [adv.]) 할 수 없이 (9)

Chongno ("Bell Road") 종로(鍾路) (3)

choose 뽑- (6)

chop 도장(刀匠) (14)

chopped (be / get ~) 찍히- (6)

Chosŏn era 조선시대(朝鮮時代) (6)

chubby (be~) 뚱뚱하- (3)

cigar 시가 (4)

circular (be ~) 동그랗- (동그래, 동그란) (18)

circumstance (extenuating) 사정(事情) (6)

circumstances 형편(形便) (19)

city hall 시청(市廳) (1,2)

city 도시(都市) (17)

clamorous (be ~) 요란(搖亂)스러w- (~스럽다) (17)

clan burial site 산소(山所) (3)

class president / leader 반장(班長) (9)

class (basic / elementary ~) 기초반(基礎班) (7)

class (first ~) 일등(一等) (2)

classifier for events 건(件) (9)

classifier for places 군데 (9)

claw 할퀴- (13)

clean (adv.) 깨끗이 (9)

clean up / away 치우- (12)

cleanly 깨끗이 (9)

clear (be ~) 맑- (12); 뻔하- (17)

clear it up / away 치우- (9)

clear up (weather) 개- (1)

clear up / away 치우- (12)

clear (be ~) 분명(分明)하- (6)

cleared away (be / get ~) 풀리- (11)

cleared away (one's doubts are ~) 풀리- (1)

climax (reach a ~) 고조(高潮)(가) 되- (7)

clogged (traffic) (be / get ~) 밀리- (2)

close (intransitive) 닫히- (11)

close to (thirty years) 가까이 (30 년 ~) (14)

close(ly) 가까이 (13)

closed (be / get ~) 닫히- (11)

closed (be / get ~) 닫히- (6)

cloudburst 소나기 (14)

clumsy (be ~) 미련하- (18)

coach 고속(高速)버스 (4)

coffer 금고(金庫) (17)

coincidentally 우연(偶然)히 (3)

coins 동전(銅錢) (2)

cold (to the touch) 차 - ; 차가w– (차갑다) (13)

cold rice 찬밥 (13)

cold sweat (a ~) 식은 땀 (3)

cold ([food] goes ~) 식 - (3)

collapse 쓰러지 - (11)

collide with 부딪치 - (8)

collision ([rear-end] ~) 추돌(追突) (2)

color (be a pearly, misty ~) 뿌옇 - , 뿌얘요 (8)

color of one's face (the ~) 안색(顔色) (1)

colorful traditional costume 색동옷 (2)

column 칸 (2)

comb (one's hair) 빗 - (14)

comb (sb's hair) 빗기 - (14)

combine 합(合)하 - (9)

come about 생겨나 - (6)

come about 생기 - (19)

come across 건너 오 - (14)

come back to life 되살아나 - (14)

come calling 찾아오 - (19)

come having done it 해(서) 오 - (2)

come into being 생겨나 - (6)

come into the world 태어나 - (14)

come near 다가 오 - (2)

come out (alcohol's taste ~) 술맛이 나 - (9)

come running out 뛰쳐나오 - (18)

come running 달려오 - (17)

come to a conclusion 결론(結論)을 내리 - (12)

come to feel / sense 느껴지 - (14)

come to love sb (but not necessarily romantically) 정(情)
(이) 드 - ㄹ - (들다) (1)

come up to the standard 합격(合格)(을) 하 - (14)

come (do it and then ~) 해(서) 오 - (2)

comes (do sth before one ~) 해(서) 오 - (2)

command (a ~) 명령(命令) (6)

command 명령(命令)(을) 하 - (2)

command 지휘(指揮) (14)

commit a crime / sin 죄(罪)(를) 지(ㅅ) - (짓다) (6)

commit an indiscretion 실수(失手)(를) 하 - (4)

commit suicide 자살(自殺)(을) 하 - (18)

common (be ~) 흔하 - (4)

common (in ~) 공통적(共通的) (6)

communicate well 마음(이) 잘 통(通)하 - (2)

communicate with 통(通)하 - (2)

company (magazine ~) 잡지사(雜誌社) (9)

comparatively 비교적(比較的)(으로) (12)

compare 비교(比較)(를) 하 - (12)

compared to (NOUN) NOUN에 비해서 (9)

comparison 비교(比較) (12)

compete in sports 경기(競技)(를) 하 - (8)

competition 경기대회(競技大會) (2)

complete (a number) 채우 - (14)

complete sth 완성(完成)(을) 하 - (18)

completely 완전(完全)히 (8)

completion of a sixty–year cycle 환갑(還甲) (17)

complexion 안색(顔色) (1)

complicated (be ~) 곤란(困難)하 - (3)

compose a sentence 작문(作文)(을) 하 - (3)

composed of (be / get ~) 구성(構成)(이) 되 - (6)

composition (write a ~) 작문(作文)(을) 하 - (3)

computer drive 드라이브 (6)

conceal sth 묻 - (11); 숨기 - (14)

concealed (be / get ~) 묻히 - (11)

concern oneself 염려(念慮)(를) 하 - (18)

concern (a matter for ~) 걱정거리 [- 꺼리] (7)

concern (it causes ~) 궁금하 - (7)

concerned about (be ~) 관심(關心)을 가지 - (NB: processive) (12); 신경(神經)(을) 쓰 - (NB: processive) (19)

conclude 결론(結論)을 내리 - (12)

conclusion 결론(結論) (12)

concrete object 구체(具體) (8)

condition 조건(條件) [- 껀] (6)

conditions and demands 요구조건(要求條件) (6)

conduct a ritual ceremony 제사(祭祀)(를) 지내 - (6)

conduct one's day-to-day life 생활(生活)(을) 하 - (3)

conduct 행동(行動) (12)

confidence (with ~) 자신감(自信感)을 가지고 (18)

confidence 자신(自信) (18); 자신감(自信感) (18)

confidently 자신감(自信感)을 가지고 (18)

confused (be ~) 당황(唐慌 / 唐惶)하 - (NB: processive)
(1)

conquer 정복(征服)(을) 하 - (18)

conscious of (be ~) 느끼 - (14)

consent 동의(同意)(를) 하 - (13)

conservatism 보수(保守) (8)

considerate of others (be ~)자상(仔詳)하 - (19)

consistently persistent (be ~) 꾸준하 - (6)

constantly 늘 (6)

consult with 상의(相議)(를) 하 - (19)

contact 연락(連絡)(을) 하 - (1)

contain in 담 - (6)

contained (be / get ~) 담기 - (11)

contamination 오염(汚染) (14)

contemporary 현대(現代) (9)

content(s) 알맹이 (19)

contents 내용(內容) (1)

contest (have a ~) 경기(競技)(를) 하 - (8)

contingency 비상(非常) (17)

continually 자꾸 (1)

continuously 내내 (3); 계속(繼續) (1)

continuously 자꾸 (12)

contrary to expectations 오히려 (6)

contribution 성금(誠金) (18)

conveyance (get on the wrong ~) ("ride in error") 잘못 타 - (2)

cooked (be / get ~) 익 - (11)

cooking 요리(料理) (1)

cool as a cucumber (be ~) 아무렇지도 않 - (3)

Correct Sounds for Instructing the People 훈민정음(訓民正音) (name of the native Korean script, and of the book that promulgated it in 1446) (8)

cosmetic surgery 성형수술(成形手術) (5)

costume (colorful Korean traditional ~) 색동옷 (2)

cough 기침(을) 하 - (1)

counseling agency / office 상담소(相談所) (18)

counseling fees 상담비(相談費) (18)

counseling 상담(相談) (18)

count 세 - (4)

counter for apparel 벌 (16)

counter for events 건(件) (9)

counter for places 군데 (9)

counterpart 상대방(相對方) (18)

country bumpkin-ish 촌스러w– (촌스럽다) (9)

countryside (one's home / house in the ~) 시골집 [- 찝] (7)

countryside (the ~) 시골 (7)

couple (married ~) 부부(夫婦) (2)

courage 용기(勇氣) (6)

course ahead (in life) 진로(進路) (18)

course (basic ~) 기초반(基礎班) (7)

course 과목(科目) (4)

courteous (be ~) 정중(鄭重)하 - (17)

courtesy 예의(禮儀) (6)

courtyard 마당 (1)

cover 덮개 (11); 뚜껑 (11)

cover (blanket) 이불 (13)

cover sth 덮 - (11,13)

covered (be / get ~) 덮이 - (11)

cow's horn 쇠뿔 (6)

cow shed 외양간 [- 깐] (14)

coward 겁쟁이 (14)

cowardly (be ~) 겁(怯) (이) 많 - (14)

crack 틈 (11)

cramming (last-minute ~) 벼락치기 (9)

crane 학(鶴) (9)

cranny (in every nook and ~) 샅샅이 (1)

crawl around 기어 다니 - (12)

crawl 기 - (12)

create trouble 말썽(을) 부리 - (12)

creative writer 작가(作家) (18)

creeps (give one the ~) 끔찍하 - (4)

crime (commit a ~) 죄(罪)(를) 지(ㅅ) - (짓다) (6)

criminal 범인(犯人) (18)

crisis 위기(危機) (17)

criticize 흉(을) 보 - (1)

cross over 건너 - (14)

crow tit 뱁새 (6)

crow 까마귀 (19)

crowded (be ~) 붐비 - (NB: processive) (8)

cucumber 오이 (7)

cuisine 요리(料理) (1)

culprit 범인(犯人) (18)

culture 문화(文化) (8)

cure 치료(治療)(를) 하 - (3)

curiosity 호기심(好奇心) (1)

curious to know about (be ~) 궁금하 - (7)

cussing 욕(辱) (6)

custom 습관(習慣) (2)

cut (e.g., one's finger) 베 - (16)

cut (the price) 깎 - (8)

cut down on (cigarettes, booze) 줄이 - (7)

cut in 끼어드 - ㄹ - (끼어들다) (8)

cut off (be / get ~) 끊기 - (11)

cut off (get ~) 끊어지 - (6)

cut off 끊 - (3)

cut one's hair 머리(를) 자르 - (13)

cut sth off 끊 - (11)

D

daily life 일상생활(日常生活) (6)

damaged (be / get ~) 손상(損傷)(이) 되 - (6)

darkness 어둠 (17)

dash in ("dash and enter") 뛰어드 - ㄹ - (뛰어들다) (8)

dash out 달려나가 - (8)

data 데이터 (6)

date (designated ~) 기일(期日) (2)

dating relationship (a ~) 애인(愛人) 사이 (2)

dawn 새벽 (1)

day-to-day life (conduct one's ~) 생활(生活)(을) 하 - (3)

day before yesterday 그제 ← 그저께 (16)

day (a working ~) 평일(平日) (1)

day (the previous ~) 전(前)날 (1)

daybreak 새벽 (1)

days ago (a few ~) 엊그제 (7)

days (a few / several ~) 며칠 (3)

days (How many ~?) 며칠 (3)

daytime 낮 (6)

dazzled (be ~)부시 - (눈이 ~) (14)

dead person 사망자(死亡者) (6)

deadline 기일(期日) (2)

deal with 다루 - (6)

dear (be ~) 소중(所重)하 - (14)

dear (be ~) 아까w– (아깝다) (4)

death by shooting 사살(射殺) (11)
death rate 사망률(死亡率) (6)
debt (incur ~) 빚(을) 지 - (6)
deceive 속이 - (6)
deceived (be ~) 속 - (NB: processive) (6)
decided (be / get ~) 결정(決定)(이) 되 - (6)
declare 선언(宣言)(을) 하 - (4)
decorum 예의(禮儀) (6)
deduct 더 - ㄹ - (덜다) (11)
deep emotion 감동(感動) (14)
deep (be ~) 깊 - (6)
deeply moved (be ~)느끼 - (14)
defame 훼방(毀謗)(을) 놓 - (14)
defend 지키 - (13)
deficient (be ~) 모자라 - (14)
deficit (financial ~) 적자 (赤字) (3)
definitely 꼭 (14)
defy 대드 - ㄹ - (대들다) (18)
delete 삭제(削除)(를) 하 - (6)
deliberately 일부러 (18)
demand 요구(要求) (6)
dementia (touch of ~) 노망(老妄)기 [- 끼] (11)
dense (be ~) 둔(鈍)하 - (18)
depart 출발(出發)(을) 하 - (7)
department (at a university) 과(科) (16)
department chief 부장(部長) (6)
depressed (be ~) 우울(憂鬱)하 - (14)
designated date 기일(期日) (2)
designed (be / get ~) 설계(設計)(가) 되 - (6)
desire 원(願)하 - (17)
desist 마 - ㄹ - (말다) (14)
dessert 후식(後食) (5)
detached (be / get ~) 떨어지 - (13)
determined (be / get ~) 결정(決定)(이) 되 - (6)
develop (~ the country) 나라(를) 발전(發展)시키 - (6)
develops (an event) 벌어지 - (3)
devoted affection 정성(精誠) (14)
dexterity (manual) 솜씨 (17)
dexterity involving hands 솜씨 (1)
dialect 사투리 (4)
Diamond Mountains 금강산(金剛山) (6)
diet (go on a ~) 다이어트(를) 하 - (1)
digestion 소화(消化) (18)
digestive medicine 소화제(消化劑) (18)
dim-witted 멍청하 - (14)
diminish 줄이 - (7)
dining table 식탁(食卓) (11)
direction(s) 지휘(指揮) (14)
directly 곧바로 (17)
dirty (be ~) 지저분하 - (17)
dirty (be ~) 더러w– (더럽다) (1)

disappointed (be ~) 섭섭하 - (2)
disappointed (become ~) 실망(失望)(을) 하 - (2)
disappointment (to one's ~) 섭섭하게도 (2)
discard 버리 - (1)
discontinue 중지(中止)(를) 하 - (5)
disease 질병(疾病) (6)
disgusting (be ~) (in a horrific, scary way) 끔찍하 - (4)
dish 접시 (4)
dishes (the ~) 설거지 (9)
disparage 흉(을) 보 - (1)
dispelled (one's doubts are ~) 풀리 - (1)
dissuade sb 말리 - (14)
distantly 멀리 (13)
distinguished (be ~) 잘나 - (3); 귀(貴)하 - (8)
distressed (be ~) 속(이) 상하 - (12)
distressed (be ~) 속(이) 상하 - (NB: processive) (8)
disturb 흔드 - ㄹ - (흔들다) (14)
disturbance 난리(亂離) (16)
divide 나누 - (4)
division chief 부장(部長) (6)
divorced (be / get ~) 이혼(離婚)(을) 하 - (2)
dizzy (be / feel ~) 어지러w–, (어지럽다) (2)
do a slipshod job of it 설치 - (9)
Do as you think best. 알아서 하세요. (9)
do it and then come 해(서) 오 - (2)
do sth before one comes 해(서) 오 - (2)
do the favor that sb asks 부탁(을) 들어 주 - (듣다) (2)
dodge 피(避)하 - (8)
doggie 강아지 (2)
doing(s) 짓(12); 행동(行動) (12)
doll 인형 (人形) (5)
Don't worry. 염려(念慮)(를) [하지] 마세요. (2)
donation 성금(誠金) (18)
door to vestibule / entrance 현관문(玄關門) (17)
doorbell 초인종(招人鐘) (17)
doubt 의문(疑問) (1)
doubtful-looking (be ~) 수상(殊常)하 - (17)
down Kyŏngsang Province-way 경상도(慶尙道) 쪽에는 (16)
down (fall ~) 넘어지 - (1)
down (to put sth ~ [for future use / reference]) 내려 놓 - (9)
downpour 소나기 (14)
drama 극(劇) (8)
dramatic role 역(役) (18)
dreams (in one's ~) 꿈 속에서 (3)
dress sb 입히 - (11)
dress shirt 와이셔츠 (12)
drilled through (be / get ~) 뚫리 - (18)
drinking (feel like ~) 술맛이 나 - (9)
drinks a lot (sb who ~) 술고래 (9)

drive it 모 - ㄹ - (몰다) (8)
drive (computer ~) 드라이브 (6)
driven by necessity to (do) 하다못해 (17)
driver's license 운전면허증(運轉免許證) (2)
driving license 운전면허(運轉免許) (18)
driving (drunk ~) 음주운전(飮酒運轉) (2)
drop by (~[and then be on one's way again]) 들렀다(가) - (3)
drop by 들르 - (3)
drop in 들렀다 가 - (3)
drop 떨어지 - (13)
dropping back to a distance 멀리 떨어져서 (13)
drunk driving 음주운전(飮酒運轉) (2)
drunk with alcohol (be ~) 술에 취(醉)하 - (NB: processive) (7)
drunk with sleep (be ~) 잠에 취(醉)하 - (NB: processive) (7)
drunk (get ~) 취(醉)하 - (2)
dry sth 말리 - (14)
dull (be ~) 둔(鈍)하 - (18); 모자라 - (NB: processive)(14)
during normal times 평소(平素)에 (5)

E

ear 귀 (12)
early stage(s) 초기(初期) (7)
earnest (be ~)알뜰하 - (16); 정중(鄭重)하 - (17)
earring 귀걸이 (14)
ease (be / feel at ~) 안심(安心)하 - (2)
ease (feel ill at ~) 곤란(困難)하 - (3)
East Asia 동양(東洋) (9)
East (the Far ~) 동양(東洋) (9)
Eastern Country of Propriety 동방예의지국(東方禮義之國) (6)
eaten (be / get ~) 먹히 - (11)
economic situation 경제형편(經濟形便) (4)
economical 경제적(經濟的) (1)
eel 장어 (6)
effect on one's stomach (have a bad ~) 체하 - (2)
effect 효과(效果) [- 꽈] (16)
effort(s) (make ~) 애(를) 쓰 - (3); 노력(努力)(을) 하 - (6)
effort(s) 노력(努力 / 努力) (6)
efforts (go over the top in one's ~) 무리(無理)하 - (7)
elbowroom (time-wise ~) 시간적 여유(時間的 餘裕) (8)
elbowroom 여유(餘裕) (19)
elder 어른 (6)
elected (be / get ~) 뽑히 - (11)
electric (as modifier) 전기(電氣) (18)
electric iron 전기(電氣) 다리미 (18)
electricity 전기(電氣) (18)
elementary class 기초반(基礎班) (7)

elevate 높이 - (14)
eliminate 없애 - (14)
elude 모면(謀免)(을) 하 - (17)
embarrassing (be ~) 곤란(困難)하 - (3)
embrace 안 - (11)
embraced (be / get ~) 안기 - (11)
emergency bell 비상벨 (17)
emergency situation 비상상태(非常狀態) (14)
emergency 비상(非常) (17)
emotion 감정(感情) (8)
employment (finding ~) 취직(就職) (1)
empty (be ~)비 - (비었어요) (17,19)
encourage 용기(를) 주 - (6)
end (in the ~) 결국(結局) (2)
end of the day (at the ~) 결국(結局) (14)
end 끝 (6)
endowed with (naturally ~) 타고나 - (2)
endure it 참 - (4)
engineering faculty / college 공대(工大) (5)
enjoyable (be ~) 즐거w– (즐겁다) (1)
enlarge sth 늘리 - (14)
enough (be not ~) 모자라 - (NB: processive) (1)
enter (insert and ~) 끼어드 - ㄹ - (끼어들다) (8)
enterprise 사업(事業) (12)
enterprise 사업(事業) (9)
enters (affection ~) (grow fond of) 정(情)(이) 드 - ㄹ - (들다) (1)
entirely 온통 (8)
entirely 완전(完全)히 (8)
entirety (in its ~) 전부(全部) (9)
entrance hall 현관(玄關) (17)
entrust with / to 맡기 - (14)
envelope 봉투(封套) (19)
enveloped (be / get ~) 싸이 - (11)
environment 환경(環境) (6)
envisions (as one ~) 자기 뜻대로 (3)
epoch-making 획기적(劃期的) (8)
equality of the sexes 남녀평등(男女平等) (5)
equip 갖추 - (7)
era 시절(時節) (18)
erase 지우 - (6)
erect sth 세우 - (14)
errand boy 심부름꾼 (7)
errand ([go on] an ~) 심부름(을) (가 -) (7)
error (an ~) 잘못 (2)
error (in ~) (adv.) 잘못 (2)
error (ride in ~) 잘못 타 - (1)
error (to make an ~) 실수(失手)(를) 하 - (4)
escape 도망(逃亡)(을) 가 - (16,17); 모면(謀免)(을) 하 - (17)
especially 유난히 (9)

especially 특(特)히 (17)

establish 세우 - (18)

establish 세우 - (6)

esteemed (be ~) 귀(貴)하 - (8)

etc. 등(等) (7)

ethnos 민족(民族) (6)

etiquette 예절(禮節) (2)

evade 모면(謀免)(을) 하 - (17)

event develops (an ~) 벌어지 - (3)

events (counter / classifier for ~) 건(件) (9)

events (unaffected by ~) 아무렇지도 않 - (3)

ever since I was born 태어나서 지금까지 쭉 (14)

ever so (much) 너무나 (3)

every nook and cranny (in ~) 샅샅이 (1)

every time 매번(每番) (6)

everybody 모두들 (17)

everyone 모두 (6)

evince a reaction 반응(反應)(을) 보이 - (3)

exactly the same 똑 같은 (8)

exactly 꼭 (8)

exaggerate 과장(誇張)(을) 하 - (8)

exam (fail an ~) 시험(試驗)에 떨어지 - (1)

exam (pass an ~) 시험(試驗)에 붙 - (1)

examine 살피 - (12)

examining room 진찰실(診察室) (19)

example (for ~) 예(例)를 들어(서) (6)

example 예(例) (6)

exasperate sb 약(을) 올리 - (16)

exasperated (be / feel ~) 속(이) 상하 - (12)

exasperated 속(이) 상하 - (8)

except for me 나 말고는 (1)

excited (feel ~) 흥(이) 나 - (6)

exclaim 감탄(感歎)(을) 하 - (13,19)

exert oneself unreasonably 무리(無理)하 - (7)

exert oneself 노력(努力)(을) 하 - (6)

exhausted (get ~) 지치 - (4)

exhaustion 피로(疲勞) (16)

exhibition 전시회(展示會) (19)

exit 나 - (14)

expand (intransitive) 느 - ㄹ - (늘다) (14)

expand it 늘리 - (14)

expect 예상(豫想)(을) 하 - (17)

experience 겪 - (6)

experience 경험(經驗) (6)

experience 느끼 - (14)

expert (be ~)능숙(能熟)하 - (17)

explain 설명(說明)(을) 하 - (11)

express one's surprise 감탄(感歎)(을) 하 - (13,19)

expression (a facial ~) 표정(表情) (3)

expression (a verbal ~) 표현(表現) (3)

extenuating circumstance 사정(事情) (6)

extinguish a light 불(을) 끄 - (14)

extra space / room / time 여유(餘裕) (19)

extract sth 뽑 - (11); 빼 - (18)

extract 빼 - (6)

extracted (be / get ~) 뽑히 - (11)

extraordinary (mind be ~) 비상(非常)하 - (14)

extravagance 사치(奢侈) (6)

extravagant (be ~) 사치(奢侈)스러w– (~스럽다) (6)

extremely 심(甚)하게 (6)

eyes wide open (watch with one's ~) 눈을 뜨고 보 - (4)

eyes (be fresh / vivid "before one's ~") 눈에 선하 - (7)

eyes (to open one's ~) 눈(을) 뜨 - (4)

eyesight 시력(視力) (7)

F

face (make a ~) 표정(表情)(을) 지(ㅅ) - (짓다) (3)

face (the color of one's ~) 안색(顔色) (1)

face 낯 (11)

face 얼굴 (6)

facial expression 표정(表情) (3)

fact (as a matter of ~) 원래(原來 / 元來) (4)

factory 공장(工場) (5)

fade 시드 - ㄹ - (시들다) (12)

fail an exam 시험(試驗)에 떨어지 - (1)

fail to turn up 빠지 - (4)

faint 기절(氣絶)(을) 하 - (16)

fall and go out 빠져나가 - (11)

fall asleep 잠(이) 드 - ㄹ - (들다) (1)

fall behind 뒤떨어지 - (6)

fall down 떨어지 - (13); 쓰러지 - (11)

fall in love at first sight ("at first eye") 첫눈에 반하 - (1)

fall into 빠지 - (8)

fall over / down 넘어지 - (1)

fall semester 가을 학기(學期) (5)

familiar (face) (be ~)낯(이) 익 - (11)

familiar with (be ~)익 - (11)

family burial site 산소(山所) (3)

family in mourning (a ~) 초상(初喪~)집 [- 찝] (2)

famous (be ~) 유명(有名)하 - (1)

far (adv.) 멀리 (13)

far and wide 널리 (6)

far as (go as ~) 닿 - (4)

Far East (the ~) 동양(東洋) (9)

farfetched (be ~) 엉뚱하 - (6)

farming (engage in ~) 농사(農事)를 지(ㅅ) - (짓다) (14)

farsightedness 원시(遠視) (7)

fashion 패션 (19)

fashion show / exhibition 패션 전시회(展示會) (19)

fasten sth 잠그 - (11)

fastened (be / get ~) 잠기 - (11)

fat (get ~) 살(이) 찌 - (19)

fat (be ~) 뚱뚱하 - (3)
fatigue accumulates 피로(疲勞)(가) 쌓이 - (16)
fatigue and miseries 몸살(이) 나 - (17)
fatigue 피로(疲勞) (16)
faute de mieux 하다못해 (17)
favor (do the ~ that sb asks) 부탁(을) 들어 주 - (듣다) (2)
favorite restaurant / bar (one's ~) 단골집 [- 찝] (4)
fear 겁(怯) (19)
feast (ceremonial ~) 잔치 (1)
fee (negligence ~) 과태료(過怠料) (2)
feed 먹이 - (14)
feel (~ pulse) 짚 - (6)
feel *Abschiedsschmerzen* 섭섭하 - (2)
feel an inclination 내키 - (19)
feel at a loss 당황(唐慌 / 唐惶)하 - (1)
feel at ease / unworried 안심(安心)하 - (2)
feel better 마음(이) 풀리 - (16)
feel burdened 번거로w- (번거롭다) (17)
feel embarrassed 무안(無顏)하 - (11)
feel heavy on the stomach 체하 - (2)
feel ill at ease 곤란(困難)하 - (3)
feel insecure 불안(不安)하 - (11)
feel like (doing) 내키 - (19)
feel like crying 코끝이 찡하 - (14)
feel like drinking 술맛이 나 - (9)
feel merry / excited 흥(이) 나 - (6)
feel out of sorts 괴로w- (괴롭다) (6)
feel pent-up frustration 억울하 - (2)
feel reassured 마음(이) 풀리 - (16)
feel relieved 마음(이) 풀리 - (16)
feel tormented 괴로w- (괴롭다) (6)
feel unworried 안심(安心)하 - (2)
feel 느끼 - (1)
feel 느끼 - (14)
feeling of confidence 자신감(自信感) (18)
female gender 여성(女性) (6)
few (a ~) 두어 (4)
few (a ~) 서너 (19)
few days (after / within ~) 며칠 만에 (18)
few days ago (a ~) 엊그제 (7)
few days (a ~) 며칠 (3)
few times (a ~) 서너 번(番) (14)
fiction 소설(小說) (8)
fierce (be ~) 매서w- (매섭다) (18)
fill (intransitive) 담기 - (11)
fill up 채우 - (14)
filled with (be / get ~) 담기 - (11)
filthy (be ~) 더러w- (더럽다) (1)
filthy (be ~) 지저분하 - (17)
finally 하다못해 (17)
financial deficit 적자(赤字) (3)

financial surplus 흑자(黑字) (3)
find a job 취직(就職)(을) 하 - (1)
finding employment 취직(就職) (1)
fine (negligence ~) 과태료(過怠料) (2)
fine (to pay a ~) 벌금(罰金)(을) 내 - (9)
finger 손가락 [- 까락] (11)
fingers (pick up sth small with one's ~) 주w-, (줍다) (9)
finish it 끝마치 - (7)
finish sth 끝내 - (14); 마치 - (17)
finish sth 끝내 - (2)
firm (be ~) 굳 - (6)
firmly (chew ~) 꼭 (14)
first anniversary 돌 (1)
first boat (the ~) 첫배 (1)
first class 일등(一等) (2)
first off 일단(一旦) (9)
first place / prize (get ~) 일등(一等)(을) 하 - (2)
first sight (fall in love at ~) ("at first eye") 첫눈에 반하 - (1)
first stage(s) 초기(初期) (7)
first time in one's life (for the ~) 생전(生前) 처음 (5)
first (ceremony in honor of baby's~ birthday) 돌 잔치 (1)
fish (in its uncooked state) 물고기 [물꼬기] (12)
fish 낚시(를) 하 - (13)
"fishy" (be ~) 수상(殊常)하 - (17)
fit one's physical constitution 체질에 맞 - (6)
fit perfectly 딱 맞 - (16)
flaw 티 (11)
flee 도망(逃亡)(을) 가 - (16,17); 도망(逃亡)(을) 치 - (17)
flip one's pencil around 연필(을) 돌리 - (14)
float away 떠내려가 - (16)
float 뜨 - (12)
float 뜨 - (3)
floating bouncingly 동동; 둥둥 (12)
floats up (into my head)(a thought ~) 생각(이) 떠오르 - (3)
flooding happens 물난리(亂離)(가) 나 - (16)
flustered (be / feel ~) 쩔쩔매 - (3); 당황(唐慌)하 - (1)
fly 나 - ㄹ - (날다) (9)
fly (intransitive) 나 - ㄹ - (날다) (14)
fly away 날아가 - (9)
fly sth 날리 - (14)
fold sth 접 - (9)
folk customs 민속(民俗) (14)
folk games 민속놀이 (14)
folklore (as field of study) 민속학(民俗學) (14)
folkways 민속(民俗) (14)
follow (sb) around 쫓아다니 - (7)
follow 따르 - , 따라요 (2)
fond of (grow ~) 정(情)(이) 드 - ㄹ - (들다) (1)

fool 속이 - (6)

fooled (be ~) 속 - (NB: processive) (6)

foolish (be ~) 미련하 - (18)

foot (go about / attend on ~) 걸어다니 - (1)

foot (top of the ~) 발등 [- 뜽] (6)

footwear 신발 (8)

for a long time 오래 (19); 오랫동안 (11)

for a long time 오래 (6)

for example / instance 예(例)를 들어(서) (6)

for fun 장난으로 (12)

for quite a while 한참 (4)

for some reason or other 왠지 (5)

for sure (will do) 반드시 (2)

for the 1st time in one's life 생전(生前) 처음 (5)

for the most part 주(主)로 (6)

for what reason? 웬일로 (2)

foreign-goods shop 양품점(洋品店) (16)

foreign particle 티 (11)

foresee 예상(豫想)(을) 하 - (17)

foresee 예상(豫想)(을) 하 - (3)

forget completely 까마득하게 잊 - (19)

forgive 용서(容恕)(를) 하 - (16)

form (pitiful / derogatory ~) 꼴 (6)

form 모양(模樣) (17); 형태(形態) (11)

form 모양(模樣) (2)

Formal Style speech 존댓말 (1)

formed (be / get ~ 형성(形成)(이) 되- (6)

fortnight 보름 (14)

fortunate (be ~) 복(福)(을) 받 - (NB: processive) (6)

fortunate (it is ~) 다행(多幸)이 - (1)

fortunately 다행(多幸)히 (8)

fortune (it is a great ~) 다행(多幸)이 - (1)

foundation 기초(基礎) (7)

"fraidy-cat" 겁쟁이 (14)

free from care 마음 놓고 (4)

free meals (get ~) 얻어 먹 - (6)

free of commitments (be ~) 한가(閑暇 / 閑暇)하 - (16)

freeload 얻어 먹 - (6)

freeze sth 냉동(冷凍)하 - / 시키 - (9)

frequently 흔히 (6)

fresh "before one's eyes" (be ~) 눈에 선하 - (7)

fresh (be ~)싱싱하 - (12)

fresh air (take / get some ~) 바람(을) 쐬 - (3)

fresh in one's mind / memory (be ~) 눈에 선하 - (7)

fresh (be ~ before one's eyes/in one's mind/memory) 선하 - (7)

friends (a "just ~" relationship) 친구 사이 (2)

friendship 우정(友情) (6)

frightened (be ~) 놀라 - (11,19)

from nearby 가까이에서 (12,13)

from the first 원래(原來 / 元來) (16)

from the very beginning 전(前)부터 (4)

from up close 가까이에서 (12,13)

frugal (be ~) 알뜰하 - (16)

frustrated (feel ~) 억울하 - (NB: descriptive) (2)

fulfill 채우 - (14)

full bloom, full swing (in ~) 한창 (7)

full of people (be ~) 붐비 - (NB: processive) (8)

full to the brim (be ~) 꽉 차 - (NB: processive) (8)

full up (be ~) 꽉 차 - (NB: processive) (8)

full 가득 / 가뜩 (14); 잔뜩 (11)

fumble 뒤지 - (12)

fun 장난 (12)

fun 즐거w- (즐겁다) (1)

function 기능(機能) (8)

fundament 기초(基礎) (7)

funny (be ~) 웃기 - (NB: processive) (14)

funny story 우스갯소리 (19)

furnish 갖추 - (7)

further 더 이상(以上) (14)

G

gaffe 실수(失手) (4)

gain experience 견문(이) 생기 - (6)

gait 걸음 (1)

gallery (art ~) 미술관(美術館) (9)

game of ball 공장난(12)

game of *yut* 윷놀이(14)

game (a practice ~) 연습경기(練習競技) (2)

game (baseball ~) 야구경기(野球競技) (2)

game 장난 (12)

gap 틈 (11)

garlic 마늘 (18)

gasoline 석유(石油) (6)

gather (intransitive) 모이 - (16)

gathering 모임 (2)

gaze at 바라보 - (13); 쳐다보 - (14)

gene 유전자(遺傳子) (6)

genetics 유전(遺傳) (6)

genial (be ~)인심(人心)(이) 좋 - (14)

gentle (be ~)얌전하 - (12)

gentlemen! (ladies and ~) 여러분 (3)

genuine and pure (be ~) 순진(純眞)하 - (18)

gesture with feet 발짓 [- 찟] (17)

gesture with hands 손짓 [- 찟] (17)

get a cramp in the leg 다리에 쥐가 나 - (2)

get a haircut 머리(를) 자르 - (13)

get a hoarse throat 목(이) 쉬 - (6)

get a job 취직(就職)(을) 하 - (1)

get a ticket 딱지(를) 떼이 - (2)

get along with (~ sb) 어울리 - (1)

get angry 화(火)가 나 - (1)

get away from 피(避)하 - (8)
get better (sickness) 병(病)(이) 낫다, 나아요 (1)
get dry 마르 - (14)
get exhausted 지치 - (4)
get fat 살(이) 찌 - (19)
get free meals 얻어 먹 - (6)
get in contact with 연락(連絡)을 하 - (1)
get it 이해(理解)(가) 되 - (1)
get lost 길(을) 잃어버리 - (6)
get old 나이(가) 드 - ㄹ - (들다) (19)
get on the wrong vehicle 잘못 타 - (2)
get rid of 없애 - (14)
get rid of 제거(除去)(를) 하 - (6)
get selected in a drawing 당첨(當籤)(이) 되 - (4)
get sick 병(病)(이) 나 - (1)
get smacked 맞 - (6)
get sopping wet in the rain 비(를) 쫄딱 맞 - (16)
get sth ready 장만(을) 하 - (7)
get through to 통(通)하 - (2)
get through ("[one's words] ~") 통(通)하 - (2)
get undressed 벗 - (14)
get up sb's nose 약(을) 올리 - (16)
get used to 익 - (11)
get wet 젖 - (14)
get (~ [a license]) 따 - (2)
getting a job 취직(就職) (1)
girlfriend 애인(愛人) (2)
give (sth) in return 갚 - (18)
give (to sb esteemed) 올리 - (14)
give a brilliant answer 명답(名答)(을) 하 - (5)
give a reaction 반응(反應)(을) 보이 - (3)
give a ride (to sb]) 태우 - (14)
give in to 들어 주 - (6)
Give me a break once. 한 번만 봐 주세요. (11)
Give me a break. 봐 주세요 (11)
give one the creeps 끔찍하 - (NB: descriptive) (4)
give sb a break 잘 봐 주 - (2)
give sb a day off 놀리 - (14)
give sth back 돌려 주 - (19)
give up 포기(抛棄)(를) 하 - (12)
glazed over 멍하 - (14)
go a round (of fighting)한바탕(을) 하 - (16)
go about on foot 걸어다니 - (1)
go across 건너 - , 건너가 - (14)
go ahead of 앞서 가 - (1)
go around 다니 - (16)
go at 대드 - ㄹ - (대들다) (18)
go away on an official trip 출장(出張)(을) 가 - (1)
go away on business 출장(出張)(을) 가 - (1)
go bad (food) 상하 - (음식이 ~) (16)
go beyond 넘치 - (4)

go fishing 낚시(를) 하 - (13)
go hiking 등산(登山)(을) 하 - (6)
go into debt 빚(을) 지 - (6)
go off (food) 상하 - (음식이 ~) (16)
go on a diet 다이어트(를) 하 - (1)
go out 외출(外出)(을) 하 - (19)
go over the top in efforts 무리(無理)하 - (7)
go so far as to 하다못해 (17)
go straight 쭉 가 - (12)
go to the bottom 가라앉 - (11)
go up to 다가가 - (13)
go well together 어울리 - (1)
go well with (clothes) 어울리 - (1)
go well with 어울리 - (19)
go (up and ~) 가 버리 - (1)
go; round (of fighting) 바탕 (16)
goal 목적(目的) (17)
gobsmacked (be ~) 깜짝 놀라 - (NB: processive) (3)
god / God 하느님 ← 하늘 + 님 (18)
goes as far as 닿 - (4)
good-hearted (be ~) 인심(人心)(이) 좋 - (14)
good-hearted (be ~) 착하 - (3)
good-looking (be ~) 잘나 - (3)
good in studies (be ~) 글(을) 잘하 - (NB: processive) (6)
good memory (have a ~) 기억력(記憶力)(이) 좋 - (19)
good on (look ~) 어울리 - (3)
good rest (have a ~) 푹 쉬 - (4)
good (be ~ [at heart]) 착하 - (3)
goods 물건(物件) (6)
goof off 노 - ㄹ - (놀다) (14)
govern 다스리 - (18)
government 정부 (2)
grace 덕분 (4)
gradually 점점(漸漸) (17)
gradually점 점(漸漸) (7)
grain (rice ~) 쌀 (2)
grave (be ~) 정중(鄭重)하 - (17)
grave way (in a ~) 심(甚)하게 (4)
great-grandfather 증조(曾祖) 할아버지 (18)
great mass 산더미 [- 떠미] (12)
great (be ~) 잘나 - (3)
greatest 최고(最高) (16)
greatly 썩 (14)
grin and bear it 참 - (4)
grit 티 (11)
grow (~ a beard = 수염) 수염을 기르 - (12)
grow (up) 자라 - (12)
grow fond of 정(情)(이) 드 - ㄹ - (들다) (1)
guard 지키 - (13)
guest in sb's home (stay as a paying ~) 민박(民泊)(을) 하 - (8)

gumption (have ~) 영악하 - (NB: descriptive) (18)

H

haberdashery 양품점(洋品店) (16)
habit 습관(習慣) (2)
habits (have bad ~) 버릇(이) 없 - (2)
haircut (get a ~) 머리(를) 자르 - (13)
half-assed job of something (do a ~) 설치 - (9)
half 절반(折半) (6)
hamper 바구니 (11)
hand in 제출(提出)(을) 하 - (4)
hand stamp 도장(圖章) (14)
handle 다루 - (6)
handle 핸들 (8)
handled (be more than can be ~) 넘치 - (NB: processive) (4)
handsome (be ~) 잘 생겼어요 (3); 잘나 - (3)
handwriting 글씨 (11)
handwriting 글씨 (6)
hang out (the laundry) 널어 놓 - (1)
hang sth 거 - ㄹ - (걸다) (11)
hang up (the phone) 끊 - (16)
happened (be / remain as if nothing ~) 태연(泰然)하 - (3)
happenings (counter / classifier for ~) 건(件) (9)
happens ([sth] ~) 벌어지 - (3)
happy (be ~) 행복(幸福)하 - (13)
hard time of it (have a ~) 혼(魂)(이) 나 - (6,7)
hard (be ~) 굳 - (6)
hard (try ~) 애(를) 쓰 - (3)
harmful (be ~) 해(害)(가) 되 - (6)
hateful (be ~) 미w- (밉다) (13)
hateful (more than 밉다)(be ~) 얄미w- (얄밉다) (13)
have a go 한바탕(을) 하 - (16)
have a thing ready 갖추 - (7)
have an interest in 관심(關心)을 가지 - (12)
have gumption 영악하 - (NB: descriptive) (18)
have maturity 철(이) 있 - (14)
"have much fear" 겁(怯)(이) 많 - (14)
have poor orientation sense 길눈(이) 어두w- (어둡다) (NB: descriptive) (16)
have sb bathe / wash 감기 - (14)
have sb call 불리 - (14)
have sb catch 잡히 - (14)
have sb walk 걸리 - (14)
have sense 철(이) 있 - (14)
have spare time 한가(閒暇 / 閑暇)하 - (16)
he himself 자기(自己) (16)
he 걔 = 그애 (8)
head for the hills 도망(逃亡)(을) 가 - (16,17)
head (inside my ~) 머릿속으로 (3)

head (section ~) 과장(課長) (2)
headquarters (administrative ~) - 청(廳) (2)
heal 치료(治療)(를) 하 - (3)
healthy (be ~) 건강(健康)하 - (7)
heap sth 쌓 - (11)
heard (be / get ~) 들리 - (11)
hearts (two people's ~ communicate well) 마음(이) 잘 통(通)하 - (2)
heat sth 데우 - ; 덥히 - (14)
heated (get ~) 다 - ㄹ - (달다) (6)
heavy on the stomach (feel ~) 체하 - (2)
heel 굽 (7)
heighten 돋우 - (14)
heightened (be / get ~) 고조(高潮)(가) 되 - (7)
held (be / get ~ (up) in the hands) 들리 - (9)
help 도w- (돕다) (14)
herd it 모 - ㄹ - (몰다) (8)
here and there 군데군데 (17)
here and there 여기저기 (3)
heredity 유전(遺傳) (6)
hero(ine) 주인공(主人公) (11)
hick (be ~) 촌스러w- (- 스럽다) (9)
hide sth 숨기 - (14)
high-class (be ~) 고급(高級)스러w- (~스럽다) (6)
high blood pressure 고혈압(高血壓) (6)
high point / climax (reach a ~) 고조(高潮)(가) 되 - (7)
high speed 고속(高速) (4)
high (be ~) 높 - (14)
highly prized article 보물(寶物) (11)
Highway (the Seoul-Pusan ~) 경부(京釜) 고속도로(高速道路) (4)
highway bus 고속(高速)버스 (4)
hike 등산(登山)(을) 하 - (6)
hints of dementia 노망(老妄)기 [- 끼] (11)
hire 뽑 - (6)
history 역사(歷史) (8)
hit (get ~) 맞 - (6)
hitch 탈 (18)
hoarse (get a ~ throat) 목(이) 쉬 - (6)
hold in 담 - (6)
hole 구멍 (18)
holiday from work 휴가(休暇) (17,19)
holiday 휴가(休暇) (4)
holidays (school ~) 방학(放學) (8)
hollow (be ~)비 - (비었어요) (17)
home in the countryside (one's ~) 시골집 [- 찝] (7)
home (leave the ~) 가출(家出)(을) 하 - (2)
home (stay as a paying guest in sb's ~) 민박(民泊)(을) 하 - (8)
homestay do a (long-term, study-related ~) 홈스테이(를) 하 - (8)

homestay (do a short ~ on a vacation) 민박(民泊) (을) 하 - (8)
honest person (be an ~) 착하 - (3)
Honey! 여보! (17)
honor (ceremony in ~ of baby's first birthday) 돌 잔치 (1)
hoof 굽 (7)
horizons (broaden one's ~) 견문(이) 생기 - (6)
horn (cow's ~) 쇠뿔 (6)
horrible (be ~) 끔찍하 - (4)
horrid (be ~) 끔찍하 - (4)
horse around 떠드 - ㄹ - (떠들다) (2)
hostage 인질(人質) (14)
hot pepper powder (red ~) 고춧가루 (2)
hot (become very ~) 다 - ㄹ - (달다) (6)
house in mourning (a ~) 초상집(初喪~) [- 찝] (2)
house in the countryside (one's ~) 시골집 [- 찝] (7)
housewarming celebration 집들이 (16)
housework 집안일 (9)
how-many-eth? 몇 번째? (14)
How many days? 며칠 (3)
hug 안 - (11)
huge amount 산더미 [- 떠미] (12)
human being 인간(人間) (18)
human race 인류(人類) (6)
humanity 인류(人類) (11)
humiliated (be ~) 욕(을) 당하 - (NB: processive) (6)
humiliation (suffer ~) 욕(을) 당하 - (6)
humiliation 욕(辱) (6)
hung (be / get ~) 걸리 - (11)
hunger 시장 (6)
hungry (go ~) 굶 - (14)
hungry (make go ~) 굶기 - (14)
hurriedly 급(急)하게 (3)
hurt oneself 다치 - (1)
husband (folksy)서방(書房) (13)
husband and wife 부부(夫婦) (2)

I

I'm used to it. 습관(習慣)이 됐어요. (2)
ignorant (be ~) 무식(無識)하 - (6)
ill at ease (be ~) 불안(不安)하 - (11)
ill at ease (feel ~) 곤란(困難)하 - (NB: descriptive) (3)
ill fortune 불우(不遇) (18)
ill luck 불우(不遇) (18)
immediately 얼른 (14)
immerse sth 잠그 - (11)
import 수입(輸入) (을) 하 - (6)
important (be ~) 소중(所重)하 - (14)
importune (sb) 재촉(을) 하 - (1)
impressive (be ~) 감탄스러w– (~스럽다) (13)
improve 느 - ㄹ - (늘다) (14)

in accord with one's wishes 뜻대로 (3)
in actual fact 실제(實際)로 (6)
in all cases 모두 (6)
in any case 좌우간(左右間) (9)
in every nook and cranny 샅샅이 (1)
in full bloom; in full swing 한창 (7)
in just one day 하루만에 (14)
in my direction 내 쪽 (14)
in one big lump 몽땅 (14)
in one breath / stroke 한꺼번에 (1)
in particular 특(特)히 (17)
in real life 실제(實際)로 (6)
in the end 결국(結局) (2)
in the front (~ [of here, where we are]) 요 앞 = 이 앞 (16)
in the main 주(主)로 (6)
in the nick of time 마침 (11)
in total 몽땅 (14)
inadvertently 무심(無心)코 (5)
incite (anger) 돋우 - (화(火)를 ~) (14)
increase sth 늘리 - (14)
increase 느 - ㄹ - (늘다) (14)
increase 늘어나 - (7)
incredible beauty 대단한 미인(美人) (5)
incredibly 무지무지 (16); 무척 (16)
incur debt 빚(을) 지 - (6)
indebtedness 덕분(德分) (4)
indigenous 고유(固有) (8)
indiscretion (to commit an ~) 실수(失手) (를) 하 - (4)
individual 인물(人物) (8)
induce wonder 감탄스러w– (~스럽다) (NB: descriptive) (13)
infected (be / get ~) 감염(感染) (이) 되 - (6)
inform 알리 - (14)
inform 알리 - (7)
infringe 위반(違反) (을) 하 - (2)
ingest (medicine) 복용(服用) (을) 하 - (18)
inherent 고유(固有) (8)
initial period 초기(初期) (7)
injured (be / get ~) 손상(損傷) (이) 되 - (6)
injurious (be ~) 해(害) (가) 되 - (NB: processive) (6)
injury 부상(負傷) (11)
insert and enter 끼어드 - ㄹ - (끼어들다) (8)
insert sth 꽂 - (13)
inside my head 머릿속으로 (3)
insolvency 파산(破産) (4)
instance (for ~) 예(例)를 들어(서) (6)
instant 순간(瞬間) (17)
insufficient (be ~) 모자라 - (NB: processive) (1)
intact 그대로 (1)
intends (as one ~) 뜻대로 (3)
intention 의지(意志) (18)

intentionally 일부러 (18)

interested in (be ~) 관심(關心)을 가지 - (NB: processive) (12)

interfere with 훼방(毀謗)(을) 놓 - (14)

interpret 해석(解釋)(을) 하 - (8)

interpretation 통역(通譯) (18)

interrupt 중지(中止)(를) 하 - (5)

interrupted (be ~) 중단(中斷)(이) 되 - (NB: processive) (2)

interval 틈 (11)

Intimate Style speech 반말 (1)

invade 쳐들어오 - , 쳐들어가 - (9)

invasion 침략(侵掠) (11)

invention 발명(發明) (8)

investigate 조사(調査)(를) 하 - (11)

invite 초대(招待)(를) 하 - (2)

iron 다리 - (12)

iron 다리미 (12)

it causes concern 궁금하 - (7)

it is fortunate 다행(多幸)이 - (1)

It is so, isn't it? 그치 ← 그렇지 (16)

item 물건(物件) (6)

J

jam in 처넣 - (9)

jammed (with traffic) (be / get ~) 길(이) 막히 - (1)

jammed 밀리 - (2)

Japanese language 일어(日語) (5)

Japanese words 일본(日本) 말들 (5)

jelly (from acorns, etc.) 묵 (11)

job (a ~) 일거리 [- 꺼리] (7)

job (get / find a ~) 취직(就職)(을) 하 - (1)

job (getting / landing a ~) 취직(就職) (1)

join 합(合)하 - (9)

joke 농담(弄談) (19); 우스갯소리 (19)

jokingly 농담 삼아 (19)

jot down 적 - (3)

journey (a ~) 여행 (旅行) (1)

joy 낙(樂) (6)

jump 뛰 - (14)

jungle 정글 (11)

junior from school (one's ~) 후배(後輩) (3)

just about to... 막 (17)

just as it is / was 그대로 (1)

just as it was / had been 있던 그대로 (8)

just as you are 그대로 (1)

just as / when... 막 (13)

just friends(a "~" relationship) 친구(親舊) 사이 (2)

just in time 마침 (11)

just like... 마치... 듯이 (11)

just right (fit ~) 딱 맞 - (16)

just 단지(但只) (2)

K

Kangnam (area south of the Han River in Seoul) 강남(江南) (9)

keep a watchful eye on 지켜보 - (13)

keep an appointment / promise 약속(約束)(을) 지키 - (4)

keep away from 피(避)하 - (8)

keep in 담 - (6)

keep on doing 자꾸 (1)

keep on VERBing 자꾸 VERB (12)

keep out of (rain) 피(避)하 - (8)

Keep quiet a moment. 가만히 있어! (11)

keep secret 숨기 - (14)

keep 지키 - (13)

key 열쇠 [- 쐬] (12)

key to sth 비결(秘訣) (1)

kidneys 신장(腎臟) (6)

kill 죽이 - (12)

kind (be ~) 친절(親切)하 - (17)

kitchen 부엌 (6)

knack (manual) 솜씨 (17)

knack to sth 비결(秘訣) (1)

knee 무릎 (16)

know (let ~) 알리 - (7)

Korean drink like Seven-Up 사이다(13)

Korean house (courtyard inside a traditional ~) 마당 (1)

Korean sickle 낫 (6)

Korean style (in the ~) 한국식(韓國式)으로 (3)

Korean traditional costume (colorful ~) 색동옷 (2)

Korean traditional medicine 한방(韓方) (5)

Korean way (in the ~) 한국식(韓國式)으로 (3)

L

lack maturity 철(이) 없 - (14)

lack sense 철(이) 없 - (14)

lack 모자라 - (14)

lacking alternatives 하다못해 (17)

ladder 사다리 (15)

ladies and gentlemen! 여러분 (3)

landing a job 취직(就職) (1)

large meeting 대회(大會) (12)

laser 레이저 (6)

last-minute cramming 벼락치기 (9)

late autumn 늦가을 (7)

late (arrive ~) 지각(遲刻)(을) 하 - (3)

late (be ~) 늦 - (14)

late (sleep ~) 늦잠(을) 자 - (1)

lately 요즘 (1)

later (a little while ~) 이따가 (3)

later (postpone / put off until ~) 다음으로 미루 - (9)

laughing matter (no ~) 웃지 못 할 일 (13)

laughingstock 웃음거리 [- 꺼리] (7)

launder 빠 - ㄹ - (빨다) (12)

laundromat, launderette 세탁소(洗濯所) (3)

laundry (do the ~) 세탁(洗濯) (을) 하 - (3)

laundry machine 세탁기(洗濯機) (3)

laundry to do 빨래거리 [- 꺼리] (11)

laundry (do the ~) 빨래(를) 하 - (1)

laundry (hang out the ~) 널어 놓 - (1)

laundry (the ~) 빨래 (1)

laundry 빨래 (11)

law (according to the ~) 법규(法規)에 따라 (2)

law (the ways ["~"] of Rome) 로마법(法) [- 뻡] (2)

lawyer (a ~) 변호사(辯護士) (4)

lay out 펴 - (3)

lazy (act ~) 게으름(을) 피우 - (6)

lazy (be ~) 게으르 - (1)

leader (the class ~) 반장(班長) (9)

leap 뛰 - (14)

leave sb with 맡기 - (14)

leave (of absence) 휴가(休暇) (17,19)

leave alone, "leave be" 내버리 - (3)

leave an impression 인상(印象)을 남기 - (14)

leave in sb's charge 맡기 - (14)

leave left over / undone 남기 - (14)

leave of absence 휴가(休暇) (4)

leave on holiday / vacation 휴가(를) 떠나 - (17)

leave out 빼 - (18)

leave sth (behind) 남기 - (14)

leave sth behind by accident 두고 오 - (1)

leave the home 가출(家出)(을) 하 - (2)

leave work for home 퇴근(退勤)(을) 하 - (3)

leave 가 버리 - (1)

leaving (be sad that someone is ~) 섭섭하 - (2)

leeway (time-wise ~) 시간적 여유(時間的 餘裕) (8)

leeway 여유(餘裕) (19)

left (behind) (be ~) 남 - (NB: processive) (14)

leg (get a cramp in the ~) 다리에 쥐가 나 - (2)

legislation (traffic ~) 교통법규(交通法規) (2)

leisure (be at ~) 한가(閑暇 / 閑暇)하 - (16)

length 길이 (14)

lengthen 느 - ㄹ - (늘다) (14)

less than satisfactory way (do sth in a ~) 설치 - (9)

lessen 더 - ㄹ - (덜다) (11)

lessen 줄이 - (7)

let go (be ~) 풀려나 - (NB: processive) (14)

let know 알리 - (7)

let live 살리 - (12)

Let me think. 가만히 있자 (11)

let sb eat 먹이 - (14)

let sb hear 들리 - (14)

let sb know 알리 - (14)

let sb play 놀리 - (14)

let sb see 보이 - (14)

let sth fly 날리 - (14)

let sth go around 돌리 - (14)

letter (a reply ~) 답장(答狀) (7)

li (about ⅓ mile) 리(里) (18)

li (one thousand ~) 천리(千里) (6)

license (driver's ~) 운전면허증(運轉免許證) (2)

lid 덮개 (11); 뚜껑 (11)

life (conduct one's day-to-day ~) 생활(生活)(을) 하 - (3)

life (daily ~) 일상생활(日常生活) (6)

life (one's station in ~) 분수(分數) (6)

life 생활(生活) (6)

lift (up) 돋우 - (14)

lift sth briskly 번쩍 (4)

lift 올리 - (14)

light (in weight) (be ~)가벼w– (가볍다) (11)

lightning strikes 벼락(이) 치 - (9)

like the others 남들처럼 (2)

like (if it had been ["~"] any other day) 다른 날 같았으면 (2)

listen to request for favor 들어주 - (17)

little (a ~) 약간(若干) (11)

little (be ~) 조그맣 - (조그매, 조그만) (12)

little while later (a ~) 이따가 (3)

little (a ~) 약간(若干) (2)

living room 거실(居室) (9)

living room 마루 (14)

living (conduct one's day-to-day ~) 생활(生活)(을) 하 - (3)

lock (intransitive) 잠기 - (11)

lock sth 잠그 - (11)

lodge 묵 - (1)

lodging fees 하숙비(下宿費) (4)

logic 논리(論理) (8)

long ago (not too ~) 얼마 전에는 (7)

long time (for a ~) 오래 (19); 오랫동안 (11)

long time (for a ~) 오래 (6)

look a certain way 생기 - (3)

look alike 닮았다 (6, 7)

look back / behind oneself 돌아다 보 - (1)

look back 돌아 보 - (4)

look good on 어울리 - (3)

look (turn around and ~) 돌아 보 - (4)

look (turn around and ~) 돌아다 보 - (1)

loose (be ~) 늦 - (14)

loosen sth 늦추 - (14)

lose face 무안(無顏)하 - (11)

lose one's way 길(을) 잃어버리 - (6)

lose sth 잃어버리 - (1)
lose weight 마르 - (2)
lose weight 살(을) 빼 - (4); 살(이) 빠지 - (1)
loss as to what to do (be at a complete ~) 쩔쩔매 - (NB: processive) (3)
loss as to what to do (feel at a ~) 당황(唐慌 / 唐惶)하 - (1)
lost (get ~) 길(을) 잃어버리 - (6)
lottery ticket 복권(福券) (4)
loud (be ~) 요란(搖亂)스러w- (~스럽다) (17)
love at first sight (fall in ~) ("at first eye") 첫눈에 반하 - (1)
love sb (come to ~) (but not necessarily romantically) 정(情)(이) 드 - ㄹ - (들다) (1)
lower back 허리 (11)
luckily 다행(多幸)히 (8)
luckily 마침 (11)
luggage 짐 (16)
luggage 짐 (9)
luxurious (be ~) 사치(奢侈)스러w- (~스럽다) (6)
luxury 사치(奢侈) (6)

M

machine (laundry / washing ~) 세탁기(洗濯機) (3)
made up of (be / get ~) 구성(構成)(이) 되 - (6)
made (get ~) 만들어지 - (6)
magazine company 잡지사(雜誌社) (9)
magnifying glass 돋보기 (11)
main character 주인공(主人公) (11)
main entrance 정문(正門) (5)
main (in the ~) 주(主)로 (6)
mainly 주(主)로 (6)
maintain (into the future) 지켜 나가 - (6)
make ("wrap") (*kimpap*) 싸 - (김밥을 ~) (13)
make a challenge 도전(挑戰)(을) 하 - (18)
make a declaration 신고(申告)(를) 하 - (11)
make a face 표정(表情)(을) 지(ㅅ) - (짓다) (3)
make a fuss 말썽(을) 부리 - (12)
make a plan 계획(計劃)(을) 세우 - (19)
make a public pledge 공약(公約)(을) 하 - (6)
make a resolution (to do) 결심(決心)(을) 하 - (3)
make a ruckus 떠드 - ㄹ - (떠들다) (2)
make an error 실수(失手)(를) 하 - (4)
make efforts 애(를) 쓰 - (13)
make efforts 애(를) 쓰 - (3); 노력(努力)(을) 하 - (6)
make go hungry 굶기 - (14)
make it stand 세우 - (12)
make it turn 돌리 - (2)
make live 살리 - (14)
make narrow 좁히 - (14)
make people laugh 웃기 - (14)
make progress 느 - ㄹ - (늘다) (14)

make ready 차리 - (13)
make sb do sth 시키 - (3)
make sb hear 들리 - (14)
make sth dry 말리 - (14)
make sth fly 날리 - (14)
make sth go around 돌리 - (14)
make sth increase 늘리 - (14)
make sth wet 적시 - (14)
make stick to 붙이 - (19)
make take off (clothing) 벗기 -
make the grade 합격(合格)(을) 하 - (14)
make up one's mind 결심(決心)(을) 하 - (3)
make up one's mind 마음(을) 먹 - (14)
make up with 화해(和解)(를) 하 - (16)
make up 채우 - (14)
make wear 입히 - (19)
makings for soup 국거리 (7)
malaria 말라리아 (6)
male gender 남성(男性) (6)
male 사나이; 사내 (12)
man 사나이; 사내 (12)
manage 다스리 - (18)
manager 과장(課長) (2); 관리자(管理者) (6)
mankind 인류(人類) (6)
manner (do sth in a less than satisfactory ~) 설치 - (9)
manner (in such a ~) 그런 식으로 (3)
manners (have no ~) 버릇(이) 없 - (2)
many days? (How ~) 며칠 (3)
margin (time-wise ~) 시간적 여유(時間的 餘裕) (8)
married couple 부부(夫婦) (2)
married ([man] get ~) 장가(를) 가 - (4)
married ([woman] get ~) 시집(을) 가 - (19)
married ([woman] get ~) 시집(을) 가- (4)
marry off (one's daughter) 시집(을) 보내 - (3)
marvelous (be ~) 감탄스러w- (~스럽다) (13)
massage cream 마사지 크림 (17)
master (folksy) 서방(書房) (13)
match one's physical constitution 체질에 맞 - (6)
match (have a ~) 경기(競技)(를) 하 - (8)
match 어울리 - (1)
matchmaking date (go on a sort of ~; often set up by the parents) 선(을) 보 - (4)
matter (with you)? (what's the ~) 웬일이세요? (2, 4)
matter for concern (a ~) 걱정거리 [- 꺼리] (7)
matter of course (as a ~) 자연(自然) (6)
matter of fact (as a ~) 원래(元來 / 原來) (4)
matter 알맹이 (19)
mature 익 - (11)
maturity 철 (14)
max (to the ~) 잔뜩 (11)
meal 식사(食事) (2)

meaning 뜻 (19)

means 방법(方法) (6)

meet sb (humbly) 만나 뵈 - ~ 뵙 - (19)

meet (athletic ~) 경기대회(競技大會) (2)

meeting 모임 (2)

meeting (have a preliminary ~ with a prospective spouse) 선(을) 보 - (4)

melt (intransitive) 녹 - (11)

memorize 외우 - (3)

memory (–power) 기억력(記憶力) (19)

memory (be fresh in one's ~) 눈에 선하 - (7)

memory 기억(記憶) (19)

men 남성(男性) (6)

mental agony 고민(苦悶) (1)

mental state 정신(情神) (11)

mentality 정신(精神) (8)

merely 단지(但只) (2)

merriment 흥(興) (6)

merry (feel ~) 흥(이) 나 - (6)

mess (a ~) 엉망 (9)

mess (be a ~) 형편(形便) 없 - (4)

method 방법(方法) (6)

middle school 중학교(中學校) (18)

middle, midst of (the ~) 가운데 (8)

military 군대(軍隊) (18)

military 군대(軍隊) (5)

mind (be fresh in one's ~) 눈에 선하 - (7)

mind (in my ~) 머릿속으로 (3)

mind (make up one's ~ [to do]) 결심(決心)(을) 하 - (3)

minds (two people's ~ communicate well) 마음(이) 잘 통(通)하 - (2)

mingle (intransitive) 섞이 - (11)

minister 신하(臣下) (18)

minor 미성년(未成年) (3)

minority 소수(小數) (2)

mirror 거울 (18)

mirth 흥(興) (6)

mischief 장난 (12)

mischievous child 장난꾸러기 (12)

miser 구두쇠 (18)

misfortune 불우(不遇) (18)

mistake (make a ~) 실수(失手)(를) 하 - (4)

mistake for 오해(誤解)(를) 하 - (13)

mistake (it's my ~) 내 잘못이에요 (2)

mistake 잘못 (2); 실수(失手) (4)

mistakenly (adv.) 잘못 (2)

misty color (be a ~) 뿌옇 - , 뿌얘요 (8)

misunderstand 오해(誤解)(를) 하 - (13)

misunderstood (be / get ~) 오해(誤解)(를) 받 - (6)

mitigate 더 - ㄹ - (덜다) (11)

mix 섞 - (11)

mixed (be / get ~) 섞이 - (11)

modern 현대(現代) (9)

modest (be ~)얌전하 - (12)

moistened (get / become ~) 젖 - (14)

moment (a ~) 순간(瞬間) (3)

moment 순간(瞬間) (3)

momentarily 순간적(瞬間的)으로 (3)

money (spending / pocket ~) 용돈 [- 똔] (2)

monkey 원숭이 (6)

monsoons 장마 (7)

moral (to a story) 교훈(敎訓) (6)

more (any ~) 더 이상(以上)(14); 더욱 (12)

more or less 그런대로 (9)

more than can be handled (be ~) 넘치 - (NB: processive) (4)

mosquito 모기 (6)

most part (for the ~) 주(主)로 (6)

mote 티 (11)

Mother's Day 어머닐날 (3)

motion 동작(動作) (17)

motorcycle 오토바이 (8)

Mount Sŏrak 설악산(雪嶽山) (16)

Mount T'aebaek 태백산(太白山) (18)

mourning (a family / house in ~) 초상집(初喪~) [- 찝] (2)

mouthful (a ~) 모금 (usually with liquids) (4)

move an inch (can't ~) 꼼짝도 못 하 - (2)

move out 가출(家出)(을) 하 - (2)

move sth 옮기 - (9)

move (both transitive and intransitive) 움직이 - (6, 9)

movement (of the body) 동작(動作) (17)

Mr. (familiar Style) 서방(書房) (13)

much (so) (very ~) 무척 (3)

much more so 훨씬 (9)

much (so ~ so that) 하도 (7)

muddy (be ~) 지 - ㄹ - (질다) (11)

muggy (be ~)후덥지근하 - (17)

mugwort 쑥 (18)

my son (humble) 아들 녀석 (12)

myth 신화(神話) (18)

N

naive (be ~) 순진(純眞)하 - (18)

name chop 도장(刀匠) (14)

namely 즉(卽) (6)

narrow sth 좁히 - (14)

narrow (be ~) 좁 - (14)

nation-state 국가(國家) (6)

nation (the people of a ~) 국민(國民) (6); 국가(國家) (6)

nation; ethnos; race 민족(民族) (6)

native 고유(固有) (8)

natural (be ~) 자연(自然)스러w– (- 스럽다) (16)

naturally endowed with 타고나 - (2)
naturally 자연(自然) (6)
naturally 자연(自然)스럽게 (16)
nature 자연(自然) (6)
near (come ~) 다가오 - (2)
nearby 가까이 (13)
nearly (all, etc.) 거의 (3)
nearly (~ [did sth]) 하마터면 (8)
nearsightedness 근시(近視) (7)
necklace 목걸이 (14)
need to make a phone call 전화(電話)할 데 있 - (19)
needle 바늘 (6)
needless to say 물어 볼 것도 없이 (12)
needlework 바느질 ← 바늘 (11)
negligence fee / fine 과태료(過怠料) (2)
neighbor 이웃 (12)
neighboring house 이웃집 (12)
nephew 조카 (17)
nervous (be ~) 궁금하 - (7)
new student 신입생(新入生) (12)
New Year's Day 설 / 설날 (3)
news 소식(消息) (7)
niece 조카 (17)
nigh on (thirty years) 가까이 (30 년 ~) (14)
night (spend the ~) 묵 - (1)
night 밤(을) 새우 - (4)
nimble (be ~) 재빠르 - (17)
no laughing matter 웃지 못 할 일 (13)
no sooner than 그러자 (11)
noble (be ~) 귀(貴)하 - (8)
noisy (be ~) 요란(搖亂)스러w- (~스럽다) (17)
nook and cranny (in every ~) 샅샅이 (1)
normal times (during ~) 평소(平素)에 (5)
normally 평소(平素)에 (5)
North Pole 북극점(北極点) (18)
nose gets itchy (tear up) 코끝이 찡하 - (14)
not (...at all) 전(全)혀 (+ NEGATIVE) (13)
not enough (be ~) 모자라 - (NB: processive) (1)
(not) even a penny 한 푼도 (14)
not long ago 얼마 전에 (13)
not recognize sb 몰라보 - (19)
not the case, then (if that is ~) 아니면 (3)
not too long ago 얼마 전에는 (7)
notepad 수첩(手帖) (9)
nothing happened (be / remain as if ~) 태연(泰然)하 - (3)
notify 신고(申告)(를) 하 - (11)
novel 소설(小說) (8)
number of personnel 인원수(- 數) [- 쑤] (14)
number of persons 인원(人員) (14)
number 번호(番號) (2)

O

object 항의(抗議)(를) 하 - (11)
objective 목적(目的) (17)
objectivity 객관(客觀) (8)
observe 지키 - (13)
obvious (be ~) 뻔하 - (17)
obvious (be ~) 분명(分明)하 - (6)
occasion 시절(時節) (14)
occasions (on some ~) 어떨때는 (4)
occupation 직업(職業) (14)
occurs to (me) (a thought ~) 생각(이) 떠오르 - (3)
odd (be ~) 이상(異常)하 - (7)
oddly 이상(異常)하게 (7)
odious (be ~) 미w- (밉다) (13)
odious (more than 밉다) (be ~) 얄미w- (얄밉다) (13)
Of course. 그치 ← 그렇지 (16)
office (ticket ~) 매표소(賣票所) (1)
officer (police ~) 경찰관(警察官) (2)
official trip (go away on an ~) 출장(出張)(을) 가 - (1)
official trip 출장(出張) (1)
old (get ~) 나이(가) 드 - ㄹ - (19)
old (be ~ [of things]) 낡 - (1)
"old lady" 마누라 (pejorative or jocular term for one's wife) (7)
oldest son 맏아들 (14)
omit 빼 - (18)
on account of what thing? 웬일로 (2)
on purpose 일부러 (18)
on some occasions 어떨 때는 (4)
on time (be ~) 시간(을) 지키 - (16)
on time 제 시간에 (2)
once (all at ~) 한꺼번에 (1)
once 언젠가(는) (2)
one's heart's content 실컷 (14)
one's own 제 (6)
one's pace, steps 걸음 (1)
one's personal experience 견문(見聞) (6)
one-day affair (outing / trip) 당일치기 (16)
one breath / go / stroke (in ~) 한꺼번에 (1)
one thousand li 천리(千里) (6)
one word 말 한 마디 (13)
onerous (be ~) 괴로w- (괴롭다) (6)
oneself 자기(自己) (17)
onlooker(s) 관객(觀客) (18)
only 단지(但只) (2)
open (~ eyes, ears) 뜨 - (11)
open (eyes, ears ~) 뜨이 - (11)
open (a book) 펴 - (3)
open (a letter) (편지를 ~) 뜯 - (12)
open (intransitive) 열리 - (11)
open one's eyes 눈(을) 뜨 - (4)

open (watch with one's eyes wide ~) 눈을 뜨고 보 - (4)

opened (be / get ~) 뜨이 - (11); (be / get ~) 열리 - (11)

opinion 의견(意見) (2)

opponent 상대방(相對方) (18)

opportunely 마침 (11)

opportunity 기회(機會) (11)

opposite (one's ~) 상대방(相對方) (18)

optimistic 낙천적(樂天的) (18)

opus 작품(作品) (18)

or 아니면 (3)

order (an ~) 명령(命令) (6)

order (sb to do sth) 시키 - (3)

order sth (as in a restaurant) 시키 - (3)

order 명령(命令)(을) 하 - (2)

original (be ~) 독특(獨特)하 - (11)

originally 원래(原來 / 元來) (16)

originally 원래(原來 / 元來) (4)

other than me 나 말고는 (1)

other (sb or ~) 누군가 (2)

other (sth or ~) 무언가 (2)

others (like the ~) 남들처럼 (2)

others 남 (14)

others; other people 남 (3)

our son (humble)아들 녀석 (12)

out of sorts (feel ~) 괴로w– (괴롭다) (6)

out (move ~) 가출(家出)(을) 하 - (2)

outrageous (be ~)엉뚱하 - (12)

outrageous (be ~) 엉뚱하 - (6)

outsiders 남 (14)

oven 오븐 (9)

over sth unpleasant (pass ~) 넘기 - (3)

over the top (be ~) 무리(無理)이 - (14)

over the top in efforts (go ~) 무리(無理)하 - (7)

over (fall ~) 넘어지 - (1)

overcome 이기 - (18,19)

overdo it 무리(無理)하 - (7)

overflow 넘치 - (4)

own (one's ~) 제 (6)

owner 주인(主人) (17)

ox horn 쇠뿔 (6)

P

P'yŏngch'angdong 평창동 (17)

pace 걸음 (1)

pack (bags) 짐(을) 싸 - (16)

pack (one's bags) 싸 - (짐을 ~) (16)

painter 화가(畫家) (8)

paper (scholarly ~) 논문(論文) (4)

paper 백지(白紙) (9)

pare 벗기 - (14)

Parent's Day 어버이날 (3)

park (a car) 세우 - (2)

park (a vehicle) 주차(駐車)(를) 하 - (13)

park a vehicle 주차(駐車)(를) 하 - (5)

parking lot 주차장(駐車場) (13)

parrotbill 뱁새 (6)

part-time work on the side (do ~) (usually said of students) 아르바이트(를) 하 - (3)

part 부분(部分) (8)

particle 티 (11)

particular (in ~) 특(特)히 (17)

particular 특별(特別)하 - (2)

particularly 유난히 (9)

pass (a message) on 전(傳)하 - (7)

pass (test) (시험에 ~) 합격(合格)(을) 하 - (14)

pass an exam 시험(試驗)에 붙 - (1)

pass out 기절(氣絶)(을) 하 - (16)

pass sth around 돌리 - (14)

passenger (a ~) 승객(乘客) (1)

passes (it ~) 지나 - (3)

passive (in grammar) 피동(被動) (11)

passport 여권(旅券) [여꿘] (12)

past week 지난 주일(週日) (3)

past (get ~) 넘기 - (3)

pastime 오락(娛樂) (13)

path in life 진로(進路) (18)

patient (be ~) 참 - (4)

patient 환자(患者) (19)

patient 환자(患者) (7)

pay a fine (to ~) 벌금(罰金)(을) 내다 (9)

pay a visit to 찾아오 - (19)

pay attention 주의(注意)(를) 하 - (6)

pay back 갚 - (18)

pay in advance 가불(假拂)(을) 하 - (17)

pay the bill (in a restaurant) 계산(計算)(을) 하 - (16)

pay 내 - (14)

paying guest in sb's home (stay as a ~) 민박(民泊)(을) 하 - (8)

peace of mind (with ~) 마음 놓고 (4)

peach 복숭아 (11)

peak (at its ~) 한창 (7)

peak (the ~) 꼭대기 (1)

pearly color (be a ~) 뿌옇 - , 뿌얘요 (8)

peculiar (be ~) 독특(獨特)하 - (11)

peel 껍질 (14)

peel 벗기 - (14)

penetrated (be / get ~) 뚫리 - (18)

penmanship 글씨 (11)

pent-up frustration (feel ~) 억울하 - (2)

people's hearts communicate (two ~) 마음(이) 잘 통(通)하 - (2)

people from one's "out-group" 남 (14)

people of a nation (the ~) 국민(國民) (6)
people (a ~) 민족(民族) (6)
people (full of ~) 붐비 - (8)
pepper powder (red hot ~) 고춧가루 (2)
pepper (black ~) 후추 (2)
perchance...? 혹시(나)...? (18)
perfectly (fit ~)딱 맞 - (16)
permission 허락(許諾) (2)
person in charge 책임자(責任者) (14)
person responsible 책임자(責任者) (14)
person (stubborn ~) 고집쟁이 (9)
person; personage 인물(人物) (8)
personal character 성품 (2)
personnel 인원(人員) (14)
perspective 관점(觀點) [- 쩜] (8)
persuade 설득(說得) (을) 시키 - (2)
photo (a ~) 사진(寫眞) (9)
physical constitution 체질(體質) (6)
physical education 체육(體育) (12)
pick up (sth small) with fingers 주w– (줍다) (9)
pick up in fingers 집 - (11)
pick up 집 - (2)
pick 뜯 - (12)
picked up in fingers (be / get ~) 집히 - (11)
picked (be / get ~) 뽑히 - (11)
pickle (kimch'i) 담그 - , 담가요 (3)
picture 그림 (17)
piece of work (a ~) 일거리 [- 꺼리] (7)
pierced (be / get ~) 뚫리 - (18)
pig 돼지 (18)
piggy bank 돼지 저금통(貯金桶) (14)
pile sth 쌓 - (11)
pile up (intransitive) 쌓이 - (11)
piled up (be / get ~) 쌓이 - (11,12)
pinchpenny 구두쇠 (18)
pitiful (be ~)아까w– (아깝다) (13)
pitiful (be ~) 아까w– (아깝다) (4)
place or other (some ~) 어디선가 (2)
place sth on top of sth 올려 놓 - (9)
place up on top of 올려 놓 - (12)
place (get first ~) 일등(一等) (을) 하 - (2)
place 장소(場所) (1)
places (counter / classifier for ~) 군데 (9)
Plain Style speech 반말 (1)
plain to see (be ~)뻔하 - (17)
plan (set up / make a ~) 계획(計劃) (을) 세우 - (19)
plank 널 (14)
plant 심 - (6)
plastic surgery 성형수술(成形手術) (5)
plate (a ~) 접시 (4)
play *paduk* (Korean go) 바둑 (을) 두 - (19)

play the guitar 기타(를) 치 - (13)
play with NOUN (을) 가지고 장난하 - (12)
play 노 - ㄹ - (놀다) (14)
plaything 장난감 [- 깜] (12,16)
Please give me a break. (한 번만) 봐 주세요 (11)
pleases (as one ~) 제 마음대로 (9)
pleasure 낙(樂) (6)
pluck 뜯 - (12)
pocket money 용돈 [- 똔] (2)
pocket 주머니 (13)
pocketbook 지갑(紙匣) (1)
poem 시(詩) (9)
poet 시인(詩人) (9)
poetry (recite ~)풍월(~을 읊 -) (6)
poetry 풍월(風月) (6); 시(詩) (9)
point of view 관점(觀點) (8)
point 손가락질 하 - (11)
police (the ~) 경찰(警察) (2)
police officer 경찰관(警察官) (2)
police state 경찰국가(警察國家) (2)
police station 경찰서(警察署) (2)
police(man) 경찰(警察) (17)
Polite Style speech 존댓말 (1)
politeness 예절(禮節) (2)
polluted (be / get ~) 오염(汚染) (이) 되 - (9)
pollution 오염(汚染) (14)
pool (swimming ~) 수영장(水泳場) (3)
poor at navigation (be ~) 길눈 (이) 어두w– (어둡다) (16)
poor manners (have ~) 버릇 (이) 없 - (2)
poorly (sleep ~) 잠 (을) 설치 - (9)
pope (the ~) 교황(敎皇) (2)
popular vote 국민투표(國民投票) (6)
popular (be ~ [of people]) 인기(人氣) (가) 있 - (1)
population 인구(人口) (5)
porter (at apt. entrance) 경비(警備) 아저씨 (12)
portion 부분(部分) (8)
position 입장(立場) (14)
position 입장(立場) (8)
possibly...? 혹시(나)...? (18)
postpone until later 다음으로 미루 - (9)
postpone 늦추 - (14)
pour 따르 - , 따라 (4)
pout 뽀로통하 - (14)
powder (red hot pepper ~) 고춧가루 (2)
powder 가루 (16)
powdered soap 가루비누 (16)
practice game (a ~) 연습경기(練習競技) (2)
practice (putting into~) (as opposed to theory) 실천(實踐) (2)
prank 장난 (12)
precede 앞서 가 - (1)

precious (be ~) 소중(所重)하 - (14); 아까w- (아깝다) (13)

precious (be ~) 귀(貴)하 - (8)

precious 아까w- (아깝다) (4)

precocious (be ~) 조숙(早熟)하 - (9)

predict 예상(豫想)(을) 하 - (3)

preferable (be ~) 나(ㅅ) - (낫다) (6)

preliminary meeting (have a ~ with a prospective spouse) 선(을) 보 - (4)

prepare 차리 - (13)

prepare (kimch'i) 담그 - , 담가요 (3)

preposterous (be ~)엉뚱하 - (12)

preposterous (be ~) 엉뚱하 - (8)

present (to sb esteemed) 올리 - (14)

president (of a country) 대통령(大統領) (4)

president (class ~) 반장(班長) (9)

press (clothes) (옷을 ~) 다리 - (12)

press on 재촉(을) 하 - (1)

pretend to be sth great 잘난 척하 - (3)

pretty (be ~) 고w- (곱다, 고와) (6)

prevent sb from doing 말리 - (14)

previous day (the ~) 전(前)날 (1)

primarily 원래(原來 / 元來) (16)

prisoner of war 포로(捕虜) (12)

prize (get first ~) 일등(一等)(을) 하 - (2)

problem 탈 (18)

problematic (be ~) 곤란(困難)하 - (3)

produce (~ [from your pocket, a bag, etc.]) 꺼내 - (4)

production (of art, etc.) 작품(作品) (18)

project 상영(上映)(을) 하 - (18)

promise (keep a ~) 약속(約束)(을) 지키 - (4)

pronunciation 발음(發音) (9)

properly 제대로 (9)

proprietor 주인(主人) (17)

propriety 예의(禮儀) (6)

protagonist 주인공(主人公) (11)

protrude 돋 - (14)

proverb 속담(俗談) (6)

provide oneself with 장만(을) 하 - (7)

provinces (one's home / house in the ~) 시골집 [- 찝] (7)

provoke anger 화(火)(를) 돋우 - (14)

provoke sb 약(을) 올리 - (16)

public pledge / promise (make a ~) 공약(公約)(을) 하 - (6)

publications 서적(書籍) (12)

puddle (a ~) 웅덩이 (8)

pull oneself together 기운(을) 내 - (14)

pull out 빼 - (18)

pull to pieces 뜯 - (12)

punish 처벌(處罰)(을) 하 - (2)

punished (be / get ~) 벌(罰)(을) 받 - (6)

puppy 강아지 (2)

purse (where people keep their money) 지갑(紙匣) (1)

push 미 - ㄹ - (밀다) (11)

pushed (be ~) 밀리 - (NB: processive) (2)

pushed 밀리 - (11)

put down (for later use) 놓아 두 - (12)

put in the care of 맡기 - (14)

put in (be / get ~) 담기 - (11)

put off until later 다음으로 미루 - (9)

put on (glasses) 끼 - (6)

put on (makeup, etc.) 바르 - (17)

put on a brave face 기운(을) 내 - (14)

put on airs 잘난 척하 - (3)

put on top of 덮 - (11,13)

put out a fire 불(을) 끄 - (14)

put sth down (~ [for future use / reference]) 내려 놓 - (9)

put sth in a vessel 담 - (11)

put sth on (sb's feet) 신기 - (14)

put up at 묵 - (1)

put up with sth 참 - (4)

put (be / get ~) 놓이 - (11)

put / take out 내 - (14)

putting into practice 실천(實踐) (2)

Q

quality (of goods) 품질(品質) (14)

quarrel (husband and wife) 부부(夫婦) 싸움 (16)

question 의문(疑問) (1)

quiet down 가라앉 - (11)

quietly 가만히 (11,12)

quietly 조용히 (2)

quilt 이불 (13)

quit (smoking) 끊 - (담배를 ~) (12)

quite a while (for ~) 한참 (4)

quite 썩 (14)

quite; rather 썩 (9); 꽤(6); 상당히 (7)

R

race along 달리 - (2)

race (human ~) 인류(人類) (6)

race 민족(民族) (6)

radical (in Chinese characters) 부수(部首) (9)

rained on (get ~) 비(를) 맞 - (4)

rains (the seasonal ~) 장마 (7)

rainy season (the ~) 장마철 (7)

raise (~ a subject)이야기(를) 꺼내 - (6)

raise (up) 높이 - (14); 돋우 - (14); 올리 - (14)

raise 기르 - (12)

rally one's strength 기운(을) 내 - (14)

rally 대회(大會) (12)

random (be ~)엉뚱하 - (6)

rascal 녀석 (12)

rather serious matter 웃지 못 할 일 (13)

rather 썩 (14)

rather; quite 썩 (9); 꽤 (6); 상당히 (7)

raw fish 생선회 (16)

raw fish / meat 회(膾) (13)

reach a conclusion 결론(結論)을 내리 - (12)

reach a high point / climax 고조(高潮)(가) 되 - (7)

reach an amicable settlement 화해(和解)(를) 하 - (16)

reach 도착(到着)(을) 하 - (1)

reaches (it ~) 닿 - (4)

react 반응(反應)(을) 하 - (8)

reaction (give ["show / evince"] a ~) 반응(反應)(을) 보이 - (3)

reader 독자(讀者) (6)

reading sutras to a cow's ear 소귀에 경(經) 읽기 (16)

ready (have a thing ~) 갖추 - (7)

real life (in ~) 실제(實際)로 (6)

reality 현실(現實) (6)

realize 느끼 - (14)

realized (get so that it is ~) 느껴지 - (14)

rear (children) (아이를 ~) 기르 - (12)

reason (a ~) 이유(理由) (2)

reason? (for what ~) 웬일로 (2)

reassured (feel ~) 마음(이) 풀리 - (16)

rebellion 난리(亂離) (16)

recall sth 생각(이) 나 - (19)

recall 생각(이) 나 - (1)

receive it (as soon as you ~) 받는 대로 (7)

recite (poetry) 읊 - (6)

recite from memory 외우 - (3)

reckon 계산(計算)(을) 하 - (16)

recognize sb 알아보 - (19)

reconciled (become ~) 화해(和解)(를) 하 - (16)

recreation 오락(娛樂) (13)

red beans 팥 (6)

red hot pepper powder 고춧가루 (2)

red (be in the ~) 적자(赤字) (3)

reduce 줄이 - (7)

refined (be ~ [in the social sense]) 고급(高級)스러w - (~스럽다) (6); 세련(洗練)(이) 되 - (9)

reflected (be / get ~) 반영(反影 / 反映)(이) 되 - (6)

refreshing (be ~) 시원하 - (13)

refuge (take ~) 피(避)하 - (8)

refuse 거절(拒絶)(을) 하 - (8)

regret (to one's ~) 섭섭하게도 (2)

regret 후회(後悔)(를) 하 - (6)

regrettable (be ~) 아까w - (아깝다) (13)

regrettable (be ~) 섭섭하 - (2)

regrettable (be ~) 아까w - (아깝다) (4)

regular restaurant / bar (one's ~) 단골집 [- 찜] (4)

regulations (traffic ~) 교통법규(交通法規) (2)

reign over 다스리 - (18)

reiterate 반복(反復)(을) 하 - (6)

rekindle 되살아나 - (14)

relationship (a "just friends" ~) 친구(親舊) 사이 (2)

relationship (a dating ~) 애인(愛人) 사이 (2)

relationship 사이 (2)

relatively 비교적(比較的)(으로) (12)

released (be ~) 풀려나 - (14)

relieved (feel ~) 마음(이) 풀리 - (16)

relocate it 옮기 - (9)

rely on 믿 - (6)

remain as if nothing happened 태연(泰然)하 - (3)

remain unaffected 태연(泰然)하 - (NB: descriptive) (3)

remain 남 - (14)

remember 기억(記憶)(을) 하 - ; 기억(記憶)(이) 나 - (19)

remove (a covering) 벗기 - (14)

remove (and put away) 떼어내 - (17)

remove (clothing) 벗기 - (6)

remove 떼 - (17); 빼놓 - (19)

remove 제거(除去)(를) 하 - (6); (~ [glasses]) 빼 - (6)

removed (be / get ~) 떨어지 - (13)

removed (one's doubts are ~) 풀리 - (1)

repay sth 갚 - (6)

repay 갚 - (18)

repeat 반복(反復)(을) 하 - (6)

reply letter (a ~) 답장(答狀) (7)

report (written) 보고서(報告書) (1)

report card 성적표(成績表) (14)

report 신고(申告)(를) 하 - (11)

representative (job title) 대리(代理) (16)Republic of Korea대한민국 (大韓民國) (12)

repulsive (be ~) 미w - (밉다) (13)

repulsive (more than 밉다) (be ~) 얄미w - (얄밉다) (13)

research 연구(硏究) (8)

resemble 닮 - (6)

resolution (make a ~ [to do]) 결심(決心)(을) 하 - (3)

resolve 푸 - ㄹ - (풀다) (11)

resolve (to do) 결심(決心)(을) 하 - (3)

resolved (be / get ~) 풀리 - (11)

respectful (be ~) 정중(鄭重)하 - (17)

rest (have a good / thorough ~) 푹 쉬 - (4)

restaurant (one's favorite or regular ~) 단골집 (4)

restorative 보약(補藥) (6)

result 결과(結果) (6)

resume one's studies 복학(復學)(을) 하 - (5)

return it 돌려 주 - (19)

revive 되살아나 - (14); 살리 - (14)

ri (about ⅓ mile) 리(里) (18)

ri (one thousand ~) 천리(千里) (6)

rice grain 쌀 (2)

rice paddy 논 (18)
rice (uncooked ~) 쌀 (2)
rich person 부자(富者) (6)
rid of (get ~) 제거(除去) (를) 하 - (6); 치우 - (9)
ride in error 잘못 타 - (2)
ride sth 타 - (14)
ride (give a ~ to) 태우 - (14)
ridicule (butt of ~) 웃음거리 [- 꺼리] (7)
ridiculous (be ~) 엉뚱하 - (12)
right (smack) in the middle 한가운데 (17)
right away 곧바로 (17); 얼른 (14)
right through the holidays 방학 내내 (8)
ring (intransitive) 울리 - (17)
ripen 익 - (11)
rise up 뜨 - (3)
ritual ceremony (conduct a ~) 제사(祭祀) (를) 지내 - (6)
road is blocked 길 (이) 막히 - (1)
rock (usually quite large) 바위 (11)
role 역(役) (18)
Rome (the ways ["law"] of ~) 로마법(- 法) [- 뻡] (2)
Romeo 로미오 (18)
room where parents sleep 안방(~房) [안빵] (12)
rose 장미(꽃) (12)
round (be ~) 동그랗 - (동그래, 동그란) (18)
round (of fighting) 바탕 (16)
ruckus (make a ~) 떠드 - ㄹ - (떠들다) (2)
rule over 다스리 - (18)
rules (traffic ~) 교통법규(交通法規) (2)
rummage 뒤지 - (12)
rumor 소문(所聞) (6)
run away 도망(逃亡) (을) 가 - (16,17)
run away 도망(逃亡) (을) 치 - (17)
run down 흉 (을) 보 - (1)
run in ("dash and enter") 뛰어드 - ㄹ - (뛰어들다) (8)
run out 달려나가 - (8)
run 달리 - (2)
run 뛰 - (14)
rush about 서두르 - (1)
rush (in a ~) 급(急)하게 (3)
rush 서두르 - (1)
Russia 러시아 (4)
Russian (a ~ [person]) 러시아인 (4)
rustic (be a bit ~) 촌스러w- (~스럽다) (9)

S

sad that sb is leaving (be ~) 섭섭하 - (2)
safe (be ~) 안전(安全)하 - (1)
safe 금고(金庫) (17)
safely 무사(無事)히 (14)
salty (be [too] ~) 짜 - (8)
same as ever (be the ~) 여전(如前)하 - (2)

same ([which is] exactly the ~) 똑 같은 (8)
sashimi 생선회 (16)
satisfactory manner (do sth in a less than ~) 설치 - (9)
satisfied (be ~) 만족(滿足)하 - (NB: processive) (14)
save (a computer file) 저장(貯藏) (을) 하 - (6)
save 살리 - (12)
sawing 톱질 ← 톱 (11)
scarcely 겨우 (17)
scholar 학자(學者) (4)
scholarly paper 논문(論文) (4)
school holidays (right / all the way through the ~) 방학 내내 (8)
school (one's junior from ~) 후배(後輩) (3)
school (one's senior from ~) 선배(先輩) (3)
school (traditional village ~) 서당(書堂) (6)
scratch 할퀴 - (13)
screen 상영(上映) (을) 하 - (18)
screw up one's courage 기운 (을) 내 - (14)
script 문자(文字) [- 짜] (8)
sea bream 조기 (12)
sea cucumber 해삼(海蔘) (11)
seal 도장(刀匠) (14)
search 뒤지 - (12)
seaside (the ~) 바닷가 (1)
season (the rainy ~) 장마철 (7)
seasonal rains (the ~) 장마 (7)
seat sb 앉히 - (14)
secret to sth (the ~) 비결(秘訣) (1)
secret you might tell sb (a ~) 비밀(秘密) (1)
section chief / head 과장(課長) (2)
security guard 경비(警備) 아저씨 (12)
seen (be ~) 보이 - (NB: processive) (11)
seesaw 널뛰기 (14)
select sth 뽑 - (11)
select 뽑 - (6)
selected in a drawing (get ~) 당첨(當籤) (이) 되 - (4)
selected (be / get ~) 뽑히 - (11)
self's 제 (6)
self 자기(自己) (17)
self 자기(自己) (3)
sell (well) 팔리 - (11)
senile dementia 치매(癡呆) (7)
senile person 치매환자 (7)
senior from school (one's ~) 선배(先輩) (3)
sense 느끼 - (1)
sense 느끼 - (14)
sense 철 (14)
senses 정신(情神) (11)
sentence (compose a ~) 작문(作文) (을) 하 - (3)
Seoul-Pusan Highway (the ~) 경부 고속도로(京釜高速道路) (4)

Seoul Grand Park 서울대공원(大公園) (17)

Seoul Station 서울역 [- 력] (12)

separate 떨어지 - (13)

separate 떼 - (17)

serious way (in a ~) 심(甚)하게 (4)

set off 출발(出發)(을) 하 - (7)

set the table 상(床)(을) 차리 - (19)

set up a plan 계획(計劃)(을) 세우 - (19)

set up 세우 - (12, 18)

set up 세우 - (6)

settle one's account 갚 - (18)

sever 끊 - (3)

several days 며칠 (3)

several times 여러 번 (12)

severe (be ~) 매서w– (매섭다) (18)

severely 심(甚)하게 (6)

shake off / out 터 - ㄹ - (털다) (11)

shake 떨리 - (7)

shake 흔드 - ㄹ - (흔들다) (14)

shaking terribly (like a leaf) 후들후들 (7)

shape (pitiful / derogatory ~) 꼴 (6)

shape 모양(模樣) (2)

shape 모양(模樣)(17); 형태(形態) (11)

share sth with sb 나누어 주 - (4)

share sth 나누 - (4)

sharp (be ~) 영악하 - (18)

she (formal / written) 그녀 (1)

she herself 자기(自己) (16)

she 걔 = 그애 (8)

sheaf 다발 (18)

shift sth 옮기 - (9)

shirk 모면(謀免)(을) 하 - (17)

shirk 피(避)하 - (8)

shoes 신발 (8)

shooting (death by ~) 사살(射殺) (11)

short of (be ~) 모자라 - (NB: processive) (14)

shove in 처넣 - (9)

show a reaction 반응(反應)(을) 보이 - (3)

show up 나타나 - (17)

show 보이 - (14); (~ a film) 상영(上映)(을) 하 - (16)

show 전시회(展示會) (19)

shrewd (be ~) 영악하 - (18)

shrivel up 일그러지 - (13)

shut (be / get ~) 닫히 - (6)

"shut-eye" (get some ~) 붙이 - (눈을 ~) (19)

sick person 환자(患者) (19)

sick person 환자(患者) (7)

sick (get ~) 병(病)(이) 나 - (1)

sick (worry oneself ~) 애(가) 타 - (7)

sickle (Korean) 낫 (6)

side dishes to go with rice 반찬(飯饌) (12)

side dishes with rice 반찬(飯饌) (6)

sight (fall in love at first ~) ("at first eye") 첫눈에 반하 - (1)

sight (pitiful / derogatory ~) 꼴 (6)

silly gaffe 엉뚱한 실수(失手) (4)

silver 동전(銅錢) (2)

similar (be ~) 비슷하 - (3)

simply 단지(但只) (3)

simultaneous interpretation 동시통역(同時通譯) (18)

sin (commit a ~) 죄(罪)(를) 지(ㅅ) - (짓다) (6)

since I was born until now 태어나서 지금까지 쭉 (14)

sincerity 정성(精誠) (14)

sink down 가라앉 - (11)

sink to the ground 쓰러지 - (11)

sip (a ~) 모금 (4)

situation (the ~) 형편(形便) (4)

situation 입장(立場)(14); 형편 (形便) (19)

sixty-first birthday party 환갑잔치 (17)

sixty-first birthday 환갑(還甲) (17)

skill (manual) 솜씨 (17)

skill with the hands 솜씨 (1)

skill(s) 재주 (2)

skillful (be ~) 능숙(能熟)하 - (17)

skillful and fast (be ~) 재빠르 - (17)

skinny 마르– (NB: processive) (2)

skip (a meal) 굶 - (2)

slander 훼방(毀謗)(을) 놓 - (14)

sleep (get some ~) 붙이 - (눈을 ~) (19)

sleep in / late 늦잠(을) 자 - (1)

sleep (be drunk / woozy with ~) 잠에 취(醉)하 - (NB: processive) (7); (~ poorly) 잠(을) 설치 - (9)

sleeping medicine 수면제(睡眠劑) (18)

sleepy (be / feel ~) 졸리 - (7)

slender (be ~) 날씬하 - (4)

slightly 약간(若干) (11)

slim (be ~) 날씬하 - (4)

slipshod job of sth (do a ~) 설치 - (9)

slow-witted (be ~) 둔(鈍)하 - (18)

slushy (be ~) 지 - ㄹ - (질다) (11)

smacked (get ~) 맞 - (6)

small (be ~) 조그맣 - (조그매, 조그만) (12)

smart (be ~) 영악하 - (18)

smash sth 부수 - (17)

smeared (be / get ~) 묻히 - (11)

smeared (be / get ~) 묻히 - (8)

smile sheepishly 씩 웃 - (14)

smiles (be all ~) 싱글벙글하 - (NB: processive) (7)

smudged (be / get ~) 묻히 - (8)

snack 간식(間食) (5)

snap sth 끊 - (11)

snatch away 빼앗 - (11)

snatched away (be / get ~) 빼앗기 - (11)

sneakers 운동화(運動靴) (13)

so (~ [much so that]) 하도 (7)

soak 담그 - , 담가요 (3)

soaked (get / become ~) 젖 - (14)

soap 비누 (14,16)

soft (be ~) 부드러w– (부드럽다) (18)

soil quality 토질(土質) (5)

sold (be / get ~) 팔리 - (11)

solid (be ~) 굳 - (6)

solidarity of the populace 국민(國民)의 단결(團結) (6)

solve 푸 - ㄹ - (풀다) (11)

solved (be / get ~) 풀리 - (11)

some occasions (on ~) 어떨 때는 (4)

some place or other 어디선가 (2)

some reason or other (for ~) 왠지 (5)

somebody or other 누군가 (2)

someone who drinks a lot 술고래 (9)

something (or other) 뭔가 ~ 무언가 ← 무엇인가 (14,18)

something happens 벌어지 - (3)

something or other 무언가 (2)

sometime or other (~ [I don't remember]) 언젠가(는) (2)

sometime 언제 ← 언젠가는 (16)

sometimes 어떨 때는 (4)

somewhat 약간(若干) (2)

somewhere or other 어디선가 (19)

son (my / our ~ [humble]) 아들 녀석 (12)

sonorous (voice) (be ~) 굵 - (13)

sons and daughters (one's ~) 자식(子息) (12)

soon as you receive it (as ~) 받는 대로 (7)

sopping wet in rain (get ~) 비(를) 쫄딱 맞 - (16)

sorry state (be in a ~) (said of a country's economy, for example) 형편(形便) 없 - (4)

sorry (be / feel ~) 섭섭하 - (NB: descriptive) (2)

sorts (feel out of ~) 괴로w– (괴롭다) (6)

soul 혼(魂) (11)

sound (intransitive) 울리 - (17)

soup (makings for ~) 국거리 (7)

soy sauce 간장(~醬) (8)

Soyang Dam 소양댐 (1)

space between (the ~) 사이 (2)

space (a ~) 칸 (2)

space 틈 (11)

spaced-out (be ~) 멍하 - (14)

speak ill of 흉(을) 보 - (1)

special characteristics 특성(特性) (6)

special (be ~) 특별(特別)하 - (2)

speck 티 (11)

spectacles 돋보기 (11)

spectator(s) 관객(觀客) (18)

speed ("high ~") 고속(高速) (4)

spend the night 묵 - (1)

spending money 용돈 [- 똔] (2)

spherical (be ~) 동그랗 - (동그래, 동그란) (18)

spill sth 쏟 - (8)

spin a top 팽이(를) 돌리 - (14)

spirit 혼(魂) (11)

spoil (food) 상하 - (음식이 ~) (16)

spoonful (one ~) 한술 (6)

sporting event (have a ~) 경기(競技)(를) 하 - (8)

sports meet 체육대회(體育大會) (12)

sports shoes 운동화(運動靴) (13)

sports (compete in ~) 경기(競技)(를) 하 - (8)

spread (intr.) 퍼지 - (6)

spread sth open 펴 - (3)

square meters 평방(平方) 미터 (5)

stable 외양간 [- 깐] (14)

stadium (a ~) 경기장(競技場) (2)

staff 인원(人員) (14)

staff; staff member 스태프 (8)

stain sth 묻 - (11)

stained (be / get ~) 묻히 - (11)

stained (be / get ~) 묻히 - (8)

staircase 계단(階段) (11)

stairs 계단(階段) (11)

stamp one's name chop 도장(刀匠)(을) 찍 - (14)

stand 서 - (14)

stand in a long line 줄(을) 쭉 서 - (16)

stand sth up 세우 - (12)

stand up to 대드 - ㄹ - (대들다) (18)

stand (~ [on an issue]) 입장(立場) (8)

standpoint 입장(立場) (8)

stands up abruptly / suddenly 벌떡 (4)

stare at 바라보 - (13); 처다보 - (14)

start with (to ~) 원래(原來 / 元來) (16)

starters (for ~) 일단(一旦) [- 딴] (9)

startled (be ~) 놀라 - (NB: processive) (11,19)

starve sb 굶기 - (14)

starve 굶 - (14)

starve 굶 - (2)

state of affairs 형편 (形便) (4)

state of mind 정신(情神) (11)

state (police ~) 경찰국가(警察國家) (2)

state (be in a sorry ~) (said of a country's economy, for example) 형편(形便) 없 - (4)

statesman 신하(臣下) (18)

station in life (one's ~) 분수(分數) (6)

station (police ~) 경찰서(警察署) (2)

stay as paying guest 민박(民泊)(을) 하 - (8) in sb's home

stay up all night 밤(을) 새우 - (4)

steadfast (be ~) 꾸준하 - (6)

stealing 도둑질 ← 도둑 (11)

steaming hot (be ~) (푹푹) 찌 - (NB: processive) (13,17)

steep sth 잠그 - (11)

steep 담그 - , 담가요 (3)

steering wheel 핸들 (8)

step on 밟 - (11)

step on 밟 - (6)

step 걸음 (1)

stepped on (be / get ~) 밟히 - (11)

stew 찌개 (2)

stick sth in 꽂 - (13)

stick sth to 붙이 - (19)

"stick to" an exam (pass an exam) 시험(試驗)에 붙 - (1)

stick to sth 묻 - (11)

stick up / out 돋 - (14)

still more 더욱 (12)

stimulate the appetite 입맛(을) 돋우 - (14)

stimulate 돋우 - (14)

stock (keep in ~) 갖추 - (7)

stomach upset (gets a ~) 배탈(이) 나 - (1)

stomach (feel heavy on the ~) 체하 - (2)

stone (usually quite large) 바위 (11)

stop 멈추 - (13)

stop (intransitive) 끝나 - (14)

stop by 들렀다 가 - (3)

stop in 들르 - (3)

stop sb 말리 - (14)

stop sth (e.g., a car) 세우 - (12)

stop sth 끝내 - (14)

stop VERBing 그만 + VERB (13)

stop (~ [a car]) 세우 - (2)

stop 막 - (6)

stork 황새 (6)

straight (go ~) 쭉 가 - (12)

straight away 곧바로 (17)

straight through 꼬박 (19)

strain (be a ~) 무리(無理)이 - (14)

strange (be ~)신기(神奇)하 - (19); 이상(異常)하 - (12)

strange (be ~) 이상(異常)하 - (7)

strangely 이상(異常)하게 (7)

strawberry 딸기 (18)

"street-eyes are dark" 길눈(이) 어두w- (어둡다) (16)

streetlights 가로등(街路燈) (17)

stress about 신경(神經)(을) 쓰 - (2)

stretch it 늘리 - (14)

strict (be ~) 매서w- (매섭다) (18)

strike 부딪치 - (8)

strikes (lightning ~) 벼락(이) 치 - (9)

strip (off) 벗기 - (14)

strive 애(를) 쓰 - (13)

stroke (in Chinese characters) 획(劃) (9)

strong (be ~) 강(强)하 - (6)

strong (be ~) 튼튼하 - (14)

strongbox 금고(金庫) (17)

stubborn person 고집쟁이 (9)

stubborn (be ~) 고집(을) 부리 - (NB: processive) (9)

student life 학생생활(學生生活) (18)

study 서재(書齋) (14)

stupid (be ~) 모자라 - (NB: processive) (14); 미련하 - (18); 멍청하 - (14)

stupid mistake 엉뚱한 실수(失手) (4)

sturdy (be ~) 튼튼하 - (14)

style (in the Korean- ~) 한국식(韓國式)으로 (3)

subject (in school) (a ~) 과목(科目) (4)

subject of talk (a ~) 이야깃거리 (7)

subject (raise a ~)이야기(를) 꺼내 - (6)

subject 신하(臣下) (18)

subjectivity 주관(主觀) (8)

submerged (be / get ~) 잠기 - (11)

submit 제출(提出)(을) 하 - (4)

subside 가라앉 - (11)

substance 알맹이(19)

subtract 더 - ㄹ - (덜다) (11); 떼 - (17)

succeed 성공(成功)(을) 하 - (2)

such a way (in ~) 그런 식으로 (2)

sudden wrench (with a ~) 확 (8)

suddenly (stand up ~) 벌떡 (4)

suddenly 갑자기 (1)

suffer from fatigue 몸살(이) 나 - (17)

suffer humiliation 욕(을) 당하 - (6)

suffer it 참 - (4)

suffer 겪 - (6)

suffer 고생(苦生)(을) 하 - (12)

sufferer (from a disease) 환자(患者) (7)

suffering 고생(苦生) (6)

suit one's tastes 입맛에 맞 - (7)

suit someone 어울리 - (19)

suit 어울리 - (1)

sulky (be ~) 뾰로통하 - (14)

summit 꼭대기 (1)

sunk (be / get ~) 잠기 - (11)

sunlight 햇빛 ← 해 + 빛 (18)

supervision 지휘(指揮) (14)

sure to... (be ~) 꼭 (14)

surplus (financial ~) 흑자(黑字) (3)

surprised (be ~) 놀라 - (NB: processive) (11, 19)

surprised (be / get utterly ~) 깜짝 놀라 - (3)

surprising (be ~) 놀라w- (놀랍다) (4)

surrender 포기(抛棄)(를) 하 - (12)

suspend 중지(中止)(를) 하다

suspended (be / get ~) 중단(中斷)(이) 되 - (2)

suspicious (be ~) 수상(殊常)하 - (17)

sway 흔드 - ㄹ - (흔들다) (14)

swearing 욕(辱) (6)

sweat (a cold ~) 식은 땀 (3)

swells (it ~) 부(ㅅ) - (붓다) (1)

swim 수영(水泳)(을) 하 - (3)

swimming pool 수영장(水泳場) (3)

swimming suit 수영복(水泳服) (16)

swoon 기절(氣絶)(을) 하 - (16)

symbol 상징(象徵) (3)

T

tackle 대드 - ㄹ - (대들다) (18)

tail 꼬리 (6)

take ("bear") responsibility 책임(責任)(을) 지 - (14)

take (medicine) (약을 ~) 복용(服用)(을) 하 - (18)

take after 닮 - (6)

take an all-nighter 밤(을) 새우 - (4)

take and put away 가져다 놓 - (12)

take away 떼 - ; 떼어내 - (17)

take care of 다루 - (6)

take charge of 맡 - (14)

take good care of oneself 몸조리(~調理)(를) 하 - (4)

take note of 적 - (3)

take off (clothes) (옷을 ~) 벗 - (14)

take off (~ [glasses]) 빼 - (6)

take off 가 버리 - (1)

take off 떼 - (17); (~ sb's clothes) 벗기 - (14)

take out (~ one's anger) 화풀이(를) 하 - (6)

take out 꺼내 - (4); 빼 - (6)

take out 빼 - (18)

take refuge 피(避)하 - (8)

take responsibility for 맡 - (14)

take up (with the fingers) 집 - (2)

take (~ a photo) 찍 - (9)

talent(s) 재주 (2)

talk (a subject of ~) 이야깃거리 (7)

talking to a brick wall 소귀에 경(經) 읽기 (16)

Tan'gun 단군(檀君) (18)

tape 테이프 (12)

taste appears / comes out (the alcohol's ~) 술맛이 나 - (9)

tastes (suit one's ~) 입맛에 맞 - (7)

tattoo 문신(文身) (12)

tear apart 뜯 - (12)

tear out 뜯 - (12)

teeter-totter 널뛰기 (14)

telephone call is called in (a ~) 전화(電話)가 걸려 오 - (9)

tell (a secret you might ~ sb) 비밀(秘密) (1)

Temple (Ch'ŏngp'yŏng ~) 청평사(淸平寺) (1)

tent 텐트 (13)

terribly 몹시 (12)

terribly 무척; 심(甚)하게 (4); 매우 (9); 너무나 (3)

test (paper) 시험지(試驗紙) (6)

that is to say 즉(卽) (6)

that (after ~) 그리고는 (1)

the end 끝 (6)

theft 도둑질 ← 도둑 (11)

then (and ~) 그리고는 (1)

then (if that is not the case, ~) 아니면 (3)

there (here and ~) 여기저기 (3)

thesis 논문(論文) (4)

thick (be ~) 굵 - (13)

"thick" (dumb) (be ~) 둔(鈍)하 - (18)

thief 도둑 (6)

thin (be~) 마르 - (2) (NB: processive)

thing 물건(物件) (6); (the whole ~) 전부(全部) (9)

things to be washed 빨래거리 [- 꺼리] (11)

think best (Do as you ~) 알아서 하세요 (9)

think of (sth) 생각(이) 나 - (19)

think of 생각(이) 나 - (1)

think (as I ~ / in the way I ~) 제 생각대로 (9)

thirsty (be ~) 목(이) 마르 - (14)

thorough rest (to have a ~) 푹 쉬 - (4)

thoroughly 꼭 (14)

thought occurs to (me) (a ~) 생각(이) 떠오르 - (3)

thought occurs to one 생각(이) 드 - ㄹ - (들다) (13)

thousand li 천리(千里) (6)

three or four 서너 (19)

thrifty (be ~) 알뜰하 - (16)

throat (get a hoarse ~) 목(이) 쉬 - (6)

through the school holidays (right / all the way ~) 방학 내내 (8)

through to (get ~) 통(通)하 - (2)

through ([one's words] get ~') 통(通)하 - (2)

throughout (all ~) 내내 (3)

throw away 버리 - (1)

throw 던지 - (4)

thwart 훼방(毀謗)(을) 놓 - (14)

ticket office 매표소(賣票所) (1)

ticket (get a ~) 딱지(를) 떼이 - (2)

tidings 소식(消息) (7)

tidy up 치우 - (12)

tiger 호랑이 (18)

tiger 호랑이 (6)

tightwad 구두쇠 (18)

time-wise leeway 시간적 여유(時間的 餘裕) (8)

time being (for the ~) 일단(一旦) [- 딴] (9)

time of it (have a hard ~) 혼(魂)(이) 나 - (7)

time (ahead of ~) 미리 (2)

time (all the ~) 자꾸 (1)

time (as in time flies') 세월(歲月) (7)

time (every / all the ~) 매번(每番) (6)

time (on ~) 제 시간에 (2)
time 시절(時節) (18); 틈 (11)
timely (be ~) 시간(을) 지키 - (NB: processive) (16)
timid (be ~) 겁(怯)(이) 많 - (14)
tip 꼭대기 (1); 끝 (6)
tired wreck (become a ~) 녹초가 되 - (9)
tired (be / get ~) 지치 - (4)
tiredness piles up 피로(疲勞)(가) 쌓이 - (16)
tiredness 피로(疲勞) (16)
title for unmarried male 서방(書房) (13)
to start with 원래(原來 / 元來) (16)
to the brim / max / top 가득 / 가뜩(14); 잔뜩 (11)
to wit 즉(即) (6)
today (as of ~) 오늘로 (3)
together ([people] go well ~) 어울리 - (1)
together (come ~) 맞드 - ㄹ - (6)
toilet tissue 화장지(化粧紙) (16)
toilet 변소(便所) (not an elegant word) (5)
tonic 보약(補藥) (6)
too much (be ~) 무리(無理)이 - (14)
top in one's efforts (go over the ~) 무리(無理)하 - (7)
top of sth (place sth onto the ~) 올려 놓 - (9)
top of the foot 발등 [- 뜽] (6)
topic 이야깃거리 (7)
topple 쓰러지 - (11)
tormented (feel ~) 괴로w – (괴롭다) (NB: descriptive) (6)
tormenting (be ~) 괴로w – (괴롭다) (6)
totally 몽땅 (14)
totally 완전(完全)히 (8)
touch of dementia 노망(老妄)기 [- 끼] (11)
tough (be ~) 질기 - (11)
tournament 대회(大會) (12)
toward me 내 쪽 (14)
toy 장난감 [- 깜] (12,16)
track-and-field stadium 경기장(競技場) (2)
traditional costume (colorful Korean ~) 색동옷 (2)
traditional game 민속놀이 (14)
traditional Korean house (courtyard inside a ~) 마당 (1)
traditional village school 서당(書堂) (6)
traffic rules / regulations 교통법규(交通法規) (2)
train accident 기차사고(汽車事故) (4)
train 기차(汽車) (4)
translate 번역(飜譯)(을) 하 - (18)
translation 번역(飜譯) (18)
transparent (be ~)맑 - (12)
traveler 여행객(旅行客) (1)
travelling 여행(旅行) (1)
tray 쟁반(錚盤) (9)
tread on 밟 - (6)
treasure 보물(寶物) (11)
treat (medically) 치료(治療)(를) 하 - (3)

tremble (intr.) 떨리 - (7)
trembling terribly (like a leaf) 후들후들 (7)
trick (the "~") 비결(秘訣) (1)
trip (go away on an official ~) 출장(出張)(을) 가 - (1)
trip (official / business ~) 출장(出張) (1)
trip 여행(旅行) (1)
trodden on (be / get ~) 밟히 - (11)
trouble 탈 (18)
troublemaker 말썽꾸러기 (12)
troubles (has tummy ~) 배탈(이) 나 - (1)
trust with 맡기 - (14)
truth 진리(眞理) (6)
try hard 애(를) 쓰 - (3)
try to do sth 애(를) 쓰 - (13)
tummy troubles (has ~) 배탈(이) 나 - (1)
tumult (there is a ~) 난리(가) 나 - (16)
turn (intransitive) 도 - ㄹ - (돌다) (11)
turn against 대드 - ㄹ - (대들다) (18)
turn around and look 돌아다 보 - (1)
turn down 거절(拒絶)(을) 하 - (8)
turn out a certain way 생기 - (3)
turn sth 돌리 - (14)
turn sth 돌리 - (2)
turn up (fail to ~) 빠지 - (4)
turned on (be / get ~) 켜지 - (17)
two or three 두어 (4)
typewriter 타자기(打字機) (17)

U

U-turn 유턴 (2)
ultimately 결국(結局) (14)
ultimately 결국(結局) (2)
unaffected by events (be ~) 아무렇지도 않 - (3)
unaffected (remain ~) 태연(泰然)하 - (3)
uncle (on father's side) 삼촌(三寸) (18)
uncle (on father's side) 삼촌 (三寸) (5)
uncle (on mother's side) 외삼촌 (18)
unclothe 벗기 - (14)
uncooked rice 쌀 (2)
under coercion / duress 억지로 (14)
underage person 미성년(未成年) (3)
undergo 겪 - (6)
understand (sth spoken) 알아들 - (알아듣다) (1)
understand each other 마음(이) 잘 통(通)하 - (2)
understand 이해(理解)(를) 하 - ; 이해(理解)(가) 되 - (1)
undertaking 사업(事業) (12)
undress (sb) 벗기 - (6)
undress sb 벗기 - (14)
uneasy (be ~) 불안(不安)하 - (11)
unflagging (be ~) 꾸준하 - (6)
unfold 벌어지 - (3)

unfortunate (be ~) 불행(不幸)하 - (17)
unique (be ~) 독특(獨特)하 - (11)
unity of the populace 국민(國民)의 단결(團結) (6)
unkempt (be ~) 더러w- (더럽다) (1)
unreasonable (be ~) 무리(無理)이 - (14)
unreasonably (exert oneself ~) 무리(無理)하 - (7)
unsatisfactory (have an ~ sleep) 잠(을) 설치 - (9)
unusually 유난히 (9)
unworried (feel ~) 안심(安心)하 - (2)
up and go 가 버리 - (1)
up (rise ~) 뜨 - (3)
uproar (there is an ~) 난리(가) 나 - (16)
upset (be ~) 속(이) 상하 - (12); 속상하 - (16)
upset (be / get ~) 속(이) 상하 - (8)
upset (get a stomach ~) 배탈(이) 나 - (1)
urchin 녀석 (12)
urge on (sb) 재촉(을) 하 - (1)
urgent (be ~) 급(急)하 - (3)
urgently 급(急)하게 (3)
used to (get ~) 익숙해지 - (2)
used (be / get ~) 쓰이 - (6)
used (I'm ~ to it.) 습관(習慣)이 됐어요. (2)
useless (be ~) 소용(所用)(이) 없 - (16)
usually 흔히 (6); 평소(平素)에 (5)
utterly surprised (be / get ~) 깜짝 놀라 - (3)

V

vacant (be ~) 비 - (비었어요) (17)
vacation (school ~) 방학(放學) (8)
vacation 휴가(休暇) (4)
valuable (be ~) 아까w- (아깝다) (13)
valuable (be ~) 아까w- (아깝다) (4)
various places (in ~) 군데군데 (17)
Vatican 교황청(教皇廳) (4)
vent (~ one's anger) 화풀이(를) 하 - (6)
verbal expression 표현(表現) (3)
very 몹시 (12); 무지무지 (16)
very beginning (from the ~) 전(前)부터 (4)
very hot (become very ~) 다 - ㄹ - (달다) (6)
very much (so) 무척 (3)
very much 무척(16); 썩 (14)
very 매우 (9); 너무나 (3))
vestibule 현관(玄關) (17)
vexing (be ~) 곤란(困難)하 - (3)
vicinity 근처(近處) (17)
victim; casualty 사망자 (死亡者) (6)
view from behind (one's ~) 뒷모습 (4)
viewer(s) 관객(觀客) (18)
viewing of it is distasteful 보기 흉(凶)하 - (11)
village school (traditional) 서당(書堂) (6)
village 촌(村) (9)

violate 위반(違反)(을) 하 - (2)
violent (be ~) 매서w- (매섭다) (18)
violent wrench (with a ~) 확 (8)
virility (boost ~) 정력(精力)(을) 돋우 - (6)
virility 정력(精力) (6)
virtually (all, etc.) 거의 (3)
visible (be ~) 보이 - (NB: processive) (11)
vivid "before one's eyes" (be ~) 눈에 선하 - (7)
vivid (be ~) 선하 - (7)
voice 목소리 (14)
volcano 화산(火山) (5)
volition 의지(意志) (18)

W

wage(s) 임금(賃金) (6)
waist 허리 (11)
wake sb up 깨우 - (14)
wake up 깨 - (14)
walk 걸 - (걷다) (14)
walk (have sb ~) 걸리 - (14)
walking 걸음 (1)
wallet 지갑(紙匣) (1)
want 원(願)하 - (17)
war 난리(亂離) (16)
warm sth up 데우 - ; 덥히 - (14)
wash (clothes) 빠 - ㄹ - (빨다) (12)
wash 감 - (14)
washing machine 세탁기(洗濯機) (3)
washing up (the ~) 설거지 (3)
washing 빨래 (11)
waste 낭비(浪費) (11)
watch closely 지켜보 - (13)
watch over 지키 - (13)
watch with one's eyes wide open 눈을 뜨고 보 - (4)
water disaster occurs 물난리(亂離)(가) 나 - (16)
water quality 수질(水質) (14)
water quality 수질(水質) (5)
watermelon (one ~) 수박 한 통 (3)
watermelon 수박 (3)
watery (be ~) 지 - ㄹ - (질다) (11)
way ahead (in life) 진로(進路) (18)
way I think (in the ~) 제 생각대로 (9)
way (any old which ~) 아무렇게나 (1)
way (in such a ~) 그런 식으로 (3)
way (in the Korean ~) 한국식(韓國式)으로 (3)
way (lose one's ~) 길(을) 잃어버리 - (6)
ways ("law") of Rome (the ~) 로마법(~法) [- 뻡] (2)
weak-willed (be ~) 마음(이) 약(弱)하 - (14)
weak stomach (have a ~) 마음(이) 약(弱)하 - (NB: descriptive) (14)
wear around 쓰고 다니 - (7)

wear around 입고 다니 - (7)

weather a trying moment 넘기 - (3)

weather forecast 일기예보(日氣豫報) (6)

webmaster 관리자(管理者) (6)

wedge it in 꽂 - (13)

week (last ["past"] ~) 지난 주일 (3)

weekday 평일(平日) (1)

weight 무게 (19)

weight (lose ~) 마르 - (2)

weight (lose ~) 살(을) 빼 - (4); 살(이) 빠지 - (1)

weighty (be ~) 소중(所重)하 - (14)

welcome party 환영회(歡迎會) (19)

welcome 환영(歡迎)(을) 하 - (19)

well behaved / brought up (be ~) 얌전하 - (4)

well brought up (be ~) 얌전하 - (12)

well together ([people] go ~) 어울리 - (1)

well with ([clothes] go ~) 어울리 - (1)

West (the ~) 서양(西洋) (9)

wet (get / become ~) 젖 - (14)

wet sth 적시 - (14)

whale 고래 (9)

What's the matter? 웬일이세요? (2, 4)

what's with the...? 웬 = 무슨 (16)

what all? 뭐뭐 (12)

what for? 웬일로 (2)

what reason? (for ~) 웬일로 (2)

what sort of? 웬 = 무슨 (16)

what thing? (On account of ~) 웬일로 (2)

wheel (steering ~) 핸들 (8)

where all? 어디어디 (12)

whereupon (first person) 그랬더니; (non-first person) 그러더니 (4)

whereupon 그러자 (11)

which way (any old ~) 아무렇게나 (1)

which (after ~) 그리고는 (1)

while later (a little ~) 이따가 (3)

while (for quite a ~) 한참 (4)

while (in a ~) 이따가 (3)

who all? 누구누구? (12)

whole body 온몸 (16)

whole thing (the ~) 전부(全部) (9)

wholly 온통 (8)

why? 웬일로 (2)

wide open (watch with one's eyes ~) 눈을 뜨고 보 - (4)

wide (be ~) 넓 - (14)

wide (far and ~) 널리 (6)

widen sth 넓히 - (14)

wife (husband and ~) 부부(夫婦) (2)

wild boar 산돼지 [- 돼지] (18)

wild strawberry, raspberry 산딸기 (18)

will 의지(意志) (18)

wilt 일그러지 - (13)

win (on a lottery ticket) 복권(福券)에 당첨(當籤)(이) 되 - (4)

win 이기 - (18, 19)

wind and moon 풍월(風月) (6)

window 창(窓) (3)

wipe something 닦 - (3)

wire 철사(鐵絲) (13)

wisdom tooth 사랑니 (18)

wisdom 지혜(智慧 / 知慧) (6)

with confidence 자신감(自信感)을 가지고 (18)

with peace of mind 마음 놓고 (4)

wither 시드 - ㄹ - (시들다) (12); 일그러지 - (13)

within a few days 며칠 만에 (18)

without a chance to rest 쉴 새 없이 (14)

without anxiety 마음 놓고 (4)

"without face" 무안(無顏)하 - (11)

without fail (will do) 반드시 (2)

without fail 꼭 (14)

without incident 무사(無事)히 (14)

without NOUN (NOUN ~) 없이 (12)

without realizing it 무심(無心)코 (5)

without sleeping a wink 꼬박 (19)

wits' end (be at one's ~) 쩔쩔매 - (3)

women's quarters 안방(~房) [안빵] (12)

women 여성(女性) (6)

wondrous (be ~) 신기(神奇)하 - (19)

woozy with sleep (be ~) 잠에 취(醉)하 - (7)

word (a ~) 말 한 마디 (13)

word 소식(消息) (7)

work (of art, etc.) 작품(作品) (18)

work of fiction 소설(小説) (8)

work on the side (do part-time ~) (usually said of students) 아르바이트(를) 하 - (3)

work (a piece of ~) 일거리 [- 꺼리] (7)

worked up about sth (get ~) 신경(神經)(을) 쓰 - (2)

working day (a ~) 평일(平日) (1)

world 세계(世界) (8)

worn out 지치 - (4)

worried, worrisome (be ~) 궁금하 - (7)

worry about 신경(神經)(을) 쓰 - (19)

worry oneself sick 애(가) 타 - (7)

worry (Don't ~) 염려(念慮)(를) [하지] 마세요. (2)

worry 고민(苦悶) (1)

worry 고민(苦悶) (19); 염려(念慮)(를) 하 - (18)

worry 신경(神經)(을) 쓰 - (2)

wrap 싸 - (11)

wrapped (be / get ~) 싸이 - (11)

wreck (become a tired ~) 녹초가 되 - (9)

wrench (with a sudden, violent ~) 확 (8)

write a composition 작문(作文)(을) 하 - (3)

write down 적 - (3)
write for sb 써다 주 - (9)
writing system 문자(文字) [- 짜] (8)
writing 글씨 (6)
written report 보고서(報告書) (1)
written (be / get ~) 쓰이 - (11)
wrong conveyance (get on the ~ ["ride in error"]) 잘못 타 - (2)
wronged (feel ~) 억울하 - (NB: descriptive) (2)

Y

y'all 여러분 (3)
yard inside Korean house 마당 (1)
yawn 하품(을) 하 - (8)
younger cousin 사촌동생(四寸同生) (5)
youngest (son, daughter) 막내 (3)
yut (game of ~) 윷놀이 (14)

English Translations for the Main Texts

LESSON ONE
I Couldn't Figure Out Why He Was Doing That

It happened last winter when I took a trip to Ch'ŏngp'yŏng Temple near Ch'unch'ŏn.

As it was a regular weekday, and I had taken the first boat from Soyang Dam, there was nobody else other than me going to Ch'ŏngp'yŏng Temple. And yet, after heading up [the mountain] for about five minutes, I could see a man walking in front of me.

I figured it must be a traveler who had stayed in the area overnight. He also must have sensed that I was following him, because he kept looking back. And then he would pick up his pace, lest I pass him. My curiosity was piqued, so I hurried up, whereupon he, too, walked even faster. I could not figure out for the life of me why he was doing that.

But a few moments later, when I saw the still-closed ticket booth for Ch'ŏngp'yŏng Temple, my question was answered. He was the man selling tickets there.

LESSON TWO
But They Say, "When in Rome, Do as the Romans Do," Don't They?

Once, some time ago, I went to Rome and lived there for two years. At the time, the most difficult thing for me was getting used to the driving customs of the Romans.

There was one time when all the cars were backed up near the Vatican because of a big traffic accident. So I was sitting in my car for a good thirty minutes without being able to move even an inch. At that point, the cars around me started making U-turns. If it had been any other day, I would have waited a bit longer, but because I had an important appointment that day, I turned my car around like the others. Then—out of nowhere—a police officer came up to me and ordered me to pull over to the side of the road. He then asked me to show him my driver's license. I was a bit worried but, using the Italian that I had been learning all that time, said to him:

"But they say, 'When in Rome, do as the Romans do,' don't they? The only thing I did was to do just like the Romans did."

But these words didn't cut it with the police officer. And so I ended up getting a ticket.

LESSON THREE
Better Not Speak in English Ever Again

As of today, it has been exactly one year since I came to Korea. When I first came to Korea, I had a difficult time because I wasn't able to communicate. Let me tell you an interesting story that happened back then.

When Koreans walk down a street, they often ask directions, even of total strangers. I must look similar to Koreans because sometimes, there would be Koreans who would ask me for directions, too. Every time it happened, I would freak out and be unable to answer.

On one such day, I had a really great idea. The idea was, when asked, instead of struggling to answer in Korean, it would be OK to answer in English. After a few days passed, some lady asked directions from me. When I said in English, "I'm sorry. I don't speak Korean," the lady was all surprised and walked off. Afterwards, too, I got through several such trying moments in this fashion.

But one day, something unexpected happened. I was on my way to a tabang on Chongno to meet a friend.

Suddenly, someone said something to me. I made an uncomprehending face and said in English that I didn't speak Korean. When I replied in English, the person asked again, in English. Aha, [I thought,] it seems like this person speaks good English.

I was so flustered, but pretending nothing was the matter, I concocted a sentence busily inside my head and then answered him in English. After he was gone, I wiped away the cold sweat [on my brow], and resolved to myself: "Better not speak in English ever again!"

LESSON FOUR
In My Country, Vodka Is So Common We Have More Than Enough to Go Around

A Russian, a Cuban, and an American were travelling with an American lawyer on a train.

After they had been enjoying an interesting conversation for some time, the Russian produced a large bottle of vodka. He poured each of them a glass, and then tossed the bottle—which still had more than half remaining—out the window. Amazed, the American asked him why he would throw away such a precious thing. The Russian told him that in his country, vodka was so common they had more than enough to go around.

A little bit later the Cuban handed out a cigar to each of them. And then he, too, after two or three puffs, threw his cigar out the window.

"Wait a minute. I heard things aren't so good in Cuba. Why are you throwing it away without smoking it all?"

"In Cuba, cigars are so common we have more than enough to go around."

When the American heard this, he suddenly jumped up, picked up the lawyer, and threw him out the window.

LESSON SIX
Proverbs

Every language has proverbs. There is no way to know who first thought up any of the proverbs or when they came into being, but we can say that proverbs are words of wisdom created by the experience of our culture and passed down to us from our ancient ancestors.

Proverbs are pithy sayings, but their meanings are deep and vast. The reason we don't easily forget proverbs once we hear them is because their meaning comes across clearly in just a few words.

Moreover, because proverbs contain the lives and thoughts of our ancestors, they teach us many morals for our everyday lives.

There is a proverb that goes, "The village schoolhouse dog recites poetry after three years." This proverb means that even uneducated people, if they spend a lot of time with people who are studious, naturally come to acquire knowledge of the world. There is another proverb that goes, "If your tail is too long, it gets stepped on." Needless to say, this means that you can fool somebody once or twice, but if you keep on doing it over and over again you are bound to get caught.

Besides these, there is the proverb, "He doesn't even know the letter ㄱ' (k) if you place a sickle in front of him." The shape of a Korean sickle is similar to the hangul letter ㄱ. If you still don't know the letter ㄱ after seeing a Korean sickle, doesn't that mean you're truly ignorant?

Do you know the proverb "Get slapped on Chongno then go to the Han River to vent one's anger"? It means being unable to say anything right then and there when one's been offended, and ending up venting one's anger somewhere else. Also, rumors that get transmitted from mouth to mouth end up spreading far and wide in an instant. That's why, as the saying goes, "Horses [a homonym with 말 word(s)'] without feet go a thousand *li*," as once a rumor spreads, nobody can stop it.

Have you heard the proverb, "After suffering comes joy?" It means that after undergoing something difficult or upsetting, nice and enjoyable things are bound to come. You can use this to show sympathy for a friend who is having trouble with something.

Besides these, there are also all sorts of proverbs composed primarily of Chinese characters. For example, there is a saying "Even the Diamond Mountains should be seen after eating," which means that no matter how captivating something might be, you can only really get into it on a full stomach. Likewise, the saying "Two birds, one stone" means to "kill two birds with one stone", and the proverb "One hundred hearings are not like one seeing" means that hearing about something a hundred times doesn't stack up to seeing it once. That is, it means that seeing something once in real life is better than hearing about it several times in words alone.

LESSON SEVEN
Annie, I Kept Thinking about You a Lot
Dear Annie:

How are you, Annie? I'm doing fine.

My, it's already been nearly two months since you left Korea. Time sure does fly, eh? I mean, the times we spent together in Seoul seem like just yesterday. Even now when I close my eyes, the days I spent together with you are fresh in my mind.

I'll fill you in on some of the news here. Do you remember teacher Ch'oe who taught us in the beginner's class? Apparently, [they say'] he's getting married on December 25. Who knows if that's what he's so happy about these days, but he is all smiles.

Also, not long ago I went to Mt. Tobong with our classmates. You have no idea how much trouble it was to get all the way to the top. On the way down my legs were trembling so much it drove me nuts.

It would have been nice if you had gone, too; I kept thinking about you the whole time.

How are you doing? Is life at school fun? I'm curious to know how you're doing, so as soon as you receive this letter, write me back, okay?

I would like to see you soon. You're definitely going to come back next summer, right?

Well, Annie, don't forget to write back, and take care of yourself.

From Mori in Seoul, Oct. 28, 2004

LESSON EIGHT
What on Earth Happened to Make You Look Like That?

A few days ago, I was on my way to work riding a small motorbike. Because very few cars travel on the road from my house to the office, I was driving the motorbike very fast. But suddenly, a big dog dashed out into the middle of the road. I almost crashed into the dog. In my surprise, I jerked the handlebars to the right in order to avoid the dog. In the next instant, I fell off the motorbike and ended up landing in a puddle at the side of the road.

Because I didn't have sufficient time to go back home and change clothes, I had no choice but to go to work with my clothes all mud-stained just as they were. When I got to the office, my colleagues all stared at me in surprise and asked,

"What on earth happened to make you look like that?" I told them, with slight exaggeration, what had happened on the way to work. After hearing my story, one of my colleagues said:

"Wait a minute—if the dog was so big, why did you try to avoid it? You should have just driven between its legs!"

LESSON NINE

It Happened Last Sunday, Which Was Unusually Busy for a Weekend

It happened last Sunday, which was unusually busy for a weekend. As I had two weddings to go to that day, as well as an article I had to write and hand in to the magazine publisher's office by Monday, I was losing my mind. So, I postponed doing housework until later and started writing the article.

Due to working the night before and only sleeping for two hours, everything was finished at around 11 a.m. Next, I hurriedly got myself ready, and dropped by the two weddings in Kangnam before coming back home. I was completely wiped out physically.

But then the phone rang. It was from some college classmates I hadn't seen for about two years, and the gist of it was that they were about to come to our house. At that moment, I started cleaning the house like a mad person. Because I hadn't cleaned the house properly for several days, the place was a mess. I was able to clean my bedroom and the living room OK, but didn't have time to do the dishes. So I had no choice but to throw the dirty dishes inside the oven.

A few moments later my friends arrived, and in their hands was a frozen pizza.

LESSON ELEVEN

Like, We Wouldn't Know That?

An anthropologist went to investigate a village in the African jungle.

When the scholar arrived, the young children were playing a peculiar game, standing up and sitting down, standing up and sitting down. Thinking to himself that this had worked out nicely, the scholar was just about to take a photograph when—wouldn't you know, the children were all shouting and pointing their fingers, as if objecting.

The somewhat embarrassed scholar went up to the children and began to explain that their souls wouldn't escape when he took their picture. And he also told them this and that about the camera. The children tried to interrupt him and say something several times, but the scholar didn't give them a chance to speak.

A short while later, after he figured that the children understood what he had said, the scholar gave the children an opportunity to speak, whereupon they said, "We know perfectly well that our souls won't leave us when you take a photograph. We just wanted to tell you that the camera lens cap was on."

LESSON TWELVE

But Fish Need to Live in Water, Right?

If you take care of children for a while, you end up both amazed and amused at the silliest things.

I have one son and one daughter. Our daughter grew up as a comparatively well-behaved child without any shenanigans. But the boy was so full of mischief that he made life difficult for me and my wife from the time he started to crawl.

One time, the following episode happened. It was when he was about four years old. My wife had just returned from the market and was claiming that the two *chogi* fish she had put on the kitchen table had disappeared. At first I didn't pay it any mind, but because my wife kept looking around for them and saying how strange it was, I started to look with her.

My wife said that she had clearly put the fish on the kitchen table in order to make side dishes for our supper. But, she claimed, the *chogi* had disappeared when she went into the *anpang* briefly to put down her purse. We turned the kitchen upside down, but the *chogi* were nowhere to be seen. So, we concluded that the cat from next door must have come in and made off with them, and we gave up looking. My wife seemed to be really upset. But, a few moments later my wife called to me in a loud voice from the bathroom. When I went into the bathroom, I discovered two *chogi* floating in the bathtub. Needless to say, it was the work of our son. But even more amusing was our son's response to our questioning: "But fish need to live in water, right? That's why I put them in the water."

LESSON THIRTEEN

Think Nothing of It!

Lately I've been working at a parking lot. Now, among our customers there are sometimes people who leave their keys in the ignition and lock the car door behind them. Whenever this happens, I use a piece of thick wire to open the door for them.

But recently there was an episode that was quite serious. Perhaps it was because the rainy season had just finished, but the weather was steaming hot. Thinking to buy myself a refreshing beverage or something, I went to the convenience store. I bought myself a *saida* and was just leaving the store when I saw two young ladies struggling to open their car door in front of the store. I was going to pretend not to notice and just walk right by, but then I stopped to watch the ladies' actions.

The women struggled to get the door open, but the door wouldn't open. Thinking I should probably help them, I took out the wire from my back pocket and walked up to the car. It took not even a minute to open the door. With a look of amazement on their faces, the ladies thanked me. I felt great. But one phrase that came out wrong distorted the look on their faces, which dashed my spirits:

"Think nothing of it! This is how I make my living."

LESSON FOURTEEN

To My Dear Wife

Today is my wife's birthday. For a few days now, I have been agonizing over what to give my wife for her birthday. I have lived with my wife for close to thirty years now. The older I get, the more precious my wife feels to me. So this time I resolved to give my wife a present full of my love and sincerity—a present that would amaze her. But no matter how much I thought about it, no good ideas came to mind. So yesterday I had no choice but to go to a department store and buy a necklace.

But, since I really don't like this present, here I am this morning at the crack of dawn lying awake under the covers and still thinking. After thinking about this and that, I recalled something that happened fifty years ago.

It happened when I was eleven years old. Because our family was in farming, our parents worked constantly without a break. And because I was the eldest son, I had to help my parents. What I hated most was getting up early in the morning and feeding the cow. My father came into our room every morning and shook awake his son who didn't want to get up.

My father's birthday was coming up soon. I wanted to make my father happy, this man who was always suffering for us. But I had no money. Then, I had a really neat idea.

On the day of my father's birthday, I got up about an hour and a half earlier than the time my father usually woke me, and then went outside. And ever so quietly, so as to not wake my parents, I boiled up the cow's mush, fed the cow, and came back to my room. "What kind of face will Father make when he sees that?" I lapsed into happy thoughts like this as I lay beneath the covers.

A few moments later I heard the sound of my father's voice calling me along with the sound of the door to my parents' room opening. Although I had heard the sound of my father calling, at first I stayed quiet and pretended not to hear. Then, after my father had called three or four times, I got up and went outside. As my father was passing by the stable, he saw that the cow was already eating its mush. Then, startled, he stared over in my direction. I just gave a quiet, sheepish smile.

As I thought these thoughts, the emotions from that time came back to me, and I felt a sudden urge to cry. And then it occurred to me what would be the best present to give my wife. I got up immediately, crossed over to my study, and began to compose a letter to my wife:

"To my dear wife..."

LESSON SIXTEEN

Am I Busy Lately or What?

(on the phone)

"Sŏnyŏng, is that you? It's me, Sumi. What're you doing?"

"Oh, good, so I guess you have a little time to chat. Boy, am I upset."

"Lately the students from our department get together in the mornings and study, you see? But there's this one student who never shows up on time. I mean, for him, thirty minutes late is early, and usually he's an hour late every time. And am I busy lately or what? So I told him once before to be on time, but of course it's just no use. He was a good hour or so late again today, so I scolded him again. But then he's the one who gets all angry!"

"And you know, it wasn't like I'd told him just once or twice. I told him so many times before! Anyway, you can talk to him as many times as you like—it's like talking to a brick wall. Really—I've never seen anything like it. If I ever do anything with him again, take me out back and shoot me."

"But now that I've spoken with you, I feel a bit better. Before I called just now, I was in such a bad mood. Hey would you look at that, we've been talking for quite a while. I'm going to let you go now. Sorry... I did all the talking. I'll call again. Bye!"

LESSON SEVENTEEN

Even If She Ran for It, It Was Obvious She Would Be Caught Nearby

Everyone had gone away on vacation, and the city seemed empty. It seems everybody thought that, rather than stay in the middle of town in such sweltering weather, it would be better to leave town.

This was especially true of P'yŏngch'angdong, where many rich people live. All that was there were streetlights illuminated here and there. But a woman appeared in the darkness and, with deft movements, entered a house.

She went straight up to the study on the second floor and, with expert dexterity, removed a painting. The moment she opened the secret safe behind it, an alarm began to ring. For a moment, the woman was at a loss. In about three minutes, the police would likely come running. Even if she ran for it, it was obvious she would be caught nearby.

As anticipated, a few minutes later the doorbell rang. The sound of the doorbell gradually grew louder and louder. Just at the moment when the police officers were about to force their way in through the main door, a lady with a shower cap on her head and massage cream all over her face opened the door. It seemed as if she had just finished her shower. Now it was the police who were at a loss.

"I was hoping somebody would come, and you did! The emergency alarm started ringing, and I didn't know what to do."

"Wait a minute—who are you, miss?"

"I'm the niece of the owner of this house. I've come to watch the house for a few days. Please come in quickly and make that alarm stop."

The policemen came in, stopped the alarm, went so far as to explain everything kindly to the woman, and then went away. About ten minutes later, the young lady who had just said she was the homeowner's niece left the house carrying what she had come for.

LESSON EIGHTEEN
Surely a Bear Couldn't Have Become a Human?

"Daddy, when did Korea come into existence? Who made it?"

My daughter, who had just turned six, must have had a lot of questions on her mind, as she was always pestering me. So I explained to her the Tan'gun myth in an easy-to-understand way.

"I'm going to tell you now, so listen closely. This is a story from a long, long time ago when tigers smoked pipes. There was this god living in heaven called Hwanin, you see? He had a son called Hwanung, and Hwanung wanted to come down to earth and live here. So Hwanung asked his father to let him come down to earth and live here, whereupon his father gave him ministers to control the wind, the rain, and the clouds, three thousand people, and told him to go down to earth and live here.

"Hwanung came down to Mount T'aebaek and was living there when one day, a bear and a tiger call on him and tell him they want to become humans. So Hwanung told them that if they ate mugwort and garlic without seeing the sunshine for one hundred days, then they can become humans. So the bear and the tiger each took a bundle of garlic and mugwort and went into a cave. But whereas the bear stuck it out until the very end, the tiger was unable to endure and came running out of the cave after a few days."

"Seems like the bear was able to last because it's dumb and slow-witted."

"Anyway, after a hundred days had passed, the bear turned into a very pretty woman, and married Hwanung. The child they gave birth to is our ancestor, granddaddy Tan'gun. When grandfather Tan'gun grew up, he founded the state called Ancient Chosŏn, and that was all five thousand years ago."

"Come on—surely a bear couldn't have become a human? And there's one other strange thing. I mean, Koreans now really like tigers—so why is our ancestor a bear and not a tiger? It'd be better if it was a tiger."

"Hmm... I wonder why? Daddy doesn't know, either."

LESSON NINETEEN
I'm Afraid to Go Out

If you work in a hospital for a while, all manner of strange patients come in.

Three or four months ago, a woman came to see me and said,

"I'm concerned about how overweight I am; is there no way for me to lose weight?"

So I said jokingly, "Actually, there are no secret tricks or anything to losing weight."

But the woman kept complaining about how she was so fat that she couldn't wear the clothes she wanted to, how she looked older, and was afraid to go out with her husband.

I told her about the methods I knew. But, she asked if there wasn't any other method. She had already tried the methods I had mentioned, but she said it was all no use.

Joking again, I told her a funny story I had read once before somewhere. It was the method of losing weight by pinning up a photo of a slim woman in a swimming suit inside the fridge. The story went that you'll end up seeing the photo every time you open the fridge door, and when you see the photo, you'll end up resisting your desire to eat.

After the patient left, I forgot all about the visit. But today, with there being no patients and all, I was thinking I should go get some lunch and was just about to leave the consultation room when a slender young lady came in.

"Do you remember me?"

"Now who were you again? You'll have to forgive me, but I can't recall."

"I'm the person who came in once to ask about ways to lose weight."

When she said this, I remembered her. She had truly become slim beyond recognition.

"Doctor, your method was really effective. What do you think—pretty amazing, eh?"

When I expressed my amazement and wonder, she told me of a new concern.

"My husband has gained ten kilograms; is there no way for him to lose weight?"

KOREAN-ENGLISH PATTERN INDEX

ENGLISH-KOREAN PATTERN INDEX

ANSWER KEY

Chapter 1, page 27, exercise 2

1. 하루 종일 날이 흐리더니 저녁부터 비가 내리기 시작했습니다. (It had been cloudy since morning but it started raining in the evening.)
2. 며칠 잠을 못 잤더니 좀 피곤하네요. (I haven't slept for a few days so I'm a bit tired.)
3. 어제 저녁을 많이 먹었더니 배가 아파요. (I ate too much for dinner yesterday and now my stomach hurts.)
4. 오랜만에 만났더니 많이 컸더라! (It had been a while since I had met him—boy had he grown!)
5. 어제는 추웠더니 오늘은 덥네요. (Yesterday was cold but today is hot.)
6. 어젠 전화 목소리가 힘이 없더니 오늘은 기분이 많이 좋아진 것 같네요. (Yesterday your voice sounded weak on the phone but it seems you are much better today.)
7. (네가) 빵을 사더니 왜 (네가) 밥을 먹니? (You bought bread, so why are you eating rice?)
8. (내가) 빵을 샀더니 왜 (내가) 밥을 먹니? (I bought bread, so why are you eating rice?)
9. (내가) 수미를 오랜만에 만났더니 못 알아보겠더라. (I saw Sumi for the first time in a while and I didn't recognize her.)
10. (네가) 수미를 오랜만에 만나더니 할 이야기가 그렇게 많았니? (It had been a long time since you'd seen Sumi, but did you really have that much to talk about?)

Chapter 1, page 27, exercise 3

1. 로비에서 한 시간 기다렸다가 그냥 갔어요. (I waited for an hour in the reception room and then left.)
2. 밥을 먹다가 갑자기 안색이 이상해졌어요. (He was eating and then suddenly his complexion became strange.)
3. 젓가락을 쓰다가 포크로 바꿨어요. (I was using chopsticks but switched to a fork.)
4. 밤 늦게까지 보고서를 쓰다가 잤어요. (I was writing my report until late in the night and then fell asleep.)
5. 버스에서 내리다가 넘어졌어요. (I fell down getting off the bus.)
6. 생선만 며칠 동안 먹다가 병이 났어요. (For a few days I ate nothing but fish and now I'm sick.)
7. 뉴스를 보다가 너무 지루해서 텔레비전을 그냥 껐어요. (I was watching the news but it was so boring I just switched the TV off.)

8. 집에 가다가 도서관에 들러야겠어요. (On the way home I'll have to stop by the library.)
9. 학교에 오다가 영진 씨를 만났어요. (On the way to school I met Yangjin).
10. 비가 오다가 갑자기 그쳤어요. (It was raining and then suddenly it stopped.)
11. 한국에서 회사에 다니다가 캐나다에 왔습니다. (I was working for a company in Korea and then came to Canada.)
12. 도서관에 가다가 친구를 만났어요. (On the way to the library I met a friend.)
13. 사무실을 청소하다가 이 사진을 찾았어요. (I happened to find this photo while I was cleaning my office.)
14. 운동을 하다가 다리를 다쳤어요. (I injured my knee while exercising.)
15. 음악을 듣다가 여자친구 생각이 났어요. (As I was listening to music my thoughts turned to my girlfriend.)

Chapter 2, page 43, exercise 4

1. 저쪽에 가서 앉으시라고 했다. (I told Man'gu to go over there and sit down.)
2. 후추 좀 집어 달라고 했다. (I asked Chuyŏn to put some pepper in for me.)
3. 내일 약속을 잊어버리지 마시라고 했다. (I told Sujan not to forget tomorrow's appointment.)
4. 용돈 좀 달라고 했다. (I asked my mother for some pocket money.)
5. 아무한테도 얘기하지 말라고 했다. (I told Sŏnyŏng not to tell anybody.)
6. 미진이한테 물 좀 주라고 했다. (I told Sumi to give Mijin some water.)
7. 사전 좀 빌려 달라고 했다. (I asked Albert to lend me his dictionary.)

Chapter 2, page 44, exercise 6

1. 동전이 이것뿐입니다. (This is all I have in the way of change.)
2. 내일 아침 일찍 나올 수 있는 사람은 우리뿐입니다. (We're the only ones who can come out early tomorrow morning.)
3. 나를 정말로 걱정해 주는 사람은 부모님뿐입니다. (The only people who really worry about me are my parents.)
4. 그냥 한두 번 만나 보았을 뿐, 특별한 사이가 아닙니다. (All we did was meet once or twice; we don't have a special relationship.)
5. 아픈 데는 없고 그냥 좀 피곤할 뿐인데 걱정하지 마십시오. (I'm not in pain anywhere; it's just that I'm a bit tired, so please don't concern yourself.)
6. 어제 밤을 새웠을 뿐인데 좀 어지럽습니다. (It's just that I stayed up all night

last night; I'm a bit dizzy.)

Chapter 3, page 62, exercise 6

1. 수미는 머리가 길다고 합니다. → 수미는 머리가 길답니다.
2. 말이 빨라서 알아들을 수 없다고 합니다. → 말이 빨라서 알아들을 수 없답니다.
3. 정아는 친구한테 전화를 건다고 합니다. → 정아는 친구한테 전화를 건답니다.
4. 진호는 아침마다 수영을 배우러 다닌다고 합니다. → 진호는 아침마다 수영을 배우러 다닌답니다.
5. 선영이는 영화를 보러 갔다고 합니다. → 선영이는 영화를 보러 갔답니다.
6. 어제는 아주 바빴다고 합니다. → 어제는 아주 바빴답니다.
7. 내일부터는 늦지 않겠다고 합니다. → 내일부터는 늦지않겠답니다.
8. 비가 올 것 같다고 합니다. → 비가 올 것 같답니다.
9. 영수는 뚱뚱하지 않다고 합니다. → 영수는 뚱뚱하지 않답니다.
10. 진호는 술을 별로 좋아하지 않는다고 합니다. → 진호는 술을 별로 좋아하지 않는답니다.
11. 내일은 한글날이라고 합니다. → 내일은 한글날이랍니다.
12. 어제는 설날이었다고 합니다. → 어제는 설날이었답니다.
13. 친구를 만나러 갈 것이라고 합니다. → 친구를 만나러 갈 것이랍니다.
14. 집에 가서 쉬고 싶다고 합니다. → 집에 가서 쉬고 싶답니다.

Chapter 3, page 63, exercise 7

1. 착해요 → 착하대요.
2. 재미없어요 → 재미없대요.
3. 써요 → 쓴대요.
4. 걸어요 → 건대요.
5. 갔어요 → 갔대요.
6. 피곤했어요 → 피곤했대요.
7. 가겠어요 → 가겠대요.
8. 올 것 같아요 → 올 것 같대요.
9. 크지 않아요 → 크지 않대요.
10. 피우지 않아요 → 피우지 않는대요.
11. 독일 사람이에요 → 독일 사람이래요.
12. 지난달에는 적자였어요 → 적자였대요.
13. 나갈 것이에요 → 나갈 것이래요.
14. 싶어요 → 싶대요.

Chapter 3, page 63 exercise 8B

7. 진호는 전화를 거는가 봅니다.
8. 선영이는 친구를 만나러 갔는가 봅니다.
9. 어제는 아주 피곤했는가 봅니다.

10. 아침 일찍 가겠는가 봅니다. Or아침 일찍 갈 것인가 봅니다.
11. 비가 오는가 봅니다.
12. 영수는 키가 크지 않은가 봅니다.

Chapter 3, page 63, exercise 9
1. 내일부터는 일찍 집에 들어가야지.
2. 내일부터는 술을 마시지 말아야지.
3. 내일부터는 게으르지 말아야지.
4. 살을 빼야지.
5. 내일부터는 매일 제시간에 와야지.
6. 내일부터는 수업에서 졸지 말아야지.

Chapter 4, page 76, exercise 2
1. 날씨 좋으냐고 물었습니다. (asked if the weather is good)
2. 어디에 가느냐고 물었습니다. (asked where somebody is going)
3. 어제 누구를 만났느냐고 물었습니다. (asked whom he met yesterday)
4. 이번 휴가 때 뭐 할 거냐고 물었습니다. (asked what she's going to do during her time off this time)
5. 누구한테 전화 거느냐고 물었습니다. (asked who she's calling)
6. 비가 올 것 같으냐고 물었습니다. (asked if it looks like it's going to rain)
7. 기분이 어떠냐고 물었습니다. (asked how he's feeling)
8. 1억 원이 생기면 뭐 하겠느냐고 물었습니다. (asked what they would do if they suddenly had a hundred million wŏn)
9. 수미 씨가 아는 사람이냐고 물었습니다. (asked if Sumi was somebody she knew)
10. 영화를 좋아하느냐고 물었습니다. (asked him if he likes movies)
11. 여기가 어디냐고 물었습니다. (asked where this place is)
12. 오늘 아침 버스에 사람이 많았느냐고 물었습니다. (asked if there were a lot of people on the bus this morning)
13. 기분이 좋지 않으냐고 물었습니다. (asked if he was in a bad mood)
14. 개를 좋아하지 않느냐고 물었습니다. (asked if he didn't like dogs)
15. 갈비를 맛있게 구웠느냐고 물었습니다. (asked if they had grilled the ribs nicely)
16. 오후에 어디에 갈 거냐고 물었습니다. (asked where they were going to go in the afternoon)
17. 언제 한국에 왔느냐고 물었습니다. (asked when she had come to Korea)
18. 보통 몇 시에 일어나느냐고 물었습니다. (asked her what time she usually gets up)
19. 어제 만난 여자 어떠냐고 물었습니다. (asked him how the woman was he had yet yesterday)
20. 가방이 무거우냐고 물었습니다. (asked if the bag is heavy)

Chapter 4, page 77, exercise 3
1. 무엇을 합니까? What are you doing? →
(a) 무엇을 하느냐니다. (Present: asks)
(b) 무엇을 하느냈습니다. (Past: asked)
2. 누구를 만나러 갑니까? Whom are you going to meet?
a. 누구를 만나러 가느냐니다.
b. 누구를 만나러 가느냈습니다.
3. 무슨 책을 읽습니까? What book are you reading?
a. 무슨 책을 읽느냐니다.
b. 무슨 책을 읽느냈습니다.
4. 무슨 생각을 하고 있습니까? What are you thinking about?
a. 무슨 생각을 하고 있느냐니다.
b. 무슨 생각을 하고 있느냈습니다.
5. 그 책 재미있습니까? Is that book interesting?
a. 그 책 재미있느냐니다.
b. 그 책 재미있느냈습니다.
6. 어디 아픕니까? Where does it hurt?
a. 어디 아프냐니다.
b. 어디 아프냈습니다.
7. 기분 좋습니까? Are you in a good mood?
a. 기분 좋으냐니다.
b. 기분 좋으냈습니다.
8. 쉬고 싶습니까? Do you want to rest?
a. 쉬고 싶으냐니다.
b. 쉬고 싶으냈습니다.
9. 비가 올 것 같습니까? Does it look like it's going to rain?
a. 비가 올 것 같으냐니다.
b. 비가 올 것 같으냈습니다.
10. 피곤하지 않습니까? Aren't you tired?
a. 피곤하지 않으냐니다.
b. 피곤하지 않으냈습니다.
11. 진수 씨는 오지 않습니까? Isn't Chinsu coming?
a. 진수 씨는 오지 않느냐니다.
b. 진수 씨는 오지 않느냈습니다.
12. 저 사람 누구입니까? Who is that?
a. 저 사람 누구냐니다.
b. 저 사람 누구냈습니다.
13. 토마스 씨는 어느 나라 사람입니까? What country is Thomas from?
a. 토마스 씨는 어느 나라 사람이냐니다.
b. 토마스 씨는 어느 나라 사람이냈습니다.
14. 어제 뭐 했습니까? What did you do yesterday?
a. 어제 뭐 했느냐니다.
b. 어제 뭐 했느냈습니다.
15. 많이 아팠습니까? Did it hurt a lot?
a. 많이 아팠느냐니다.
b. 많이 아팠느냈습니다.
16. 전에도 여기가 커피숍이었습니까? Was this a coffee shop before, too?
a. 전에도 여기가 커피숍이었느냐니다.
b. 전에도 여기가 커피숍이었느냈습니다.

17. 뭐 먹겠습니까? What would you like to eat?
a. 뭐 먹겠느냐니다.
b. 뭐 먹겠느냈습니다.
18. 저 영화 재미있겠습니까? Do you think that movie will be interesting?
a. 저 영화 재미있겠느냐니다.
b. 저 영화 재미있겠느냈습니다.

Chapter 4, page 77, exercise 4
7. 나만큼 약을 많이 먹는 사람은 없을 겁니다.
8. 한국만큼 아들을 좋아하는 나라가 없을 겁니다.
9. 나만큼 여자친구를 잘 돌봐 주는 사람은 없을 거예요.
10. 우리는 참을 수 없을 만큼 속상했습니다.
11. 여기 학생들은 놀라울 만큼 공부를 많이 합니다.
12. 나는 꼼짝도 못할 만큼 진이 다 빠졌습니다.
13. 모두 다 셀 수 없을 만큼 사람이 많이 왔습니다.

Chapter 4, page 78, exercise 6
7. 나는 김치를 담글 줄 몰라요.
8. 젓가락질 할 줄 알아요?
9. 시내로 갈 줄 알아요?
10. 진호가 정말 우리집으로 올 줄을 몰랐어요.
11. 복권에 당첨될 줄 몰랐어요.
12. 눈이 이렇게 올 줄은 누가 알았겠어요?
13. 그녀가 유학을 갈 줄은 전혀 몰랐어요.
14. 요리를 이렇게 잘 하는 줄 몰랐어요!
15. 비가 온 줄 몰랐어요.
16. 비가 오는 줄 몰랐어요.
17. 비가 올 줄 몰랐어요.
18. 아이들은 작은 줄 알았는데 전혀 아니네요.

Chapter 4, page 80, exercise 8
1. 다음 주일에 미국에 간다면서요? Is it true you're going to the United States next week?
2. 그 술집은 이 교수님의 단골집이라면서요? Is it true that that bar is Professor Lee's regular hangout?
3. 내일 눈이 온다면서요? Is it true that it's going to snow tomorrow?
4. 전쟁 때 고생을 많이 했다면서요? Is it true that he suffered a lot during the war?
5. 그런 영화는 보기 싫다면서요? Is it true that you hate movies like that?
6. 에릭 씨 아버님이 유명한 학자시라면서요? Is it true that Eric's father is a famous scholar?
7. 아버지가 수영하러 가고 싶어하신다면서요? Is it true that your father wants to go swimming?

8. 민희 씨가 지금 밖에서 가방을 들고 있다면서요? Is it true that Minhee is holding your bag outside now?

9. 수철 씨는 교통사고로 죽었다면서요? Is it true that Such'ŏl died in a car accident?

10. 김치 없으면 못 산다면서요? Is it true that you can't live without kimch'i?

11. 회사가 파산을 해서 난리가 났다면서요? Is it true that there was big trouble because the company went bankrupt?

12. 병이 나았지만 몸조리를 잘 못하고 있다면서요? Is it true that even though you're not sick anymore you're not taking good care of yourself?

13. 대통령을 모시러 간다면서요? Is it true that you're going to escort the president?

14. 결국에는 오래 가지 못하고 파산을 선언했다면서요? Is it true that in the end they couldn't last long and declared bankruptcy?

15. 친구가 장가를 간다면서요? Is it true that your friend is going to get married?

16. 저 여자분은 아주 얌전하시다면서요? Is it true that that lady is very well-mannered?

17. 4월에 논문을 제출해야 하다면서요? Is it true that you have to submit your thesis in April?

18. 상범이하고 수영 배우러 다닌다면서요? Is it true that you're attending swimming lessons with Sangbŏm?

Chapter 6, page 102, exercise 2

1. 아침에 먼저 세수를 하고서 머리를 감아요. In the morning first I wash my face then I shampoo my hair.

2. 거짓말을 하고서 얼굴이 확 빨개지더군요. He told a lie and then his face suddenly turned red.

3. 옷을 입고서 아침을 먹지요. I get dressed and then I eat breakfast.

4. 식사 후 이를 닦고서 버스 정류장으로 나가요. I brush my teeth after eating my meal and then go out to the bus stop.

5. 그렇게 게으름을 피우고서 언제 일을 다 끝내겠어요? If you're going to be so lazy, when are you going to finish all your work?

6. 학교에 와서 도서관에서 숙제를 마치고서 수업에 들어가요. I go to school and finish my homework in the library and then I go to class.

7. 돈을 다 내지 않고도 물건을 가지고 가면 되나요? Is it okay to not pay all of the money and take the goods with me?

8. 오후에는 피아노를 연습하고서 운동장에 나가요. In the afternoon I practice piano and then I go to the gym.

9. 옷을 갈아입고서 운동을 좀 하지요. Let's change clothes and do a little exercise.

10. 남의 물건을 훔치고도 부끄러운 줄을 모르나 봐요. It seems he has no concept of shame even after stealing somebody else's things.

11. 저녁에는 집에 와서 쉬고서 부엌에서 저녁식사를 준비해요. In the evening I come home and rest and then I prepare dinner in the kitchen.

12. 엄마가 부르는 소리를 듣고도 못 들은 척했어요. I heard Mom calling me but nevertheless pretended I hadn't heard.

13. 마시고도 안 마신 척했어요. I drank but nevertheless pretended I hadn't drunk.

14. 진수는 시험에 떨어지고도 놀기만 하네요. Chinsu failed the test and yet only plays.

15. 아까 그렇게 많이 먹고도 벌써 배가 고프니? You ate so much just now and yet you're still hungry?

16. 젊어서 하는 고생은 돈을 주고도 못 산다. The troubles of youth cannot be bought for gold.

Chapter 6, page 103, exercise 3

1. 죄를 지으면 벌을 받는 법이다. If you break the law you will be punished.

2. 돈을 빌리면 반드시 갚아야 되는 법이다. If you borrow money you definitely have to pay it back.

3. 착한 사람은 복을 받는 법이다. Good people are generally blessed with good fortune.

4. 약속은 꼭 지켜야 하는 법이다. You should always keep promises.

5. 공부를 하지 않으면 시험을 못 보는 법이다. If you don't study you don't do well on tests.

6. 교통 법규를 어기면 딱지를 떼이는 법이다. When you violate traffic laws you get ticketed.

7. 아프면 집 생각이 나는 법이다. When you're sick you think of home.

8. 밥을 자주 굶고 잠도 제대로 못 자면 건강이 나빠지는 법이다. If you skip meals and don't sleep properly your health will decline.

9. 공부를 열심히 하면 성공하는 법이다. If you study hard you will succeed.

10. 여름은 덥고 겨울은 추운법이다. Summer is hot and winter is cold.

Chapter 6, page 103, exercise 4

1. 그렇게 게으르게 시간을 보내다가는 후회하는 날이 꼭 올 거야. If you spend your time so lazily the day will surely come when you regret it.

2. 게으름을 <u>피우다가는</u> 시험에 떨어지는 수가 있어. If you're lazy you could fail the test.

3. 그렇게 신경을 많이 <u>쓰다가는</u> 병이 나고 마는 법이다. If you worry so much you'll end up getting sick.

4. 그렇게 놀기만 <u>하다가는</u> 남한테 뒤떨어지기가 쉬워. If all you do is play you're likely to fall behind other people.

5. 그 사람만 <u>믿다가는</u> 믿는 도끼에 발등 찍히는 꼴이 될 거야. If you trust only him you'll end up as an example of the proverb 'trust is the mother of deceit' ['getting stabbed in the top of your foot by your trusty axe'].

6. A: 고향으로 돌아가신다고요? I heard you're going back to your hometown?
B: 예, 조금 더 <u>있다가는</u> 돌아가기가 싫어질 것 같아서요. Yes, because I figured that if I stayed any longer I wouldn't feel like going back anymore.

7. A: 술을 끊으셨다고요? I heard you stopped drinking alcohol?
B: 예, 이렇게 날마다 술을 <u>마시다가는</u> 건강이 나빠질 것 같아서요. Yeah, because it seemed if I kept drinking alcohol every day like this my health would suffer.

8. A: 왜 식사를 조금만 하세요? Why are you eating so little at meals?
B: 계속해서 많이 <u>먹다가는</u> 뚱뚱해질 것 같아서요. Because it seemed I'd get fat if I kept eating so much.

9. A: 왜 여기서 TV를 보면 안 돼요? Why can't we watch TV from here?
B: 그렇게 가까이에서 TV를 <u>보다가는</u> 눈이 나빠질 테니까요. If you watch TV from so close, your eyes will go bad.

10. A: 왜 갑자기 컴퓨터를 배우려고 하세요? Why are you suddenly trying to learn about computers?
B: 컴퓨터를 <u>모르다가는</u> 뒤떨어질 것 같아서요. Because I figured I'd fall behind if I remained ignorant about computers.

11. A: 늦을 때마다 집에 연락하세요? Do you call home whenever you're going to be late?
B: 그럼요. <u>전화하지 않다가는</u> 어머니한테 야단을 맞을까 봐서요. Of course. Because I'm afraid that if I don't call, my mother will scold me.

12. 그렇게 사치스럽게 <u>살면</u> 돈을 곧 다 써 버릴 겁니다. If you live so extravagantly, you'll soon use up all your money.

13. 매번 얻어먹기만 <u>하다가는</u> 친구들이 싫어해요. If you let yourself be treated to meals every time, your friends will hate you.

14. 운동은 하지 않고 먹기만 <u>하다가는</u> 살이 쪄요. If you don't exercise and only eat, you will gain weight.

15. 돈을 벌지 않고 쓰기만 <u>하다가는</u> 빚을 지는 법이다. If you don't earn money and only spend it, you will go into debt.

Chapter 6, page 104, exercise 5

1. 시내에 나온 김에 백화점에 들러서 쇼

핑이나 할까요? Seeing as we're down-town, shall we drop in at a department store and do some shopping?

2. 생각이 난 김에 그 사람한테 전화나 겁시다. While we're thinking of it, let's call her.

3. 이왕 준비를 하는 김에 보고서를 잘 씁시다. As long as we're preparing them anyway, let's write the reports well.

4. 이왕 사는 김에 괜찮고 보기 좋은 것을 삽시다. Since we're buying one any-way, let's buy a decent nice-looking one.

5. 영국까지 가는 김에 프랑스 구경도 좀 하고 옵시다. Since we're already going all the way to England let's do some sightsee-ing in France, too, before coming back.

6. 도서관에 온 김에 신문이나 보고 가 야겠어요. Since I've come to the library anyway, I suppose I should read a newspa-per or something.

7. 우리 집에 오신 김에 점심이나 드시고 가시지요. Since you've already come to my house, why don't you eat lunch or something before you go.

8. 청소를 하는 김에 내 방도 좀 청소할 래요? As long as you're cleaning, will you clean my room too?

9. 빨래를 하는 김에 이 바지도 좀 빨아 줄래요? Since you're doing laundry any-way, could you please wash these trousers for me too?

10. 한국어를 배우는 김에 한자도 좀 배워야겠지요? As long I'm learning Korean anyway, I guess I should learn some Chi-nese characters too?

11. 일어난 김에 그 창문 좀 닫아 줄래? Seeing as you're already up could you please close that window for me?

12. 우체국에 가는 김에 편지도 부쳐 주실 래요? As long as you're going to the post office, could you mail a letter for me?

13. 떡을 본 김에 제사를 지냅시다. [속 담!] Do things when the opportunity pre-sents itself [proverb: 'Since you've espied a rice-cake, you might as well conduct an ancestral rite'].

14. 말이 나온 김에 이 일도 좀 해 주세요. Since the topic has come up, please do this for me too.

15. 생각난 김에 친구 부모님도 찾아뵈었 어. While I was thinking of it, I also visited my friend's parents.

Chapter 6, page 104, exercise 6

1. A: 이 약은 어디에 쓰는 약이에요? (모기를 잡아요)
   B: 그 약은 모기를 잡는 데에 쓰는 약이에요. This medicine is used for killing mosquitoes.

2. A: 이 USB 드라이브 뭐에 써요? (데이터를 저장해요)

B: 그것은 데이터를 저장하는 데에 사용하는 드라이브예요. This drive is used for saving data.

3. A: 친구 사이에 사과라는 것을 꼭 해야 하나요? (우정을 지켜 나가요)
   B: 그럼요. 우정을 지켜 나가는 데에 필요한 예의는 반드시 지켜야죠. Of course. One should always observe the proper etiquette necessary to preserving friendship.

4. A: 한국말 배우는 게 이렇게 시간이 많이 걸릴 줄은 몰랐어요. (외국어를 배워요)
   B: 외국어를 배우는 데에 가장 필요한 건 시간과 노력이라고요. When you learn a foreign language, the most essential things are time and effort.

5. A: 한 번에 시험에 붙는 좋은 방법이 없을까요? (시험을 잘 봐요)
   B: 시험을 잘 보는 데에 가장 중요한 건 꾸준한 노력이랍니다. When you want to do well on a test, the most impor-tant thing is consistent effort [they say].

6. A: 선진국이 되기 위해서 무엇이 필요하다고 생각하세요? (나라를 발전시켜요)
   B: 나라를 발전시키는 데에 국민이 모두 노력해야 합니다. In developing their country, all citizens have to put in an effort.

7. A: 이거 하면 어떻게 도움이 되는 겁니까? (선택을 하세요)
   B: 여러분께서 선택을 하시는 데에 도움이 될 것입니다. It will be of use to you all in making your choice.

8. A: 사람들이 장어를 왜들 그렇게 좋아하지요? (정력을 돋워요)
   B: 장어는 정력을 돋우는 데에 좋다고 알려졌어요. Eating eel is known to be good for increasing your stamina.

9. A: 숙제를 하는 데에 도움이 있었습니까? (보고서를 써요)
   B: 보고서를 쓰는 데에 한국인 룸메이트한테 도움을 좀 받았습니다. When I was writing my report I got some help from my Korean roommate.

Chapter 6, page 104, exercise 7

1. A: 무슨 일로 예약을 취소하게 되었어요? (사정)
   B: 사정에 의해서 여행을 못 가게 되었어요. Due to extenuating circumstances it turned out that I couldn't go on my trip.

2. A: 사람의 성격은 어떻게 형성되지요? (환경과 유전)
   B: 대개 환경과 유전에 의해서 형성되지요. People's characters are usually formed by their environment and heredity.

3. A: TV에서 6시에 야구중계를 한다고 신문에 나와 있는데, 왜 안 할까요? (방송국 사정)

B: 방송국 사정에 의해서 안 해요. They're not showing it because of extenu-ating circumstances at the broadcasting station.

4. A: 좋은 책과 나쁜 책은 어떻게 결정됩니까? (독자)
   B: 그건 독자에 의해서 결정됩니다. That is decided by the readers.

5. A: 한국에서 대통령은 어떻게 뽑아요? (국민투표)
   B: 대통령은 국민투표에 의해서 뽑아요. They elect the president by citizens' vote.

6. A: 사장님은 분명히 내일 가라고 하셨는데요. (부장님 명령)
   B: 나는 부장님 명령에 의해서 가요. I'm going on account of my department chief's orders

7. A: [웹사이트 게시판에서] 이쪽 글이 왜 안 보이지요? (관리자)
   B: 관리자에 의해서 삭제됐어요. It was deleted by the administrator.

8. A: 사람이 똑똑하고 똑똑하지 못한 것은 어떻게 결정되지? (유전자)
   B: 유전자에 의해서 결정돼요. It's determined by genetics.

9. A: 그 사람 신장이 나쁘다면서요? (고혈압)
   B: 네. 고혈압에 의해서 손상됐어요. Yes. It was damaged by high blood pressure.

Chapter 6, page 106, exercise 8

1. 열심히 노력했지만 결과가 좋지 않게 나타나는 수 가 있다. Sometimes even when you work hard the results can turn out not so good.

2. 요즘같이 교통이 복잡할 때는 택시보다 지하철이 더 빠르는 수 가 있다. At times like recently when the traffic is congested, the subway can be faster than a taxi.

3. 복잡한 버스 안에서는 잘못해서 다른 사람의 발을 밟는 수 가 있다. On a crowded bus you can sometimes step on other people's feet by accident.

4. 시험 볼 때 당황하면 아는 문제도 틀리는 수 가 있다. If you get flustered when you're taking a test, sometimes you can miss questions you know the answer to.

5. 거짓말을 많이 하면 들키게 되는 수 가 있다. If you tell a lot of lies, you might get caught.

6. 일하지 않고 잘 사는 수 가 있다? Is it possible to live well without working?

7. A: 비행기 도착 시간이 10분이나 지났는데 왜 소식이 없지요?
   B: 날씨가 나쁘면 원래 도착 시각보다 늦게 도착하는 수 가 있다. When the weather is bad, planes can sometimes arrive later than their original arrival time.

8. A: 지난번엔 그 집을 못 찾아서 아주 고생했어요.
   B: 그 곳은 비슷한 곳이 많아서 주의 하지 않으면 길을 <u>잃어버리는 수 가 있다</u>. There are so many places that look similar there that if you aren't careful you can lose your way.

9. A: 김 선생님을 찾아 갔는데 못 뵈었어요.
   B: 바쁘신 분이라서 미리 약속을 하지 않으면 <u>못 만나는 수 가 있다</u>. He is a busy person so if you don't make an appointment in advance you might not be able to meet with him.

10. A: 이 과목은 꼭 하는 건가요?
    B: 학생이 너무 적으면 <u>취소되는 수 가 있다</u>. If there are too few students it might be cancelled.

11. A: 이 보약이 몸에 좋다는데 한번 먹어 볼까요?
    B: 체질에 맞지 않으면 오히려 해가 <u>되는 수 가 있다</u>. If it doesn't agree with your constitution it could actually be detrimental.

12. A: 믿을 수 있는 사람이니까 걱정 안 하셔도 돼요.
    B: 그러다가 믿는 도끼에 발등을 찍 <u>히는 수 가 있다</u>. However if you're not careful, you could be stabbed in the back. [속담!]

Chapter 6, page 106, exercise 9

1. 고장이 났는지 문이 잘 안 <u>닫아지는 데요</u>. Maybe the door is broken or something—it doesn't close.

2. 잉크가 <u>굳어져서</u> 쓸 수가 없어요. The ink has hardened so you can't use it to write.

3. <u>불이 꺼지고</u> 영화가 곧 시작 되었다. The lights went out and the movie started right away.

4. 잘 <u>써지는</u> 볼펜 있으면 좀 빌려 주세요. If you have a ballpoint pen that writes well will you lend it to me?

5. A: 한글은 언제 생겨났어요?
   B: 조선시대 때 <u>만들어졌어요</u>. It was made during the Chosŏn era.

6. A: 연세대학교가 언제 <u>세워졌어요</u>? When was Yonsei University established?
   B: 1885년에 언더우드라는 사람에 의해 <u>세워졌어요</u>. It was established in 1885 by a man named Underwood.

7. A: 티셔츠에 뭐라고 쓰여 있어요?
   B: 학교 티셔츠인데 오래 되어서 글씨 가 다 <u>지워졌어요</u>. It's a school T-shirt but it's so old that all of the writing has rubbed off.

8. A: 어디에서 모자를 잃어버리셨어요?
   B: 모르겠어요. 지하철 안에서 <u>벗겨졌나</u> 봐요. I don't know. I guess it must have come off in the subway.

9. A: 이 책은 언제 <u>써진</u> 책이에요? When was this book written?
   B: 이 책은 지금으로부터 100년 전에 <u>써진</u> 것이에요. This book was written 100 years ago.

Chapter 7, page 127, exercise 6

Part One

1. 들어오는 대로 전화해 달라고 전해 주 세요. Please tell her to call me as soon as she gets in.

2. 결정되는 대로 알려 줄게요. As soon as it's decided I'll let you know.

3. 보는 대로 빨리 연락하라고 전해 주세 요. As soon as you see her please tell her to contact me right away.

4. 침대에 눕는 대로 자 버려요. As soon as I lie down in bed I fall asleep.

5. 일이 끝나는 대로 집에 빨리 오세요. As soon as work finishes, hurry home.

6. 보는 대로 연락해 주세요. As soon as you see her, please contact us.

Part Two

1. 선생님이 시키시는 대로 하세요. Do as the teacher says.

2. 일을 끝내는 대로 갈 거예요. I'm going to go as soon as I finish work.

3. 아버지가 한국에서 도착하시는 대로 바로 이사 갈 예정입니다. We plan to move as soon as our father arrives from Korea.

4. 제가 부르는 대로 한 번 써 보세요. Please try writing it down according to how I say it.

5. 회의가 끝나는 대로 얼른 집에 와요. Come home as soon as the meeting is over.

6. 준비가 다 되는 대로 떠납시다. Let's leave as soon as all the preparations are finished.

7. 눈이 그치는 대로 출발할까요? Shall we depart as soon as the snow stops?

Chapter 7, page 127, exercise 7

1. 어제 하나도 못 잤어요. 언니하고 밤늦 게까지 이것저것에 대해서 이야기하 고 있었거든요. I couldn't sleep at all last night. I was talking with my older sister about this and that late into the night.

2. 요즘 너무 바빠서 죽겠어요. 지난 주일 에 개학을 했거든요. Lately I'm so busy it's killing me. It's because school started last week.

3. 손이 아파서 죽겠어요. 어제 다쳤 거든요. My hand is killing me. I hurt it yesterday.

4. 나는 바다에 가지 않고, 산에 갈래요. 수영을 못 하거든요. I'd rather go to the mountains than to the sea. I can't swim.

5. A: 아니, 손이 왜 이렇게 차가워요? Why are your hands so cold?

B: 밖이 춥거든요. It's cold outside.

6. 거기 가지 마세요. 위험하거든요. Don't go there. It's dangerous.

7. 요즘 매일 수영을 해요. 수영장이 우리 집에서 가깝거든요. Recently I've been swimming everyday. The pool's close to our house.

8. 따뜻한 옷을 가지고 가야 돼요. 산에서 는 날씨가 잘 변하거든요. I have to take warm clothes with me. The weather in the mountains often changes.

9. 비옷을 가지고 가야지. 금방 비가 쏟 아지는 일이 많거든. I have to take rain gear. Soon there will be many days of heavy rain.

10. 한자를 열심히 공부하고 있어요. 재미 있거든요. I'm studying Chinese characters diligently. It's interesting.

Chapter 7, page 128, exercise 8

1. 있잖아요! 쉿~ 비밀인데요... You know what? Shh~ it's a secret...

2. "왜 그거, 그거 있잖아" 등의 표현 이 늘어납니다. 당신도 초기 치매 환자군요. Expressions like "Well, you know—whatchamacallit" and the like are increasing. You're starting to sound like an Alzheimer's patient!

3. 시력 있잖아요. 제가 근시가 있었는데 난시가 생겼거든요. So, about my vision: I used to have myopia, but now I've got astigmatism.

4. 있잖아 비밀이야. [익명게시판] Know what? I've got a secret. [Anonymous bulletin board]

5. 있잖아요... 제가 인터넷에서 봤는 데... Guess what? I saw this thing on the Internet...

6. 있잖아요, 나무는요... So, you know, about this tree...

7. 저~ 있잖아요. Uhh..., you know what?

8. 입학 장학금 있잖아요~~ [경성대학 교 게시판] So, about entrance scholarships... [Kyŏngsŏng University bulletin board]

9. 왜 그럴 때가 있잖아요. 분위기가 한창 고조되는데 갑자기 남자의 어떤 말 때 문에... You know how there are times like this, right? The atmosphere is great, then suddenly because of something one guy says...

Chapter 8, page 140, exercise 8

1. 한국의 역사적 인물은 누구누구 아십 니까? Who all do you know from among historical figures of Korea?

2. 세계를 보는 관점은 주관적 입니다. Our view of the world is subjective.

3. 연구를 할 때는 데이터를 객관적으 로 해석해야 됩니다. When you are

doing research you have to analyze data objectively.

4. 구체적 예를 하나 주시겠습니까? Can you give a concrete example?

5. 피카소는 세계적으로 유명한 화가입니다. 어떤 사람들은 피카소의 그림이 추상적이라고 생각합니다. Picasso is a globally famous artist. Some people think his art is abstract.

6. 우리 한국어 선생님이 좀 보수적인 것 같지 않아요? Doesn't our Korean teacher seem a bit conservative?

7. A: 완전히 이해했습니까? Did you understand everything?
B: 아니오, 부분적으로만 이해했습니다. No, I only partially understood.

8. 너무 감정적으로 반응하지 말고 한 번 논리적으로 생각해 보세요. Don't react too emotionally, but try to think about it logically once.

9. 그분은 극적인 표현을 많이 쓰십니다. That person uses a lot of dramatic expressions.

10. 그 사람은 정신적으로 건강합니까? Is that person mentally healthy?

Chapter 11, page 168, exercise 6

1. A: 누가 문을 열어 주었습니까? Who opened the door for you?
B: 문이 열려 있어서 그냥 들어왔습니다. The door was open so I just came in.

2. A: 장사 잘 됩니까? Is business going well?
B: 네, 요즘은 더워서 음료수가 많이 팔립니다. Yeah, it's hot lately so drinks are selling well.

3. A: 선생님, 글씨가 작아서 안 보입니다. Teacher, the writing is too small to see.
B: 네, 좀 더 크게 써 줄게요. OK, I'll write it a little bigger.

4. A: 젓가락으로 음식을 먹습니까? Do you eat food with chopsticks?
B: 네, 먹기는 하는데, 젓가락으로 잘 안 집혀 먹기가 힘듭니다. Yes, I eat food with chopsticks, but nothing catches well with chopsticks so it is hard to eat with them.

5. A: 이게 무슨 소리입니까? What kind of sound is this?
B: 글쎄요, 바람 부는 소리처럼 들립니다. Well, it sounds like the wind blowing.

6. A: 어디로 여행 갈 겁니까? Where are you going to go on vacation?
B: 눈으로 덮인 설악산 쪽으로 갈까 합니다. I'm thinking of going to snow-covered Sŏraksan.

7. A: 너 나한테 잡히면 죽어. If you're caught by me I'll kill you.
B: 잡을 수 있으면 잡아 봐. Try to catch me if you can!

8. A: 고기가 질겨서 안 씹힙니다. The meat is tough and can't be chewed.
B: 이쪽에 있는 걸로 드십시오. Eat the pieces on this side.

9. A: 왜 집에 들어가지 않고 밖에 서 있습니까? Why are you just standing outside instead of going inside?
B: 문이 닫혀 있어서 못 들어갑니다. The door is shut so I can't go in.

10. A: 수미 씨, 내일은 일요일이니까 푹 쉬십시오. Sumi, tomorrow is Sunday so get a good rest.
B: 집에 할 일이 너무 많이 쌓여 있어서 쉴 수도 없습니다. There's so much to do piled up at home that I can't even rest.

11. A: 전화가 왜 이러지요? 자꾸 끊깁니다. What's up with the phone? It keeps getting disconnected.
B: 고장났다고 신고해야겠습니다. We'll have to report that it's broken.

12. A: 롯데 백화점에 가서 샀습니까? Did you go to Lotte Department Store and buy it?
B: 아니오, 롯데 백화점에 갔는데 문이 잠겨 있어서 신세계 백화점에 가서 샀습니다. No, I went to Lotte but it was closed ("the door was locked") so I went to Shinsegae Department Store and bought it there.

13. A: 아, 아파. Ouch, it hurts.
B: 왜 그럽니까? What's wrong?
A: 옆 사람한테 발을 밟혔어. I got my foot stepped on by the person next to me.

14. A: 보물이 어디에 있을까요? Where could the treasure be?
B: 저 바위 밑에 묻혀 있을 겁니다. It's probably hidden under that rock.

Chapter 14, page 202, exercise 4

1. 새벽까지 책을 읽다가 잤으니 지금 깨우지 마십시오. I read books until midnight and then went to sleep so don't wake me now.

2. 오빠가 무언가를 보고 있다가 내가 방에 들어갔더니 얼른 채널을 돌렸어요. My older brother was watching something or other but when I entered the room he quickly changed the channel.

3. 1 달 동안 써야 될 용돈을 하루만에 한 푼도 남기지 않고 다 써 버렸습니다. I spent my month's allowance in one day without leaving even a penny.

4. 요즘 봄이라서 그런지 입맛이 없으니까 입맛 돋우는 음식 좀 해 주세요. Maybe because lately it's spring or something, but I don't have much of an appetite, so please make some food that will increase my appetite.

5. 엄마, 우리 반 애들이 자꾸 나를 돼지라고 놀려요. Mom, the kids in my class keep teasing me and calling me a pig.

6. 수미 씨, 결혼할 때 꼭 알려 주세요. Sumi, please be sure to let me know when you get married.

7. 내일은 만우절이니까 친구들을 좀 속일 거예요. Tomorrow is April Fool's Day so I'm going to play tricks on my friends.

8. "보물찾기" 란 안 보이는 곳에 숨긴 물건을 찾는 게임입니다. "Treasure hunt" is a game where you search for things hidden in an unknown place.

9. 선영 씨, 음악 소리가 너무 큽니다. 소리 좀 줄여 주세요. Sŏnyŏng, the music is too loud. Turn it down a bit, please.

10. 매일 한 시간만 공부해서는 한국어를 잘 할 수 없습니다. 공부하는 시간을 좀 늘려야 합니다. Studying just an hour each day you can't speak Korean well. You have to increase your study time a little.

11. 요즘 좀 우울해. 어디 가서 웃기는 영화 보고 실컷 웃었으면 좋겠다. Lately I'm feeling a little depressed. It would be nice to go and see a funny movie and laugh to my heart's content.

12. 원숭이들도 바나나 먹을 때 껍질을 벗겨 먹습니까? Do monkeys also peel bananas when they eat them?

13. 돼지 저금통에 동전을 가득 채웠어요. I fill my piggy bank with coins.

14. 길이 좁아서 길이 많이 막히네요. 좀 넓혀야겠어요. The road is so narrow that the traffic is quite congested. They should widen it a bit.

15. 진수는 벌레를 무서워해서 그런지 바퀴벌레도 못 죽인대요. Maybe because Chinsu is afraid of bugs or something, but he says he can't even kill a cockroach.

16. 영진아, 너는 수준이 너무 높아서 우리가 따라가지를 못하겠다. 수준 좀 낮춰 주세요. Yŏngjin, your level is so high we can't follow along. Please lower it a little.

17. 정윤이가 전에도 비슷한 일을 많이 했으니까 이 일은 정윤이한테 맡겨야겠니다. Chŏngyun has done a lot of similar work before so I'll have to entrust this job to her.

18. 아기한테 뭘 먹여 줘서 아기가 이렇게 튼튼합니까? What do you feed the baby to make him so strong?

19. 8시에 출발하는 것은 무리입니다. 시간을 좀 늦춰야겠습니다. Leaving at 8 o'clock is going to be difficult. We'll have to delay the time a bit.

20. 이 성적표 집에 가서 어머니께 보여 드리고 여기에다 도장 받아 오십시오. Take this report home and show it to your mother, have her stamp here, and bring it back.

Chapter 16, page 219, exercise 2

1. 나 어제 남대문 시장에 옷 사러 갔었

다. 그런데 옷이 아주 <u>싼 것 있지</u>. I went to Namdaemun Market yesterday to buy clothes. But you know how clothes there are so cheap?

2. 어제 영화 보러 갔다가 못 보고 그냥 왔어. 표가 다 팔려서 <u>못 보고 온 거 있지</u>. I went to see a movie yesterday, but ended up coming back without seeing it. Wouldn't you know it—the tickets were all sold out.

3. 나 어제 야구 구경하러 갔다가 <u>비를 쫄딱 맞은 거 있지</u>. I went to watch baseball yesterday but wouldn't you know it—I was caught out completely in the rain.

4. 며칠 전에 길에서 우연히 희수 봤다. 그런데 걔가 나를 못 본 척하고 <u>간 거 있지</u>. A few days ago I ran into Hŭisu by chance in the street. But wouldn't you know it—she pretended not to see me and just kept going.

5. 아침에 일찍 일어나려고 하는데도 잘 <u>안 되는 거 있죠</u>. I keep trying to get up early in the morning but it just doesn't happen—you know what I mean?

6. 그 집 음식 값이 <u>너무 비싼 거 있지</u>. 계산하려고 값을 물어 보고 깜짝 놀랐어. That restaurant's food is so cheap, hey? I went to pay and asked the price and was quite taken aback.

Chapter 16, page 219, exercise 3

1. A: 진수가 제일 먼저 왔다면서요? I heard Chinsu was the first to come?
   B: 네, <u>걔가 좀 부지런합니까</u>? Yeah, is she hard-working or what?
   새벽부터 와서 짐 싸는 것부터 다 했어요. She came at the crack of dawn and did everything, starting with packing the bags.

2. A: 어디가 어딘지 하나도 모르겠습니다. I don't have a clue about where anything is.
   B: 서울이 좀 <u>많이 달라졌습니까</u>? Has Seoul really changed a lot, or what?

3. A: 지난 번 노래방에 갔을 때 철민 씨가 그렇게 인기 있었다면서요? I heard last time you went to *noraebang* Ch'ŏlmin was really popular?
   B: <u>노래를 좀 잘합니까</u>? Is he a good singer or what?

4. A: 어릴 때 언니랑 나랑 참 많이 싸웠

다, 그치? When we were little big sister and I fought a lot, didn't we?
   B: 그래, <u>좀 많이 싸웠니</u>? Boy, did you ever!

5. A: 정민이 때문에 기분 나빠 죽겠어요. 말하고 싶지 않은데 계속 이것저것 묻는 거예요. Because of Chŏngmin I'm so angry I could die. I didn't want to say anything but he kept asking me about this and that.
   B: 걔가 <u>원래 좀 못됐습어요</u>? Has he always been clueless or what?

6. A: 일요일 날 설악산에 갔다 왔더니 힘들어 죽겠습니다. On Sunday I went on a day trip to Sŏraksan and it was so tiring I could die.
   B: <u>좀 멉니까</u>. 그런데 당일치기로 갔다 왔습니까? Isn't that a bit far, or what? So you went there and back on the same day?

Chapter 16, page 220, exercise 5

6. A: 수미한테 빌리지 왜 샀습니까? You should have borrowed one from Sumi—why'd you buy one?
   B: 빌려 달라고 얘기했는데 <u>안 빌려 주더라고요</u>. 그래서 그냥 샀습니다. I asked her to lend me one, but she wouldn't. So I just bought one.

7. A: 영민이가 우리가 준 선물 보고 기뻐했어요? Was Yŏngmin pleased when he saw our present?
   B: 네, 아주 좋아했어요. 그리고 <u>몸에 딱 맞더라고요</u>. Yes, he was very happy. And it fit him perfectly.

8. A: 토마스 씨, 대학에서 공부하는 게 어때요? 말은 다 알아들어요? Thomas, how is studying at university? Do you understand everything?
   B: 아니요, 말이 빠르고 모르는 단어가 많아서 <u>못 알아듣겠더라고요</u>. No, they speak quickly and there is a lot of vocabulary I don't know so I can't understand it all.

9. A: 친구 애기 돌이라는데 뭘 사 가지고 가면 좋을까요? It is the first birthday of my friend's child; what should I buy to bring him?
   B: 옷이나 장난감 같은 게 어때요? 내 친구들 보니까 그런 거 많이 <u>사 가지고 가더라고요</u>. How about clothes or toys? Thinking of my friends, that's the

sort of thing people often bring along.

10. A: 어머, 선주야. 너 그 옷 어디서 샀니? 참 예쁘다. Say, Sŏnju—where did you buy those clothes? They're really pretty.
    B: 며칠 전에 요 앞 옷가게를 지나가는데 이게 밖에 <u>걸려 있더라고</u>. 마음에 들어서 샀어. A few days ago I was passing the clothes shop in front of here and these were hanging outside. I liked them so I bought them.

11. A: 선영아, 너 기분 좋은 것 보니까 남편이랑 화해한 모양이구나. Sŏnyŏng, you look like you're in a good mood; you must have made up with your husband.
    B: 응, 철민 씨가 잘못했다고 빌었어. 그래서 용서해 줬지, 뭐. Yeah, Ch'ŏlmin admitted he was wrong and apologised. So I forgave him.
    A: 그래서 부부싸움은 칼로 물 <u>베기라고 하더라고요</u>. That's why they say that lovers' quarrels are soon mended.

Chapter 17, page 231, exercise 5

1. 다음 주 일요일에 결혼을 합니다. I'm getting married next week.
   바빠도 꼭 와 주셨으면 합니다. However busy you might be I hope you can come.

2. 일이 다 끝나 가니까 저쪽에서 잠깐만 기다려 주셨으면 합니다. The work is almost finished, so would you be so kind as to wait a moment over there?

3. 돈 좀 빌려 주셨으면 합니다. Would you please be so kind as to lend me some money?

4. 여보세요, 과장님이십니까? 저 이영진인데요, 몸살이 나서 오늘 집에서 쉬었으면 합니다. Hello? Is that the kwajang? This is Yi Yŏngjin speaking. I've got a bad cold and am hoping I can rest at home today.

5. 작년 휴가 때는 바다로 갔으니까 이번에는 산으로 갔으면 합니다. Because we went to the ocean last year for our holiday, this time I'd like to go to the mountains.

6. 들어오는 대로 저희 집에 전화 좀 해 달라고 전해 주셨으면 합니다. Would you please be so kind as to ask him to call me at home as soon as he comes in?

Online Contents
www.tuttlepublishing.com/advanced-korean

PREFACE TO THE ONLINE CONTENTS
Advanced Korean and *Advanced Korean: Sino-Korean Companion*
www.tuttlepublishing.com/advanced-korean

Advanced Korean: Sino-Korean Companion by Ross King, Chungsook Kim, Jae Hoon Yeon and Don Baker, is an optional online companion volume to the textbook *Advanced Korean* by *Ross King, Chungsook Kim,* and *Jaehoon Yeon.* First, then, let us provide some background about *Advanced Korean. Advanced Korean* is an updated and improved version of 한국어 3, first published in 1986 by the (then) 민족문화연구소 or Research Center for Korean Culture at Korea University (고려대학교) in Seoul as part of their multilevel and multivolume textbook series. For more information on the old 한국어 3 and its reincarnation as *Advanced Korean,* please refer to the preface of the latter.

In addition to, and parallel with, the two volumes of *Advanced Korean,* Ross King, Chungsook Kim, and Donald Baker have developed the *Advanced Korean: Sino-Korean Companion* as an optional online supplement for learners wishing to commence the study of Chinese characters as they are used in Korean. The *Sino-Korean Companion* is designed to serve as a kind of "parallel universe" for *Advanced Korean*—it assumes a knowledge of the main texts, example sentences, vocabulary, and structural patterns introduced in *Advanced Korean,* and introduces five hundred Chinese characters (漢字, i.e., 한자, typically pronounced [한짜]) in their Korean readings with a view to helping students do two things: (1) improve their knowledge of and intuitions about Sino-Korean vocabulary in Korean and (2) teach themselves 한자 as they continue their lifelong journey of Korean language learning.

Most of the hard work in preparing both *Advanced Korean* and *Advanced Korean: Sino-Korean Companion* has been carried out by research assistants working with Ross King at the University of British Columbia (UBC). With specific respect to the *Sino-Korean Companion,* the three coauthors' contributions were as follows: Chungsook Kim was the lead author of the Korea University team that wrote the Main Texts and Example Sentences for each lesson in the original 한국어 3. Don Baker was responsible for the initial selection of Chinese

characters to be targeted for teaching in each of the twenty lessons. Ross King has modified the work of both Chungsook Kim and Don Baker slightly and is responsible for everything else. UBC graduate students Dafna Zur, Kiyoe Minami, and Sinae Park worked many hours on the Sino-Korean materials in the initial stages of the project. Most recently and most notably, Jung Hwang and especially Sunah Cho, Leif Olsen, and Cindy Chen put in many hours of work on the files and made numerous helpful suggestions on content and format. Moreover, several cohorts of UBC students have suffered through beta versions of the *Sino-Korean Companion* since 1995 when Ross King began developing the materials. The authors are grateful to all these students for their patience and feedback. Most recently, Sunny Oh, Yoon Chung, Mike Whale, and Andrew Pugsley of the 2005–2006 "Korean 300" cohort have caught numerous problems and errors in the beta files.

The authors also owe a debt of thanks to several colleagues who have published useful reference works and textbooks in recent years. Please refer to the preface of *Advanced Korean* for a more detailed list of sources consulted for that book, but here we wish to record our appreciation for the excellent but now out-of-print Myongdo textbooks, especially the *Intermediate Korean: Part I* volume, which has provided the inspiration for the Main Text in Lesson 6 on proverbs. The authors are also grateful for the existence of numerous study aids, manuals, learner dictionaries, and websites targeted toward Korean native speakers (see the section "Learning 한자: Methodological and Sociolinguistic Premises and Preliminaries" section below for some references), but we are especially grateful to two works in particular: Bruce Grant's classic *Guide to Korean Characters* and Choo and O'Grady's *Handbook of Korean Vocabulary.* Any serious student of Korean should own both of these books.

Finally, the authors wish to thank the Korea Foundation for the teaching materials development grant that funded this project at UBC.

References

Choo, Miho, and William O'Grady. 1996. *Handbook of Korean vocabulary: A resource for word recognition and comprehension.* Honolulu: University of Hawai'i Press.

Grant, Bruce K. 1979/1982. *A guide to Korean characters: Reading and writing* hangŭl *and* hanja. 2nd rev. ed. Elizabeth, NJ: Hollym.

Myongdo Language Institute, Franciscan Friars. 1977. *Intermediate Korean: Part I.* Seoul: Myongdo Language Institute.

About the Authors

Ross King completed his BA in linguistics and political science at Yale in 1983, then his MA (1985) and PhD (1991) in linguistics at Harvard. Currently he is professor of Korean and head of department in the Department of Asian Studies, University of British Columbia, Vancouver, Canada. His e-mail: ross.king@ubc.ca.

Chungsook Kim completed her BA in Korean language and linguistics at Korea University in 1984 and subsequently earned her MA (1986) and PhD (1992) from the same institution. Currently, she serves as professor in Korea University's Department of Korean Language and Literature. Her e-mail: kmjane@korea.ac.kr.

Donald Baker completed his PhD in Korean history in 1987 at the University of Washington. As a specialist in late Chosŏn history, thought, and religion, he deals with Sino-Korean and *hanmun* on a daily basis. His e-mail: don.baker@ubc.ca

MORE ABOUT THE ONLINE CONTENTS

About the Lessons

Each lesson consists of the following sections:

Main Text

Each lesson begins with a Main Text, the contents of which are identical to the Main Text of the corresponding lesson in *Advanced Korean*. However, any Sino-Korean vocabulary that has been introduced in previous lessons and/or in the current lesson is highlighted in **bold text**. Sometimes the Main Text is followed by one or more of the Example Sentences from the body of the corresponding lesson in *Advanced Korean*, in which case these sentences carry new Chinese characters meant to be learned in the current lesson. Here, too, any Sino-Korean items that are "fair game" for the learner are in bold.

New Vocabulary

The "New Vocabulary" section glosses only those words from the Main Text (and Example Sentences). The idea is to avoid a situation where the student of the *Sino-Korean Companion* is forever having to look up vocabulary in the back of *Advanced Korean*.

The fact that the Main Text (plus any Example Sentences) and New Vocabulary sections are identical between *Advanced Korean* and *Advanced Korean: Sino-Korean Companion* creates some unavoidable duplication between the two titles—somewhere along the lines of 6 to 8 percent of the total volume of each set of books. But this overlap—this creation of a "parallel universe"—is essential to the teaching philosophy of the book, for which see more in "Learning 한자: Methodological and Sociolinguistic Premises and Preliminaries" below.

새 한자 (New Chinese Characters)

This section lists, in order of appearance, the new Chinese characters to be learned in the current lesson. Each box contains all the essential information for each new character: 훈(訓) (Korean gloss or moniker); 음(音) (Korean pronunciation[s]); (rough) English meaning; total stroke count; radical, radical name, and rough English gloss as well as radical pronunciation (if it has one) and radical stroke count; information about the phonetic element hinting at the character's pronunciation (if there is one)—all rounded off by the radical stroke count plus number of remaining strokes to reach the total stroke count, e.g.:

病 (병)	훈음: 병들 병 뜻: disease; sickness 총획수: 10획 부수: 疒 (병질엄 sickness: 5획)	Phonetic 丙(병) 5 + 5 = 10획

`丶 一 广 广 疒 疒 疒 病 病 病`

새 부수 *(New Radicals)*

This section is identical in form to that of "새 한자 (New Chinese Characters)" above, but focuses on all the new radicals associated with the new Chinese characters to be learned.

Building Word Power with 한자

This section lists, in order of appearance, all new Chinese characters introduced in the lesson, followed by a list of words (primarily compounds or "binoms" that combine two or more Chinese characters, but occasionally a Chinese character and a native Korean element) that incorporate the Chinese character in question. Each list begins with Chinese character compounds, *both* components of which have been introduced in the current or previous lessons. Such compounds are always listed with the Chinese characters first, in **bold**, followed by the 한글 reading in parentheses. These "known" compounds are followed by additional compounds incorporating the Chinese character in question, but where the other character(s) is (are) unknown to the learner from this course. Thus, the word list for 病(병) just above (from Lesson 15) starts like this:

病院(병원)	hospital
傳染病(전염병) [−뼝]	contagious/communicable disease
重病(중병) [−뼝]	serious illness
...	
질병(疾病)	disease
병균(病菌)	(disease) germ
병환(病患)	sickness (hon.)

The assumptions are that students will memorize the new vocabulary items in bold and develop at least a passive acquaintance with the other compounds in each list. In this way, students should acquire a growing number of the fundamental building blocks of Sino-Korean vocabulary, as well as begin to develop intuitions about the structure of this huge sector of the Korean lexicon.

새 부수에 대하여 *(About the New Radicals)*

This section is formatted along the same lines as the "Building Word Power with 한자" sections, with two exceptions. Firstly, the characters introduced here are all radicals. If the radical in question is one of the many radicals that functions both as a radical and as an independent character, and if the character has not already been introduced in the "Building Word Power" section, then a list of compounds incorporating the character-cum-radical in question is given. Secondly, this section also presents any facts and tips about the radical deemed to be useful to the learner: whether or not the radical also functions independently as a character, any alternate shapes, information about the radical's Korean name, relationship to other characters, etc.

About the New Phonetics

This section repeats each of the new phonetic determinatives learned in the lesson and gives examples of other characters that contain the same phonetic. The numerous characters given here as illustrations *are not for memorization!* The point is to get into at least two habits: (1) analyzing Chinese characters into their constituent building blocks, which are often a radical and a phonetic; (2) taking advantage of the (admittedly imperfect) phonetic clues lurking in Chinese characters so as to facilitate the recognition and learning of other, graphically related characters. Our definition of a "phonetic" here is generous and includes both genuine core phonetic elements that rarely function anymore as independent characters on their own and entire freestanding characters that get rolled into new 한자 through the addition of another graphic element (usually a radical), all the while preserving the pronunciation of the original character. All together, this book alerts students to some 250 different phonetic elements, which, if mastered along the way, position the learner to acquire hundreds more characters at a discount.

New 한자 Combinations

This section brings together all the new Chinese character combinations in the lesson that consist of characters introduced thus far in the course—that is, all the compounds presented in **bold** typeface in the "Building Word Power with 한자" and "새 부

수에 대하여 (About the New Radicals)" sections. Understandably, this section tends to grow in size with each successive lesson, as the learner's repertoire of Chinese character building blocks grows.

한자 문장 연습 *(Practice Sentences)*

This section consists of 25–30 sentences exemplifying some (but by no means all) of the new vocabulary from the lesson—both **bold** combinations and otherwise. At a minimum, students should familiarize themselves with these practice sentences. But they are also advised to seek out more authentic examples-in-context on their own, especially for all the **bold** combinations in each lesson, using common web-based resources. Thus, a useful exercise, whether for use in a classroom setting or for learners using these materials on their own, is to seek out and translate into English another ten to twenty (or more) sentences by using (a) the search function in search engines like Google, Yahoo!, etc., or (b) online Korean-language corpora (말뭉치) like the 용례검색기 (Web-based Corpus Analysis Tool) at Korea University's 민족문화연구원 (http://corpus.korea.ac.kr/), the KAIST Concordance Program http://semanticweb.kaist.ac.kr/research/kcp/, or Yonsei University's 한국어사전 site (http://kordic.britannica.co.kr/sear_frame.asp?keyword=%20&keykind=all&sear_type=part). This latter resource is highly recommended: the site is fast, the words listed are all current and useful, and the example sentences (usually two per word) are excellent. We have taken many of the Practice Sentences from this site.

Supplementary Vocabulary

This is a (usually) one-page list of vocabulary items designed to aid students working their way through the 한자 practice sentences. Only items deemed difficult for an advanced-level learner or not already introduced in the body of the lesson are listed.

한자 연습 *(Practice)*

These pages give the student an opportunity to practice writing the new characters (and radicals) according to the correct stroke orders.

Reference Section

Korean-English New 漢字 Combinations Glossary
English Translations for Main Texts
漢字 Finder List
부수 (Radical) Finder List
List of Phonetics

Note that the "Reference Section" does not include any vocabulary glossaries other than a comprehensive listing of those Sino-Korean compounds where both component characters have been covered in the book. To include any more such alphabetized listings would have made the volumes exceedingly bulky, and any learner at the stage where he or she is undertaking the study of Sino-Korean should own a dictionary (whether paper or electronic) and be adept at using it.

About Contact Hours

Few Korean language programs in Anglophone universities include instruction in Chinese characters as a regular feature of their courses of study. Thus, the authors assume that most purchasers of this book will be using it for self-study. However, in the case of adoption of this book as a textbook for a course, and assuming that most university Korean language courses in the United States, Canada, United Kingdom, Australia, and New Zealand meet four or five hours per week, the authors would recommend covering one lesson for every six to ten classroom hours. The ideal situation would be to take this course either in tandem with a separate course based on just *Advanced Korean*, or after first completing *Advanced Korean* or a course similar to it in coverage of vocabulary and grammatical patterns. But the authors recognize that different students and different courses proceed at different paces; certainly it would be an achievement to complete all twenty lessons during the course of a typical two-semester school year.

About Vocabulary

This textbook introduces a lot of vocabulary: some two thousand items in all in just the case of **bold** Sino-Korean combinations. The authors are skeptical of approaches to introducing vocabulary based on statistical frequency lists, since these frequency lists are never based on the vocabulary needs of university students, businessmen, or adult Anglophone learners of Korean in all their diversity. This book includes many sophisticated adult, intellectual vocabulary items—some more immediately useful than others—but all the sorts of words that mature, educated Korean adults know and that mature, educated learners of Korean as a foreign language would likely want to be able to produce (or at least recognize) once they have reached an "advanced" level in Korean and have begun to learn Chinese characters. Furthermore, since Korean does not give the English speaker as many shortcut vocabulary "freebies" as does French or Spanish or German, it is a hard fact of life that students need to spend more time on vocabulary building, and this is precisely the point of this book: to provide advanced learners with the fundamentals of Chinese characters with a view to building vocabulary.

It is also the view of the authors that some vocabulary items cost more than others to learn. This view is reflected in the layout of the vocabulary sections, where certain words are indented beneath others to indicate that these items are related to the main vocabulary item in question, and thus cost less to learn.

Other features of the vocabulary sections to be born in mind are these: (1) all verb bases are given in the special notation introduced in King & Yeon's *Elementary Korean*; (2) processive and descriptive bases are distinguished from each other by their English glosses—descriptive verbs are always preceded by *be* (e.g. be blue, be sad), while processive verbs are not.

About the English Translations and Glosses

In a number of cases the English translations of Korean expressions and patterns are structured to resemble as closely as possible the Korean meaning. In some cases, students and teachers may feel that certain English renditions are not typical English usage. The authors ask for indulgence on this matter.

Abbreviations used in This Book

hon	honorific
lit.	literally
pron.	pronounced
sb	somebody
sth	something

About Linguistic Symbols

Our use of linguistic symbols amounts to a special kind of code which is designed to streamline the learning process for the student, and to streamline the book presentation. Once the teacher and students have mastered the few simple symbols below, they should have no trouble following the exposition in the book.

SYMBOL	COMMENTS
–	The dash is used to demarcate boundaries and bound forms. Because the abstract Korean verb stems (we call them bases) to which students must attach endings are all bound forms (that is, they cannot be used and do not occur in real speech without some ending), verbs in each lesson's Vocabulary List are listed as a base, that is, as a bound form, followed by a dash to its right (e.g., 사−ㄹ− *live*). The same goes for all verb endings in Korean—they are abstract notions which only occur in Korean when attached to a verb base; they are bound forms, and always appear in the book with a dash to their left.
+	The plus sign means "plus" or "added to / in combination with."
[...]	Phonetic notations are enclosed by square brackets. This notation is used to indicate the actual pronunciation of a Korean form when this is not indicated in the Korean orthography. Another usage of the square brackets is to indicate optional material.
*	The asterisk is used to mark grammatically unacceptable utterances.
→	This arrow sign means "becomes/gives/yields/produces."
←	This arrow sign means "comes from / is a product of / derives from."
~	The tilde is used to represent an alternation, and means *in alternation with*. It is also used to indicate "insert here" in glossary phrase definitions and the 한글 portion of a Sino-Korean blend, such as 말문 (~門).

LEARNING 한자:
Methodological and Sociolinguistic Premises and Preliminaries

If the field of Korean language pedagogy (한국어 교육) as a whole is still rather young and lacking in a wide variety of teaching materials for the Anglophone learner, the question of Chinese character education (한자교육) within Korean language education is even more under-researched, under-theorized, and simply unprovided for. This *Sino-Korean Companion* hopes to become a useful resource for the Anglophone learner commencing the study of Chinese characters and their substantial role in Korean.

But because this particular subfield of Korean language pedagogy has been so neglected, and in particular because of the significant changes in the sociolinguistic status of Chinese characters in South Korea in the past generation or two, it is necessary—both for the authors and for any potential users of the book (whether as learners or as teachers)—to disclose here the main premises that underlie the design and structure of this *Sino-Korean Companion*.

First Things First: 한문 vs. 한자

Common Korean parlance makes no clear distinction between the concepts 한문(漢文) and 한자 (漢字). Technically speaking, the former should be reserved for the meanings of "Classical Chinese" or "Literary Sinitic" as a separate linguistic code, i.e., as a separate language—the cosmopolitan written language that bound together the "Chinese character cultural sphere" or 한자문화권(漢字文化圈) in premodern times. Properly speaking, the term 한자 should be reserved for the individual graphic units themselves—the Chinese characters divorced from any particular language. In spoken Korean, it is not unusual for a Korean to ask a Korean language learner huddled over a 한자 manual, "아, 한문도 배우세요?" And it is not difficult to encounter even well-educated Koreans who are convinced that a good knowledge of 한자 is equivalent to knowing 한문. Nothing could be further from the truth!

This seemingly harmless conceptual muddle has very real (and pernicious) consequences for Chinese character education, both for Koreans themselves and for non-Koreans learning Korean. For Koreans themselves, this muddle has led to a situation where the boundaries between Classical Chinese, Sino-Korean holophrase (whole strings plucked from Classical Chinese with the odd concession to Korean in the form of a particle or two), and Chinese characters become blurred, as school curricula and extracurricular cram school programs alike teach a mishmash of Chinese character-based materials, including the 천자문(千字文) (*Thousand Character Classic*), stock phrases and famous quotations (from, say, Mencius and Confucius), and 한시(漢詩) (Chinese poetry). This is confusing enough for Korean schoolchildren, but creates even more confusion if carried over to the teaching of Chinese characters to non-Koreans still learning Korean.

So let us be clear about our purpose here: this book teaches the basics of Chinese characters (한자), not 한문. Except for just two or three common 한자-based proverbs in Lesson 6, the focus throughout is on individual Chinese characters as they function in Korean word-building (in particular, on how they participate in creating binoms composed of two Chinese characters).

Chinese Characters in Korean: Why Bother?

Travel to either North or South Korea today, and you will see little evidence of extensive usage of Chinese characters around you in daily life. In North Korea, you will be hard put to find any Chinese characters at all in daily life, and such has been the case since the late 1940s. In South Korea today, the odd newspaper or current events magazine (typically those of a more conservative, right-wing persuasion) still uses (some) Chinese characters, as do many academic publications in the humanities, but the impression is that one can easily get by without knowing them. So the obvious question is, why bother? Here are some reasons.

The tradition

Korea and Koreans have been using Chinese characters for more than two millennia. Educated Koreans have always been well grounded in Chinese characters, right up to the present day. Anybody wishing to access written materials from South Korea before the mid-1980s, and from anywhere in Korea before 1945, needs to know a *lot* of Chinese characters. (Needless to say, anybody wishing to access the written culture of Korea before 1910 also needs to know 한문.)

Korean schools (North and South) and your peers

Assuming that you, the reader, are a university-educated adult, your peers in both North and South Korea have finished obligatory middle and high school curricula that include the study of at least 1,800 Chinese characters. Hat'ori (1991: 267–268) shows that while the banishing of Chinese characters from everyday publications in North Korea started as early as the end of 1946, Chinese character education was revived there as early as 1953, starting with grade 5, and has consistently trained North Korean schoolchildren in a total of some 1,800 characters. South Korean Chinese character education has been less consistent, with a few years here and there when they were dropped from school curricula, but on the whole (and still today), South Korean high school graduates have had to master some 1,800 Chinese characters.

한글 orthography

Few Korean language textbooks for foreigners ever devote much space to the incredibly important issues of orthography and spelling, and when they do, they might reveal that 한글, as a true alphabet, could theoretically be written in 가로풀어쓰기 fashion, i.e., linearly. In other words, the possibility has always existed for, say, a word like 한글 to be written as ㅎㅏㄴㄱㅡㄹ. So why has Korean never adopted an orthography like this? Because of Chinese characters. The practice of 모아쓰기 or grouping individual 한글 letters into syllables is both an emulation of the graphic shape of Chinese characters and a provision to allow Chinese characters and 한글 syllables to be mixed in the same text.

But Korean orthography assumes a knowledge (however vague) of Chinese characters and their Sino-Korean pronunciations and in yet another fundamental way. Korean spelling is etymologically based, meaning it attempts, wherever possible, to render transparent graphically the etymology and/or grammatical analysis of the words being written. If Korean writing and spelling were truly "phonetic"—as naive observers often claim—we would expect spellings like 구거, 궁문, and 국자 for what are spelled 국어 (國語 *national language*), 국문 (國文 *national writing system*), and 국자 (國字 *national written graphs/letters*). Chinese characters, and the assumption that Koreans are aware of them (even if they cannot write them), always lurk just beneath the surface of Korean spelling.

Chinese characters in the East Asian twenty-first century

While it was always well known that Chinese characters and Sino-xenic (Sino-foreign) word formation played formative roles in the historical development of the languages (especially their vocabularies) of the Sinitic sphere (Chinese, Japanese, Korean, and Vietnamese for our purposes), for much of the twentieth century there existed a strain of wishful thinking that saw Chinese characters as a thing of the past, doomed eventually to fade away in the face of technological progress and modernization. This same wishful thinking has been behind attempts at script reform in China (the pinyin movement, simplified characters), Japan (the romaji and kana movements, reduction of number of characters taught in schools), and the Koreas (successful banishment from public life in North Korea, mixed results in South Korea). Only Vietnam, it would seem, has weaned itself off Chinese characters even in its education system, but a huge percentage of the Vietnamese lexicon is Sino-Vietnamese in origin, and there are indications that Chinese characters and Chinese character education are making a comeback even in Vietnam.

The closing decades of the twentieth century and the first decade of the twenty-first have witnessed developments that have conspired to strengthen rather than weaken the importance of Chinese characters in Korea and Japan (and even Vietnam). One is technology itself. Whereas in the old days, one had to know how to write a Chinese character in order to include it in a (handwritten) document, today Chinese character-savvy word processing software allows users to insert Chinese characters at the push of a button (although one still needs to choose the correct one out of a list). The same pieces of software allow one to ascertain the vernacular readings of characters one has forgotten (or never learned). Instead of hastening the demise of Chinese characters, computer technology has given them a new lease on life.

Another development has been a growing anxiety over the severed connection with tradition. For example, when in 1999, the South Korean Kim Daejung regime announced a new (and controversial) policy of 한자병용(漢字倂用) or parallel use of 한글 and Chinese characters (with 한자 in parentheses) in official government documents and public road signs, President Kim was quoted as saying that "if we ignore Chinese characters, we will have trouble understanding our classics and traditions." This policy met with shrill opposition in certain quarters, and some cynical critics accused the septuagenarian president and his septuagenarian prime minister, Kim Jong-pil, of being out of touch with the new times and the younger "한글 generations."

But vociferous opposition to anything 한자-related in South Korea seems increasingly confined to a minority of scripto-nationalists inclined to see the world in black and white: 한글 = Korean/native = good; 한자 = Chinese (and Japanese)/foreign = bad. Meanwhile, yet another series of developments has led increasing numbers of (South) Koreans to invest time and money in learning Chinese characters: both the ongoing discourses of 세계화(世界化 *globalization*) and 국제화(國際化 *internationalization*) initiated by the Kim Young-sam regime in the early 1990s, and the very tangible effects of these two processes, however one wishes to understand them. For South Koreans, it is all about the rise of East Asia in the twenty-first century. Already in the 1990s, improved relations between South Korea and Japan, and especially the opening up of South Korea to Japanese cultural imports, led to a boom, for example, in Koreans studying Japanese—and therefore rediscovering no small amount of utility in going back to review 한자. More than anything else, though, it has been the rise of China in the East Asian and world economies that has convinced South Koreans of the need for Chinese characters,

and this trend seems likely to continue unabated in the foreseeable future. Nearly everybody is learning 한자 in South Korea these days.

The Korean lexicon

Finally, a simple statistic. Depending on which experts and which dictionaries one consults, Sino-Korean words—Korean words that traditionally have Chinese characters associated with them and which can, in principle, be written in 한자 instead of 한글—comprise anywhere from a minimum of 60 percent to a maximum of 75 percent of the Korean lexicon.

Which Characters to Learn, How Many, When, and How?

As simple as these questions may seem, they are in fact complex, and we would claim that there is no one correct answer to each of them. Instead, we can only offer responses based on our own experience learning and teaching Chinese characters in an Anglophone context.

Which 한자 should be taught first?

It doesn't really matter. To be certain, Lesson 1 should not contain a barrage of complex characters composed of umpteen stroke orders, nor should an introductory book like this focus inordinately on low-frequency 한자 that do not participate in extensive word formation. Thus, we have tried to include, on the whole, 한자 with relatively fewer strokes, of relatively high frequency that can be found as constituent components of numerous other Sino-Korean vocabulary items.

Some Korean language educators might maintain that a course like this should follow some standardized list like, for example, the first few hundred Chinese characters learned by South Korean schoolchildren in the official government-approved curriculum, or that it should adhere to some other ranked listing like, for example, those of the various 한자능력시험(漢字能力試驗) or Chinese character proficiency exams popular these days in South Korea. We reject any such notion for the simple reason that the users of these materials are not South Koreans.

Instead, the approach used here is systematic in its own way, based on the notion that the learner is starting with materials he or she has already seen—the "parallel universe" with *Advanced Korean*. In other words, we have tried to avoid a learning environment where absolutely everything encountered—vocabulary, Chinese characters, politico-historical and cultural context, and structural patterns—is new and overwhelming. The learner will quickly acquire a solid basis in Chinese characters as well as the confidence and tools to tackle more advanced Sino-Korean materials on his or her own.

How many 한자 should an introductory course teach?

Because it is well known that Korean high school graduates are required to learn some 1,800 Chinese characters, and given the need for non-Korean learners to somehow "catch up" or "make up for lost time" in comparison to the educated native speaker models they are encouraged to emulate, one often encounters a rushed, "cramming" approach to Chinese character education; the more the better, and the quicker the better. Our book, though, is in no rush. Our teaching experience suggests that 500 한자 over the course of two semesters is a reasonable number, especially if the focus of learning is just as much on the associated vocabulary and vocabulary-building strategies as it is on the Chinese characters themselves. Any learner who masters the 500 한자 in this book will be well placed to go on and master another 1,500 on his or her own.

When is the best time for the Anglophone learner to start learning 한자?

Here again, one finds different approaches. For example, Rogers et al.'s *College Korean* (1992), the UC-Berkeley elementary Korean textbook, starts introducing about six to ten Chinese characters each lesson with Lesson 7, for a total of 142 in this first-year course. But it is difficult to imagine a good pedagogical reason for introducing Chinese characters in the first year of a Korean language course, even if one makes this portion "optional," as the Berkeley authors do. Our view is this: native speakers of Korean in the two Koreas do not start learning 한자 until elementary school (sometimes later), after they have already mastered all the basic patterns and vocabulary of their native tongue. Moreover, when

they begin to learn Chinese characters, they are, for the most part, learning the 한자 for Korean words that *they already know*. The authors of this book are by no means claiming that L2 ("foreign") learners of Korean should somehow follow a language-acquisition trajectory identical to that of an L1 ("native speaker") learner, but it seems eminently reasonable to hold off until at least the intermediate level—i.e., until after two years of non-intensive or one year of intensive instruction—before tackling 한자. In this way, the learner is guaranteed a minimum comfort zone and at least a modicum of that "Hey, I know this word already, but didn't know it was Sino-Korean" feeling. In short, non-Korean learners of Korean have their hands full as it is; let's hold off on Chinese characters until they know the basics, and embed the 한자 in texts simple enough to allow the learners to focus on the 한자.

How should 한자 be taught?

Simple: analytically and without mystification. Thus, students need to learn from the very beginning that the vast majority of Chinese characters are composed of two elements: a semantic determinative and a phonetic determinative. The semantic determinatives, also known as semantic classifiers, are usually referred to, somewhat inaccurately, as "radicals," and provide a very general idea as to the meaning of the character concerned. The phonetic determinative ("phonetic" for short, usually called 기본음 *basic reading* or 성부 *phonetic element*, in Korean), by contrast, gives a hint as to the pronunciation of the character. Learners of Korean, in particular, are well served by attention to phonetic determinatives because of the conservative nature of Sino-Korean phonology. Thus, Korean language learners get more mileage out of paying attention to the phonetic determinatives than do learners of Mandarin or Japanese, and this book introduces some 250 of them.

For example, in Lesson 1 the student encounters this character: 공부 課 (과). This character is composed of the "speech radical" 言 plus the phonetic element 果 (과), a component that shows up in other characters like 菓, 顆, 堁, etc. The beginning learner of 한자 need not learn these other characters, but benefits from knowledge of the high probability that any character with the element 果 in it is likely pronounced [과]. To put it another way:

> The failure [in Chinese writing] to develop a standardized set of syllabic signs, together with the elevation of the radicals to the position of key elements in the filing of characters in dictionaries, have combined to create a system whose complexity masks a partial regularity. (DeFrancis 2002: 11)

The partial regularity DeFrancis alludes to lies in the phonetic determinatives, and this partial regularity is at its most robust in Sino-Korean (compared to Mandarin or Japanese). So one noteworthy feature of this book is that it points out phonetic elements whenever possible.

How Is This Book Different from Others?

The ideographic myth

For starters, we differ from traditional accounts in eschewing any reference to Chinese characters as "pictograms" or "ideograms." As Boltz (2003: 34) points out, Chinese characters with pictographic origins comprise only a tiny fraction of the total number, and we see little utility in perpetuating what many scholars have come to designate as the "ideogram" myth: as DeFrancis (2002: 3) and Unger (1990: 395–396), among others, have shown, "ideogram" is a concept dreamed up by Westerners and taken over from them in last century or so by the Chinese, Japanese, and Koreans. Erbaugh (2002: 24) is unequivocal on this point: "Invoking the ideographic myth should by now be as embarrassing as the flat earth hypothesis."

Our book also differs from traditional approaches in its attitude toward the typological classification of Chinese characters. Most 한자 textbooks start by teaching about the 六書(육서)—the Six Categories or "six [forms of] script"—a typology of Chinese characters that dates back to the last decades of the first century BC (see Boltz 2003: 143–149). While there is no harm in knowing about this as cultural history, it has little pedagogical value today. So here they are (from Boltz 2003: 143–149),

指事 (지사): "indicating the matter"
象形 (상형): "representing the form"
形聲 (형성): "formulating the sound"
會意 (회의): "conjoining the sense"

轉注 (전주): "revolved and re-directed [graphs]"
假借 (가차): "loaned and borrowed [graphs]"

As Erbaugh (2002: 47) notes, two of these six traditional categories reinforce the ideographic myth: (1) characters categorized under the 指事 (지사) "indicating the matter" category such as 上 (상) *up; on* and 下 (하) *down; under*, and (2) the so-called 象形 (상형) or "pictograph" characters like 日 (일) *sun* and 月 (월) *moon*.

Thus, rather than reinforce an ideographic myth that mystifies and orientalizes Chinese characters with little or pedagogical payoff, we stick to an analytic approach. Of course, any "tricks," visuals, or mnemonic devices that can aid a learner in remembering the characters are fair game; but they are just that—tricks—and not an inherent feature of Chinese writing.

Lists vs. "readers"

The study materials found in the online files differ somewhat in format from the materials in Sino-Korean textbooks currently on the market, which are all in "reader" format with numerous short "canned" (inauthentic) texts carrying the Chinese characters to be learned, followed by various short exercises. Our materials also feature lessons that start with a "canned" text, but our Main Texts are previously studied texts from a "parallel universe." Moreover, our lessons feature numerous lists structured so as to maximize vocabulary learning. We also encourage learners to use online resources to seek out authentic examples-in-context of the Sino-Korean vocabulary they are learning.

The point of this book's emphasis on vocabulary lists is this: the focus is not so much on learning individual 한자 as it is on acquiring intuitions about webs of interconnected vocabulary that 한자 help create. These networks of vocabulary items are more important than the individual characters, and in Korean, especially, they are more important than being able to write the individual characters: i.e., it is more important to have an appreciation of the different words that include 나라 國 (국) *nation, country* in them—and be able to reproduce them in just 한글—than it is to be able to reproduce the Chinese character 國 itself. In other words, "knowing how a character is written has very little value in the modern Korean society" (Kim 2001:

ii), but all learners of Korean, benefit from learning the written form of the Chinese characters as part of the vocabulary-building process.

The questions of authenticity and target audience

"Authenticity" is a key concept in language education these days. The more "authentic" teaching materials are, and the more advanced learners become, the more desirable it is to base pedagogy on authentic teaching materials. But what does it mean to use "authentic" materials for a beginning course in Sino-Korean? And who are the learners wanting to learn Chinese characters in their Korean readings? In earlier days, when Chinese characters had greater visibility in South Korean print culture, the answer to the authenticity question was easy: use newspaper articles and editorials and/or academic materials. But current events articles, editorials, and academic materials quickly grow outdated, and in any case, nowadays fewer and fewer newspapers use Chinese characters; even academic materials tend to use them much less, or else employ parallel 한글 (漢字) or 漢字(한글) formats.

As for the target audience question, Anglophone Korean language students today are different from the tiny handful of students in the 1980s who were the intended consumers of books like Lukoff (1982/1989) and Francis Park (1984). Lukoff's book, with its 1,200 한자, was academically focused and targeted at rather specialized, typically nonheritage, Korean studies students who, if they weren't already graduate students, were likely considering graduate school and/or otherwise needed training in academic Korean with a heavy Sino-Korean focus. And Park's book, with a staggering 1,554 different 한자, was designed originally for intensive in-country training courses for Maryknoll missionaries. But nowadays both the numbers and diversity of Anglophone Korean language learners have increased dramatically, making it more difficult to pinpoint with any accuracy appropriately "authentic" materials for learning 한자.

The upshot of all this, we would claim, is that it makes no sense to worry about the "authenticity" of one's reading texts in a course like this, as long as they help the student learn 한자 and build the student's vocabulary. (On the other hand, this *Sino-Korean Companion* is an ideal springboard for students who, on completion of the course, want to work with materials like the Lukoff or Park books.)

Given then, that "authenticity" is a pie in the sky for a beginning 한자 textbook, we have adopted one more unauthentic convention in the Main Texts for each lesson. Because this is a beginning course with a closed and (relatively) manageable set of 한자, it is easy to track which 한자 are known and which are not with the vocabulary items in each Main Text. Sometimes, then, it can happen that a binom (e.g., 선조 ancestor(s) and 생활 life in Lesson 6) contains one character either previously learned or targeted for learning in the current lesson, and another which has not been studied yet. In cases like this, we apply a "mix-and-match" format: 先조 and 生활. By Lesson 6, the students have already learned 먼저 先 (선) and 날 生 (생), so why not write at least these characters that they know, and allow for some review? The point is to constantly analyze out the 한자 building blocks of the Korean lexicon. That such an ad hoc orthographic practice might jar the traditionally educated Korean native speaker's eye is of little consequence.

Writing the characters

On the other hand, it *is* authentic, in a Korean cultural context, to de-emphasize the ability to write from memory every character one has ever learned. Highly educated Koreans with significant Sino-Korean reading abilities, able to recognize hundreds of Chinese characters rarely, if ever, show the apparent shame often displayed by educated speakers of Chinese or Japanese when they slip up on or forget how to write a Chinese character. "Horrors!" they say. But the Korean's reaction is a shrug and a dismissive "Whatever—we've got 한글, the world's greatest writing system ever!"

Having said this, it is nonetheless important to learn both the correct strokes and the proper stroke orders and to practice writing the characters, and provisions are made for this in the *Sino-Korean Companion*. To that end, we also give here some general guidelines on basic strokes and stroke-order.

<u>The Eight Basic Strokes as Exemplified by 길 永 (영)</u>

Just as one can analyze out and distinguish different strokes in, say, English cursive handwriting or in shorthand, it is possible to distinguish a number of strokes basic to the writing of Chinese characters. One traditional method for teaching the most basic stroke types is called 永字八法(영자팔법), i.e., the "eight ways [of writing] of the Chinese character 永." Technically speaking, this character has a total stroke count of five:

永 永 永 永 永

But from a calligraphic point of view, it actually has eight hand motions, all of which are basic to the writing of Chinese characters (and each of which has a name, for the real calligraphy buffs—for details, see 위키백과 or the Korean Wikipedia, whence the image below):

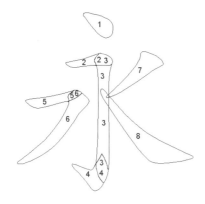

<u>General Guidelines for 한자 Stroke Order</u>

Once you know the basic hand strokes, you need to remember a few basic rules of thumb for stroke order. And don't worry—each new character in the book is accompanied by a stroke-by-stroke breakdown of the stroke order.

 Top to Bottom
(↓) e.g., 오얏 李 (이 / –리):

一 十 オ 木 杢 李 李

Left to Right
(→) e.g., 쉴 休 (휴):

ノ イ 仁 什 休 休

Horizontal before Vertical
(→↓) e.g., 열 十 (십):

Principles 1–3 are the most fundamental principles of stroke order and can be supplemented by the following four additional guidelines.

When Left and Right Are Mirror Images, Start in the Middle
e.g., 작을 小 (소):

丿 小 小

In Characters with Enclosed Elements, Start with the Enclosure
e.g., 한 가지 同 (동):

丨 冂 冃 冃 同 同

Vertical Strokes That Pierce through the Middle Come Last
e.g., 가운데 中 (중):

丨 冂 口 中

"Pedestals" May Be Written First or Last
i. Pedestals that always get written first: 走, 是
e.g., 제목 題 (제):

口 日 旦 是 是 是 題 題 題 題

ii. Pedestals that always get written last: 夂, 辶
e.g., 통할 通 (통):

ㄱ マ 孑 甬 甬 甬 甬 涌 通 通

Chinese Character Resources for Ambitious Students

Clearly, Chinese characters are a vast topic and require a huge investment of time and effort. This *Sino-Korean Companion* will provide a useful grounding in the basics. Those learners who want to supplement this book and/or go beyond it are encouraged to use some of the many useful books and electronic resources dedicated to the study of 한자.

First, books. As mentioned above, every student of Korean should own a copy of Bruce Grant's *Guide to Korean Characters*. Every student should also own a handy pocket 옥편 or Chinese character dictionary for Koreans; one of our favorites is the 동아 신 활용옥편. Lukoff (1982/1989) and Park (1984; 2000) make good follow-ons to the *Sino-Korean Companion*, and Whitlock and Suh (2001), while pricey and bulky, contains many useful mnemonic devices for memorizing characters. Kim (2001) is another useful resource that shares with us the conviction that knowledge of 한자 is empowering in numerous ways.

But the best resources for 한자 are all electronic and are too many to list here. A quick Google search in 한글 for "한자" will yield numerous South Korean sites in South Korea. We particularly appreciate the following sites:

"한자통" (http://www.hanjatong.com/)
"이야기 한자여행" (http://hanja.pe.kr/)
"존 한자사전" (http://www.zonmal.com/)
 Naver Hanja Dictionary (http://hanja.naver.com)
"OK 한문" (http://www.ok-hanmun.net/)
"맛있는 한자" (http://www.yamhanja.com/)
"한자닷컴" (http://www.hanja.com/)
 (a kids' site, but cute)
"한자야닷컴" (http://www.hanjaya.com/)
 (another good kids' site)
"공자맹자왈" (http://www.e-hanja.com)

Finally, users of this book are encouraged to navigate their way to the UBC Korean language program website at http://www.korean.arts.ubc.ca/ for its web-based Chinese character learning tool for students of Chinese, Japanese, and Korean that incorporates all of the features of this book, plus many more. The site can also be found at www.ubccjk.com, is best viewed in Mozilla/Firefox, and, at the time of writing, is being developed for an iPhone app.

References

Boltz, William. 2003. *The origin and early development of the Chinese writing system.* American Oriental Series 78. New Haven, CT: American Oriental Society.

Cho, Choon-Hak, Yeon-Ja Sohn, and Heisoon Yang. 2002. *Korean reader for Chinese characters.* KLEAR Textbooks in Korean Language. Honolulu: University of Hawai'i Press.

DeFrancis, John. 2002. The ideographic myth. In *Difficult characters: Interdisciplinary studies of Chinese and Japanese writing*, ed. Mary S. Erbaugh, 1–20. Columbus, OH: National East Asian Language Resource Center, Ohio State University.

Erbaugh, Mary S. 2002. How the ideographic myth alienates Asian Studies from psychology and linguistics. In *Difficult characters: Interdisciplinary studies of Chinese and Japanese writing*, ed. Mary S. Erbaugh, 21–52. Columbus, OH: National East Asian Language Resource Center, Ohio State University.

Hat'ori, Reikko [Hattori Reiko]. 1991. Pukhan ŭi hanja kyoyuksa [History of Chinese character education in North Korea]. In *Pukhan ŭi chosŏnŏ yŏn'gusa*, vol. 2, ed. Kim Minsu, 266–290. Seoul: Nokchin.

Jorden, Eleanor. 2002. Teaching Johnny to read Japanese: Some thoughts on Chinese characters. In *Difficult characters: Interdisciplinary studies of Chinese and Japanese writing*, ed. Mary S. Erbaugh, 92–104. Columbus, OH: National East Asian Language Resource Center, Ohio State University.

Kim, Kye-Chong. 2001. *ShipBai SaJun-I.* New York: Han Sung Group.

King, Ross. 2005. Introductory-level Korean language textbooks for the Anglophone adult learner: A survey of three recent publications. *Journal of Korean Studies* 10, no. 1: 145–190.

Lukoff, Fred. 1982/1989. *A first reader in Korean writing in mixed script.* Seoul: Yonsei University Press.

Park, Francis Y. T. 1984. *Speaking Korean, book III: A guide to Chinese characters.* Elizabeth, NJ: Hollym International.

———. 2000. *Speaking Korean, book IV: A guide to newspaper editorials.* Elizabeth, NJ: Hollym International.

Rogers, Michael C., Clare You, and Kyungnyun K. Richards. 1992. *College Korean* [Taehak Han'gugŏ]. Berkeley: University of California Press.

Tusan Tong'a Sasŏ P'yŏnjipkuk. 1975/2003. *Tonga sin hwaryong okp'yŏn.* [Tonga new practical okp'yŏn]. 2nd edition. Seoul: Tusan Tong'a.

Unger, J. Marshall. 1990. The very idea: the notion of ideogram in China and Japan. *Monumenta Nipponica* 45, no.4: 391–411.

———. 1991. Memorizing *kanji*: Lessons from a pro. In *Schriftfestschrift: Essays on writing and language in honor of John DeFrancis*, ed. Victor Mair, 49–58. Philadelphia: Department of Oriental Studies, University of Pennsylvania.

———. 2004. *Ideogram: Chinese characters and the myth of disembodied meaning.* Honolulu: University of Hawai'i Press.

Whitlock, James C., and Kyung Ho Suh. 2001. *Chinese characters in Korean: A "radical" approach—Learn 2,300 Chinese characters through their 214 radicals.* Seoul: Ilchokak.